Partnership Taxation 2017/18

Partnership Taxation 2017/18

David Whiscombe FTII Barrister Ex-HMIT
Partner, Tax Technical
BKL Tax

Bloomsbury Professional

Bloomsbury Professional
An imprint of Bloomsbury Publishing Plc

Bloomsbury Professional Ltd	Bloomsbury Publishing Plc
41–43 Boltro Road	50 Bedford Square
Haywards Heath	London
RH16 1BJ	WC1B 3DP
UK	UK

www.bloomsbury.com

British Library Cataloguing-in-Publication Data

A catalogue record for this book is available from the British Library.

ISBN: 978 152 650 308 4

Typeset by Compuscript Ltd, Shannon
Printed and bound by CPI Group (UK) Ltd, Croydon, CR0 4YY

Preface

Partnership Taxation 2017/18 aims to offer a comprehensive guide to the law and practice relating to the taxation of partnerships in the UK, including where appropriate worked examples where that is the best way to illustrate the practical effects of the legislation. A descriptive Table of Examples may be found immediately after the Contents pages.

This edition has been revised and updated to June 2017 including changes implemented by (the first) *Finance Act 2017*, as well as other developments in statute and case law which have taken place since the last published edition.

Among other topics, this year's edition includes new, expanded or rewritten commentary on:

- the responses to HMRC's Consultation Document 'Partnership taxation: proposals to clarify tax treatment' which were published in March 2017;
- the meaning of 'business' and its importance in the context of partnerships and limited liability partnerships;
- *Investec Asset Finance plc v HMRC* and the consequences of 'trading in partnership interests';
- *HMRC v Vaines* on the extent to which a partner is deemed to be carrying on his own separate business;
- the application of loan relationship rules to partnerships involving a company;
- entrepreneurs' relief, especially in its application to trust disposals;
- mixed member partnerships;
- partnership enquiries, including the relevance of cases like *King*, *Gibbs*, *Eclipse* and *De Silva*.

The Appendices set out relevant legislation referred to in the main commentary, including the *Partnership Act 1890*, the *Limited Partnerships Act 1907* and the *Limited Liability Partnerships Act 2000*. There is also guidance on Partnership Agreements and the main clauses affecting tax to be included.

I am indebted to Sarah Laing CTA much of whose excellent original text continues to be the bedrock on which this year's edition is founded; and to colleagues at BKL whose expertise I have called upon in specific areas including VAT, inheritance tax and pension provision.

It is hoped that readers will find this book a useful and practical companion to understanding the main vagaries of the UK tax system as it applies to partnerships. As always, constructive criticism and suggestions for improvements in future editions will be welcomed.

David Whiscombe FTII Barrister Ex-HMIT

June 2017

Contents

Appendices

Table of Examples

Table of Statutes

Table of Statutory Instruments, EC Regulations and other Guidance

Table of Cases

Abbreviations and References

Abbreviations

AIA	=	annual investment allowance
ANG	=	Application Note G 'Reporting the substance of transactions: Revenue Recognition'
Art	=	Article
b/f	=	brought forward
BIM	=	HMRC Business Income Manual
CA	=	Court of Appeal
CAA 2001	=	Capital Allowances Act 2001
CCAB	=	Consultative Committee of Accountancy Bodies
c/f	=	carried forward
Ch	=	Chapter
CIS	=	Construction Industry Scheme
CTA	=	Corporation Tax Act
CTC	=	Child Tax Credit
DWP	=	Department for Work and Pensions
EA	=	employment allowance
EEIG	=	European economic interest grouping
EIS	=	Enterprise Investment Scheme
ESC	=	Extra-statutory Concession
FA	=	Finance Act
FPS	=	full payment submission
FRSSE	=	Financial Reporting Standard for Smaller Entities
FYA	=	first-year allowance
GAAP	=	generally accepted accounting principles
HMRC	=	Her Majesty's Revenue and Customs
ICTA 1988	=	Income and Corporation Taxes Act 1988
IFRS	=	International Financial Reporting Standard
IHTA 1984	=	Inheritance Tax Act 1984
ISA	=	Individual Savings Account
ITA 2007	=	Income Tax Act 2007
ITEPA 2003	=	Income Tax (Earnings and Pensions) Act 2003
ITTOIA 2005	=	Income Tax (Trading and Other Income) Act 2005
LLP	=	limited liability partnership

LLPA 2000	=	Limited Liability Partnership Act 2000
LLPR 2001	=	Limited Liability Partnership Regulations 2001
LPA 1907	=	Limited Partnerships Act 1907
NICs	=	National Insurance contributions
NISA	=	New ISA
NLW	=	National Living Wage
NMW	=	National Minimum Wage
PA 1890	=	Partnership Act 1890
para	=	paragraph
PAYE	=	Pay As You Earn
PPC	=	personal pension contribution
Pt	=	Part
RAP	=	retirement annuity premium
reg	=	regulation
RTI	=	real time information
s	=	section
SA 1891	=	Stamp Act 1891
SA 2012	=	Scotland Act 2012
SAI	=	Standard Accounts Information
Sch	=	Schedule
SDLT	=	stamp duty land tax
SEE	=	small earnings exemption
SI	=	Statutory Instrument
SIPP	=	self-invested personal pension
SORP	=	Statement of Recommended Practice
SP	=	Statement of Practice
SRIT	=	Scottish rate of income tax
SRT	=	statutory residence test
SSAP	=	Statement of Standard Accounting Practice
SSAS	=	small self-administered scheme
SSCBA 1992	=	Social Security Contributions and Benefits Act 1992
TCGA 1992	=	Taxation of Chargeable Gains Act 1992
TEE	=	tax-exempt-exempt
TIOPA 2010	=	Taxation (International and Other Provisions) Act 2010
TMA 1970	=	Taxes Management Act 1970
TOCG	=	transfer of a going concern
UITF	=	Urgent Issues Task Force (Abstract)
UTR	=	Unique Taxpayer Reference
VAT	=	value added tax
VATA 1994	=	Value Added Tax Act 1994
VCT	=	Venture Capital Trust

WA 2014	=	Wales Act 2014
WDA	=	writing-down allowance
WDV	=	written-down value
WIP	=	work in progress
WTC	=	Working Tax Credit

References

AC	=	Law Reports, Appeal Cases
All ER	=	All England Law Reports
Ch D	=	Chancery Division
HL	=	House of Lords
KB	=	King's Bench Division
QB	=	Queen's Bench Division
STC	=	Simon's Tax Cases
TC	=	Official Reports of Tax Cases
VATTR	=	Value Added Tax Tribunal Reports
WLR	=	Weekly Law Reports

Chapter 1

Introduction

Signposts

- A general definition of a partnership is contained in the *Partnership Act 1890, s 1* (see **1.1 – 1.3**) and is to be distinguished from a joint venture (see **1.18**).
- Individuals, companies, trustees, nominees and even partnerships can be partners in a partnership (see **1.7 – 1.9**).
- A partner can exist only if it carries on a business: mere joint ownership of property does not constitute partnership (see **1.10 – 1.17**).
- The existence of a partnership is a question of fact. Although there are few legal formalities in establishing a partnership (other than one under the *Limited Partnerships Act 1907* or the *Limited Liability Partnerships Act 2000*), a written agreement is advisable (see **1.19 – 1.25**).
- Partners are normally jointly liable for the firm's debts (see **1.27 – 1.31**).
- 'Salaried partners' may be true partners or employees, depending on the facts (see **1.32 – 1.35**).
- For tax purposes, partnership accounts must normally comply with GAAP though in some circumstances some partnerships can use the cash basis, the simplified expenses regime or both (see **1.37 – 1.52**).
- A partnership tax return (SA 800) must be completed and submitted to HMRC, normally by 31 January following the end of the tax year but a partnership is not itself liable to tax. Instead profits are allocated between and taxable on partners (see **1.53 – 1.58**).

Partnership basics

What is a partnership?

1.1 Before looking at the tax treatment of partnerships, it is as well to consider what a partnership is. The general law on partnership is mainly contained in the *Partnership Act 1890* ('*PA 1890*') (reproduced in Appendix 1), which states that partnership is 'the relation which subsists between persons carrying on a business in common with a view of profit' (*PA 1890, s 1*).

Although *PA 1890* sets out a number of detailed rules it does not purport to be a comprehensive code and it is overlaid upon the pre-existing equity and common law position, which is expressly retained (by *s 46*) except in so far as that position is inconsistent with the express provisions of the Act.

1.2 A partnership within the meaning of *PA 1890* (often called an 'ordinary partnership') is to be distinguished both from a Limited Partnership ('LP') (see **Chapter 18**) and a Limited Liability Partnership ('LLP') (see **Chapter 19**). In this text we use the term 'ordinary partnership' where necessary to make the express distinction between a partnership under *PA 1890* and an LP or LLP.

In English law a partnership is not a separate legal entity, although partners are agents for each other in respect of the business transactions, and each is bound by the acts of the others. Scottish partnerships are, under Scots Law, separate legal persons. However, *ITTOIA 2005, s 848* provides that, unless otherwise indicated either expressly or by implication, a firm is not to be regarded for income tax purposes as an entity separate and distinct from the partners. This applies equally to Scottish as to English partnerships.

Focus

The *Scotland Act 2012* gave tax-raising powers to the Scottish Parliament. From 6 April 2016 the UK income tax rates (ie, the basic, higher and additional rates) paid by Scottish taxpayers (broadly, those mainly resident in Scotland) are reduced by 10 percentage points. The Scottish Rate of income tax is then set annually by the Scottish Parliament at any value from 0% upwards. For 2016/17, the Scottish Rate is 10% meaning that for 2016/17 Scottish taxpayers pay the same overall income tax as people in the rest of the UK.

The *Scotland Act 2016* built on this to give the Scottish Parliament the full power (from 6 April 2017) to set all rates and band thresholds that apply to all non-savings, non-dividend income of Scottish taxpayers. For 2017/18, the rates are the same as for the rest of the UK but the increase to the higher rate threshold which applies to the rest of the UK was not implemented in Scotland.

Increasingly, therefore, Scottish tax rates and bands may be expected to diverge from the rest of the UK.

1.3 The fact that a partnership is not regarded as a separate legal entity means that a partnership does not as such have a place of residence for income tax purposes. In particular it cannot be a 'Scottish taxpayer' liable to the Scottish Rate of income tax. Individual members of an English or Scottish partnership may of course be 'Scottish taxpayers' and the possibility that different partners may pay tax on profit share at different rates may arise.

1.4 The treatment of a business structure established under foreign (other than Scots) law is not completely clear. HMRC have published (at INTM 180030) a list of foreign entities together with their classification for UK tax purposes as 'transparent' or 'opaque' (meaning respectively that a member is to be charged tax on his share of the entity's profit as it arises or that a member is to be taxed only on such amounts if any as are distributed to him by the entity). However, HMRC specifically say that:

> 'The expressions 'transparent' and 'opaque' are not interchangeable with 'partnership' and 'company' or 'body corporate'. For example, a fiscally transparent entity is not necessarily a partnership. Likewise a UK company is a 'body corporate' and is opaque for the purposes of UK tax on income, but a fiscally opaque entity is not necessarily a 'body corporate' or a 'company' for UK tax purposes.'

Nonetheless it is reasonable to suppose that where a foreign entity is described in the list as 'transparent' the UK taxation treatment of profits arising from a UK business or to a UK-resident member from a non-UK business may be expected to follow substantially the same rules as those applied to partnerships.

1.5 Common ownership of property does not in itself constitute a partnership (*PA 1890, s 2(1)*). Partnership must arise from agreement between the parties, whereas co-ownership need not: for example, a brother and sister becoming joint owners as a result of inheriting property from parents would not per se constitute a partnership. Partners are, as stated at **1.2**, agents for each other, whereas co-owners are not. Partnership must also involve carrying on a business. Joint ventures are considered in **Chapter 10**.

1.6 By contrast, an unincorporated association which does not meet the requirements of being a partnership (perhaps because no business is carried on or because there is no view of profit) falls within the tax definition of a company (*CTA 2010, s 1121*). Such an association will accordingly be liable to corporation tax if it does make any profits; for example, interest received on bank deposits by members' clubs, or capital gains on the disposal of the club's property. The Blackpool Marton Rotary Club failed in its attempt to avoid corporation tax assessments on bank interest by claiming to be a partnership (*Blackpool Marton Rotary Club v Martin* (1988) 62 TC 686). The court observed that the *PA 1890* definition implied both an entitlement on the part of partners to some share of any profits and an obligation to share in any losses. Members of the Club were not in this position and it accordingly was held not to be a partnership.

Who can be a partner?

1.7 Any 'person' may be a partner. This may include individuals, companies or trustees.

1.8 The question whether a partnership can itself be a partner in a partnership is complicated. HMRC guidance (BIM82001) is clear that it cannot, unless it has distinct legal personality (see PM50800). It was therefore somewhat surprising that one of the areas covered in the Consultation Document 'Partnership taxation: proposals to clarify tax treatment' issued by HMRC in August 2016 was 'The taxation of business structures that include partnerships as partners'.

The proposal in the Consultation Document was that in a case where a partnership (a 'bottom-tier' partnership) numbers among its partners a partnership (a 'member partnership') it would be required to disclose in its tax return the identity of all the ultimate recipients of a share of partnership profit (tracing through as many tiers of intermediate 'member partnerships' as necessary) and the share of profit allocated to each recipient. The practical difficulties of meeting such a requirement are obvious: the partner filing the 'bottom tier' partnership return may not be aware of the identity of the members of a 'member partnership' even one tier up, let alone the basis on which the 'member partnership' allocates profit. The revised proposal, following representations, is that:

- where a partnership includes among its partners a partner which is itself a partnership, it must report to HMRC the details of that partner and provide to both HMRC and the partner computations of taxable profit on all four possible bases (ie, UK-resident individual, UK-resident company, non-UK-resident individual and non-UK-resident company); alternatively
- where the details of all ultimate recipients (ie, identity and amount of profit share allocated) have been provided to HMRC (and to the ultimate recipients) the partnership will have to prepare computations only on the basis appropriate to each ultimate recipient.

It is proposed that the legislation will be included in a second Finance Bill 2017 and will be effective for partnership accounting periods beginning on or after 6 April 2018.

Example 1.1 – Allocation of profit where members include an LLP

The members of XYZ LLP are Mr A, Mr B and C LLP. Profits are shared equally. The members of C LLP are Mr D and E Ltd. The taxable profits of XYZ LLP are £90,000 (computed using income tax rules) or £84,000 (computed using corporation tax rules).

XYZ LLP's return will allocate £30,000 to each of Mr A and Mr B. If XYZ LLP does not know on what basis C LLP allocates its profits it must show on its return that £30,000 is allocated to C LLP using income tax rules and £28,000 using corporation tax rules (and if the profits would be computed differently for a non-resident in either case, it must also show the amount which would be allocated in each case using the rules for a non-resident). If, on the other hand, the person filing the XYZ LLP return knows that C LLP allocates its profit equally between Mr D and E Ltd the XYZ LLP return will show £15,000 of XYZ LLP's taxable profit allocated to Mr D (using income tax rules) and £14,000 allocated to E Ltd (using corporation tax rules). He will, however, need to be careful to take account of any possible adjustments to the allocation of C LLP's profits occasioned by the 'mixed member' rules (see **Chapter 17**). This may require the exercise of judgement as to whether Mr D has 'power to enjoy' E Ltd's profits; whether E Ltd's share exceeds the 'appropriate notional profit' etc. Often the safe option will be for XYZ LLP simply to report the profit share allocated to C LLP computed on the four possible bases and leave C LLP to wrestle with the allocation of profit between its members.

1.9 The position of a person who acts as a partner in a partnership but does so as bare trustee or nominee for others has historically been less than clear. In the Consultation Document referred to at **1.8** above, HMRC asserted that 'the application of the current law is clear and a partner cannot act in the capacity of a nominee or agent for another person.'

Responses to the Consultation Document suggested that the position was not in fact at all clear and that many legal commentators argue that a partner can be a nominee for someone else.

The government's response has been to state an intention to legislate to ensure that the beneficiary of a nominee or bare trust arrangement is treated as a partner for tax purposes. Accordingly it is that person rather than the nominee or bare trustee who will be named on the partnership tax return as the partner and to whom any share of profit will be shown as allocated. It is proposed that the legislation will be included in a second Finance Bill 2017 and will be effective for partnership accounting periods beginning on or after 6 April 2018.

This assumes of course that the person signing the tax return is aware not only that the nominal partner is acting as nominee or bare trustee, but also of the identity of the beneficiary of the arrangement. How the legislation will deal with the situation where this is not the case remains to be seen.

What is a business?

1.10 Since a partnership is defined as 'the relationship which subsists between persons carrying on a business in common with a view of profit' it is plain that where there is no business there cannot be a partnership. Similarly, the incorporation of a limited liability partnership requires 'two or more persons associated for carrying on a lawful business'. So, again, without a business (and, furthermore, a lawful one) there can be no LLP.

1.11 One of the leading cases on the meaning of 'business' is *American Leaf Blending Co. Sdn. Bhd v Director-General of Inland Revenue* [1978] 3 All ER 1185, a Malaysian case heard by the Privy Council. This concerned a company which, after a short initial period during which it had traded unsuccessfully, let its former trading premises on a succession of leases to a number of unrelated tenants. Under Malaysian tax law, the trading losses could be carried forward and offset against the rental profits if the lettings amounted to the carrying on of a business, but not otherwise.

As well as confirming that '"business" is a wider concept than "trade"' the judgement observed that 'a company may carry on business as an investment or holding company deriving its gains or profits from dividends and interest from the securities it owns' and 'A property company or individual may be carrying on the business of letting premises for rents from which the gains or profits of that business are derived'.

It was held that whether in any particular case activities amount to business is a question of fact, but that a business normally requires some degree of activity: 'The carrying on of "business", no doubt, usually calls for some activity on the part of whoever carries it on, though, depending on the nature of the business, the activity may be intermittent with long intervals of quiescence in between.'

One particular point made by the Privy Council was that whether an activity is or is not a business may depend on who is carrying it on: 'In the case of a private individual it may well be that the mere receipt of rents from property that he owns raises no presumption that he is carrying on a business. In contrast …in the case of a company incorporated for the purpose of making profits for its shareholders any gainful use to which it puts any of its assets *prima facie* amounts to the carrying on of a business'.

Of course, the *American Leaf Blending* case pre-dates LLPs by many years: but the suggestion that a company's activity is *prima facie* by way of business probably applies to an LLP to the same extent as to a company. Hence it seems likely that an LLP which passively invests in property is probably carrying on a business and is validly formed, whereas a group of people who do the same thing may be less likely to be carrying on a business and thus less likely to be in partnership.

1.12 The meaning of 'business' has more recently been considered in *Elisabeth Moyne Ramsay v HMRC* [2013] UKUT 0226. In this case the taxpayer sought deferral relief under *TCGA 1992, s 162* on the transfer of a let property to a company. The relief is available only on the transfer of a business (see **Chapter 16**) and the question was thus whether the letting of the property amounted to a business. The case is less important for its conclusion (that the letting was in fact a business) than for the analysis of the case law and relevant factors, including the following:

- The word 'business' is 'an etymological chameleon; it suits its meaning to the context in which it is found' (*Town Investments v Dept of the Environment* [1978] AC 359).
- Although the *American Leaf Blending* case indicated that some degree of activity is required, it was not authority for the proposition that only a modest degree would always suffice.
- Letting furnished rooms and providing services to occupiers can amount to a business (*Griffiths v Jackson; Griffiths v Pearmain* 56 TC 583).
- VAT cases on the meaning of 'business' must be used with a degree of caution since UK law implements the definition of 'taxable person' which is contained in the relevant treaty as a person who carries out 'any economic activity, whatever the purpose or results of that activity'. A VAT 'business' may thus be wider in scope than the definition for direct tax purposes.
- Nonetheless it may be useful to consider the criteria identified in VAT cases including that of *C&E v Lord Fisher* [1981] STC 238. These included whether the activity:
    - is a 'serious undertaking earnestly pursued';
    - is an occupation or function actively pursued with reasonable or recognisable continuity;
    - has a certain measure of substance as measured by the quarterly or annual value of taxable supplies made;
    - is conducted in a regular manner and on sound and recognised business principles;
    - is predominantly concerned with making taxable supplies to consumers for a consideration;
    - involves the making of supplies which are of a kind which are commonly made by those who seek to profit by them.

The conclusion was that 'the proper approach' (in the context of *TCGA 1992, s 162*) is to construe 'business' broadly, according to its unvarnished ordinary meaning.

Finally, it should be noted that although the charge to tax on rental income lies under *ITTOIA 2005, s 264* and *s 265*, the wording of which charges income tax by reference to 'a person's UK [or overseas] property business' this does not imply that the receipt of rental income necessarily amounts to a business either as a matter of general law or for the purposes of *TCGA 1992, s 162.*

Joint ownership of property

1.13 As will be evident from the above, mere joint ownership of let property by two or more individuals does not of itself constitute a partnership: something more is required for the letting to constitute a business.

Where the letting does not amount to a business (and there is therefore no partnership) it follows that no partnership return is required. Instead, each co-owner will include his share of the rental profit or loss on his personal tax return. If a person has rental income from a property he owns personally and also a share of rental income from one or more properties of which he is co-owner, all the income is aggregated to form the profit of the 'rental business' on which he is assessed to tax.

Normally income from jointly-owned property will be shared in the proportions in which the property is owned. But (as is confirmed at PIM 1030) joint owners can if they wish agree that profits or losses will be divided in proportions that differ from the shares in ownership of the underlying property, in which case that allocation will also apply for tax purposes. Some care is needed here: where any element of bounty is involved in the allocation of profits it will be necessary to consider whether the 'settlements' legislation at *ITTOIA 2005, Pt 5, Ch 5* may be in point.

Example 1.2 – Adjusted profit sharing arrangements – no settlement

David and his sister Joan own each own 50% of a property to which they have each contributed 50% of the purchase price. David undertakes all the work involved in managing the property and they agree that sharing the income 70% to David and 30% to Joan is a commercially appropriate way to compensate him for his work. In this case there is no 'bounty' involved: David and Joan will include on their respective tax returns 70% and 30% of the property income.

Example 1.3 – Adjusted profit sharing arrangements – settlement

Ernest and his partner Harriet jointly own an investment property in the same proportions in which they have contributed capital to its purchase, namely 10% Ernest and 90% Harriet. Neither takes any active part in the management of the property. They agree that, unless and until Harriet determines otherwise, they will share the income equally. In this case the arrangement is clearly 'bounteous' and furthermore is revocable. Accordingly s 624 will apply and Harriet will remain taxable on 90% of the income.

1.14 A special rule applies where let property is jointly owned (other than in partnership) by spouses or civil partners. Where this is the case, *ITA 2007, s 836* provides that profits and losses are treated as arising in equal shares (regardless of the proportions in which it is actually owned) unless one of three exceptions applies, namely:

- the income is income to which neither of the co-owners is beneficially entitled (ie, where the property is held on trust); or
- the income arises from the commercial letting of furnished holiday accommodation in the UK or the EEA within the meaning of *ITTOIA 2005, Pt 3, Ch 6*; or
- the income is in fact shared in the same way as the underlying ownership and the co-owners jointly elect (under *ITA 2007, s 837)* that they should be treated for tax purposes as sharing income in the proportions in which they actually share it.

Where the spouse or civil partners are in partnership (that is, where the letting constitutes or forms part of a business) the normal partnership rules apply and the income is divided between them in accordance with the terms of the partnership agreement.

1.15 There are two circumstances in which the joint ownership of real property may amount to, or be part of, the carrying on of a business. The first is where there is already in existence a trade or profession carried on in partnership and the partners also, as an incident of their partnership activity, jointly own property that they let. This might be a letting of business property which is temporarily surplus to requirements; or it might be an independent but subsidiary activity carried on by the partners.

Less commonly, people who jointly own one (or, usually, more than one) property for letting might conduct themselves in such a way that, by reference to the criteria described above, the property investment activity itself amounts to the carrying on a business.

Where joint ownership of property does give rise to a partnership there are a number of tax implications:

- A partner's share of rental profits from the partnership business (or, if there is more than one such business, each of them) must be kept completely separate from any property income received by the partner from a 'sole trade' rental business. There can be no offset of expenses or losses of one against the other.
- A partnership return will be filed showing partnership profits and the allocation between partners. These profits can be allocated in whatever way the partners agree, but the commercial allocation must be followed for tax purposes.
- Where spouse or civil partners are in partnership the rule at *ITA 2007, s 836* which deems the income from jointly held property to arise in equal shares (unless a declaration is made under *s 837*) does not apply and the allocation of income for tax purposes must follow the allocation under the partnership agreement.

1.16 Where a non-trading business is carried on in partnership, the basis period for it depends on whether the partnership also carries on a trade alongside the non-trading business. Where there is no trade, the basis period for assessment of the non-trading income is always the tax year itself. Where the partnership carries on a trade (or profession or vocation) as well as having non-trading income, the basis period for the non-trading income is aligned with that of the trade. For more details and examples, see **Chapter 4**.

Example 1.4 – Rental income both within and outwith partnership

Sally is a partner in a firm of solicitors. The partnership balance sheet contains a property which was formerly occupied by the firm but has for many years been let on a long lease to a firm of accountants. Sally owns a buy-to-let flat in her own name and also lets a house (which she inherited from her parents) jointly with her brother.

Sally's personal income from letting the flat and her share of income from letting the house will be aggregated and assessed on a tax year basis, separately from her share of the firm's letting income which will be assessed by reference to the firm's accounting period.

1.17 Joint ownership of land will normally, however, be treated as a partnership for VAT purposes, requiring registration in the joint names of the owners where the rents are taxable supplies in excess of the registration threshold (see **Chapter 26**).

Joint ventures

1.18 The term 'joint venture' is not defined in general or tax law. Sometimes it means nothing more than a jointly-owned company; but the term is sometimes used as a loose general description of a venture of some kind in which two or more parties co-operate to achieve a particular result. However, what matters is not what name is attached to a structure but what its essential character is. As was colourfully put by Lord Templeman in *Street v Mountford* [1985] 2 All ER 289

> 'the manufacture of a five-pronged implement for manual digging results in a fork even if the manufacturer, unfamiliar with the English language, insists that he intended to make and has made a spade.'

Thus, in many cases so-called 'joint ventures' entail the parties carrying out a single business in common with a view to profit, sharing risk and reward in whatever manner is agreed – and thus being in partnership. See, for example, *John Gardner and Bowring Hardy & Co Ltd v CIR* 15 TC 602, *Morden Rigg & Co and R B Eskrigge & Co v Monks* 8 TC 450. Contrast that with the case where two parties each carrying on business on their own account agree to work together to their mutual gain on a project but – crucially – not to share risks or profits. For example, an entertainments promoter and a caterer may come together to run a music festival, on terms that the entertainments promoter will arrange and pay for the acts and will sell tickets, keeping the proceeds; the caterer will sell food and drink to the festival-goers and keep any profits. They might agree that they will jointly bear the other costs of the festival such as rent to the farmer, security costs and compensation to local residents. In such a case the caterer and promoter would not be trading in partnership but in joint venture: each would include his income and costs (including his share of joint costs) in his own accounts in the usual way and there would be no question of a partnership return being filed.

Establishing a partnership

1.19 In contrast to the position for Limited Partnerships or LLPs (governed by *LPA 1907* and *LLPA 2000* respectively) there are no legal formalities in establishing a general partnership. A written agreement is not even necessary, although it is advisable: a partnership may come into existence under an oral agreement. Whether or not a partnership exists is a mixed question of fact and law, and it is obviously more difficult to prove the existence of a partnership if there is no written agreement.

1.20 The question whether a particular state of affairs amounts to a partnership has come before the courts on a number of occasions, commonly where there has been dispute between HMRC and taxpayer as to whether a particular arrangement of affairs between family members amounts to a partnership. The best guidance here is often simply to go back to the statutory phraseology: are the parties carrying on a business in common with a view of profit?

1.21 The crux is often whether all the alleged partners can truthfully be said to be 'carrying on' the business. In *CIR v Williamson* [1928] 14 TC 335, for example, a farming family asserted that a partnership existed but in the absence of a partnership deed or any evidence that profits were shared (and in the light of the fact that the father appeared to make all the decisions regarding the partnership) the courts held that no partnership existed. Where there is no partnership deed questions which may need to be asked include the following.

- Was there a partnership bank account? If so, in what name was it held?
- Who were the signatories to the bank account?
- Were the supposed partners represented to the outside world as such? Were their names shown on letter-heading or other business correspondence? Was their appointment as partners notified to suppliers, customers or the bank?
- What did accounts of the business show?
- Was notification of the change given for VAT purposes?
- Is there any evidence that in practice the supposed partners were able to bind the business by making contracts on its behalf?
- Who made the key decisions regarding the management of the business?
- If the supposed partners were previously employees, what change can be shown to have taken place on the date on which they were advanced to partnership?
- What share of profit did the supposed partners in fact receive?

1.22 The receipt of a share of profit is under *PA 1890, s 2 prima facie* evidence of partnership but does not of itself prove a partnership. Thus in *Horner v Hasted* [1995] 67 TC 439 an employee who was paid a share of profits, had the status of partner within the firm, had management responsibility and was held out to clients as a partner was nonetheless held not to be a partner, though this decision was probably influenced by the fact that as a matter of law he was ineligible under the rules of the firm's professional body to be a partner in the firm.

1.23 A partnership can exist even though the partners themselves deny the existence of a partnership – see, for example, *Morden Rigg & Co and R B Eskrigge & Co v Monks* 8 TC 450 and *Fenston v Johnstone* 23 TC 29.

1.24 For a useful summary of some of the leading cases on the existence of partnerships and the analysis of the factors to be taken into account, see the First-tier Tribunal decision in *Phillips v HMRC* [2009] UKFTT 335 (TC). In this case the taxpayer sought to appeal against partnership assessments on the basis that there was on the facts no partnership in existence. Factors considered in the case included

- the presence or absence of letter-heading;
- the power to bind the partnership;
- evidence of trust between the parties;
- competition constraints;
- sharing of losses;
- VAT registration;
- profit share;
- whether partnership tax returns were filed;
- existence and content of partnership accounts.

1.25 Where a partnership deed exists there is very limited scope for HMRC to dispute the existence of a partnership even if the partnership has manifestly been entered into in order to minimise tax. HMRC will be able to succeed in setting aside the partnership only if it is in some way flawed. This might be the case if for example the rules of any relevant professional body require all partners to have a professional qualification, or the written terms of the partnership deed are patently being ignored – see *Dickenson v Gross KB* (1927) 11 TC 614 as an example of a case where a written agreement was ignored and the courts held that no partnership existed. And, of course, a deed cannot have retrospective effect – see *Waddington v O'Callaghan* (1931) 16 TC 187, where it was held on the facts that the partnership constituted by a partnership deed executed in May was effective only from the date of execution and not (as claimed) from the previous January. Some caution must be expressed here: if as a matter of fact a partnership exists from a given date, that state of affairs is not vitiated or contradicted by the fact that the position is formally documented by a written partnership agreement only at a later date. The problem in *Waddington v O'Callaghan* was essentially that there was no evidence before the Commissioners to support the existence of a partnership at any date earlier than that of the deed.

Restrictions on partnerships

1.26 There is no limit on the maximum permitted number of partners or members who may participate in a partnership or LLP. A partnership name cannot include the word 'Limited' (limited liability partnerships are denoted by 'LLP') and cannot suggest a connection with the government or a local authority. If the name does not consist of the names of all the partners, the provisions of the *Companies Act 2006* must be complied with in terms of disclosing 'particulars of ownership' on letter-headings, websites, places of business etc.

There are few restrictions on who may be a partner. Certainly a company, a trustee or a personal representative can be a partner. Minor children can be partners, though only if they have the intellectual capacity to understand the nature of the business and the obligations of partnership. It may be easier for minors to be partners in some businesses than in others: for example, minors may be able to fulfil the role of partner in a family farming partnership at a relatively young age (see HMRC guidance at BIM82065).

Liabilities of partners

1.27 Partners are normally jointly liable for the firm's debts to the full extent of their private assets, one partner not being able to settle his or her own personal position independently of the others. Someone who has obtained judgment against one or more of the partners in respect of a partnership debt can take action against another partner or partners in respect of the same debt. The implication of each partner's separate liability for the firm's debts was brought out in *VGM Schooler v C & E Commrs* [1995] 2 BCLC 610, a case concerning unpaid VAT. It was held that the joint debt of a partner was a debt owed by that partner for the purposes of the *Insolvency Act 1986, s 267(1)*, and even though one partner had entered into an individual voluntary arrangement, the debt could be enforced against the other partner.

1.28 Someone who is not as a matter of fact a partner in a firm can also be liable for partnership debts in the same way as a partner if he or she has actively or passively allowed it to be believed that he or she is a partner (*PA 1890, s 14*). This may be the case, for example, if a salaried employee is described on a business card or website as a 'partner'. However, any claimant relying on *s 14* will need to show both that reliance was placed on that 'holding out' when giving credit to the firm and that the 'partner' was complicit in the 'holding out' (*UCB Home Loans v Soni* [2013] EWCA Civ 62). Where a partner does not wish to put private assets at risk, it is possible to create a partnership under the *Limited Partnerships Act 1907* (*'LPA 1907'*) (reproduced in Appendix **2**) under which the liability of one or more partners is limited to the amount of capital the partner has agreed to contribute (see **Chapter 18**). Such partnerships must have at least one general partner who is fully liable for the firm's debts, and must register with Companies House. Limited partners are not permitted to take part in the management of the business – any partner who does so will lose the protection of limited liability. Nor may capital be returned to a limited partner during the lifetime of the partnership.

1.29 A partner registered as a limited partner in a Limited Partnership must be distinguished from a so-called 'sleeping partner' in a general partnership. Being a 'sleeping partner' (that is, desisting from taking any active part in the management of the business) does not absolve a partner in a general partnership from personal liability for the firm's debts.

1.30 Alternatively, where limited liability is required it is possible to form a LLP under the *Limited Liability Partnerships Act 2000* (*'LLPA 2000'*) (see Appendix **3**). The 'price' of this limited liability is that broadly the same obligations as regards filing information and accounts at Companies House apply to an LLP as apply to a limited company. LLPS are dealt with in more detail at **Chapter 19**.

1.31 Joint liability extends to tax liabilities which fall upon the partnership as such – for example liabilities to account for PAYE and NIC in respect of employees of the partnership, or to account for VAT (see **Chapter 26**). It does not extend to liability for UK tax payable on the profits of the partnership, because the partnership as such has no such liability: tax is payable by each partner on that partner's own share of taxable profit (see **Chapter 3**). However, it should be borne in mind that:

- if the partnership is liable to tax in an overseas jurisdiction (perhaps because it carries on trade through an overseas branch), local law will generally govern the question of liability and the possibility of joint personal liability of the partners cannot be ruled out: local advice should be taken;
- there are circumstances (see **Chapter 20**) in which partners may find themselves liable as agents to meet unpaid UK tax liabilities of a non-resident partner.

Salaried partners

1.32 It is common in professional partnerships to have 'salaried partners'. In some cases these may be genuine partners albeit that their entitlement is to a prior share of profit with little or no expectation of receiving anything (or anything substantial) in excess of that prior share. In other cases a 'salaried partner' may not in fact be a partner at all, but merely a senior employee given the title of 'partner' as a matter of status. Which side of the line the individual falls is a question of fact: ultimately it is a question of whether the 'partner' is carrying on the business in common with the other partners – that is, whether the 'partner' is truly entitled to participate as principal in the general management and conduct of the business. A 'salaried partner' who is in fact an employee will of course be charged to tax and National Insurance as an employee. Benefits in kind will also be taxable on such a 'partner' and may be subject to Class 1A National Insurance.

Focus

A salaried partner who is an employee will normally require an indemnity from the real partners (often called 'equity partners'), since by his or her inclusion on notepaper, etc, a salaried partner might be regarded as representing himself to be a partner (*PA 1890, s 14*) and thus as becoming liable for partnership debts to anyone who has relied upon that representation.

1.33 This subject of salaried partners was considered in the case of *Nationwide Building Society v Lewis & Williams* [1998] 3 All ER 143. L, who was a solicitor, invited W to join him as a salaried partner. W was shown on the firm's letterhead as a partner. The Nationwide Building Society sued L and W for negligence. The Court of Appeal held that W was potentially liable for the negligence because he acquiesced with L in allowing his name to be shown on the firm's headed paper and therefore representing himself to be a partner. However, on the facts, the Building Society's claim failed because it could not show that it had relied upon that representation.

1.34 It is however necessary that the 'salaried partner' has acquiesced in his representation as a partner. In *UCB Home Loans Corporation Ltd v Soni & Anor* [2013] EWCA Civ 6, S wrongly represented to UCB that K was a partner in the business. Since K had neither made nor acquiesced in the representation, he was not liable as partner to UCB.

> **Focus**
>
> *FA 2014* introduced provisions amending the treatment for salaried partners in LLPs (*FA 2004, s 74* and *Sch 17, Pt 1*). For full details of the changes, see **Chapter 19**).

1.35 The so-called 'Gig Economy' cases such as *Aslam, Farrar v Uber BV* [2017] IRLR 4; *Pimlico Plumbers v Smith* [2017] EWCA Civ 51; *Boxer v Excel Group Services (in liquidation)* (decision 23 March 2017); *Dewhurst v Citysprint UK Ltd* (unreported, 5 January 2017) may have relevance to salaried partners. The *Employment Rights Act 1996*, the *Working Time Regulations 1998* and the *National Minimum Wage Act 1998* all apply not only to employees but to 'workers'. This term is defined to mean an individual working under a contract whereby the individual:

> 'Undertakes to do or perform personally any work or services for another party to the contract whose status is not by virtue of the contract that of a client or customer of any profession or business undertaking carried on by the individual'.

Thus an individual working under a contract may be, depending on the facts:

- employed; or
- self-employed, but a 'worker' entitled to the protections of the *Employment Rights Act 1996* etc; or
- self-employed and not a 'worker'.

Although there are a number of cases in which salaried partners or salaried LLP members have sought on leaving the firm to establish that they were in fact 'employees' with full employment rights (see, for example, *Tiffin v Lester Aldridge LLP* [2012] EWCA Civ 35) it is not believed that thus far any salaried partners have sought to establish the proposition that they are 'workers'.

Sleeping partners

1.36 'Sleeping partner' is a non-statutory term which is generally taken to mean a partner who takes no active part in the running of the partnership business. For most purposes, whether a partner is a sleeping partner or not is of no significance for tax purposes. In particular, there is no requirement that a partner's share of profit must be 'justified' by reference to the work he has done or any other contribution he has made to the profitability of the partnership. However, note that:

- In some circumstances the award of a share of profit to a partner may constitute a 'settlement' in respect of which the legislation at *ITTOIA 2005, Pt 5, Ch 5* may need to be considered (see **Chapter 11**).
- 'Relevant UK earnings' for pension purposes is defined (in relation to a partnership) as income which is immediately derived from the carrying on of a trade, profession, vocation or UK or EEA furnished holiday lettings business 'as a partner acting personally in a partnership'. It is at least questionable whether a sleeping partner who takes no active part at all in the partnership business could be said to be meet that definition, though HMRC guidance (PTM044100) is silent on the point.
- Where a partner is 'non-active', there are restrictions on the extent to which any share of partnership tax losses may be used (see **Chapter 9**). A sleeping partner as the term is normally understood will almost always fall within the statutory definition of a 'non-active' partner, though the statutory definition is wide enough to include a partner whose activity, though limited, would be sufficient that he would not normally be regarded as a sleeping partner.
- Following a change of practice from 6 April 2013, sleeping partners are now regarded as liable to make National Insurance Contributions (see **Chapter 24**).

Partnership accounts

Generally accepted accounting practice

1.37 The general rule is that trading profits must be computed for income tax purposes in accordance with generally accepted accounting principles ('GAAP'), subject to any adjustments required or permitted by law (*ITTOIA 2005, s 25*). The *Corporation Tax Act 2009, s 46* makes equivalent provision for corporation tax purposes.

GAAP is defined in the *Income Tax Act 2007 ('ITA 2007'), s 997* to mean generally accepted accounting practice with respect to accounts of UK companies that are intended to give a true and fair view. The same definition applies to individuals, entities that are not companies, and companies that are not UK companies. This definition means GAAP applicable to companies incorporated or formed under the law of a part of the UK. It is not the GAAP relevant to another country. In relation to a company or other entity that prepares accounts under International Financial Reporting Standards ('IFRS'), this means GAAP in relation to IFRS accounts. Again, equivalent provision is made for corporation tax purposes at the *Corporation Tax Act 2010, s 1127*.

1.38 *ITTOIA 2005, s 25* gives statutory force to the view taken in the courts, in cases such as *Herbert Smith v Honour* [1999] STC 173 and *Jenners Princes Street Edinburgh Ltd v IRC* [1998] STC (SCD) 196, which held that the tax treatment should follow accounting practice except to the extent that tax law specifically provides otherwise.

1.39 Producing accounts in accordance with GAAP does not require partnerships that are not LLPs, ie ordinary partnerships, to:

- comply with the *Companies Act 2006;* or
- have the accounts audited.

1.40 For ordinary partnerships, compliance with GAAP only applies to the computation of profits and losses for tax purposes. There is nothing that requires accounts to be drawn up on any particular basis; cash accounts could still be prepared, provided that adjustments are made where necessary to convert the profit to an earnings basis (if necessary) in the tax computations.

Focus

In the case of *Sharkey v Wernher* (1955) 36 TC 275, the House of Lords ruled that, where trading stock was appropriated for personal use, it should be transferred at market value for tax purposes. After the *Finance Act 1998* introduced the requirement for taxable profits to be calculated in accordance with UK GAAP, doubts were raised whether the decision in *Sharkey v Wernher* was still relevant, bearing in mind that UK GAAP would have required the transfer to be valued at cost or the price actually paid on the disposal. The matter was put beyond doubt by the *Finance Act 2008, s 37* and *Sch 15* (introducing *ITTOIA 2005, ss 172A–172F* for income tax, and other provisions for corporation tax) for transactions occurring on or after 12 March 2008. These rules make clear that the tax treatment of changes to trading stock, otherwise than by way of trade, must reflect market value rather than the accounting result. The market value rule also applies where goods are acquired or appropriated into trading stock other than in the course of a trade.

A similar doubt about the tax treatment of transactions involving the receipt of 'money's worth' was resolved by the *Finance Act 2016, s 71* which confirms that an amount equal to the value of the money's worth must be brought into account for tax purposes.

1.41 The accounts of an ordinary partnership do not normally need to be audited or filed at Companies House. The exception is where the partnership is a 'qualifying partnership' within the meaning of The Partnerships (Accounts) Regulations 2008. These regulations apply to any partnership all of whose members are companies; they impose broadly the same audit and filing requirements as would apply to a company of the same size. Furthermore, in the case of a Limited Partnership, any limited partners are ignored in determining whether the partnership is a 'qualifying partnership' with the result that a UK Limited Partnership whose only general partner is itself a limited company will be a 'qualifying partnership'.

1.42 In contrast, an LLP is subject to broadly the same audit and filing requirements as a company. Thus, the accounts must be audited unless the LLP meets at least two of the qualifying criteria of turnover (under £10.2 million), balance sheet total (under £5.1 million) and employees (under 50). If the LLP's profits exceed £200,000, the remuneration of the highest paid member must be disclosed. Company-style disclosure is also required at Companies House, including members' home addresses (though this information is not available on the public register). An LLP is also subject to the rules regarding disclosure of 'People with Significant Control'. This will always extend to people whose interest in the assets or voting rights of the LLP exceeds 25% but may extend to others exercising 'significant influence or control'.

Focus

Figures from the partnership accounts have to be transferred to the partnership tax return. The partnership return requires accounting information to be presented in a standard format known as Standard Accounts Information ('SAI'). Accordingly, it makes sense for the partnership accounts to follow this format. Doing so makes it easier for the partners to understand the composition of the tax return entries and avoids the need to break down or combine numbers from the accounts to complete the return.

1.43 HMRC require accounts to be submitted with the partnership return only where the turnover exceeds £15 million. In this case, the SAI does not need to be completed. Where the partnership turnover is below £83,000, HMRC only require details of turnover, expenses and net profit to be entered on the return, plus the balance sheet details if one is prepared.

1.44 Regardless of the fact that HMRC do not require accounts, it is considered prudent to submit them with the return in all cases where they are prepared. Doing so may reduce the risk of an enquiry or a later 'discovery'. Whether or not the accounts are submitted, care must be taken to ensure that their content is fully reflected in the partnership return. If necessary, supplementary disclosure should be made in the 'additional information' box.

Partnership accounts should be consistent in presentation and in the categorisation of expenses and must reflect the partnership agreement. Formal approval of the accounts by all the partners is recommended.

Cash basis

1.45 From 2013/14, *ITTOIA 2005, s 31A* et seq provides that eligible small businesses may choose to use the cash basis when calculating taxable income. The cash basis is available only to unincorporated businesses including partnerships (but not LLPs) whose partners are all individuals. So in practice most Limited Partnerships (which normally have a corporate general partner) are excluded. Other exclusions are set out at *s 31C*. For full details of the operation of the scheme, see HMRC guidance at BIM 70000. At the time of writing, the Autumn 2017 Finance Bill proposes changes to the cash basis rules, including a claimed simplification of the way in which capital expenditure is treated (though whether it is in fact a simplification may be open to question). These changes will be back-dated to 6 April 2017.

An eligible business can elect to use the scheme for a tax year if its cash basis receipts for the year do not exceed an 'entry limit' of the greater of £150,000 or the VAT threshold (or, for an individual claiming universal credit, the greater of £300,000 or twice the VAT threshold). Once in the scheme, a business can continue to use it until the cash basis receipts for a tax year exceed the 'exit limit' of the greater of £300,000 or twice the VAT threshold. Once the 'exit limit' is exceeded, cash basis ceases to apply for the following year unless the receipts for that following year drop back to below the relevant 'entry limit'. The limits stated apply from 6 April 2017; before then, lower limits applied.

All businesses run by a 'person' (ie, for this purpose, a partnership or an individual) are aggregated when considering eligibility.

1.46 There are very limited aggregation rules for related businesses. Where one or more partnerships are controlled by an individual who also carries on a separate business personally, cash basis is available to the partnerships only if the aggregate of the cash basis receipts of the partnership business (or businesses) and the 'sole trade' business (or businesses) fall below the limits referred to above (and only if the individual and each of the other partnerships has also made a cash basis election in respect of the relevant businesses). Interestingly, the drafting of the legislation does not require aggregation of the receipts of a number of partnerships where there is no common control by a single individual. Thus the test for eligibility for cash basis is applied separately to different partnerships running different businesses even if the partnerships have some (or even all) partners in common, provided there is no one partner who is entitled to more than 50% of the assets or 50% of the income of any of the partnerships. Similarly if a non-controlling partner carries on a trade independently of the partnership, eligibility for cash basis for the partner and the partnership are considered independently.

1.47 When it was introduced, cash basis applied only to trades, professions and vocations. It did not apply to property businesses. Following consultation, the government undertook to extend cash basis to certain property businesses. The relevant provisions are in the Autumn 2017 Finance Bill and are to be effective from 6 April 2017. However, rather than simply extend the rules to property businesses, the legislation creates a parallel code for property businesses which is very similar, but not quite identical, to the code for trades, professions and vocations.

Property businesses carried on by companies, by LLPs or by partnerships which have a non-individual member are excluded from using cash basis, as are businesses where the cash basis receipts would exceed £150,000. But unlike trades, there is no uplifted 'exit limit' – if cash basis receipts would exceed £150,000, cash basis is not available for a property business.

For property businesses which do qualify, cash basis becomes the default basis of computation, though it remains possible to elect out of cash basis and compute profits using GAAP (a reversal of the 'opt-in' arrangements for trades, professions and vocations).

Again unlike trades etc, each property business is considered independently when applying the turnover limit. Thus there are no aggregation rules for related property businesses cognate with those described above in relation to trades etc. Where a partnership or individual carries on two property businesses (typically a UK property business and an overseas property business) the receipts of the businesses are not added together in arriving at the turnover limit; and a separate choice as to whether to accept cash basis or elect for GAAP treatment must be made for each separate business. And, rather bizarrely, where property is jointly owned under arrangements which do not constitute partnership, any election for GAAP is made independently by each co-owner so it may happen that one or more co-owners compute profits on a cash basis while one or more others have elected for GAAP. However, this rule is amended in the case of joint ownership by spouses or civil partners in circumstances where *ITA 2007, s 836* applies: in that case, if one spouse or civil partner uses GAAP (either by election or because the total of that spouse's property business income exceeds £150,000) the other spouse or civil partner must also do so.

Focus

General partnerships may use the cash basis providing:

- the partnership meets the receipts and other entry criteria;
- the partners are all individuals; and
- either there is no individual treated as controlling the partnership, or any such individual would be eligible to use the cash basis if they were conducting the business as a sole trader.

1.48 The cash basis operates by reference to the tax year. This means partnerships will be able to calculate their taxable income for the tax year by adding or subtracting:

- receipts in connection with the business received in the tax year;
- payments made in the tax year to cover allowable expenses; and
- amounts allowed for simplified expenses.

Business losses may be carried forward to set against the profits of future years, but not carried back or set off sideways against other sources of income (see **Chapter 9**).

1.49 The cash basis operates on a VAT-inclusive basis. This means that full amount of receipts and payments are counted, including any VAT element. If a partnership is registered for VAT, any VAT paid to HMRC will be an allowable expense, and any VAT refund received from HMRC will be taxable as a receipt in connection with the business.

1.50 Receipts in connection with the trade will be counted as income in the tax year in which the income is received. This will include all receipts treated as trading income by virtue of *ITTOIA 2005, Pt 2*. Receipts in the form of 'money's worth' will be included; for example, the value of goods or services received from customers. Also, a reasonable amount will need to be added to income reflecting any deficiency arising from a transaction being made other than on a commercial basis. (An example would be if, after expensing the cost of purchasing stock, an item of the stock was taken for personal use without any actual payment being made for it.)

Sale proceeds for capital assets (such as plant or machinery) whose purchase costs have previously been relieved will be taken into account as a receipt.

Where there is a significant reduction in the business use of an asset whose purchase costs have previously been relieved (eg a switch to partial private use), a reasonable amount representing the appropriate proportion of the value of the asset at the time will need to be added to income.

Focus

The following items are not treated as income under the cash basis scheme:

- capital introduced by the owners of the business for purposes of financing the business;
- changes in the form of money, eg cash withdrawals from bank accounts;
- loan capital borrowed by the business from third parties for financing purposes;
- proceeds from disposals of durable assets, eg land and property, intellectual property, shares; and
- refunds of income tax, capital gains tax ('CGT'), or tax credits.

Simplified expenses

1.51 *ITTOIA 2005, s 94B* et seq gives unincorporated businesses the option to calculate profits by claiming standardised deductions for certain costs in place of the expenses actually incurred. The expenses concerned are those relating to motor vehicles, use of home for business purposes and private use of business premises. For full details of the operation of the scheme, see HMRC guidance at BIM75000.

1.52 The scheme is available to sole traders and partnerships. Its availability is not restricted to businesses which elect to use the cash basis though many small businesses will no doubt wish to use both the cash basis and the simplified expenses regime.

The list of exclusions from cash basis at *ITTOIA 2005, s 31C* does not apply to the simplified expenses regime. In particular the regime is available to LLPs but it is not available to any partnership which has a corporate member (see *s 94C*).

Overview of taxing partnership income and gains

1.53 The income of partnerships is computed on a current year basis. This means on the net profits of the accounting year ended in the tax year. For 2015/16, a partnership with a year end of 5 April would be taxed on its profits for the accounting year to 5 April 2016. A partnership with a year end of 30 June would be taxed on its profits for the accounting year to 30 June 2015. There are special rules for opening and closing years and where accounting dates are changed.

The profits are divided between the partners in the profit-sharing ratio of the period of account.

> **Focus**
>
> Although the taxable profits have to be established at the partnership level and no partner can agree an adjustment to the partnership profits independently of the others, the partners are not jointly liable for tax on the profits. Rather, each partner is taxed individually on his or her share of the partnership profits, income and gains (*ITTOIA 2005, s 852*; *CTA 2009, s 1262*; and *TCGA 1992, s 59*).

1.54 There is comparatively little statute law specifically directed at the tax treatment of partnerships, and sometimes the procedure is derived from custom and practice. This is particularly so in the case of partnership capital gains, where some of the problems have been addressed by the issue of former Revenue and HMRC Statements of Practice.

The following chapters of the book examine in more detail the various aspects of partnership taxation, both statutory and extra-statutory, and attention is drawn to the various opportunities and pitfalls.

Partnership returns

1.55 A partnership tax return (SA 800) has to be completed and submitted to HMRC, normally by 31 January following the tax year (*Taxes Management Act 1970 ('TMA 1970'), ss 12AA* and *12AB*). For 2016/17 this means by 31 January 2018. There are automatic penalties for the late filing of returns (*FA 2009, Sch 55*).

The return comprises an eight-page core tax return showing trading profits and taxed investment income. Details of income from land and property, untaxed and foreign source income and the disposal of chargeable assets are shown on supplementary pages.

The return includes a short partnership statement which shows, for each partner, his or her name, address, National Insurance number, tax reference and date of admission to or retirement from the partnership if it occurred during the year. It also contains the individual partner's share of profits, losses, UK taxed interest, deductions under the construction industry scheme, tax deducted and partnership charges. Partnerships with untaxed non-trading income, rental income or disposals of capital assets complete a full version of the partnership statement.

The Standard Accounts Information ('SAI') encompasses trading income, expenses, adjustments for tax purposes, capital allowances and a balance sheet (where one is prepared for the partnership). The accounting information reported on the return is for the accounting period falling to be taxed in the tax year in question on a current year basis. Taxed income, partnership charges and capital disposals should be reported for the tax year and not by reference to an accounting period.

1.56 Each partner is responsible for transferring the information from the partnership return onto his or her self-assessment return and for calculating and paying the tax due after taking into account their other sources of income, deductions and allowances (*TMA 1970, s 8(1)–(1C)*).

> **Focus**
>
> It is advisable for someone within or on behalf of a partnership to be responsible for informing the individual partners of the entries and amounts required in their personal returns. Without this, even in the best regulated partnerships, no partner can ensure that his personal return reflects all the aspects and technicalities of the partnership situation as it relates to him or her. The detailed provisions on partnership tax returns are in **Chapter 21**.

Changes in the partnership

1.57 Each incoming or departing partner is treated as if he or she had started or ceased a separate business by reference to his or her personal profit share (*ITTOIA 2005, s 246*). A change in partners does not affect the basis on which continuing partners are assessed.

Partners with other business interests

1.58 Where partners have other business interests, it will sometimes be necessary to make sure that normal business transactions between the two do not give rise to taxation difficulties. For example, where an individual partner is also a participator in a company, the whole of any loan or advance made by the company to the partnership will fall within the terms of *CTA 2010, s 455* regardless of the size of the individual's interest in the partnership. If the individual is also a director of the company there may also be implications under the *Income Tax (Earnings and Pensions) Act 2003 ('ITEPA 2003'), s 173* on the basis that the individual has received a beneficial loan from the company (see *Grant v Watton (Insp of Taxes)* [1999] STC 330) though if any interest paid would have been tax-deductible for the partnership *ITEPA 2003, s 178(c)* would now be in point.

Cost of acquiring partnership interests

1.59 *Investec Asset Finance plc v HMRC; Investec Bank plc v HMRC* [2016] UKFTT 0356 deals with the very interesting question of 'trading in partnership interests'. The detailed facts were complicated and unusual (and involve a number of issues in addition to those detailed below) but the principles as regards 'trading in partnership interests' are clear and of wider application.

The Investec companies were financial dealers. In the course of their trades they acquired for consideration interests in leasing partnerships where the partnership was about to realise trading profit. Although the position of the vendors of the partnership interests was not before the Tribunal it appears that the crucial point of the arrangement as far as tax planning was concerned was that by selling their interests in the partnerships rather than the partnership assets themselves, the vendors sought in each case to avoid any realisation of the partnership assets and thus to avoid any charge to tax.

Assuming for the purposes of illustration that the company paid 90 to acquire the interest from the outgoing partner and subsequently received a share of partnership income of 100, four possible outcomes were canvassed in the case:

Under ***Result A***, it was suggested that the partnership computation would simply be ignored, and that Investec would be taxed on 10. In its sole financial trades, it would bring in income of 100 (consisting either of a look-through to the partnership income, or consisting of the distributions received from the partnership); the cost of acquiring or funding the partnership of 90 would be a deductible expense in the sole trade and the taxable profit would be 10.

Under ***Result B***, Investec would recognise the partnership income of 100 but would then sustain the claim that the costs of 90 (incurred entirely outside the partnership) were deductible, and that the partnership profits that had already been taxed should not be taxed again by being included as receipts of the sole trade, such that the total taxable profits ended up as 10, ie 100 and (0 minus 90).

Result C proceeded on the basis that the partners had respectively to recognise their share of partnership profits of 100, but that HMRC would then have succeeded in disallowing the cost of 90 on the basis that it was either capital expenditure or that if not capital expenditure it was still an expense not incurred wholly and exclusively for trading purposes. Having disallowed the expenditure of 90, the resultant taxable profits became 100 rather than 10.

Result D again assumed that the partnership profits of 100 had to be allocated to the partners with Investec succeeding in undermining HMRC's claims that the expense of 90 was either a capital expense or an expense that was not incurred wholly and exclusively for trading purposes. HMRC's fall-back contention was then that if the 90 constituted an expense of the sole trade, then Investec should be taxed on the profits of that trade as a separate and distinct matter from its liability to tax on the partnership profits. Accordingly, Investec was subject to tax on both 100 (as share of partnership profit) and then it was also taxable on the net profits made in its sole trade, ie 10 (distributions or see-through profits of 100 minus costs of 90), so that the total taxable profits were 110.

After lengthy and detailed analysis the Tribunal concluded that Investec was carrying on separate trades – the sole trade of financial dealing and the trades which it carried on in partnership. It concluded that Result B was the preferred analysis: the share of partnership profit taxable in full but the cost of buying the partnership interest was deductible as an expense of the financial trade. And to the extent that that resulted in the financial trade being loss-making, any loss could be relieved against other profits of the company, subject to the usual rules.

It is important to note the significance in the Investec case of the fact that the cost of the partnership interests was regarded as revenue expenditure. This was because 'They were conducted by companies that carried on financial trades and the transactions were short-term transactions in which the appellants had no interest in making a capital acquisition and drawing income.' The same analysis would not apply to the purchase of a partnership interest as a capital acquisition: see **Example 1.5**.

Example 1.5 – Sale and purchase of a partnership interest

A and B form an equal partnership to buy, develop and sell a piece of land. The land costs £1m of which A and B each contribute £500,000. Before the development is complete, B runs into financial difficulty and needs to realise his investment in the partnership. By this time, A and B have each put a further £100,000 into the project and the partnership assets have an open market value of £1.6m. B accordingly negotiates to sell his partnership interest to C for £800,000, who pays B that amount and steps into B's shoes as a partner. A and C each contribute a further £200,000 to the project to bring it to completion and the development eventually realises a total of £2.4m, which is shared equally between A and C.

The partnership therefore makes a profit of £800,000 (being the excess of the £2.4m sale proceeds over the £1m cost of the land and the £600,000 development costs). This profit is divided equally between A and C, so £400,000 each.

This is the 'right' result for A: he has contributed £800,000 and received £1.2m. C will be less happy to find that he is paying tax on £400,000 since from his perspective his 'real' profit is only £200,000 (being the difference between (a) the £800,000 paid for B's partnership interest plus the further contribution of £200,000 and (b) the £1.2m proceeds).

The moral is that in any case of purchase of a partnership interest the tax consequences for vendor and purchaser should be carefully analysed.

Chapter 2

Computation of Partnership Income and Gains

Signposts

- The rules for calculating the taxable income and gains of partnerships consisting of individuals are the same as the rules for individual traders (see **2.1**).
- Where non-residents or companies are involved, multiple computations may be required using the rules appropriate to each type of partner (see **2.2 – 2.3**).
- Trading profits are computed using the rules appropriate to each type of partner but there are a number of areas in which specific issues arise (see **2.4 – 2.18**).
- On a cessation of business rules on post-cessation receipts will need to be considered (see **2.19 – 2.28**)

Introduction

2.1 Where all partners in a partnership are individuals, the taxable income of the partnership (whether from trading or from any other source) is computed using the same rules as apply to individuals. Where a partnership includes individuals who are not resident in the UK, income is computed (in relation to those individuals) using the rules applicable to non-UK-residents.

For more on the tax implications if one or more of the partners are not resident in the UK for tax purposes, see **Chapter 20**.

2.2 Where a partnership includes one or more companies, the profit share of corporate partners is computed using, broadly speaking, the computational rules applying to companies – see **Chapter 17**.

Often the computational rules for a particular source will be the same for UK resident and non-resident individuals and for companies: but in theory where a partnership includes both non-resident individuals and companies it may be necessary to produce up to four separate computations of each source of income using different sets of computational rules for resident and non-resident individuals and resident and non-resident companies.

2.3 Chargeable gains on disposals of partnership assets are computed using the normal principles of calculation of chargeable gains and are charged as appropriate to capital gains tax ('CGT') in the hands of individual partners or corporation tax in the hands of corporate partners (see **Chapter 12**).

Trading or professional profits

Introduction

2.4 The normal rules on determining the taxable profits of a trade apply equally to partnerships. Thus for those partnerships who choose not to (or are ineligible to) use the cash basis, profits must be computed in accordance with generally accepted accounting practice ('GAAP') (*ITTOIA 2005, s 25*), subject to any adjustment required or authorised by law in calculating profits for tax purposes (see **Chapter 1**). This might include deducting non-taxable credits or adding back non-tax-deductible expenses, deducting capital allowances (see **Chapter 8**) and claiming appropriate reliefs including relief for averaging profits. We assume in this chapter a knowledge of the general rules of computing profit from various sources and we deal with some particular issues which may arise in the context of a partnership.

> **Focus**
>
> There is, therefore, no deduction for expenses that are not wholly and exclusively for the purposes of the business (*ITTOIA 2005, s 34*), nor for those of a capital nature. Thus the legal costs of drawing up partnership agreements, including dissolution agreements, are not allowable in computing profits, since they relate to matters between the partners, as distinct from the trade or profession which is being carried on. Until recently HMRC took the view that the costs of recruiting equity partners were also non-deductible as relating to the capital structure of the firm. It is now recognised (see PM30800) that such costs will normally be deductible as revenue expenses.

Specific areas of difficulty

2.5 The main areas of doubt or difficulty which arise specifically in regard to partnerships relate to transactions between the partnership and the partners.

Drawings and profit share

2.6 Partners' drawings and salaries are an appropriation of profit, not a deduction in calculating it (*PDC Copyright (South) v George* [1997] STC (SCD) 326, SpC 141). However, this does not mean that no payment made by the partnership to a partner is deductible: the true character of the payment must be identified.

For example, it may be that the partnership agreement allocates a slice of profit between partners by reference to the amount of capital each has invested in the partnership. That allocation of profit remains an allocation of profit and not a payment of interest, however it may be described. But it is equally possible for a partner to loan money to the partnership under a separate documented loan agreement providing for the payment of interest. This might be the case if, for example, the arrangements required that the interest was paid by the partnership even if there were no profits out of which to pay it. If that is the case, what has been paid by the partnership and received by the partner will be interest and not profit share, which will be tax-deductible for the partnership to the same extent and subject to the same rules as any interest paid to any other lender: and taxable on the hands of the lending partner in the same way as interest received from any other source.

Similarly, the partnership agreement may allocate an enhanced share of profit to a partner who personally owns the property from which the partnership trades. Such an enhanced profit share remains profit share and not rent. But it is equally possible that a partner may enter into a formal lease or licence agreement which requires the partnership to pay rent for occupation of the property. In that case the partner is taxed on the rent like any other landlord, with the partnership having a deduction in calculating its profits in the same way as if the rent had been paid to any other landlord (so long as the rent in relation to the property is not so excessive as to fall foul of the 'wholly and exclusively' rule).

The leading case establishing the principle is *Heastie v Veitch & Co* 18 TC 305. In this case, a partnership of chartered accountants carried on its business from premises which were owned by the senior partner and for which the partnership paid a rent which was found by the General Commissioners to be a fair and proper rent. It was held by the Court of Appeal that the rent was deductible by the partnership in computing the partnership profit. But it is clear from the judgement in the Court of Appeal that the principle is not limited to rent but extends to any goods or services provided by a partner independently of his position as partner:

> 'suppose two people are carrying on business in partnership as hotel proprietors and it is necessary for the purpose of carrying on that hotel, that business, that they should be supplied from time to time with wine, and suppose one of the partners is carrying on a wholly independent business on his own account in the wine business and supplies wine to the partnership, it would be idle to suggest, would it not, that for the purpose of ascertaining the profits of the hotel you could not deduct the sums paid to the partner who was the wine merchant?' (Romer LJ at p 319)

Salaries, fees, etc

2.7 It is not unusual for partners in a professional partnership to hold offices or employments in the course of the partnership business on terms that the income from them is regarded as partnership income and divided between partners in accordance with the partnership profit-sharing arrangements. Subject to ESC A37 (see below), the income remains taxable as employment income and the normal rules of taxing employment income apply to it. It remains taxable as employment income in the hands of the partner earning it and the same limited expenses are deductible for tax purposes as for any other employment income (see *ITEPA 2003, s 336*). In particular, costs of travelling to the place of employment are not deductible for tax purposes, nor are any other incidental expenses such as secretarial or support costs. Where these costs are borne for convenience by the partnership they will not be incurred 'wholly and exclusively' for the purposes of the partnership business and will not be deductible in computing partnership profits. Even if it is clearly demonstrable that the employment itself was undertaken at the instigation of the other partners for reasons closely connected with and beneficial to the partnership business the illogical and unsatisfactory decision by the House of Lords in the case of *Mitchell and Edon v Ross HL* (1961) 40 TC 11 presents an insuperable hurdle to any claim to deduct expenses of the employment in computing the taxable income of that business.

2.8 In certain circumstances Extra-Statutory Concession A37 provides that earnings of a partner as director of a company (but, it should be noted, not earnings as an employee) may be treated as part of the professional income of the partnership and brought into the calculation of the profits of the partnership, with expenses incurred being allowed in the normal way. ESC A37 will apply if:

- the fees are only a small part of the profits;
- the directorship is a normal incident of the profession and of the particular practice concerned;
- there is an agreement between the partners that the fees from the appointment are to be treated as partnership income and divided between the partners, and that arrangement actually happens in practice; and
- all the partners agree that the income is to be treated as part of the partnership profits for tax purposes, and written confirmation of this is given to HMRC.

ESC A37 is paralleled by a similar treatment in respect of National Insurance Contributions ('NICs') under *SI 2001/1004, reg 27* – see **Chapter 24**.

2.9 Where a person, in the course or furtherance of a trade profession or vocation, accepts any office, services supplied by him as the holder of that office are treated as supplied in the course or furtherance of the trade, profession or vocation (*Value Added Tax Act 1994, s 94(4)* so will normally bear VAT. Note that *s 94(4)* applies only to offices, not employments; but it applies even if the conditions for ESC A37 are not fulfilled (or the benefit of ESC A37 is not taken) such that the income from the office in question is charged to tax as employment income of the individual concerned. In other words, in cases where *s 94(4)* applies it is not possible to avoid the imposition of VAT by accepting or procuring that the income is treated as employment income rather than as business income of the partnership. Further complexities of the VAT position are discussed in **Chapter 26**.

2.10 Where ESC A37 cannot apply, or where it is more practical for the partner concerned to retain the income outside the partnership, the profit-sharing arrangements may need to be varied accordingly to preserve equity between the partners.

Example 2.1 – Partner retaining income outside the partnership

A firm of five equal partners has profits of £190,000 *after* A has kept £10,000 directors' fees.

	Total	*A*	*B*	*C*	*D*	*E*
	£000	*£000*	*£000*	*£000*	*£000*	*£000*
Profits	190					
Adjustment	10	(10)				
	200	40	40	40	40	40
	190	30	40	40	40	40

Interest paid by the partnership

2.11 Normally interest paid by a partnership is deductible in computing profits or losses of a business subject to the usual requirements including that it be incurred wholly and exclusively for the purposes of the business. The position may however be more complex.

If a partner's capital account becomes overdrawn, HMRC may argue that part of the partnership's borrowing has been used to fund the overdrawn account such that tax relief for interest on partnership borrowings should be restricted. In the simple case of a sole trader preparing accounts on a cash basis with a bank overdraft, an overdrawn capital account and few business assets it may be reasonable to say that the overdraft has funded the excess drawings. But things will rarely be that simple, even for a sole trader. If there are both liabilities and assets in the balance sheet, who is to say that the business assets have not been financed by the overdraft and the overdrawn capital account by the business creditors? Or if the capital account has become overdrawn because of losses, how much of the loss is attributable to non-cash items such as depreciation or amortisation? The potential complexity of the analysis is apparent from HMRC's somewhat superficial analysis at BIM 45690.

The Special Commissioners case of *Silk v Fletcher* [1999] STC (SCD) 220 gives some guidance, but not much. In that case the taxpayer was originally in partnership but he then worked as a sole practitioner. His capital account was substantially overdrawn and for many years his drawings exceeded his profits. The taxpayer sought, in calculating profits, to deduct the interest incurred on several loans. The Special Commissioner held that, even if the capital account was not overdrawn, it would not necessarily follow that the interest would be tax deductible. It had to be ascertained how much of the borrowed money was actually used for business purposes. As drawings exceeded profits, the implication was that at least part of the interest was used to fund private expenditure. The taxpayer also argued that his capital account was not overdrawn because the accounts did not reflect goodwill. The former Special Commissioner disagreed with this contention, although the appeal was allowed in part after making adjustments for depreciation, debtors and creditors.

2.12 If the matter is complicated even for a sole trader, it is that much more complicated for a partnership. If one partner's capital account is overdrawn but others are in credit it may well be possible to argue that the overdrawn account is being funded not by any partnership bank borrowings but by the positive capital accounts of the remaining partners, such that no restriction to tax relief on interest paid by the partnership should be made. However, each situation will depend on its own facts: at the end of the day the question to be asked is – what was the purpose for which any interest was paid?

A partner may borrow money to acquire an asset personally but permit the partnership to use the asset on the understanding that the partnership will pay the interest on the loan and charge it in the partnership accounts. The interest payable by the partnership will normally be allowable in this situation as a substitute for payment of rent to the partner. It is a moot point whether strictly speaking the partner should treat himself both as receiving rent equal to the interest paid on his behalf and as paying out the interest which has been paid on his behalf. In practice HMRC do not seem to take the point. Difficulties will arise if the amount of the interest paid by the partnership exceeds the market value of occupancy of the property or part of the property occupied by the partnership – the excess is in effect a distribution of profit to the partner and is not deductible for the partnership.

The effect on CGT and inheritance tax reliefs on holding property outside the partnership should be considered (see **Chapters 12**, **13**, **15** and **23**).

For partnerships using the cash basis, interest payments are only permitted up to a maximum of £500 (*ITTOIA 2005, s 57B*).

Expenses incurred by partners

2.13 In some cases partners incur and bear personally expenditure which is nonetheless incurred 'wholly and exclusively' for the purposes of the partnership business. Common examples include motoring expenses and the use of the home for business purposes. In the context of a corporate member of a partnership (see **Chapter 17**) the expenses borne by the partner might also extend to remuneration of a director (including pension contributions) or other expenses of the company.

All expenses, including those incurred at the partner level, must be claimed on the partnership return, There is no scope for a partner to make a personal claim for expenses of this kind outside of the partnership return. Preparing the partnership return correctly involves adding together the partnership expenditure and the expenditure incurred by the individual partners in order to arrive at the total expenditure figure for the partnership. This is then included in the Standard Accounts Information.

HMRC say (at BIM 82075) that it is necessary that 'the adjustments are made before apportionment of the net profit between the partners' and instruct that officers 'should not accept any deductions for expenses from the net profits allocated to a partner'. In practice, HMRC generally accept that tax relief should be effectively given to the partner incurring the relevant expense, as in **Example 2.2**.

Example 2.2 – Expenditure incurred outside the partnership

Tony and Julia are osteopaths. They share profits equally and do not use the cash basis in preparing their accounts. Tony uses his car for work 75% of the time. His expenditure (reduced by 25% for private use) is £2,500 a year. Julia often works from home. She incurs expenses of £780 in doing so. Tony and Julia have agreed that each should bear these business expenses out of their own profit shares. The partnership profits are £50,000 before the partners' expense claims are deducted (so that the taxable profits are £46,720).

The profits will be allocated as follows:

	Total	Tony	Julia
	£	£	£
Partnership profits before personal expenses (shared 50:50)	50,000	25,000	25,000
Less:			
Tony's motor expenses	(2,500)	(2,500)	
Julia's use of home	(780)		(780)
Adjusted profits	46,720	22,500	24,220

However, care must be taken to differentiate between the payment by a partner of expenses which are incurred wholly and exclusively for the purposes of the partnership business and expenses which are incurred by a partner for his own personal purposes albeit in some way related to his participation in the partnership. An example of this is interest on a loan taken personally by a partner for the purpose of investing in a partnership: any relief for such interest will be available if at all under the provisions of *ITA 2007, s 383* – see **Chapter 3**.

Partner recruitment costs

2.14 In the past, HMRC have resisted claims to tax relief on the costs of recruiting partners on the basis that they, like the costs of drawing up a partnership agreement, are in the nature of capital costs. HMRC now accept that recruitment costs are normally allowable as revenue expenditure, save where there is some additional factor involved. They give as examples of relevant factors (at PM30800):

- whether the admission of the partner has a fundamental impact on the structure of the firm's business involving more than a mere expansion of the business;
- whether the partner is recruited as part of the acquisition of a business;
- whether the new partner's capital contribution is a material factor in the recruitment.

Costs of partnership agreements and disagreements

2.15 The costs of drawing up or amending a partnership agreement will usually be disallowable as capital expenditure. This would extend to costs of transferring a partnership's business to a limited company or to an LLP. Similarly the costs of dissolving a partnership will be capital in nature.

However, it is likely that the legal and professional costs which an ongoing partnership business incurs in getting rid of (or otherwise settling a dispute with) a recalcitrant partner will be viewed in the same light as those of recruiting a partner, with similar factors determining the tax-deductibility of the expense. This is to be contrasted with the position where a partnership dispute is resolved by a splitting of the business, with two or more groups of partners each taking part of the business and going their separate ways: the costs in such a case are likely to be capital in nature.

Termination payments to partners

2.16 The treatment of any payment made to a partner on leaving a partnership depends on its true character. In some circumstances a payment may simply be an additional share of profit which will be taxable in the usual way. In others the payment may be in settlement of some alleged grievance which the leaving partner has against the firm which will usually be tax-free. In the conjoined First-tier Tribunal cases of *Self and Morgan v Commissioners of HMRC* [2009] UKFTT 78 (TC) the payments in question were held to be taxable as being in each case an allocation of profits made to the appellant in the capacity of partner and not as 'entirely collateral payments made to them otherwise than in their capacity as partners'.

2.17 However, there are occasions when a payment will not be an allocation of profits, as in *AB v HMRC* [2011] UKFTT 685 (TC). The taxpayer had received termination payments from two unconnected partnerships on two successive occasions. On each occasion the relationship between AB and the partnership had broken down and on each occasion a payment had been made by the partnership on AB's leaving. On the first occasion the payment was described as and held to be a share of profit: in the other it was held to be in the nature of compensation for the adverse treatment AB had suffered at the hands of the partnership. The discussion in the case of the factors to be considered and the reasons why different conclusions were reached in respect of the two payments are well worth reviewing.

Although in the cases cited the Tribunal was required only to determine the treatment of the receipts in the hands of the ex-partner concerned (rather than the treatment of the payment in the hands of the partnership) it would seem that the payment would be deductible in computing partnership profits if and only if it had the character of compensation. For another point arising in the *Self and Morgan* case, see **Chapter 21**.

Payments to partnership service companies

2.18 For treatment of payments to service companies, see **Chapter 17.**

Valuation of work in progress on a cessation to trade

2.19 The valuation of work in progress is covered by statute in the case of a cessation of business.

If trading stock and work in progress are sold to another UK trader, the value of the consideration for the sale is regarded as a trading receipt of the one and as a trading expense of the other unless the parties are connected, as defined by *ITTOIA 2005, s 179*. Partners are treated as connected with their fellow partners (and their spouses, civil partners, and relatives) for this purpose. Further, parties are connected if one is a partnership and the other has a right to a share in the partnership (which would include of course any partner in the partnership); if both are partnerships that have one or more common partners; or if one is a partnership and the other a company and the same person or persons have control of each.

On a transfer between connected persons, the stock and work in progress are to be valued at the amount that would have been realised in an arm's-length transaction.

If this value exceeds both:

(a) the actual sale price; and

(b) the amount that would have been taken into account as the cost if the stock had been sold in the ordinary course of trade;

the parties may jointly elect to substitute the greater of (*a*) and (*b*) for the arm's-length value. The election must be made on or before the first anniversary of the filing date for the tax year in which the trade is discontinued (*ITTOIA 2005, s 178*). If trading stock and work in progress are not sold to another UK trader, they are valued at the amount they would have realised in an arm's-length transaction (*ITTOIA 2005, s 175(4)*).

This may in theory cause difficulty where a partnership business is transferred to a company in exchange for shares. The value of the consideration (ie, the shares) will normally reflect the full market value of the stock being transferred, so that arguably an election under *s 178* may not be possible. This may particularly an issue on incorporation of a property development business, where the market value of the land may greatly exceed its cost. In practice HMRC do not seem to take the point, and accept a *s 178* election provided both the company and the partnership treat the property as having been sold and acquired at its original cost to the partnership.

2.20 Where trading stock is sold or transferred on cessation together with other assets to an unconnected party, and falls to be valued at the amount realised on sale (*ITTOIA 2005, s 176*), the sale proceeds or value of the consideration are apportioned on a just and reasonable basis between the assets.

2.21 Where work in progress is transferred for money or other valuable consideration to another trader carrying on a profession or vocation in the UK, and the consideration exceeds cost, the excess over cost need not be brought into the computation of profits or gains for the period immediately before the discontinuance. Instead, it can be taxed as if it were an amount received after discontinuance, ie a post-cessation receipt (*ITTOIA 2005, s 185(1)*). An election for this treatment must be made not later than 12 months after the 31 January following the tax year of discontinuance (*ITTOIA 2005, s 185(2)*).

Post-cessation receipts and expenses

2.22

> **Focus**
>
> For 2013/14 onwards, if, immediately before the trade permanently ceases, an election to use the cash basis under *ITTOIA 2005, s 25A* has been effected in relation to that trade, a sum will be treated as a post-cessation receipt only if it would have been brought into account in calculating the profits of the trade on the cash basis had it been received at that time (*ITTOIA 2005, s 246(2A)*).

2.23 Income may arise after a partnership has ceased trading which is not included in the final accounts. This income is charged to tax by *ITTOIA 2005, Pt 2, Ch 18,* normally as income of the year in which it is received. This charges tax:

(a) on sums received after discontinuance but not brought into account for a period prior to discontinuance (because they had not then arisen or could not be ascertained); and

(b) on deductions allowed in computing profits up to discontinuance, in respect of debts incurred, which are subsequently released (other than as part of a statutory insolvency arrangement).

2.24 Where post-cessation receipts are received and taxed as such, expenses incurred which would have been allowed as a deduction had the business continued are deductible in calculating the taxable amount. Any excess expenditure can be carried forward for relief against post-cessation receipts in later years (*ITTOIA 2005, s 255*).

2.25 If the income before discontinuance was treated as earned income, the amount chargeable is likewise treated as earned income (*ITTOIA 2005, s 256*). This may be of importance for the calculation of funding limits for personal pensions.

2.26 There may be occasions where the person receiving the post-cessation receipt would prefer it to be treated as income arising at the date of cessation of the business (perhaps because personal allowances or other reliefs are available in that tax year, or the marginal rate of tax for that year is lower). Accordingly, *ITTOIA, s 257* provides for an election to that effect to be made.

The election may be made in respect of sums received in any tax year beginning not later than *six* years after the discontinuance. The election is by notice in writing to HMRC within one year from the 31 January next following the tax year in which the amount was received, and the effect is that the sum received is treated as received on the date on which the discontinuance took place. The *tax payable* on the post-cessation receipt will then be calculated by reference to the tax position in the earlier year, although the *claim* will relate to the tax year in which the sum is received and will result in the tax being treated as additional tax payable for that later year.

The question whether the election is to be made by the partnership representative partner on behalf of the whole partnership, or whether each partner has the right to choose to make or not make the election in respect of his share of the post-cessation receipt, is not clear: probably the former applies.

2.27 If expenditure in the seven years after cessation is incurred:

- for remedying defective work done, goods supplied or service provided in the course of the former business or by way of damages in respect of such defective work etc; or
- for indemnity insurance or legal or professional services in relation to such defective work etc; or
- for debt collection;

a claim may be made against *any* income of the tax year of payment. Such a claim cannot be made to the extent that the payments are relieved in some other way (eg, against post-cessation receipts), and any amounts recovered must be brought into account. The time limit for the claim is one year from 31 January following the end of the tax year in which the liability, etc is ascertained (*ITA 2007, s 96*).

2.28 Adequate provision for bad debts should be made in respect of bills rendered but unpaid prior to the cessation, and any amounts recovered for which provision has been made are assessed as post-cessation receipts. Any under-provision is treated in the same way as post-cessation expenditure and may be relieved against other income of the year.

Chapter 3

Taxation of Partners

Signposts

- Assessments are made at the partner level, with each partner responsible for self-assessing his or her individual share of partnership income on the basis of the partnership statement (see **3.1 – 3.6**).
- Special rules have developed to deal with the case where a partner disagrees with the amounts allocated on a partnership statement (see **3.7**).
- Capital disposals (rather than gains) are disclosed at partnership level, with gains computed by partners on their individual self-assessment returns (see **3.8**).
- Profits are allocated by reference to profit-sharing arrangements in the relevant period. Different sources may be allocated in different ways (see **3.9 – 3.10**).
- Relief for interest on a partner's qualifying loan is claimed in the partner's personal self-assessment return or corporation tax return (see **3.11 – 3.16**).
- Claims and elections which affect the computation of the partnership profits must be made in the partnership return (see **3.17 – 3.20**).

Self-assessment

3.1 For each tax year in which a firm carries on a trade (the 'actual trade'), each partner's share of the firm's trading profits or losses is treated, for the purposes of *ITTOIA 2005, Pt 2, Ch 15* (basis periods), as profits or losses of a trade carried on by the partner alone (the 'notional trade') (*ITTOIA 2005, s 852*). For the effect of this on basis periods, see **Chapter 4**.

However, although a partner is treated for these purposes as carrying on his own business with its own basis period and its own overlap relief, the legislation does not go so far as to treat membership of successive partnerships as being a single activity. A 'serial partner' does not, for tax purposes, carry on a single overarching business comprising his membership of successive partnerships: he carries on a number of businesses in succession, each time carrying on the business in question jointly with the other partners. This has important implications for the deduction of expenses and losses attributable to the separate businesses. *HMRC v Vaines* [2016] UKUT 2 (TCC) is the leading (indeed, so far the only) case on the point.

Until 31 December 2005, V was a member of the HH partnership. In connection with the business of HH, a German bank ('BL') claimed to be entitled to certain amounts from the former partners of HH including V. V believed that the risk of challenging the claim through the courts was unacceptably high because if BL were successful there was a possibility that he would be made bankrupt and prevented from practising as a member of SSD LLP, a firm he had subsequently joined. V accordingly paid €300,000 to settle the claim in January 2008 and sought for tax purposes to deduct it in computing his professional income from SSD.

V succeeded before the First-tier Tribunal. This was essentially on the basis that the effect of *ITTOIA 2005, s 852* was that he (personally) was to be treated for tax purposes as carrying on his own business. This single business was first carried on jointly with the other partners of HH and subsequently with the other members of SSD. The €300,000 was spent wholly and exclusively for the purposes of that business and was deductible in computing his profits from it.

The Upper Tribunal found that that was a misunderstanding of the law. Regardless of the fact that assessments were made on partners and not on a partnership, it remained the case that each partnership carried on its own business. The proper question was therefore not whether the €300,000 was spent for the purposes of V's business; for there was no such business. Rather, it was whether the expenditure was incurred for the purposes of the business of SSD (the only business in which V was involved at the time). As a matter of fact it was not – it had no real connection at all with the business of SSD – and it was therefore not deductible.

3.2 Partnership income is computed for the whole partnership by reference to the various sources of income for each accounting period.

Allocation of partnership profit

3.3 The partnership is required to make a return of its taxable income under each income heading to HMRC. The division of the profits between the partners is shown in the partnership statement.

ITA 2007, s 850 requires that taxable profit for any period of account is allocated between partners 'in accordance with the firm's profit-sharing arrangements during that period'. The firm's profit-sharing arrangements (that is, the basis on which partnership profits have been shared) is a question of fact. Partners are generally free to share profits in whatever way they wish and to vary those arrangements by mutual agreement from time to time. A share of profit need not (and often does not) bear any relation to the amount of effort or capital contributed by the partner. Partners need not share profits and losses in the same proportions; and they may choose to allocate different kinds of income in differing proportions. But the crucial point is that once they have agreed how profits of a period are to be shared in the 'real world' that same basis of allocation must be applied in allocating tax-adjusted profits between partners.

HMRC guidance (at BIM 82055) refers to the case of *Bucks v Bowers* 46 TC 275 in stating that 'The allocation of profits or losses for an accounting period cannot be varied retrospectively after the end of that accounting period'. The main problem with that assertion is that *Bucks v Bowers* does not in fact say anything of the kind. The case concerned the availability of earned income relief and it is worth recording what the judge actually said:

> 'It appears clear that, in the absence of agreement to the contrary between the partners, any part of the income of the firm which qualified for earned income relief would, for the purpose of such relief, have to be apportioned rateably between the partners in proportions corresponding to their shares of the entire income under the articles of partnership. In the present case, as appears from the schedules exhibited to the Case Stated, the partners agreed on 22nd February 1968 – ie, several years after the conclusion of the year of assessment 1964–65 – to reallocate the income for that year in such proportions that the individual partners (in contradistinction to the corporate partners) took the entire income in respect of which earned income relief was claimed. It seems to me clear that the right to earned income relief, if any, crystallised once and for all at the end of the year of assessment, and that this ex post facto reallocation of income could not operate to redistribute the right to relief. Mr. Nolan relied upon *Commissioners of Inland Revenue v Sterling Trust Ltd.* (1925) 12 TC 868, where the question was as to the allocation of an outgoing to a particular part of the company's income. It seems to me that quite different considerations arise in that connection from those which arise in relation to the allocation of shares of profit. However, as I have said, that question does not arise here and I need say nothing further.'

Essentially the question in the case was whether one could notionally identify within the partnership's total trading profit an element which was eligible for Earned Income Relief and allocate that part to the individual partners who could benefit from such relief. It was held that one could not, especially having previously made in the accounts an allocation of profits which took no account of Earned Income Relief. This is a long way from saying that a decision on the allocation of profits of losses of an accounting period between partners must, if it is to be effective for tax purposes, be made before the last day of the accounting period. In many partnerships the basis on which profit for a period is allocated is not agreed until after the end of the period when the relative performance and profitability of the partners is assessed. There is, in fact, no previously-made allocation to vary. At most, *Bucks v Bowers* underlines the fact that once an allocation is finally made for commercial purposes, that allocation is binding for tax purposes.

3.4 The August 2016 Consultation Document, 'Partnership taxation: proposals to clarify tax treatment' included proposals dealing with profit-sharing arrangements and allocation of tax-adjusted profit to partners.

Proposal 5 in the Consultation Document addressed government concerns arising from the 'potential for uncertainty where partners dispute the allocation of profits made to them for tax purposes on the basis that the actual profit-sharing arrangements are different from the written agreement or as stated by the nominated partner'. The original proposal was that legislation should be introduced to confirm that the arrangements set out in the partnership or LLP agreement should be conclusive unless overridden by notification to HMRC from the nominated partner. Following consultation, it is now proposed that the profit allocation stated in the partnership return will be 'the first point of reference for HMRC in determining the taxable profits of each partner' but that where that allocation is disputed by a partner 'the Government intends to legislate to protect the partners from being taxed on incorrect profit shares'.

The second Finance Bill of 2017 proposes to amend the law to introduce a mechanism to allow any dispute between partners as to the allocation of profit between them to be referred for adjudication to the First-Tier Tax Tribunal. This change will apply to returns relating to the tax year 2018/19 or any subsequent tax year.

Proposal 6 in the Consultation Document identified Government concerns that flexibility in allocating profits 'is seen by some partnerships as an opportunity to manipulate profit, loss and capital gains allocations for tax purposes. For example, by allocating specific items of income and expenditure to particular partners or classes of partner or by determining profit shares after the end of the accounting period'. Following consultation it is proposed that 'to reduce the scope for allocating profits for purely tax-motivated purposes', the following changes will be made:

- clarifying (presumably by legislation) how to apply a firm's profit-sharing arrangements consistently in allocating taxable profits among the partners, including in cases where different partners' taxable profits are computed on different bases;
- passing legislation that will provide that any retrospective variation to a partnership's profit-sharing arrangements made after the period-end will not apply. How this will work where there is no agreed allocation of profit at all until after the end of the period is not yet clear;
- where a partner joins or leaves a partnership during an accounting period, legislation will provide that such partners will be treated as taxable on their share in profits or losses that arose during the period in which they were partners or members. The profit arising during the part of the accounting period when a person is a partner should be used as a basis and the allocation agreement in force at that time (the time of their joining the partnership) will be applied to that proportion to determine the partner's share of taxable profit.

In each case it is expected that legislation will appear in a second 2017 Finance Act and will be effective for periods of account starting after 5 April 2018.

3.5 Taxable profit is allocated between partners 'in accordance with the firm's profit-sharing arrangements during that period' (*ITTOIA 2005, s 850(1)*). This is easy enough where profits are shared on a simple percentage basis – see **Example 3.1.**

Example 3.1 – Simple profit-sharing ratios

A, B and C agree to share profits 40% 30% 30%. Their commercial profit is £100,000 allocated £40,000 to A, £30,000 to B, £30,000 to C. Their tax-adjusted profit is £120,000. This will be allocated for tax purposes £48,000 £36,000 and £36,000.

Although the phrase is simple enough, in some circumstances it may not be clear what it means. Examples in HMRC's guidance notes suggest that the preferred method may be to allocate tax-adjusted profits by applying to them the same formula as has been used commercially. But this can give capricious results – as in **Example 3.2** below where Brown, despite having 50% of the commercial profit, has a smaller tax charge than Smith, who has 31.25% of the commercial profit.

Example 3.2 – Complex profit-sharing ratios

Smith, Jones and Brown share profits as follows:

	Smith	*Jones*	*Brown*
First £30,000 (salary)	£20,000	£10,000	£0
Next £50,000 (return on capital)	£5,000	£5,000	£40,000
Balance	45%	45%	10%
Allocation of commercial profit £80,000	£25,000	£15,000	£40,000
Allocation of tax adjusted profit £130,000	£47,500	£37,500	£45,000

An alternative, which would also arguably meet the statutory requirement of allocation 'in accordance with the firm's profit-sharing arrangements', and which would seem fairer, would be to allocate taxable profits in the same proportion as commercial profits. Probably either method would be acceptable to HMRC if agreed between the partners and applied consistently. The second Finance Bill of 2017 proposes to amend the law such that only this second method will be acceptable: taxable profit will be allocated in accordance with the 'partner's percentage' (defined as equal to the partner's percentage share of the commercial profit). This change will apply for periods of account (or company accounting periods) beginning on or after Royal Assent – expected to be late autumn 2017.

Whatever method is used, the total amount allocated between partners must be no more and no less than the total of the tax-adjusted profit. If the allocation gives some different answer – typically because of partnership salaries or interest – it must be adjusted to accord with this requirement:

Example 3.3 – Partnership salaries creating 'loss'

Profits of a four-person partnership are shared equally, after allocating a salary of £80,000 to each of three partners. The profits, before deduction of these salaries, are £160,000 and this is also the tax-adjusted profit. Then, commercially, each of the three salaried partners will show a profit of £60,000 (being £80,000 minus the 25% share of the partnership 'loss' of £80,000) while the remaining partner will show a loss of £20,000. There can however be no question of assessing the partners on a higher figure than the partnership's tax-adjusted profit: so the three partners who actually shared in the profit will each be assessed on their proportionate share of the taxable profit, namely £53,333.

One further commercial point should be considered here. One not uncommonly sees arrangements whereby a guarantee is given to one or more partners that his or her share of profit will not fall below a minimum figure. This is not quite the same as the sort of prior share of profit discussed in **Example 3.3**, for the partner with the guarantee is then being indemnified against any share of loss. This kind of arrangement, which has historically been fairly common in businesses in the financial dealing sector, can give some anomalous results:

Example 3.4 – Guaranteed profit shares

A is sole trader. He takes B and C into partnership with him. He guarantees that their share of profit in the first year will be not less than their previous salary of £55,000 each.

The partnership loses a large customer and the first year's results show a profit (also the tax-adjusted profit) of only £50,000 in total. Commercially, A suffers a loss of £60,000 (ie the 'guaranteed minima' of £110,000 less the actual profit of £50,000).

B and C will each pay tax on £25,000 of profit. A gets no tax relief for his commercial loss of £60,000 (for there is in fact no partnership loss to be relieved). The planning point here is that any guarantee given by A should be stated in the partnership agreement in terms of after-tax not pre-tax income, or should provide for suitable tax indemnities.

3.6 Each partner is responsible for obtaining the relevant details from the partnership statement, completing his or her own personal tax return and paying the tax due. The partnership will usually provide each partner with a copy of the relevant section of the partnership statement to assist them to complete their return. It is not acceptable to enter 'see partnership return' on a personal tax return. The actual income and profit figures have to be entered on the form, and HMRC will check the partners' personal returns against that of the partnership to ensure that they agree.

3.7 It may happen that a partner disagrees with the figure of profit that is allocated to him or her on the partnership return. This may be either because there is disagreement as to the quantum of the partnership profit for tax purposes or because there is disagreement as to how the partnership profit is allocated for tax purposes. This was the case in *Morgan and Self v HMRC* [2009] UKFTT 78 (TC). In the event the Tribunal held that the figures allocated to the relevant partners on the partnership return were correct. But the Chairman expressed the view that where a partner disagreed with the figure of taxable profit allocated to him or her on the partnership statement the correct procedure was for the partner to self-assess on the basis of the amount believed to be the correct figure but also to disclose in the return the amount shown in the partnership statement. See also **Chapter 21** for further discussion of the point and regarding the technical matter in dispute in the case.

The second Finance Bill of 2017 proposes to reverse the position established by Morgan and Self by introducing a mechanism to allow any dispute between partners as to the allocation of profit between them to be referred for adjudication to the First-Tier Tax Tribunal. This change will apply to returns relating to the tax year 2018/19 or any subsequent tax year. This will apply only to disputes as to how the taxable profit is allocated: if the dispute is about the quantum of the partnership taxable profit the usual appeal processes described in Chapter 21 will apply.

3.8 The position for capital gains is slightly different. When a partnership asset is disposed of, each partner may make a chargeable gain on his or her share of that asset but the gains made by each partner will vary. This may be because:

- some partners own a smaller or greater share of the asset;
- partners will have owned the asset for differing lengths of time;
- each partner's entitlement to reliefs and allowances depends on his or her personal situation.

Focus

There is no such thing as a partnership capital gain. The partnership is simply required to enter the proceeds from the disposal of the asset on the partnership return. This in turn is allocated between the partners in the appropriate ratio and each partner self-assesses the tax due on his or her chargeable gain. The partnership may need to provide the individual partners with further information about the asset, for example the acquisition details and incidental costs of sale, so that they can complete their capital gains tax computation.

Example 3.5 – Self-assessment of partnership profits

For 2016/17, Adams and Baker, who have for some years practised in partnership as solicitors, sharing profits equally, report the following details on their partnership tax return and statement:

Details	*£000*
Professional profit	120
Untaxed interest	20
Rent from sub-letting part of the office	10
	150
Disposal proceeds on sale of office	200

Each partner will include the following entries on his personal tax return and self-assess the tax due:

Details	*Adams*	*Baker*
	£000	*£000*
Practising profit	60	60
Untaxed interest	10	10
Rent from letting part of the office	5	5
	75	75

Details		*Adams*	*Baker*
		£000	*£000*
Disposal proceeds on sale of office	The disposal proceeds are used by each partner to calculate his or her chargeable gain	100	100

3.9 As can be seen from **Examples 3.5** and **3.6**, the taxable income of the partnership is divided between the partners in the profit-sharing ratio of the period of account. **Example 3.7** illustrates this point further with more complex profit-sharing arrangements.

Example 3.6 – Change in profit-sharing arrangements

The established partnership of Michael, Rose and Alexander prepares accounts to 31 December and has shared profits equally after the following partnership salaries and interest on capital:

	Salaries	*Interest on capital*
	£	*£*
Michael	10,000	1,000
Rose	8,000	1,600
Alexander	6,000	2,000

From 1 April 2015, it was decided that Alexander's salary should be increased to £10,000, that Rose's salary should cease, and that the balance of the profits should be shared in the following proportions: Michael 1/2, Rose 1/3, and Alexander 1/6. Interest on capital remained unchanged.

Recent profits, as adjusted for tax purposes, were:

	£
Year to 31 December 2014	80,000
Year to 31 December 2015	70,000

The tax position is as follows:

	Michael	*Rose*	*Alexander*	*Total*
	£	*£*	*£*	*£*
2014/15				
Salaries	10,000	8,000	6,000	24,000
Interest on capital	1,000	1,600	2,000	4,600
Profits (equally)	17,134	17,133	17,133	51,400
	28,134	26,733	25,133	80,000

	Michael	*Rose*	*Alexander*	*Total*
	£	*£*	*£*	*£*
2015/16				
1.1.15–31.3.15				
Salaries (three months)	2,500	2,000	1,500	6,000
Interest on capital (three months)	250	400	500	1,150
Profits (three months equally)	3,450	3,450	3,450	10,350
	6,200	5,850	5,450	17,500
1.4.15–31.12.15				
Salaries (nine months)	7,500	0	7,500	15,000
Interest on capital (nine months)	750	1,200	1,500	3,450
Profits (nine months 1/2:1/3:1/6)	17,025	11,350	5,675	34,050
	25,275	12,550	14,675	52,500
	31,475	18,400	20,125	70,000

Example 3.7 – More complex profit-sharing arrangements

Between 6 April 2015 and 5 April 2016, the long-established partnership of Afon, Pentre and Felin shares its profits as follows:

	Afon	*Pentre*	*Felin*	*Total*
	£000	*£000*	*£000*	*£000*
Prior share				
First slice	4	4	–	8
Interest on capital				
Second slice	3	2	1	6
Partnership salaries				
Third slice	10	15	12	37
Special purposes				
Fourth slice	7	9	4	20
Income-sharing ratio				
Fifth slice	11	11	11	33
Special efforts				
Sixth slice	15	2	20	37
Expenses re special efforts				
Seventh slice	(5)	(3)	(4)	(12)
Division of profit between those dates	45	40	44	129

The profits will be allocated on the partnership return for 2015/16, and the individual partners will self-assess their share of the profits on their personal returns for 2015/16, the total of the profit share in each case reflecting exactly what was allocated by reference to their arrangements.

Dealing with different sources of income

3.10 Although a partner is likely to regard his share of partnership income as arising from 'the partnership' without differentiating the underlying sources, it will be necessary for tax purposes to identify the various sources of income of the partnership and apply the appropriate rules to compute taxable income from each source before allocating income and gains between partners in accordance with partnership agreement.

In principle it is possible for the partnership agreement to allocate different kinds of partnership income in different ways. For example, the agreement may provide that trading profits are shared equally between partners but rental income arising from letting of surplus accommodation may be shared in proportion that the property is owned by partners. Where this is the case, the different allocations of different sources of income must also be followed for tax purposes.

Example 3.8 – Identifying sources

The profits of a professional partnership are as follows:

	£000
Fees	100
Salaries from lecturing appointments	20
Investment income and interest received	10
	130
Expenses	(50)
Net profit	80

The expenses of £50,000 include £2,000 for travelling by the partners to their lecturing appointments and £1,000 in respect of management fees attributable to receipt of investment income.

Assuming that the cash basis is not being used, taxable income will be as follows:

		Fees	*Salaries*	*Investment income*
	£000	*£000*	*£000*	*£000*
Income as listed		100	20	10
Expenses	50			

		Fees	*Salaries*	*Investment income*
	£000	*£000*	*£000*	*£000*
Less: relating to salaries, investment income and interest	(3)*			
		(47)		
Taxable:		53	20	10
Total taxable			83	

* The expenses relating to the salaries, investment income and interest cannot be set against the salaries and interest, since the charging rules for those sources of income do not permit such deductions.

Interest paid by partners

3.11 Where a partnership pays interest in respect of partnership borrowings the interest may be deductible in computing partnership profits subject to the normal rules for computing profits from the relevant source. Thus interest on a loan taken wholly and exclusively for the purposes of a trade or profession carried on by the partnership is normally deductible in computing trading profits: a loan taken wholly and exclusively for the purposes of a property business is deductible in computing rental profits (subject to the restrictions at *ITTOIA 2005, s 272A* where the loan is a 'dwelling-related loan').

Quite separately and independently from the provisions relating to borrowings of the partnership, *ITA 2007, s 383* gives tax relief in certain circumstances in respect of interest paid by an individual partner on loans taken personally outside the partnership where the money is used for a qualifying purpose. Where interest relief is available, a claim is required and relief is then given by deducting the amount eligible for relief in calculating the individual's net income for the tax year in which the interest is paid (see Step 2 of the calculation provided for by *ITA 2007, s 23*).

The provisions specifically applicable to loans taken by an individual partner are:

- *ITA 2007, s 388* (loan to buy plant or machinery for partnership use);
- *ITA 2007, s 398* (loan to invest in a partnership).

In each case it is the purpose of the loan that matters, rather than the security for it. Thus relief is not affected where the borrowing is secured on private property (often the dwelling house) owned jointly by the partner and his or her spouse or civil partner, provided the interest is borne solely by the partner and otherwise meets the criteria for relief.

3.12 *ITA 2007, s 388* gives relief for interest on a loan used for capital expenditure on the provision of plant or machinery if:

- the plant or machinery is owned by the partner but is used for the purposes of a trade, profession or 'ordinary property business' (that is, a property business other than a furnished holiday lettings business) carried on by the partnership; and

- the partnership is entitled to a capital allowance (or liable to a balancing charge) in respect of the plant or machinery for the period of account in which the interest is paid (see **8.6**).

As regards the second bullet point, if the partnership has been entitled to a capital allowance (or liable to a balancing charge) for any period of account it is treated as continuing to be so entitled or liable until the period of account in which it is required to bring in a disposal value. This is apparently to ensure that eligibility for relief is maintained even after full allowances have been given (perhaps under the rules for Annual Investment Allowance).

However, *ITA 2007, s 389* provides that interest is eligible for relief only if:

- the individual is a member of the partnership at the time the interest is paid; and
- the interest falls due and payable not later than three years after the end of the period of account in which the loan was made.

Thus if a loan to acquire an asset is expected to extend beyond the end of three years after the end of the period of account of the partnership in which the loan was taken, it will be more tax-efficient for the partnership to borrow and for the asset to be a partnership asset.

If the machinery or plant is used partly for the purposes of the partnership's trade, profession or ordinary property business and partly for another purpose, relief is given for such part of the interest as is attributable to the trade (etc) as is just and reasonable having regard to all the relevant circumstances.

Example 3.9 – Relief for interest under s 388 (1)

Eric is senior partner of Idle & Co, a firm of solicitors. He borrows £25,000 on a three-year loan to purchase a BMW (used 50% for business) and he pays interest of £1,500 per year. The car is written off in an accident before it is a month old and under the terms of the insurance policy Eric's insurance company replaces it with an identical model. In the period of account in which the car is written off, Eric pays £500 of interest. He will be able to claim tax relief for £250 but will not be entitled to claim relief for any interest paid in any subsequent period of account.

Example 3.10 – Relief for interest under s 388 (2)

David is also a partner in Idle & Co. He also borrows £25,000 on a three-year loan to purchase a BMW, used 50% for business and also pays interest of £1,500 per year. During the term of the loan he leaves Idle & Co and joins Diligent & Co as a partner where he continues to use the same car to the same extent for business purposes. He will be entitled to claim tax relief for 50% of the interest throughout.

If on leaving Idle & Co David had joined Diligent & Co as an employee, he would not be entitled to tax relief for interest paid after the date of leaving Idle & Co.

3.13 *ITA 2007, s 398* gives relief for interest paid by a partner on a loan that is used to:

- purchase a share in a partnership;
- contribute money to a partnership, by way of capital or premium, that is used wholly for the purposes of the trade or profession (but not, it should be noted, property business) carried on by the partnership;
- advance money to a partnership that is so used; or
- repay a loan used for any of the three preceding purposes.

If the partnership in question is a limited partnership registered under the *Limited Partnerships Act 1907*, relief is not available to a limited partner. And if the partnership is an 'investment LLP' (meaning one whose business consists wholly or mainly of the making of investments and the principal part of whose income is derived from investments) relief is not available to any member. But, subject to that, there is no requirement that the partner should be actively involved in the business – sleeping partners may qualify for relief if all other conditions are satisfied. Furthermore, *s 399(5)* provides that where a partnership carries on a profession (but not a trade) senior employees can be treated for this purpose as if they were partners if in dealing with clients they are allowed to act independently and in such a way generally as to be indistinguishable from actual partners.

If, between the time that the loan is applied until the time the interest is paid the individual has recovered any amount of capital from the partnership, he is treated as having applied that amount in repayment or part repayment of the loan, and relief for interest is restricted accordingly. For this purpose an individual is treated (under *ITA 2007, s 407*) as recovering an amount of capital if:

- the individual receives consideration of that amount for the disposal of all or part of his interest in the partnership or of a debt due to him from the partnership (or would have done so if the disposal had been by way of a bargain at arm's length); or
- the partnership repays that amount of a loan or advance from the individual; or
- the partnership returns that amount of capital to the individual.

Relief under *ITA 2007, s 398* is available only so long as the borrower is a partner. Interest paid after a partner leaves the partnership is not available for relief, even if the funds cannot immediately be withdrawn from the partnership.

3.14 The fact that interest paid by a partnership is allowable in computing trading profits, so long as it does not arise through the overdrawing of a partner's capital or current account, means that it will be tax efficient for a partnership sensibly to limit the capital requirement from the partners and enable them to retain more of their personal funds to meet personal and private expenditure or to redeem tax inefficient personal loans.

> **Focus**
>
> If a partnership experiences financial difficulties, care needs to be taken to ensure that partners' capital or current accounts do not become inadvertently overdrawn. It is at least possible that repaying an overdrawn capital or current account would not be regarded as 'contributing money to a partnership' and that tax relief could be denied to the extent that the introduction merely replaces the monies withdrawn.

Particular care must also be taken with contrived schemes for loaning funds to a partnership. In *Lancaster v IRC* [2000] STC (SCD) 138, the senior partner of a firm of chartered accountants withdrew £30,000 from his capital account and gave it to his wife, for the purposes of inheritance tax planning. She then made a loan of £30,000 to her husband which he in turn invested in the firm. The taxpayer claimed relief for £3,000 of interest paid on the loan under the former *Income and Corporation Taxes Act 1988* ('*ICTA 1988*'), *s 362* (now *ITA 2007, s 398*). The Special Commissioner held that the transaction did not come within *s 362* since the net result of the circular transaction was that no money was contributed to the partnership which it did not already have. Furthermore, the interest had not actually been paid, although it had on one occasion been offset against his wife's share of a family holiday (which he would previously have paid for himself). Tax relief was refused.

3.15 None of the foregoing should be confused with the position where a partner borrows money to acquire real property which is let to the partnership. Where that is the case, the interest will simply be deductible from rents along with any other expenses of the partner's property business in the usual way.

3.16 A corporate partner which pays interest on a loan taken out to invest into a partnership may be entitled to tax relief under the loan relationship rules. Interest on such a loan will rank as a 'non-trading debit' which will be added to any other non-trading debits and netted against any non-trading credits (such as interest received) to arrive at a non-trading profit or a non-trading deficit.

Where the result is a non-trading deficit, the default position is that the deficit will be carried forward and set against non-trading profits of the company for subsequent accounting periods. Often a corporate partner may have little or no non-trading profit so will wish to make a claim under *CTA 2009, s 459* to set the deficit against profits of the period in which the deficit arose (the 'deficit period'). Those profits will include any share of partnership profit. A deficit may also be carried back and used against income arising under the loan relationship rules for accounting periods ending within the period of 12 months immediately preceding the deficit period, or surrendered as group relief. It is not necessary that the whole deficit be used in the same way: a company may claim to relieve different parts of the deficit in different ways but the aggregate amount of the different claims cannot exceed the total deficit.

Any claim to set the deficit (or part of it) against profits of the deficit period must be made within two years of the end of the deficit period. Where other reliefs are also claimed an order of priority is given by *CTA 2009, s 461* – the deficit is set against profits after relief for any trading loss brought forward, but before relief for property losses, trading losses of the same period or carried back from a subsequent period or any non-trading deficit carried back from a subsequent period.

For further detail on the application of the loan relationship rules to partnerships involving a company, see **Chapter 17**.

Claims and elections

3.17 Claims and elections which affect the computation of the partnership profits must be made in the partnership return. This includes claims for pre-trading expenses and capital allowances (*TMA 1970, s 42(7)*), where appropriate. It therefore follows that individual partners cannot make supplementary capital allowances claims; rather, they must all be included in the partnership claim.

3.18 Claims and elections which only affect the tax liability of an individual partner must be made by that partner in his or her personal tax return. This includes claims for loss relief (*TMA 1970, s 42(1)* and *(2)*). Relief for claims will be given automatically, subject to HMRC's verification and enquiry procedures.

3.19 The time limit for making claims, where not otherwise specified, is four years from the end of the tax year to which the claim relates (*TMA 1970, s 43*). Supplementary claims can be made where an error or mistake has been discovered, provided that the time limit for making the original claim has not expired.

3.20 Eligible partnerships may choose to use the cash basis when calculating taxable profits from 2013/14. In essence, most claims procedures should be simplified, if not eliminated, for those using the scheme.

Chapter 4

Basis Periods for Assessment

Signposts

- Income from a partnership is charged to tax on the current year basis (see **4.1 – 4.3**).
- Overlap profits are divided between the partners in their profit-sharing ratios. A new partner joining a partnership may also have overlap profits (see **4.4 – 4.10**).
- Choosing the right year end may help with business administration, minimise the risk of paying interest and potentially assist with cashflow (see **4.11 – 4.13**).
- Special rules apply in the year in which a partner leaves the firm or the business ceases (see **4.14 – 4.15**).
- The basis period rules applying to non-trading income differ according to whether the non-trading income is taxed or untaxed (see **4.16 – 4.20**).

4.1 For each tax year in which a firm carries on a trade ('the actual trade') each partner's share of the firm's trading profits or losses is treated, for the purposes of working out basis periods for assessment, as profits or losses of a trade carried on by the partner alone (the 'notional trade'). (*ITTOIA 2005, s 852*). For this purpose 'trade' includes a profession (see *s 847(2)*).

The 'notional trade' is treated as commencing when the firm starts to carry on the actual trade or, if later, the date the partner becomes a partner in the firm. It is treated as ceasing when the firm ceases to trade or, if earlier, the date the partner ceases to be a partner in the firm. But if the partner carries on the partnership business as a sole trader either before others join him in partnership or after all other partners retire from the partnership, the partner is treated as starting to trade on the date the earlier sole trade starts and as ceasing when the later sole trade ceases, as the case may be.

4.2 It follows that an established partner in an established partnership will pay tax by reference to the share of profits earned in the partnership's accounting year ending in the relevant tax year. For example, an established partner in an established partnership with a year end of 31 August will be taxed in 2016/17 on the share of tax-adjusted trading profits and other untaxed profits for the year ending on 31 August 2016. Special rules apply on commencement and cessation of the partner's notional trade and any change of accounting date of the notional trade (which will occur if there is a change in the accounting date of the 'actual trade' carried on by the partnership). For the detailed rules on changes of accounting date see **Chapter 6**.

Where the commencement or cessations rules apply to a partner on joining an existing partnership or leaving a partnership whose business continues after his departure, the basis periods of existing or continuing partners will differ from those of the partner joining or leaving. In this situation, continuing partners and new (or leaving) partners may pay tax on the profits of the same partnership accounting period in different years.

4.3 One of the effects of each partner carrying on a separate 'notional trade' and being assessed by reference to the basis periods of that notional trade is that 'overlap periods', 'overlap profit' and 'overlap relief' are personal to each partner. The concept of overlap period, overlap profit or overlap relief of a partnership as such is meaningless. Although profits are calculated at the partnership level, they are assessed at the partner level.

If a partnership carrying on a trade also has untaxed non-trading income a partner's share of the untaxed non-trading income from one or more sources is taxed as if it arose from a separate deemed trade. This separate deemed trade will give rise to its own overlap relief. For most years the basis periods for the 'notional trade' and the 'deemed trade' will coincide. However, in some circumstances they will not, and it may happen that overlap profits arise or overlap relief is given at different times for the 'notional' and 'deemed' trades. For more detail on the deemed trade relating to untaxed non-trading income, see **4.16** below.

Where a trading partnership has non-trading income which has borne tax at source ('taxed income') this is always taxed on an actual tax year basis.

Overlap profits

4.4 In the first year in which a partner is a member of a partnership (whether that is because it is a new partnership or the partner is joining an existing partnership) the partner's taxable income is based on the actual profits of the tax year (time-apportioned where the partnership accounting date is anything other than 5 April). Unless the partnership's accounting date is 5 April this inevitably means that the move to tax profits in subsequent years by reference to the profits of the partnership accounting year will result in some profits being taken into account in computing taxable profits of a partner for more than one tax year. Such profits are known as overlap profits (*ITTOIA 2005, s 204*). Similarly, overlap profits can arise in the context of a continuing business where an accounting date is shifted to a date earlier in the tax year: again there will be a period the profits of which have been taken into account in computing taxable profits of more than one tax year.

4.5 When a partner ceases to have income from the partnership (either because the partnership ceases to trade or because the partner ceases to be a member of it) or on a change of year end of the partnership resulting in an accounting period of more than 12 months (see **Chapter 6**), relief is given ('overlap relief') by deducting all or part of the overlap profits as a trading expense. The relief given on a change of accounting date is the fraction A/B of the available relief where A is the excess of the basis period over 12 months and B is the length of the overlap period. For example, if the overlap period is nine months and the basis period for the tax year 16 months, 4/9ths of the overlap relief will be given against the profits of the 16-month period and the overlap period remaining for any subsequent application of the rule is reduced by four months. Strictly, taxable profits and overlap relief must be calculated by apportioning in proportion to the number of days in the relevant period though apportionment by reference to weeks or months will be acceptable to HMRC provided the method chosen is reasonable and is applied consistently (see *ITTOIA 2005, s 220(4)* and HMRC guidance at BIM81065). Exceptionally, where the profit for the period can be identified as arising from a small number of discrete transactions it may be more accurate to allocate profit between different parts of the period by reference to when those transactions took place rather than by time-apportionment. This was the case in *Marshall Hus & Partners Ltd v Bolton* [1980] 55 TC 539 but the facts in that case were unusual.

Any overlap relief remaining unallowed at the time at which the partner ceases to have income from the partnership (that is, on retirement or cessation) is given as a deduction in computing taxable profit for the final year.

The overall effect in every case is that over the lifetime of the business the amount charged to tax (after deducting overlap relief) will exactly equal the taxable profits of the business. The choice of accounting date (and any changes made to it during the lifetime of the business) may affect the years in which profits fall to be taxed: but they do not affect the total profits ultimately charged to tax.

4.6 Capital allowances, where due, are treated as a trading expense of the accounting period in question, and balancing charges are treated as a trading receipt. Hence capital allowances reduce both overlap profits and overlap relief.

Deduction of overlap relief will give rise to a loss if the relief exceeds the profits of the period for which it is deducted. Where this relates to the partner's 'notional trade', losses will be relieved in the usual way (see **Chapter 9**). Where deduction of overlap relief for the partner's 'deemed trade' relating to untaxed non-trading income results in a loss, see **4.18** below.

4.7 HMRC accept that accounts drawn up to the last five days of the tax year may (unless the taxpayer wishes otherwise) be treated as the same as those drawn up to 5 April (*ITTOIA 2005, s 209* and HMRC guidance at BIM81020). This means that, if a business commences in the period from 1 April to 5 April, the profits for the first year will be nil and there will be no overlap profits or overlap relief – a considerable simplification.

Opening years

4.8 The rules for the opening tax years are as follows (*ITTOIA 2005, ss 198–201*):

Year 1 Profit from date of commencement to the end of the tax year.

Year 2
(a) If there is an account of at least 12 months ending in the second tax year, profits of 12 months to the end of that account (as in **Example 4.1**, parts (i) and (iii)).

(b) Where the first account ends in the second tax year but is for less than 12 months, profits of 12 months from commencement (as in **Example 4.1**, part (ii)).

(c) Where no account ends in the second tax year, profits of the tax year itself (as in **Example 4.1**, part (iv)).

Year 3 onwards Normally profits of accounting year ending in the tax year, but with special rules for changes of accounting date, under which the basis period will never be less than 12 months but may be longer.

If, however, the tax year is the first year in which there is an accounting date not less than 12 months after commencement (as in the third year 2014/15 in **Example 4.1**, part (iv)), the profits of 12 months to the accounting date are taken, even though the accounting period itself is longer.

Example 4.1 – Assessable profits in the early years

The partnerships in (i) to (iv) below started on 1 January 2014:

12-month period of account ending in the second year of assessment

(i) The partnership made up accounts annually to 31 December, with the following results in the first two years:

	£000
Year to 31 December 2014	120
Year to 31 December 2015	150
	270

The assessable profits for division between the partners and overlap profit arising would be:

			£
2013/14	1.1.14–5.4.14	95/365 × 120	31,232
2014/15	Yr to 31.12.14		120,000
2015/16	Yr to 31.12.15		150,000
			301,232
Overlap profit (95 days):		1.1.14–5.4.14	31,232

Short period of account ending in second year of assessment

(ii) The partnership made up accounts with profits as follows:

				£
Nine months to 30 September 2014				90,000
Year to 30 September 2015				140,000
				230,000
The position would be:				
2013/14	1.1.14–5.4.14	95/273 × 90		31,318
2014/15	1.1.14–31.12.14			
	First nine months		90	
	92/365 × 140		35,287	125,287
2015/16	Yr to 30.9.15			140,000
				296,605
Overlap profit (187 days):		95/273 × 90	31,318	
		92/365 × 140	35,287	66,605

Long period of account to 31 March ending in second year of assessment

(iii) The partnership made up accounts with profits as follows:

			£000
15 months to 31 March 2015			150
Year to 31 March 2016			180
			330
The position would be:			
2013/14	1.1.14–5.4.14	3/15 × 150	30
2014/15	1.4.14–31.3.15	12/15 ×150	120
2015/16	Yr to 31.3.16		180
			330

Overlap profit five days from 1.4.14–5.4.14, but no overlap arises since accounts are drawn to 31 March.

Long period of account to a non-5 April date ending in third year of assessment

(iv) The partnership made up accounts with profits as follows:

	£
16 months to 30 April 2015	160,000
Year to 30 April 2016	180,000
	340,000

The position would be:

2013/14	1.1.14–5.4.14	95/485 × 160	31,340
2014/15	6.4.14–5.4.15	365/485 × 160	120,412
2015/16	1.5.14–30.4.15	365/485 × 160	120,412
			272,164
2016/17	1.5.15–30.4.16		180,000
			452,164

Of the profits of the first 485-day accounting period, the profits of the 340-day period 1 5 14 – 5 4 15 have been taken into account in computing taxable profits of both 2014/15 and 2015/16 so overlap relief is 340/485 × 160,000 = 112,164

Relief for his or her share of the overlap profits will be given to each partner on leaving the partnership, or when the business ceases completely or on an earlier change of accounting date, to the extent that more than 12 months' profits would otherwise be taxed in one year.

Short period of account ending in the first year of assessment

4.9 Particular problems arise where accounts are prepared for a short period falling into the first year of assessment, because it will be necessary to prepare a second set of accounts in order to compute the first assessment. If the second set of accounts is drawn up for a 12-month period, this may mean that both the partnership return and the partners' tax returns will have to be completed with provisional figures, and partners may face interest charges if they pay too little tax.

Example 4.2 – Short period of account ending in the first year of assessment

Anil and Zoe start trading in partnership as hairdressers on 1 June 2014. They prepare their first accounts to 31 December 2014 and then annually to 31 December. The results for the first 31 months are as follows:

	£
7 months to 31 December 2014	15,000
Year to 31 December 2015	40,000
Year to 31 December 2016	45,000

The assessable profits will be:

2014/15	1.6.14–31.12.14	15,000
	1.1.15–5.4.15 – £40,000 × 95/365	10,410
		25,410
2015/16	Year to 31 December 2015	40,000
2016/17	Year to 31 December 2016	45,000

The overlap period will be the period from 1 January 2015 to 5 April 2015 (95 days). Overlap profits of £10,410 will be divided between the partners in their profit-sharing ratios.

The tax return for 2014/15 will be due to be submitted to HMRC by 31 January 2016. In order to calculate the profit for 2014/15, it is necessary to prepare the accounts for the year ended 31 December 2015. This gives the partners only one month to complete the accounts and returns.

Long period of account ending in the third year of assessment

4.10 **Example 4.1**, part (iv) illustrates a similar problem where the commencement accounts are prepared for a period of more than 12 months. In order to compute the taxable profits for 2013/14 it is necessary to have prepared the accounts for the 16 months from 1 January 2014 to 30 April 2015. The 2013/14 tax return will have to be submitted by 31 January 2015. This makes it necessary to complete the return with provisional figures and make an estimated tax payment for 2013/14. In addition, the payments on account for 2014/15 due on 31 January 2015 and 31 July 2015 will also be based on these provisional figures. Where this situation occurs, the accounts should be completed as quickly as possible after the accounting date. The provisional figures on the tax return should be amended within 12 months. If the partners have paid too little tax, they will be charged interest. The returns for 2014/15 must be submitted by 31 January 2016, giving only nine months for the accounts and returns to be finalised. The larger the partnership, the longer the time period that is potentially needed to agree the accounts.

Choice of accounting date

4.11 A partnership has a free choice as to selecting its accounting date. Some partnerships will choose a date for commercial reasons; for example, to fit in with a cyclical trading pattern or to fall in a slack period. Changes of accounting date are dealt with in **Chapter 6** and are subject to anti-avoidance provisions. Choosing the right year end will not only make life administratively easier and minimise the risk of paying interest but in the early years of a new partnership the choice of a year end other than 5 April can give a cash-flow advantage where the initial profits are low. A date early in the tax year may also make claiming tax credits administratively easier.

Example 4.3 – Choice of accounting date

Sandra and Toby start a graphic design partnership on 1 June 2014, sharing profits equally. The accounts to 31 May 2015 show a loss of £2,000. They expect to make profits in the year to 31 May 2016 of £72,000.

Tax year	*Accounts year*	*Period taxed*	*Months taxed*	*Profit (£)*
2014/15	1.6.14–31.5.15	1.6.14–5.4.15	Ten months, six days	0
2015/16	1.6.14–31.5.15	1.6.14–31.5.15	12	0
2016/17	1.6.15–31.5.16	1.6.15–31.5.16	12	72,000

If the partners had chosen a year end of 5 April (assuming that the profits and losses remained at the same level), the £72,000 of profits would largely arise in the year ended 5 April 2016 and would have been taxed one year earlier in 2015/16. The cash-flow benefits will be further improved by the effect of payments on account also being deferred by one year.

Many partnerships are short of funds when they commence trading, so a non-5 April year end may be attractive and beneficial. The use of a tax reserve to cover any excess tax on cessation should be considered in this situation (see **Chapter 27**). However, the sting in the tail of an accounting date early in the tax year may be revealed when the partner ceases to have partnership profits: there may be a 'bunching' of income in that year. For example, in **Example 4.3**, if profits continue at the level of £72,000 per year until Sandra leaves the partnership on 31 May 2018 to take up full-time employment, her taxable income for 2018/19 will be the aggregate of £36,000 plus her earnings from employment for the remaining 10 months of the year, which may bring her into higher rates of tax for the year. Contrast this with the position if the partnership uses a 5 April accounting date throughout – her 2018/19 partnership final year income will then be just £6,000 and the risk of paying higher-rate tax for 2018/19 will be correspondingly smaller.

4.12 For some partnerships, the only logical choice of year end is 5 April (or 31 March). This will be the case where the partnership only lasts for a short period of time. It should also be adopted to keep matters simple for partnerships with a low turnover and financially unsophisticated partners. Where partners like to keep up to date with their tax payments, the use of a 31 March/5 April year end is not the only option; a tax reserve can be set up, with the partners benefiting by receiving interest on the funds.

4.13 The number of times that the first period of account falls into aggregation will also affect the taxable profits and overlap profits and therefore the choice of accounting period.

Example 4.4 – Choice of accounting period

Lynn and Mike started a partnership as booksellers on 1 January 2014. Accounts are drawn up to 30 June. The results for the first periods of account are as follows:

	£	£
6 months to 30 June 2014	3,000	
Year to 30 June 2015	50,000	

The assessable profits will be:

2013/14	1.1.14–5.4.14 – £3,000 × 95/181		1,575
2014/15	1.1.14–31.12.14		
	1.1.14–30.6.14 – 181 days	3,000	
	1.7.14–31.12.14 – £50,000 × 184/365	25,205	
			28,205
2015/16	Year to 30 June 2015		50,000
			79,780

Overlap profits over a period of nine months will be £1,575 + £25,205 = £26,780.

If the first accounts are produced for 18 months instead of for two separate periods, with the profits for the period to 30 June 2015 being £53,000, the following taxable profits result:

		£
2013/14	1.1.14–5.4.14 – £53,000 × 95/547	9,205
2014/15	6.4.14–5.4.15 – £53,000 × 365/547	35,365
2015/16	1.7.14–30.6.15 – £53,000 × 365/547	35,365
		79,935

Overlap profits for the period from 1.7.14–30.6.15 will be £79,935–£53,000 = £26,935.

Thus assessable profits for the three years from 2013/14 to 2015/16 with two separate sets of accounts are £79,780, and overlap profits of £26,780; a single 18-month accounting period gives profits are £79,935 and overlap profits of £26,935.

The example demonstrates that even where the choice of a long accounting period does not significantly affect the gross and overlap figures, it may affect the spread of profits over the tax years concerned. In this example it may give a small cash-flow advantage: in others any cash-flow advantage may rest with a short initial accounting period. But in many cases the benefit either way may be so small as not to warrant the additional cost of performing the alternative calculations and producing two sets of accounts.

Final year

4.14 For partnerships with an accounting date of 5 April, the final assessment when either the partnership trade ceases or a partner leaves will be based on the actual profits from 6 April to the date of cessation (*ITTOIA 2005, s 202*). There will have been no overlap profits so no overlap relief is in point.

Example 4.5 Cessation

Peter and Ridley, who have made up their accounts annually to 5 April, cease their partnership on 31 October 2015. The partners' final assessments will be based on the partnership profits for the period from 6 April 2015 to 31 October 2015.

4.15 Where a partnership with a non-5 April year end ceases (or a partner leaves a partnership), the final assessment will be based on the profits arising from the end of the basis period ending in the preceding year to the date of cessation (*ITTOIA 2005, s 202*). The period may be shorter or longer than 12 months. Overlap relief will be given against the profits assessable in the final period of account.

Example 4.6 – Taxable profits on cessation with overlap relief

Georgina and Henry close down their partnership on 30 November 2015. They share profits equally. They previously made up accounts to 31 May each year. Overlap profits brought forward are £5,000 each. The profits for the last two accounting periods are as follows:

		£
Year to 31 May 2014		30,000
18 months to 30 November 2015		20,000
The taxable profits are:		
2014/15	Year to 31.5.14	30,000
2015/16	1.6.14–30.11.15	20,000

In 2015/16, each partner will have taxable profits of £10,000 less his or her share of overlap relief of £5,000. They will therefore each be taxed on £5,000.

Basis periods for non-trading income

Untaxed income

4.16 If a partnership carries on a trade, a partner's share of any untaxed non-trading income from one or more sources is taxed as if it arose from a separate deemed trade, so that the same basis periods apply as for the trading income, and the rules for overlap relief apply (*ITTOIA 2005, s 854*). This is the case even if the trading income is a minor part of the partnership. If the firm changes its accounting date, the basis periods for the deemed trade will be revised in the same way as those of the actual trade, and overlap relief in relation to the non-trading income is either created or utilised as indicated in **4.4** et seq for the trading income.

The separate deemed trade is regarded as starting when the individual becomes a partner (or, if later, when the partnership starts to carry on a trade), not when the first source of non-trading income is acquired, and as ceasing when the individual ceases to be a partner (or, if later, when the partnership ceases to carry on a trade). Note that the actual commencement or cessation of receipt of non-trading income is irrelevant.

This treatment of non-trading income applies only where there is a partnership, so it does not apply to the non-trading income of a sole trader arising before he or she is joined by one or more partners. And if someone continues in business alone when one or more partners leave, his or her overlap relief on non-trading income will be given at that time even though his or her trade continues.

If a partnership does not carry on a trade, untaxed income is assessed in the same way as an individual, ie on an actual tax year basis.

Example 4.7 – non-trading income (1)

A has been a sole trader for many years, drawing up accounts to 30 June annually. B joins as a partner on 1 July 2015. The partnership starts to let property (in addition to trading) on 1 January 2016. On 30 June 2019 the trade ceases but the letting of property continues. Basis periods are as follows:

Basis periods for the letting income are:

2015/16	1.7.15–5.4.16 (even though income is actually received only from 1.1.16)
2016/17	1.7.15–30.6.16 (overlap relief created)
2017/18	1.7.16–30.6.17
2018/19	1.7.17–30.6.18
2019/20	1.7.18–30.6.19 with overlap relief allowed

Contrast these assessments with the position if B had joined as a partner one year earlier on 1 July 2014 but the facts had otherwise remained the same: basis periods would then be:

2015/16	1 7 14–30.6.15 (but there is no assessment to tax as no income arises in the period)
2016/17	1.7.15–30.6.16 (no overlap relief created)
2017/18	1.7.16–30.6.17
2018/19	1.7.17–30.6.18
2019/20	1.7.18–30.6.19 (no overlap relief allowed)

From 1 July 2019, A and B will (depending on the facts) either be (a) conducting in partnership a business of letting property or (b) simply jointly letting property in circumstances that fall short of a business. For more on this distinction, see **Chapter 1**. In either case, letting income will be assessed for 2019/20 for the period 1.7.19 – 5.4.20 (in addition to the 2019/20 assessment shown above) and thereafter will be assessed on a tax year basis.

Property income

4.17 Rents from both furnished and unfurnished lettings of a property investment activity carried on by a trading partnership are treated as the profits of a property income business, the profits being calculated according to generally accepted accounting principles, with adjustments for amounts in arrears and in advance. The basis period for the property income business is the same as that used for the trading profits.

Example 4.8 – Non-trading income (2)

The partnership of Geoffrey, Cynthia and Tracey commences trading on 1 January 2014 and makes up accounts to 31 December each year, sharing profits 3:2:1. From the start, the partnership lets out part of its premises furnished, and receives rent of £6,000 per annum.

The rents will be taxed using the *ITTOIA 2005, Pt 2, Ch 15* basis periods. The annual rental income will be shared as follows:

Geoffrey (3/6ths)	£3,000
Cynthia (2/6ths)	£2,000
Tracey (1/6th)	£1,000

The first assessable rents, and overlap profits arising, are as follows:

		Geoffrey	*Cynthia*	*Tracey*
		£	*£*	*£*
2013/14	1.1.14–5.4.14 (95/365ths)	780	520	260
2014/15	1.1.14–31.12.14	3,000	2,000	1,000
Overlap profits (three months):		780	520	260

4.18 As and when overlap relief falls to be given on non-trading income, either when the partner leaves the firm, or the firm closes down completely, or on an earlier change of accounting date if more than 12 months' income would otherwise be taxed in one year, then if the overlap relief should exceed the partner's share of the untaxed income, the excess must be deducted from the partner's *total* income of that tax year (*ITTOIA 2005, s 856*). This is not as generous as the treatment of excess overlap relief relating to the trade, which creates a trading loss and may therefore be carried back one year against total income in a continuing business and/or carried forward against future trading profits and/or carried back against the previous *three* years' trading income if it arises in the tax year of cessation (see **Chapter 8**).

4.19 It should be noted that overlap relief in relation to non-trading income will normally arise only where that income is received in a period to which overlap relief applies in respect of the trading profits, because a partner's deemed trade in respect of the non-trading income is regarded as starting and ceasing when the partner joins and leaves the firm. If the letting in **Example 4.8** had not started until 1 January 2015, there would have been no overlapping profits in respect of the rents and overlap relief would not have arisen. However, if a sole trader with sources of untaxed non-trading income is joined by one or more partners, the notional trade in respect of the non-trading income will be deemed to start at the time the partnership is formed, so that the rules for opening years' overlap relief will apply to each partner's non-trading income at that time, even though the sole trader is regarded as continuing in business.

> **Focus**
>
> A source of non-trading income to which overlap relief applies may cease many years before the partner leaves the firm, but the overlap relief will not be given until he or she leaves, unless more than 12 months' profit is being charged as a result of a change of accounting date.

Example 4.9 – Overlap relief and non-trading income

The partnership in **Example 4.8** ceases to let part of its premises during 2016. There is no entitlement to overlap relief against the rental income at that time. In 2017/18, when there is no non-trading income, the firm changes its accounting date and makes up a 14 months' (424 day) account to 28 February 2018. The partners will be taxed on their shares of the 14 months' profits in 2017/18, reduced by 59/95 of their 95 days overlap relief on trading profits. They will also be entitled at that time to relief on 59/95 of the overlap profits on their rental income. Since there is no non-trading income against which the relief may be given, it will be given against each partner's *total* income of 2017/18 (but not against any income of any other year, should the 2017/18 income be insufficient). The remaining 36/95 of the overlap relief on trading and rental income will remain available for later relief.

Taxed income

4.20 By contrast, taxed income is taxed on a 'tax year' basis. Since, from 6 April 2016, bank interest is paid gross and dividends do not carry tax credits, the receipt of 'taxed income' by partnerships will be less common than hitherto.

Where the partnership accounts are prepared to a date other than 5 April, a strict reading of the law would require that the figures in the accounts should be analysed to identity the tax year in which each item of taxed income was received. Guidance notes to the Partnership Return in earlier years have indicated that figures for the accounting periods involved may be apportioned between tax years on a time basis if this 'gives a reasonable approximation of the actual figures for that period'. Given that it would be necessary to analyse the figures between tax years in order to know whether the time-apportionment basis does in fact give a 'reasonable approximation', the advice was puzzling. Current HMRC guidance simply indicates that 'you should apportion figures in the sets of accounts that between them cover [the tax year]' without specifically saying that the apportionment is to be made on a time basis. HMRC examples at BIM 82330 use time-apportionment without any reference to the actual dates of receipt so it may (presumably) be assumed that time-apportionment is the approved method. Of course, if a partnership prefers to use the strict method and to return income by reference to the actual date of receipt, it may do so.

Where an accounting period spans 6 April 2016 amounts of dividend income or bank interest received before 6 April 2016 will be taxed income, taxable on a 'tax year' basis for 2015/16 while such amounts received on or after 6 April 2016 will be untaxed income, taxable (where a trade is being carried on) on an accounting period basis in 2016/7. In the writer's view, time-apportionment for such an accounting period should be avoided and matters should instead be dealt with on the strict basis.

Where a partnership's only savings income is untaxed interest or alternative finance receipts paid by a banks or building societies, the only boxes which require completion are those found on the short partnership statement. If the partnership has dividends or other taxed or untaxed investment income (or indeed any other income not included elsewhere in the partnership tax return) the full partnership statement and supplementary pages SA804 must be completed.

Example 4.10 – Non-trading income all before 6 April 2016

The Golden partnership makes up its accounts to 30 June. Its results for the year ended 30 June 2014 are as follows:

	Gross	*Tax*
	£	£
Trading profit	200,000	
Dividends received – 30 September 2013	10,000	1,000
Dividends received – 1 May 2014	5,000	500
Bank interest – credited 1 April 2014	20,000	4,000

The results to 30 June 2015 are as follows:

	Gross	*Tax*
	£	£
Trading profit	250,000	
Dividends received – 30 September 2014	11,000	1,100
Dividends received – 2 May 2015	5,000	500
Bank interest – credited 1 April 2015	10,000	2,000

The partnership is completing its partnership return to 5 April 2015. The entries required are as follows:

- Trading profit – year to 30 June 2014: £200,000.
- Dividends (on strict basis) £4,500 + £9,900 (plus associated tax credits totalling £1,600).
- Bank interest (on strict basis): £10,000 (with credit for tax deducted £2,000).
- Dividends (on apportioned basis) tax year to 5 April 2015 computed as follows: year to 30 June 2014: £15,000 × 3/12 = £3,750 + year to 30 June 2015: £16,000 × 9/12 = £12,000. Total £15,750. The same proportion of the associated tax credit £1,575 will be entered in the relevant boxes.

- Bank interest (on apportioned basis) – tax year to 5 April 2015 computed as follows: year to 30 June 2014: £20,000 × 3/12 = £5,000 + year to 30 June 2015 £10,000 × 9/12 = £7,500. Total £12,500. The same proportion of the tax deducted £2,500 will be entered in the relevant boxes.

The income on the partnership statement will be allocated between the partners in the profit-sharing ratios applying to the accounting periods in which the income arose. If the Golden partnership had three partners – A, B and C – who shared profits equally in the year to 30 June 2014 and in the ratio 40:30:30 in the year to 30 June 2015, the partnership income would be allocated as follows:

2014/15	*Total*	*A*	*B*	*C*
	£	£	£	£
Profits (equally)	200,000	66,667	66,667	66,666
Dividends				
1.5.14 (equally)	4,500	1,500	1,500	1,500
30.9.14 (40:30:30)	9,900	3,960	2,970	2,970
	14,400	5,460	4,470	4,470
Bank interest				
1.4.15 (40:30:30)	10,000	4,000	3,000	3,000
	10,000	4,000	3,000	3,000

The associated tax credits will be allocated in the same ratios.

Example 4.11 – Non-trading income on or after 6 April 2016

The results of the same partnership for the year ended 30 June 2016 are as follows:

	Gross	*Tax*
	£	£
Trading profit	240,000	
Dividends received – 30 September 2015	10,000	1,000
Dividends received – 1 May 2016	5,000	500
Bank interest – credited 1 April 2016	20,000	4,000

The partnership is completing its partnership return to 5 April 2016. The entries required are as follows:

- Trading profit – year to 30 June 2015: £250,000.

- Dividends – £9,000, together with remaining dividends from 30 June 15 period not already taxed in 2014/15 (£5,000 if strict basis was applied in 2014/15, or £4,000 if time-apportionment was applied) plus associated tax credits.
- Bank interest £20,000 together with £2,500 from 30 June 2015 period if time-apportionment was applied in 2014/15 (with credit for tax deducted).

The dividends received in May 2016 are untaxed income and will be taxed (on an accounting period basis) as income of 2016/17 and will be the only dividends so taxed. Any bank interest or dividends received in the June 2017 period will be taxed as income of 2017/18: no apportionment is required.

Chapter 5

Partnership Changes

> **Signposts**
>
> - New partners joining a partnership are taxed separately on their share of the profits as if they had started a new business when they joined the partnership (see **5.1 – 5.8**).
> - Partners are treated as ceasing their own separate business when they leave the partnership (see **5.9 – 5.11**).
> - Extra care is needed where a sole trader takes on a partner or a partnership reverts to a sole tradership (see **5.12 – 5.14**).

New partners

5.1 Under the current year basis of assessment, each partner is taxed individually. New partners joining a partnership are taxed separately on their share of the profits as if they had started a new business when they joined the partnership (*ITTOIA 2005, s 850*).

5.2 The rules illustrated in **Example 4.1** (see **4.8**) apply not only when a new partnership sets up in business but also to each new partner as he or she joins the partnership.

Whilst the partnership itself continues, the rules for the opening years apply to each partner as he or she joins.

Thus, a partner's taxable profit for the first tax year in which he or she is a member of the partnership is on the profit from the date of joining to the next 5 April, apportioning accounts on a time basis.

5.3 The taxable profit for the second tax year in which the partner is a member of the partnership depends on the dates to which accounts are drawn up. If an account covering at least 12 months ends in that second tax year, the new partner's share is based on the profits of 12 months to the end of that account. If the account is for less than 12 months, the taxable profit for the second tax year is based on the first 12 months in which he or she is a partner.

Example 5.1 – Assessable profits in early years on a new partner joining the partnership (1)

(i) Johnson joins a partnership on 1 January 2014. His share of profits for the 12 months to 31 December 2014, when accounts are prepared, is £12,000.

His assessable profits are:

			£
2013/14	(1.1.14–5.4.14)	95/365	3,123
2014/15	(12 months to 31.12.14)	12/12	12,000
			15,123

(ii) Bains joins a partnership on 1 January 2014, accounts then being prepared from that date to 31 March 2015. His share of the profit of the 15 months to 31 March 2015 is £3,750.

His assessable profits are:

			£
2013/14	(1.1.14–5.4.14)	3/15*	750
2014/15	(12 months to 31.3.15)	12/15	3,000
			3,750

*The odd days being ignored as the accounting date is 31 March

(iii) A partnership prepares accounts annually to 30 June. Joan joins on 1 January 2014. Her profit shares are:

	£
First six months to 30.6.14	3,000
12 months to 30.6.15	17,000
	20,000

Her assessable profits are:

2013/14	(1.1.14–5.4.14) 95/181 × 3,000		1,574
2014/15	(1.1.14–30.6.14)	3,000	
	(1.7.14–31.12.14) 184/365 × 17,000	8,569	11,569
2015/16	(12 months to 30.6.15)		17,000
			30,143

5.4 Where a partner joins a partnership, and no account ends in the second tax year after joining, the profits of the tax year itself are assessed.

Example 5.2 – Assessable profits in early years on a new partner joining the partnership (2)

(iv) Howard joins a partnership on 1 January 2014 and the first accounts after his doing so are prepared from that date to 30 April 2015.

His share of profits for those 16 months to 30.4.15 is £4,400.

His assessable profits are:

		£
2013/14	(1.1.14–5.4.14) 95/485 × 4,400	861
2014/15	(6.4.14–5.4.15) 365/485 × 4,400	3,311
2015/16	(12 months to 30.4.15) 365/485 × 4,400*	3,311
		7,483

* Apart from failing to properly notify a change of accounting date (see **Example 6.4** at **6.6**), this is the only occasion after the second tax year where the profits of only 12 months out of a longer period of account are assessed, as distinct from the profits of the longer period being assessed and available overlap relief brought forward being deducted.

5.5 The self-assessments of the existing partners are not affected by the admission of the new partner. Each existing partner is assessed according to the normal rules on his or her share of the profit per the accounts, as adjusted for disallowable expenditure, non-taxable income and capital allowances.

5.6 The profits of the incoming partner which are assessed more than once qualify for overlap relief, viz:

Examples 5.1 and 5.2 (continued)

	(i)	*(ii)*	*(iii)*	*(iv)*
	£	£	£	£
Profits	12,000	3,750	20,000	4,400
Assessed	15,123	3,750	30,143	7,483
Overlap relief	3,123	–	10,143	3,083

5.7 Since each partner is taxed separately on his or her share of the profits, the overlap relief is a personal entitlement. The relief is given when the partner leaves the partnership, or in an earlier tax year if, because of a change of accounting date, more than 12 months' profit would otherwise be taxable in that tax year (but not so as to reduce the taxable amount to less than a 12 months' equivalent).

Example 5.3 – Assessable profits in early years on a new partner joining the partnership (3)

Cathy and Debbie have been trading for many years as beauty consultants, sharing profits equally. They have overlap profits of £3,000 each and they prepare their accounts to 30 April.

On 1 January 2014, they admitted Enya as a partner. The profit-sharing ratio after Enya's admission is 25:50:25.

The profits are as follows:

	£
Year to 30 April 2013	50,000
Year to 30 April 2014	60,000
Year to 30 April 2015	80,000

The assessable profits for the partners are as follows:

Tax year	*Comments*	*Total*	*Cathy*	*Debbie*	*Enya*
		£	£	£	£
2013/14	Year to 30.4.13 shared 50:50	50,000	25,000	25,000	
	1.1.14–5.4.14 – £60,000 × 95/365 × 25%	3,904			3,904
		53,904	25,000	25,000	3,904
2014/15	1.5.13–31.12.13 shared 50:50 – £60,000 × 245/365	40,274	20,137	20,137	
	1.1.14–30.4.14 shared 25:50:25 – £60,000 × 120/365	19,726	4,932	9,862	4,932
	1.5.14–31.12.14 £80,000 × 245/366 × 25%	13,388			13,388
		73,388	25,069	29,999	18,320
2015/16	Year to 30.4.15 shared 25:50:25	80,000	20,000	40,000	20,000

Enya's overlap profits are for the period 1 January 2014–5 April 2014 = £3,904 and for the period 1 May 2014–31 December 2014 = £13,388, a total of £17,292. Each partner has her own overlap profits to carry forward.

5.8 In **Example 5.3**, Enya must enter on her 2013/14 tax return her share of the partnership accounts for the year to 30 April 2014. The return must be submitted by 31 January 2015, giving a reasonable amount of time to complete the accounts in time to enter the actual figures on the return. If the partnership had a year end of 31 December, however, it would be much more difficult to prepare accounts in time to have final figures to enter on the return. In this case, the partner must include an estimate, advise HMRC accordingly and amend the return within 12 months. The tax payment for 2013/14 will be estimated, as will the payments on account for 2014/15. This could give rise to interest charges and cause the partner concerned administrative inconvenience.

Retiring partners

5.9 Partners are treated as ceasing their own separate business when they leave the partnership. The basis period for the tax year in which a partner leaves a firm is from the end of the basis period for the previous tax year to the date of cessation, unless a partner leaves in the second tax year, in which case his or her basis period for that tax year is from 6 April to the date of leaving (*ITTOIA 2005, s 202*).

Any overlap profit for which relief has not already been given on a change of accounting date will be deducted in arriving at the partner's assessable profit for the final tax year, and if that results in a loss, the normal loss reliefs will be available. Losses are dealt with in **Chapter 9**.

Example 5.4 – Overlap relief given on a partner leaving a continuing partnership

Howard (see **Example 5.2** at **5.4**) leaves the partnership on 31 December 2017, so that he is a partner for only nine months in the tax year 2017/18. The accounts are usually prepared to 30 April. His profit share is:

		£
12 months	to 30.4.2017	40,000
8 months	to 31.12.2017 (out of accounts for 12 months to 30.4.2018)	24,000
		64,000
Reduction for overlap relief brought forward		3,083
		60,917

5.10 The assessable profits of the continuing partners are not affected by the fact that a partner has retired, even if an intermediate account is prepared to the departure date, unless the partners intend the intermediate accounting date to be the new year end, since a change of accounting date is not effective unless HMRC are notified accordingly. Thus, in **Example 5.4**, the other partners would be taxed in 2017/18 on their shares of the profit of the year ended 30 April 2017, and in 2018/19 on their shares of the profit of the year ended 30 April 2018, even if intermediate accounts were prepared for the eight months to 31 December 2017, unless 31 December was to be the new accounting date and HMRC were notified accordingly.

Focus

Although it is important that arrangements when a partner leaves make clear how the profit share of the retiring partner is to be ascertained if his or her departure does not coincide with the normal accounting date, the ability to make up an account for commercial reasons without changing the annual accounting date prevents the retirement of a partner affecting the tax payable by continuing partners.

Example 5.5 – Partner retiring from a partnership

Using the facts in **Example 5.3**, Cathy retires as a partner on 30 September 2016. The profit-sharing ratio then becomes 60:40.

The profits are as follows:

	£
Year to 30 April 2016	85,000
Year to 30 April 2017	95,000

Tax year	*Comments*	£	*Cathy*	*Debbie*	*Enya*
2016/17	Year to 30.4.16 shared 25:50:25	85,000	21,250	42,500	21,250
	1.5.16–30.9.16 – £95,000 × 153/365 shared 25:50:25	9,955	9,955		
		94,955	31,205	42,500	21,250
2017/18	1.5.15–30.9.16 – £95,000 × 153/365 shared 25:50:25	29,867		19,912	9,955
	1.10.16–30.4.17 – £95,000 × 212/365 shared 60:40	55,178		33,107	22,071
		85,045		53,019	32,026

Cathy's overlap profits will be deducted from her assessable profits for 2016/17.

The tax liability on her ceasing to be a partner would be more easily manageable if the partnership maintained a tax reserve from the commencement of the partnership (see **Chapter 27**).

5.11 In **Example 5.5**, Cathy must enter on her 2016/17 tax return her share of the partnership accounts for the year to 30 April 2016 and her share of the profits for the period 1 May 2016 to 30 September 2016. To do this she will require the accounts to 30 April 2017. The return must be submitted by 31 January 2018, giving a reasonable amount of time to complete the accounts in time to enter the actual figures on the return. Where the partnership has an accounting date late in the tax year, it may be more difficult to prepare accounts in time to have final figures to enter on the return. In this case the partner must include an estimate, advise HMRC accordingly and amend the return within 12 months. The tax payment for 2016/17 will be estimated, which could give rise to an interest charge and cause the partner administrative inconvenience.

Switch between a sole trader and a partnership

5.12 Where a sole trader takes on a partner or a partnership reverts to a sole tradership, care needs to be exercised when completing the partnership and individual tax returns. For the partnership return the date of commencement or cessation needs to be entered. Where the change takes place during the course of a tax year, both the partnership pages and self-employed pages will need to be completed on the individual's return.

Where the change from sole trade to partnership (or vice versa) takes place other than on the normal accounting date, accounts will need to be completed for a period encompassing both the partnership and sole tradership and the partnership Standard Accounts Information completed for that period.

Example 5.6 – Consequences of a partner becoming a sole trader

Fred and Ginger, who have been in partnership for many years sharing profits equally, prepare their accounts to 31 August. Fred retires on 31 December 2014 and Ginger continues to trade. The accounts continue to be prepared to 31 August.

Partnership return and statement

The partnership return for 2014/15 must include two Standard Accounts Informations ('SAIs') for the years to 31 August 2014 and 31 August 2015.

The partnership statement will show the accounts to 31 August 2014 with the profits shared equally. A second partnership statement will show the profits allocated between Fred and Ginger for the period 1 September 2014 to 31 December 2014. The balance of the profits for the period 1 January 2015 to 31 August 2015 will be allocated to Ginger. No partnership return will be required for 2015/16.

Fred's tax return

Fred's return for 2014/15 will show the profits for the year to 31 August 2014 and for the period 1 September 2014 to 31 December 2014. Since the profit for the latter four months will not be known until after the accounts to 31 August 2015 are completed, Fred will have just five months to get the accounts agreed and the return completed.

Ginger's tax return

The return for 2014/15 will show the partnership profits for the year to 31 August 2014.

The return for 2015/16 will show the partnership profits for the period 1 September 2014 to 31 December 2014. This will be entered as the full accounts to 31 August 2015 less an adjustment for the period 1 January 2015 to 31 August 2015 to give the four months' partnership profits on the partnership pages.

The self-employment pages will show the profits to 31 August 2015 less an adjustment for the four months shown on the partnership pages.

Suitable explanation of the entries and sufficient extra detail should be given in the additional information boxes on the return.

Agreements

5.13 Partnership changes are best dealt with by formal admission and retirement agreements. This is the case whether or not there is a partnership agreement in force. Such agreements should cover the date of the change, the accounting date and any changes to it, the provision of timely information and the completion of accounts and partnership returns, the use of tax reserves, the continuing activities of the partners and any indemnities or compensation paid.

See **Chapter 6** for changes of accounting date, **Chapter 7** for mergers and demergers and **Chapter 12** for CGT consequences of partnership changes.

5.14 When a partner retires, his or her profit share from the last accounting date to that point is sometimes agreed between the partners before accounts are prepared, the profits of the other partners being affected accordingly if an otherwise strict ratio would have been used.

In these circumstances, the outgoing partner is not inconvenienced in ascertaining the profit share for his or her personal return.

Chapter 6

Change of Accounting Date

Signposts

- The tax effects of a change of accounting date are dealt with by statutory rules (see **6.1 – 6.5**).
- If the partnership fails to satisfy the conditions for a valid change of year end, the assessment will be based on the profits for the 12 months to the old accounting date (see **6.6 – 6.9**).
- Care should be taken as to what is required in order for a set of figures to constitute 'accounts' for tax purposes (see **6.10**).

6.1 Subject to special rules on commencement, cessation, or changes of accounting date, the general rule is that profits for a tax year are assessed by reference to the period of 12 months ending on the 'accounting date' in the year.

'Accounting date' means the date in the tax year to which accounts are drawn up (or, if there are two or more such dates, the later or latest of them).

The statutory treatment applies to the accounting periods of partnerships, with consequent effects on the deemed basis periods for each partner's separate notional trade (*ITTOIA 2005, ss 852, 853*). The legislation is designed to give a free choice of accounting date but is subject to anti-avoidance provisions.

A change from one accounting date to another (an 'accounting change') is treated as made in the first tax year in which accounts are not made up to the old date, or are made up to the new date, or both (*ITTOIA 2005, s 214(1)*). See **Example 6.3**.

6.2 An accounting date change cannot by definition affect the first or second years of a new business. This is because the first year basis period is always the tax year itself, so an accounting date becomes relevant only for the second year (at the earliest, and not always then). Thus the legislation needs to deal with changes only in the third or subsequent years of a new business.

If the change in made in the third year (and the business does not permanently cease in that year), the basis period is:

(a) The twelve months ending on the new accounting date; or

(b) If longer, the period starting with the end of the basis period for year two and ending on the new accounting date (*ITTOIA 2005, s 215*).

If a change is made in a later tax year, then in order for the change to become effective at the time it is made, the following conditions must be satisfied (*ITTOIA 2005, s 217*):

(a) The first account to the new date does not exceed 18 months.

(b) For partnerships, notice of the change is given to HMRC in the partnership return under *TMA 1970, s 12AA*. The normal time limit for notification is therefore 31 January next following the tax year of change (*ITTOIA 2005, s 217(2)*). The partners may nominate any partner to give the notice (*ITTOIA 2005, s 853(3)*).

(c) Either:

    (i) no earlier effective change has been made in any of the five previous tax years;

    or

    (ii) the notice under (b) sets out the reasons for the change and HMRC either are satisfied that the change is for bona fide commercial reasons or do not express their dissatisfaction within 60 days of receiving the notice. Obtaining a tax advantage is not a bona fide commercial reason. If HMRC object to the change, the taxpayer has a right of appeal (*ITTOIA 2005, s 218*).

If the above conditions are not satisfied for the first relevant year, the change is ignored in the year in which it is made and the basis period ends on the old accounting date. If the new accounting date continues to be used in subsequent years it continues to be ignored until the first year in which the conditions above are fulfilled, at which point the change becomes effective for tax purposes. (*ITTOIA 2005, ss 216(4), 219(1)*).

The requirement to give notice of a change of accounting date in order for a change to be effective means that a temporary new date may be used without affecting the normal date; for example, if an intermediate account is made up to the date of a partnership change, with an account then being made up from the date of the change to the normal accounting date.

Short periods of account

6.3 If on a change of accounting date the new accounting date falls less than 12 months after the end of the basis period for the previous year, the normal basis period rules apply and the basis period for the year of change is the period of 12 months ending on the new date (*ITTOIA 2005, ss 198, 216(2)*). In this case part of the period will have been taken into account for two tax years and overlap relief will be created.

Example 6.1 – Change of accounting date – short period of account

Profits are as shown below at the time of an accounting change that satisfies the conditions of *ITTOIA 2005, s 217:*

	£000
Year to 31.12.14	40
Nine months to 30.9.2015	20

The year of change is 2015/16. The new accounting date falls less than 12 months after the end of the basis period for 2014/15 (which ended on 31 December 2014), so the basis period for 2015/16 is the period of 12 months ending on the new accounting date.

Assessable profits			£
2014/15	Year to 31.12.14		40,000
2015/16	92/365 × 40		
(being 1.10.14 – 31.12.14)		10,082	
1.1.15 -30.915		20,000	30,082

Further overlap relief is available on £10,082, being the 92 days out of the year to 31 December 2014 that is taxed twice (*ITTOIA 2005, s 220*).

Long periods of account

6.4 If on a change of accounting date the new accounting date falls more than 12 months after the end of the basis period for the previous year, the basis period for the year of change is the period ending on the new date (*ITTOIA 2005, s 216(3)*). In this case some or all of any existing overlap relief will be deducted to compensate for the fact that the basis period exceeds 12 months. (*ITTOIA 2005, s 216*).

Example 6.2 – Change of accounting date – long period of account (1)

Pink and Red, who share profits equally, have made up accounts to 31 July for many years. They decide to change their year end to 31 January. The conditions of *ITTOIA 2005, s 217* are satisfied:

The adjusted profits are:

	£
Year to 31 July 2014	100,000
18 months to 31 January 2016	125,000

Overlap profits brought forward are £20,000 for each partner, representing 248 days 'double taxed' on commencement.

The assessable profits for each partner are as follows:

		£
2014/15	Year to 31 July 2014	50,000
2015/16	18 months to 31 January 2016	62,500

Overlap profits will be offset against the 2015/16 profits. There are 547 days assessed in 2015/16. 365 should be assessed, requiring a release of 184 days' worth of overlap relief. This means that each partner can offset overlap relief of £20,000 × 184/248 = £14,838 against the profits in 2015/16 and carry forward the balance of £5,162.

6.5 It can happen that as a result of a change of accounting date there is a tax year which does not contain an accounting date (ie, a date to which accounts are drawn up) at all. In that case, accounts are deemed to have been drawn up to the date in that year which corresponds to the new accounting date and the change of accounting date rules are applied to that year accordingly (*ITTOIA 2005, s 214*).

Example 6.3 – Change of accounting date – long period of account (2)

Profits are as shown below at the time of an accounting change that satisfies the conditions of *ITTOIA 2005, s 217*:

	£000
Year to 31.12.13	42
16 months to 30.4.2015	60

The year of change is 2014/15, since accounts are not made up to the old date in that year. The deemed accounting date in 2014/15 is 30 April (ie, the new accounting date even though accounts are not made up to that date).

Since this falls less than 12 months after the end of the basis period for 2013/14, the basis period for 2014/15 is the period of 12 months to 30 April 2014, and assessable profits are as follows:

			£
2013/14	Year to 31.12.13		42,000
2014/15	245/365 × 42,000 (1.5.13 to 31.12.13)	28,191	
	120/485 × 60,000 (1.1.14 to 30.4.14)	14,845	43,036
2015/16	Year to 30.4.15 (365/485 × 60,000)		45,154

The available overlap relief is increased by £28,191, being the profit of the 245 days out of the year to 31 December 2013 that is taxed twice.

Failure to satisfy conditions

6.6 If the partnership fails to satisfy the conditions stipulated in **6.2** for a valid change of year end (for example, because it has failed to give notice to HMRC in time, or because accounts have been prepared for a longer period than 18 months), the assessment will be based on the profits for the 12 months to the old accounting date.

Example 6.4 – Change of accounting date – failure to satisfy conditions

Porgy and Bess prepare partnership accounts to 31 May. They decide to change the year end by preparing accounts for 22 months to 31 March 2015.

The basis periods will be:

2013/14	Year to 31 May 2013
2014/15	Year to 31 May 2014 (12/22 of the accounts for the period to 31.3.15)
2015/16	1 June 2014–31 March 2016 (10/22 of the accounts for the period to 31.3.15 plus the accounts to 31.3.16 less overlap relief to reduce the assessable profits to 12 months). There will be no overlap profits to carry forward, since this is now a 31 March accounting date.

6.7 **Example 6.4** assumes that HMRC accept the accounting change for the tax year 2015/16, on the basis that *ITTOIA 2005, ss 216* and *219* allow the use of the new accounting date in the next tax year to be treated as if it were the first use of the new date. If the partnership continues to be unsuccessful in changing the date, it can keep trying until five years have elapsed, at which point the condition will be satisfied. Alternatively, it can return to the original accounting date as if there had never been an attempt to change it.

6.8 Were the new date not accepted for 2015/16, the taxable profits for that year would be: 10/12ths of year to 31 March 2015 plus 2/12ths of year to 31 March 2016, giving 12 months' profits to 31 May 2015, and so on until a valid change is accepted.

6.9 Relief for overlap profits is given to each partner whenever there is a change of accounting date which would otherwise result in tax being charged on more than 12 months' profit in one tax year, or otherwise when the partner leaves or the business ceases completely. The overlap relief given on a change of accounting date is the appropriate proportion according to the length of the period to which the overlap relief relates and the extent to which the current basis period exceeds 12 months.

Example 6.5 – Overlap relief on change of accounting date

Raven, Swift, Swallow and Robin change their accounting date to 31 December, making up accounts for the 15 months to 31 December 2017, for which the profits are £300,000. Raven retires on 31 December 2017.

The assessable profits for each partner for 2017/18 will be their shares for the 15 months' period, against which Swift, Swallow and Robin will be entitled to a three months' proportion of their overlap relief. Raven will be entitled to deduct all his overlap relief, since he has left the business. The position (assuming overlap relief of £35,000 for each partner based on a six month overlap period) is therefore as follows:

	Raven	*Swift*	*Swallow*	*Robin*
	£000	*£000*	*£000*	*£000*
Profit share	75	75	75	75
Less overlap relief:				
Full amount	35			
3/6 × 35		17.5	17.5	17.5
	40	57.5	57.5	57.5

The remaining partners still have three months of overlap relief to be given against later changes.

What are 'accounts'?

6.10 Fundamental to the rules on a change of accounting date is the need to identify what is meant by 'accounts' and the date to which accounts have been drawn up. This apparently simple question was considered by the First-tier Tribunal in *Grint v HMRC* [2016] UKFTT 537.

The taxpayer, the actor Rupert Grint, had for some years prepared accounts to 31 July until 31 July 2008. With the introduction of the 50% tax rate from 6 April 2010, he was advised to advance as much income as possible into the tax year 2009/10. If accounts had been drawn up for the period 1 August 2008 to 31 July 2009 and also for the period 1 July 2009 to 5 April 2010, the conditions for a change of accounting date 5 April would have been satisfied and the basis period for 2009/10 would have been the 20-month period to 5 April 2010 with eight months' of overlap relief allowed. As it was, however, a single set of accounts were initially drawn up for the 20-month period 1 August 2008 to 5 April 2010, presented to Mr Grint by his accountant, and signed by him. The profits shown by those accounts were then apportioned on a time basis between the first 12 months to 31 July 2009 and the last 8 months to 5 April 2010 and Mr Grint's tax return was filed showing those profits as the profits of two separate periods of account.

HMRC subsequently became aware (following a VAT visit) of the existence of the original signed 20-month accounts and opened an enquiry into the return on the basis that the 'period of account' ending on 5 April 2010 exceeded 18 months and that the basis period for 2009/10 ended on the old accounting date of 31 July 2009.

In a long and closely analysed judgment the Tribunal Chairman concluded that on the facts of the case the only 'accounts' for the purposes of the legislation were the accounts for the period 1 August 2008 to 5 April 2010 and that since this made the 'period of account' longer than 18 months the change of accounting date in 2009/10 did not meet the conditions of *s 217* and was not effective.

Chapter 7

Mergers and Demergers

Signposts

- On a merger or demerger the tax consequences as regards cessation, continuation or commencement of separate trades are heavily fact-dependent (see **7.1 – 7.5**).
- On a merger both businesses may cease (see **7.6**); one may continue (see **7.7**) or both may continue (see **7.8 – 7.9**).
- Where merging partnerships have accounted for work in progress on different bases the accounting policies of each partnership will need to be analysed correctly (see **7.10 – 7.17**).
- Care needs to be taken regarding the CGT and VAT implications of merging partnerships (see **7.18 – 7.24**).
- Demergers (see **7.25**) present similar problems and may involve the continuation of one or more existing businesses (see **7.26 – 7.27**) or cessation of the old and recommencement of new businesses (see **7.28 – 7.29**).
- Issues arising on demerger include valuation of work in progress, CGT, VAT and consideration of the special position of farming partnerships (see **7.30 – 7.33**).

7.1 Where two (or more) businesses come together the result may be:

- a cessation of both (or all) of the previous businesses and the start of a new one; or
- the continuation of both (or all) of the previous businesses; or
- the cessation of one (or some) of the businesses and the continuation of one (or some) of the businesses.

Which of these applies is a question of fact.

Similarly, where a partnership breaks up and different partners take with them different parts of the partnership activity, the result may be:

- the partnership business has ceased and two or more new businesses commence; or
- some of partners have continued what is identifiably the partnership business and others have started a new business.

In each case, HMRC guidance at SP 9/86 may be in point as well as more general HMRC guidance at BIM82400 onwards.

7.2 If the result of the merger is a new business, different in nature from either of the two previous businesses, the current year basis cessation and commencement provisions outlined in **Chapter 4** will apply.

7.3 Where two businesses carrying on similar activities in different ownership merge and the new business is then carried on by the joint owners in partnership, the new partnership may be regarded not as carrying on a new business but as carrying on both the previous businesses simultaneously. Each business, together comprising the new partnership, will be deemed to continue. It may be that on a merger of businesses of this kind some of the previous owners of the businesses cease to be involved. Cessation provisions apply to those owners in the usual way.

7.4 A third possibility is that a 'merger' is in fact simply the acquisition of the trade and assets of one business (which thereupon ceases to exist) by the owners of another, which continue in enlarged form. Cessation provisions apply to the profits of the acquired (or rather ceased) business.

Mergers

7.5 Dealing with the merger of two firms is straightforward. It is simply necessary to decide whether there is a completely new business as indicated in **7.2**, or whether the new firm may be regarded as succeeding to the old firms as in **7.3**. (But see **7.7** regarding the possibility of only one of the previous businesses being regarded as having ceased.)

Cessation of both businesses

7.6 The merger of two businesses may create a totally new business or businesses. New personnel or partners may be involved, and the new partnership may undertake a qualitatively different trade. An example of this was in *George Humphries & Co v Cook* (1934) 19 TC 121, where it was held that a merger of two complementary businesses resulted in a new business and not a continuation of either of the original businesses. In this case, the tax consequences are as follows:

- The original businesses will cease at the date of the merger. The partners will be taxed on their profit share until cessation and will offset any overlap relief to which they are entitled.
- A new business will commence on the date of the merger. The partners in the new business will be taxed according to the current year basis commencement rules.

Merger with one business continuing

7.7 A merger could result in one continuing business, for example, because a larger partnership acquires the assets of a smaller one. In this case the tax consequences are as follows:

- The cessation rules apply to the partners in the ceasing business. They can claim overlap relief against their final taxable profits.

- If some of the partners in the ceasing business join the acquiring partnership, they will be taxed using the commencement rules.
- There will be no effect on the partners in the acquiring partnership unless the partnership's year end is changed at the same time (see **Chapter 6**) or their profit shares change.

Merger with both businesses continuing

7.8 Where two businesses with the same essential characteristics merge (eg where they have similar trades and are of similar size), the combined business may be a continuation of both previous businesses. The tax consequences where both businesses continue are as follows:

- The tax position of the continuing partners will be unchanged.
- Any partners leaving the partnership will be taxed on their profits to cessation, less a deduction for overlap relief.
- If any partners outside the partnership join the merged firm, they will be taxed under the commencement provisions.
- Where the two businesses do not have coterminous year ends, the assessable profits of the merged business will initially have to be calculated by reference to separate basis periods.

Example 7.1 – Business merger with both businesses continuing

Oak and Ash are both landscape gardening partnership businesses.

Oak has two partners: Mae and Nat. They share profits equally and prepare accounts to 31 May. They each have overlap profits of £10,000.

Ash has three partners: Olive, Poppy and Quentin. The partners also share profits equally and prepare accounts to 31 December. The partners have overlap profits of £15,000 each.

The businesses merge on 1 January 2015 to form Tree Design. Olive retires on 31 December 2014. The other partners continue to share profits equally. The partnership decides to make up accounts to 31 May each year.

The profits net of capital allowances are as follows:

Year ended	*Oak*	*Ash*	*Tree Design*
	£	£	£
31 May 2013	100,000		
31 December 2013		90,000	
31 May 2014	120,000		
31 December 2014		105,000	

Year ended	*Oak*	*Ash*	*Tree Design*
	£	£	£
1 June 2014–31 December 2014	80,000		
1 January 2015–31 May 2015			80,000
31 May 2016			200,000

The assessments for 2013/2014 will be:

Mae and Nat (year ended 31 May 2013): £50,000 each.

Olive, Poppy and Quentin (year ended 31 December 2013): £30,000 each.

The assessments for 2014/15 will be:

Mae and Nat (year ended 31 May 2014): £60,000 each. The accounting period 1 June 2014 to 31 December 2014 is a temporary accounting date and will be ignored.

Olive, Poppy and Quentin (year ended 31 December 2014): £35,000 each. Olive will offset her overlap relief of £15,000, leaving her taxable on £20,000.

ITTOIA 2005, Pt 2, Ch 17 applies to both partnerships, and a continuation basis applies to all the partners except Olive.

The assessments for 2015/16 will be:

	Total	*Mae*	*Nat*	*Poppy*	*Quentin*
	£	£	£	£	£
1 June 2014–31 December 2014	80,000	40,000	40,000		
1 June 2014–31 December 2014	40,833			20,416	20,417
(7/12 from the accounts to 31 December 2014) less Olive's share = £70,000 × 7/12					
1 January 2015–31 May 2015	80,000	20,000	20,000	20,000	20,000
	200,833	60,000	60,000	40,416	40,417
Overlap profits brought forward	50,000	10,000	10,000	15,000	15,000
Additional overlap profits on change of year end	40,833			20,416	20,417
Overlap profits to carry forward	90,833	10,000	10,000	35,416	35,417

The profits are calculated on a continuing basis. Ash has a change of accounting date and additional overlap profits are created.

From 1 January 2015, Mae and Nat are participating for the first time in the profits of the 'Ash' business (albeit as part of the merged business). It might logically be thought that Mae and Nat should be treated as new partners in the Ash business, with commencement rules applying to their share of the profits of the merged business which are attributable to the Ash activities. (And by the same token that Poppy and Quentin should be treated as new partners in the Oak business). Although this would arguably be logical, it is not the approach taken by HMRC. Instead each partner is treated, for the purpose of determining basis periods, as if the merged business is (as a single business) a continuation of both the previous businesses, with the result that the basis periods are as shown above.

The assessments for 2016/17 will be:

Mae, Nat, Poppy and Quentin (year ended 31 May 2016): £50,000 each.

7.9 Both previous partnerships may change their accounting date to facilitate the merger.

Example 7.2 – Change of accounting date on merger of firms

Ambrose and Walsh commenced their partnership on 1 May 2013. Their profits for the year to 30 April 2014 were £72,000, divided 2:1.

Newport and Ripley began their business on 1 July 2013, preparing accounts to 30 June 2014, in which period their profits were £48,000, divisible equally.

Their businesses merged on 30 September 2015, and their profits to that date were as follows:

		£000
Ambrose and Walsh	1.5.14–30.9.15	170
Newport and Ripley	1.7.14–30.9.15	150

They continued to share profits up to the date of the merger as previously. The merged partnership adopts 30 September as its accounting date, and the profits of the year to 30 September 2016 are £360,000, divisible equally.

The merged business is to be regarded as a continuation of both of the previous businesses.

The taxable profits and overlap relief are:

Ambrose and Walsh

	Ambrose	*Walsh*
Taxable:	*£000*	*£000*
2013/14 (11/12 × 72 = 66)	44	22

	Ambrose	*Walsh*
2014/15 (year to 30.4.14 = 72)	48	24
Overlap relief to carry forward:		
11/12 × 72 for year to 30.4.14 used twice	44	22

Newport and Ripley

	Newport	*Ripley*
Taxable:	*£000*	*£000*
2013/14 (9/12 × 48 = 36)	18	18
2014/15 (year to 30.6.14 = 48)	24	24
Overlap relief to carry forward:		
9/12 × 48 for year to 30.6.14 used twice	18	18

		Ambrose	*Walsh*	*Newport*	*Ripley*
Taxable 2015/16		*£000*	*£000*	*£000*	*£000*
17 months to 30.9.15	170	113	57		
5 months overlap relief:					
5/11 × 44		(20)			
5/11 × 22			(10)		
15 months to 30.9.15	150			75	75
Three months' overlap relief					
(3/9 × 18 for each partner)				(6)	(6)
Taxable on each partner		93	47	69	69
Overlap relief b/f		44	22	18	18
Used		(20)	(10)	(6)	(6)
Overlap relief remaining (covering six months in each case)		24	12	12	12
Taxable 2016/17					
Year 30.9.16	360	90	90	90	90

Income recognition and work in progress

7.10 Where a partnership has carried out work but has not yet met the criteria to recognise revenue – for example, in certain circumstances where work has been performed but the ability to charge the client is contingent on a future event – work in progress will be included on the balance sheet.

Following the issue of UITF 40 (now superseded following the introduction of FRS100), many partnerships found that amounts historically recorded as work in progress related to services meeting the criteria to be recognised as revenue and accrued income on the balance sheet. Accordingly, levels of work in progress reduced significantly and, for a large number of partnerships, became nil.

The primary reason for accounting for work in progress is to satisfy the accruals basis of accounting and to ensure that expenditure relating to the work undertaken is matched with the income it generates in the correct period. The principle is to carry forward costs relating to future periods. The accruals principle is, however, subject to prudence if there is uncertainty. Where there is no uncertainty, work in progress should not be unnecessarily reduced.

If there is no expenditure, there can be no work in progress. This is particularly relevant for partnerships because there is no expenditure included in the profit and loss account in respect of the partners' time: it is simply an appropriation of profits. A partnership with no fee-earning (or productive) staff cannot, therefore, have work in progress.

7.11 Partnerships that are ineligible to use, or simply choose not to use, the cash basis from 2013/14 (see **Chapter 1**) are required to prepare accounts in accordance with GAAP – this means on an earnings basis and incorporating work in progress. Therefore, as such partnerships will account on the same basis, no mismatch will occur if two or more such partnerships merge. However, each partnership will have selected the most appropriate accounting policies to its particular business. It is therefore probable that these will not be the same. New policies will have to be selected for the merged business.

7.12 It is possible for two merging partnerships to have accounted for work in progress on different bases and to have recognised income in different ways. The accounting policies of each partnership will need to be analysed and the tax effect taken into account to ensure that the terms of the merger are fair. For example, where one partnership takes over the assets of a smaller partnership, the smaller partnership may not have been required to include work in progress in its accounts on the basis of materiality. Internal adjustments may be necessary between partners to maintain equity.

7.13 Where there is effectively a continuation of more than one partnership, there may be a change in the basis of valuing work in progress to reflect the activities of the new combined partnership. In this case, a prior year adjustment may be necessary.

7.14 In the event of both or either of the former businesses ceasing at the time of the merger, the work in progress of that business can be:

(a) sold to the new or continuing business, being:

  (i) fully included in the final accounts of the old business; or

  (ii) partly included in the final accounts of the old business and an election made for the excess over cost to be taxed as income on the old partners; or

(b) licensed to the new business to complete, the new business paying an appropriate amount to the old business which will be charged to income tax accordingly.

7.15 Licensing may be appropriate, since it may be proper for some of the profit to be included in the amount paid by the new business to the former firms.

The payment will minimise the assessments based on the profits of the first accounting period of the new business and thus the profits which are overlapped. The recipient former firms will be taxed on the payment from the new firm once only.

7.16 Where the old and new partnerships are connected, HMRC will look closely at the value used to arrive at the payment for work in progress. For trading partnerships, the provisions of *ITTOIA 2005, Pt 2, Ch 17* will apply to substitute arm's-length value for the value used, subject to the former and new partnerships being able to elect to use the lesser cost price or actual consideration, whichever of those two is the higher.

7.17 If the merging firms have different bases of accounting and/or valuation, and to bring them into line would be tax costly or disadvantageous to some partners, it is worth considering the continuation of the old firms until the fiscal disadvantages are removed.

An entirely new firm then carries on a new business comprising those partners from the existing firms who form the new firm, with appropriate commercial arrangements being made to regulate, as between all parties, the businesses carried on.

Capital gains tax

7.18 Where partnerships merge, the CGT treatment is the same as that for changes in profit-sharing ratios (see **Chapter 12**). If gains arise due to the revaluation of assets, or payment outside the accounts, the partner may be able to claim rollover relief on the share acquired in the new firm (see **Chapter 15**). See also Statement of Practice D12.

Value added tax

7.19 As far as value added tax ('VAT') is concerned, if both businesses are VAT-registered, one firm's VAT registration will usually be retained, with HMRC being notified of the entry of new partners into that firm (and, if relevant, the retirement of some of the existing partners), and any other changes, such as a change of name, within 30 days of the merger.

7.20 The firm whose registration is to be cancelled must also notify HMRC within 30 days, and must submit a final VAT return to the date of the merger and pay the amount due. The merging of the assets of that firm with those of the firm retaining its registration will be treated as the transfer of a going concern, and will not have any VAT consequences (*Value Added Tax (Special Provisions) Order 1995 (SI 1995/1268), Art 5*).

7.21 The partners of the deregistering firm will be liable for that firm's VAT liabilities up to the date of deregistration. They will not normally be liable for VAT liabilities incurred prior to the merger by the firm whose registration is retained, the *Partnership Act 1890* providing that a partner is liable for debts incurred 'while he is a partner' and *VATA 1994, s 45(5)* providing that the liability of someone who joins a firm during a return period is 'such proportion of the firm's liability as may be just'.

7.22 If any partners are retiring at the time of the merger, they remain jointly liable with other partners for supplies made up to the time at which HMRC are notified of their retirement (*VATA 1994, s 45(2)*).

7.23 If one of the firms was not VAT-registered, then the only action required would be for their entry into the VAT-registered firm to be notified, as indicated at **7.19**.

7.24 If neither firm was previously VAT-registered, the normal rules of *VATA 1994, Sch 1, para 1* would apply to determine if and when the business would become liable for registration. It is considered that only the turnover of the merged business would need to be considered, since the previous businesses were separate 'persons', neither of which was a 'taxable person', so that the provisions of *VATA 1994, s 49* requiring previous turnover to be taken into account on a transfer by a taxable person of a going concern would not apply. The merged business would therefore be able, if appropriate, to defer VAT registration until its turnover had exceeded the VAT threshold in the previous 12 months, unless the threshold would be exceeded in a single month.

Demergers

7.25 There are no statutory rules on a demerger. Again, HMRC Statement of Practice SP 9/86 deals with the assessment position without reference to the other aspects, such as work in progress. It is once again a question of fact as to whether any of the new partnerships are the same as the original partnership. The facts should be disclosed to HMRC in each case.

> **Focus**
>
> The HMRC Business Income Manual at BIM72425 states:
>
> > 'Where a business is split (demerged) into two separate parts then you [HMRC] should normally apply the cessation rules to the original business and the commencement rules to the new businesses. This is because a person cannot succeed to part of a business.
> >
> > 'But if one of the businesses formed after the demerger can be seen to be the same business as that previously carried on before the demerger, even though it has lost part of its customers and its assets, and there is either no change or only a partial change of ownership then you [HMRC] should apply the automatic continuation basis to that business.'

Demerger with one business continuing

7.26 If one partnership, carrying on a single business, splits into two or more separate partnerships, each of the new partnerships will be carrying on a separate business. It is not possible for more than one of the new partnerships to be carrying on the same business as the old partnership; whether any of them are doing so is a matter of fact. This may happen where a large proportion of the original business continues in one of the new partnerships: – for example, one or more of the former partners may leave and take with them some of the firm's existing clients, leaving the majority of the partnership business unchanged. In this situation, the tax consequences will be as follows:

- the cessation rules apply to the partners leaving the continuing partnership;
- the commencement provisions will apply to any new partners joining the continuing partnership;
- there will be no effect on the existing partners who remain in the continuing partnership unless the partnership's year end is changed at the same time, in which case overlapping profits will have to be taken into account, or the partners' profit shares change.

Demerger with two or more businesses continuing

7.27 It will be extremely unusual for a single partnership to be carrying on two separate businesses, but not quite impossible. Where, exceptionally, this happens, it may be that on a partnership demerger each of the new partnerships carries on one of the separate businesses previously carried on by the old partnership. In this situation, the partners would be taxed on a continuing basis, subject to changes in profit share and accounting date.

Cessation of business

7.28 Where (as will almost always be the case) a partnership carries on a single business and on a splitting up of the partnership neither (or none) of the new partnerships can be said to be carrying on the whole business of the old partnership in an identifiable form, the partnership split will create a new business or businesses. In this case, the tax consequences will be:

- the original partnership will cease at the date of the demerger, the partners being taxed on their share of the profits less overlap relief to the date of cessation; and
- the new businesses will commence at the date of the demerger and the partners will be taxed under the commencement rules.

Example 7.3 – Partnership demergers

The Citrus Partnership has 20 partners and five offices. Its year end is 31 March. Consider the following scenarios:

(a) Two partners leave the partnership on 31 March 2015 and take some of their clients, setting up a new firm, Lime, on 1 April 2015.

It is likely that as a matter of fact the Citrus Partnership continues. For the leaving partners, the cessation basis of assessment will apply to their profits from the Citrus Partnership, subject to any overlap relief. They will be taxed under the current year commencement rules for the profits from Lime, starting from 1 April 2015. The remaining partners in the Citrus Partnership will be taxed on a continuing basis.

(b) The partners at each office decide to split from the others with effect from 31 March 2015. Each partnership retains a 31 March year end, admits no new partners and none retire.

None of the five new partnerships can reasonably be said to be carrying on the Citrus business. Each is carrying on a part of it. All the partners will be taxed on the basis of a cessation of the Citrus business on 31 March 2015, subject to any overlap relief. The partners in the five new businesses will be taxed on a commencement basis from 1 April 2015.

(c) The partners in the Citrus Partnership fall out. Half the partners take a substantial block of fees and set up a new partnership, Orange Associates, in a new location ten miles away, on 1 June 2016. Five partners retire and the remainder (together with two new partners, previously sole practitioners, who bring their client portfolio into the business) continue to trade as the Citrus Partnership but on a much smaller scale, closing three of the previous five offices.

It is a question of fact which if either of the new partnerships has succeeded to the old business. The fact that Orange Associates trades under a different name in a different location strongly suggests that that partnership has not succeeded to the old business, despite having some partners and clients in common. It is possible that the business carried on by the remaining partners (together with the new partners) is identifiably the same as the old Citrus Partnership business despite the reduction in size and the change in the client base and the number of offices. If so, the analysis will be as (a) above. The alternative analysis is that the changes which have occurred mean that the old business has ceased to exist in any identifiable form, in which case the tax treatment will be as at (b) above. In either case, the commencement rules will apply to Orange Associates.

7.29 HMRC's approach to cessation was supported in the pre-self-assessment case of *C Connelly & Co v Wilbey* (1992) 65 TC 208, which concerned a continuation election for the purposes of the now defunct stock relief. It was held that an election for continuity could not be made where an accountancy practice that had previously carried on a combined business from two offices was split into two separate parts.

Work in progress

7.30 Work in progress will enter into the final result of the old business (or, for professional partnerships, the excess over cost will be assessed on the old partners by election) and into the first results of each of the demerged parts. (Special rules apply in relation to the valuation of the work in progress on cessation of a trading partnership – *ITTOIA 2005, s 173*.)

Capital Gains Tax

7.31 As with a merger, a demerger is likely to involve changes in the profit-sharing ratios. If gains arise on the relinquishment of an interest in some assets (or payment outside the accounts) the partner may be able to claim rollover relief in respect of any enhanced share in other assets. ESC D25 provides that the acquisition of a further interest in an asset already in use for the purposes of a trade is for roll-over relief purposes treated as the acquisition of a new asset (see **Chapter 15**).

Value added tax

7.32 On a demerger of a VAT-registered business, one of the businesses may retain the existing VAT registration. In that event, the VAT consequences for that business are similar to those outlined at **7.19**, the changes requiring notification within 30 days. However this means that the VAT obligations of the old partnership pass over to the partners in the new partnership retaining the VAT registration. Thus, where there is a dispute between the demerging partners, it may be preferable to cancel the VAT registration on demerger and to re-register the new partnerships. It should, however, be borne in mind that HMRC may (for direct tax purposes) take into account factors such as the transfer of the VAT registration when considering whether there has been a cessation or continuation of one or more partnerships.

If both seek new registrations, and in any event for the business that does not retain the old registration, the demerger would almost certainly be treated as the transfer of a business (or part of a business) as a going concern under *VATA 1994, s 49*, so that VAT would not be payable on assets transferred.

Farming partnerships

7.33 All the farming carried on by any particular person or partnership or body of persons is treated as one trade (*ITTOIA 2005, s 9(2)*). This will be the case regardless of how many separate farming trades would otherwise on first principles be considered to exist, and whether the farms are adjacent to each other, or located far apart in the UK. The legislation does not, however, combine the farming of a partnership with the farming carried on by any of the individual partners on their own account.

Chapter 8

Capital Allowances

Signposts

- Trading and professional partnerships who are not using the cash basis for calculating taxable income are entitled to claim capital allowances on qualifying partnership assets in the same way as other traders (see **8.1 – 8.5**).
- Capital allowances can be claimed on plant and machinery owned personally by partners (see **8.6 – 8.10**).
- Extracting assets for personal use of partners may require a market value adjustment (see **8.11 – 8.14**).
- All claims to capital allowances (including in respect of assets owned personally by partners) are made on the partnership return (see **8.15 – 8.23**).

8.1 Trading and professional partnerships who are not using the cash basis are entitled to claim capital allowances on qualifying partnership assets in the same way as other traders. Under the cash basis, allowable expenses include certain capital expenditure. This removes the need for capital allowance calculations and claims, and so no capital allowances will be available.

Capital allowances are not related to a tax year, but are instead treated as a trading expense of the 'chargeable period' in computing the profit or loss of the period.

8.2 In the context of a trade, 'chargeable period' means for income tax a period for which accounts are drawn up. This may be a 12-month period, or may be shorter or longer. Where the accounting period is less or more than 12 months, writing-down allowances ('WDAs') are proportionately reduced or increased. However, if the accounting period exceeds 18 months, it must be split for capital allowances into one or more periods of 12 months plus a period covering the remainder of the account, the allowances then being aggregated for the whole period.

Example 8.1 – Capital allowances – long accounting period

A partnership making up accounts to 30 June annually has a written-down value ('WDV') at 30 June 2015 of £100,000 on the plant and machinery pool. The capital allowances, if it then makes up an account for: (a) 18 months; or (b) 21 months, will be:

(a) 18-month account to 31 December 2016

	£
WDV brought forward	100,000
WDA 18% × 18/12	27,000
WDV carried forward	73,000

(*b*) 21-month account to 31 March 2017

	£
WDV brought forward	100,000
Year to 30.6.16:	
WDA 18%	18,000
	82,000
Nine months to 31.3.17:	
WDA 18% × 9/12	11,070
WDV carried forward	70,930
The total WDA for the period is (18,000 + 11,070) =	29,070
Without the rule for accounts of 18+ months, the WDA would have been	
100,000 × 18% × 21/12 =	31,500

8.3 The rate of WDAs was reduced from 20% to 18% from 6 April 2012 (1 April 2012 for corporation tax) (*Finance Act 2011 (FA 2011), s 10*). For chargeable periods which straddle this date, the rate of WDAs is a hybrid of the rates before and after the change.

8.4 For a partnership, capital allowances are given at the partnership level and are deducted in computing the profits of the partnership for the partnership chargeable period. These are allocated between the partners according to their sharing arrangements, and each partner will be taxed on his or her share. As long as any changes in the composition of the partnership do not result in its permanent cessation, allowances are given ignoring any partnership changes (*CAA 2001, s 263*).

The profit-sharing arrangements may include a specific allocation of some of the capital allowances; for example, where the assets are owned individually by the partners (see **8.6**).

8.5 If the partnership has a year-end other than 31 March or 5 April, capital allowances of a period may (like the profits of the period) be taken into account in computing the taxable profits of more than one tax year; but since they are taken into account in computing the resulting overlap relief there is no permanent double relief.

Plant and machinery owned individually

8.6 It is common in many partnerships (particularly professional firms) for certain assets (typically motor vehicles) to be owned individually by partners rather than by the partnership, perhaps to accommodate different views of different partners as to the appropriate level of expenditure on such assets.

Where the asset qualifying for allowances belongs to an individual partner but is used for the purposes of the partnership (without any charge being made to the partnership for its use), capital allowances may be claimed in the same way as if the assets were owned by the partnership (*CAA 2001, s 264*).

8.7 The capital allowances must however be claimed on the partnership self-assessment return rather than by the partners individually. This will involve adding together capital allowances computations for the partnership assets and those owned by the individual partners in order to arrive at the total capital allowances figure for the partnership.

8.8 The net taxable profit to be divided between the partners will be the profit after making all the capital allowance claims (including those in respect of assets owned individually by partners). In order to achieve the equitable arrangements desired by the partners it will usually be necessary to add back the individual partner's capital allowances claims, divide the profit according to the partnership profit-sharing ratio and then deduct the individual partner's capital allowance claim. This will then provide the correct profit share after the partner's share of partnership capital allowances and his or her own personal capital allowances.

Example 8.2 – Plant and machinery owned individually

Chris and Jo are dentists. They share profits equally. Their cars are owned by the partners personally. Chris buys a car costing £20,000 in May 2014. The car has emissions of 125g/km. He uses the car 75% for business purposes. Jo also bought a new car in May 2014. His car cost £25,000 and has emissions of 120g/km. He uses his car 25% of the time for work purposes. The profits after partnership capital allowances are £100,000.

Capital allowances will be due as follows:

	Chris	*Jo*
	£	*£*
Cost of car	20,000	25,000
WDA at 18%	3,600	4,500
Reduction for private use	900	3,375
Capital allowance claim × 75% and 25%	2,700	1,125

The partnership profits will be £100,000 less Chris's capital allowances (£2,700) less Jo's capital allowances (£1,125) = £96,175.

The profits will be allocated as follows:

	Total	*Chris*	*Jo*
	£	*£*	*£*
Partnership profits	96,175		
Add back:			
Chris's capital allowances	2,700		
Jo's capital allowances	1,125		
Adjusted profit (shared 50:50)	100,000	50,000	50,000
Less:			
Capital allowances	3,825	2,700	1,125
Taxable profit	96,175	47,300	48,875

If the adjustment had not been made, the profit of £96,175 would have been shared equally, giving each partner profits of £48,087.

8.9 On the other hand, where a partner owns an asset which is used for the purposes of the partnership business and makes it available to the partnership for consideration (ie, hires or leases it to the partnership) the partner is regarded as conducting a separate leasing business independently of the partnership and is able personally to claim capital allowances against the personal leasing income in the normal way.

8.10 If individually owned plant or machinery used without charge for the purposes of the partnership business is sold (or given) by one partner to another, the asset continuing to be used in the business, the capital allowances computation for the asset concerned would continue without taking any disposal value into account (*CAA 2001, s 264(3)*), appropriate adjustments being made as to the allocation of allowances between the partners.

Disposals other than sale at arm's length

8.11 Special capital allowances rules may apply where an asset is disposed of other than by way of sale at market value. These may affect partnerships where there are changes in the partners or when an asset ceases to be used for the partnership business including when a partnership business is incorporated.

8.12 If an asset is taken from the partnership for personal use by one of the partners or sold (perhaps to a connected person) for less than market value the asset is deemed for capital allowance purposes to have been disposed of at its market value. This value will be used by the partnership to determine whether there are balancing allowances or charges (*CAA 2001, s 61(2)*).

8.13 If a partnership business is incorporated, the basic rule is that plant and machinery is treated as sold by the partnership to the company at market value. However, *CAA 2001, s 266* provides the facility for a joint election to be made by the partners and the company, within two years after the transfer of the business, for the disposal to be treated as made at tax written-down value (WDV). This avoids a balancing adjustment on the partnership; the company will take over the assets at their WDV.

8.14 Where plant and machinery is the subject of an election under *CAA 2001, s 266*, the transfer is treated as being for an amount equal to the WDV brought forward at the end of the previous tax year.

There is no scaled-down WDA according to the length of the chargeable period of transfer.

Example 8.3 – Plant and machinery – allowances on incorporation

Incorporation takes place on 30 June 2014.

	Plant pool	*Motor car (1/4 private)*
	£	£
WDV at 5.4.14	50,000	22,000
2014/15		
(6.4.14–30.6.14)		
Deemed sale proceeds		
(giving a transfer value equal to WDV at 5.4.14)	50,000	22,000

No capital allowances are due for the period 6.4.14 to 30.6.15.

Claims for capital allowances

8.15 Claims for capital allowances (for those not using the cash basis) must be made in the partnership tax return, subject to three minor exceptions (*CAA 2001, s 3*). Under self-assessment, the profit share of a partner in his or her personal return must coincide with the allocation to him or her in the partnership return (unless, exceptionally, there is disagreement between the partner and the partnership as to the correct amount of taxable profit allocable to the partner – see **Chapter 21**). Thus it will not be possible for a partner to reduce his or her partnership income as advised to him or her by the partnership by a personal claim for capital allowances. Claims for capital allowances by individual partners on assets owned personally, therefore, must be incorporated into the partnership computation and return.

Depending of the personal circumstances of each partner, it may be that some partners would wish capital allowances for a particular year to be disclaimed or claimed in a reduced amount, while others would prefer them to be claimed in full. But because capital allowances are claimed at the partnership level, such flexibility is not possible: partners will have to agree between themselves what allowances are to be claimed, which may involve compromises between the ideal tax position for individual partners.

> **Focus**
>
> Claims for capital allowances are subject to the same time limits as other entries in the return, ie any amendment must be made within 12 months after the 31 January filing date for the return.

8.16 Depending on circumstances, the capital allowances available on plant and machinery used for the purposes of a partnership business may include:

- writing-down allowance;
- first-year allowance;
- annual investment allowance.

If the full available allowances on plant and machinery are not required, a claim may be made for a reduced amount (*CAA 2001, s 56(5)*).

Writing-down allowances

8.17 Qualifying expenditure is pooled for the purpose of determining entitlement to writing-down allowances ('WDA') and balancing allowances and liability to balancing charges. There are single-asset pools, class pools and the main pool. (*CAA 2001, ss 53, 54*)

A single-asset pool contains expenditure relating to only one asset. The two cases most often encountered are those of an asset which is used partly for business and partly privately or an asset in respect of which a 'short-life asset' election is made. The rate of WDA in a single-asset pool may be either the main rate or the reduced special rate depending on the nature of the asset.

The most common example of a 'class pool' is the pool which is maintained in respect of expenditure qualifying for WDA at the reduced 'special rate' but which is not required to be maintained in a single-asset pool (the 'special rate pool').

Any expenditure which does not fall into a single-asset pool or a class pool is allocated to the 'main pool' and WDA at the standard rate applies.

WDAs are available at the following rates for 2016/17 and 2017/18.

Standard rate	18%
Special rate	8%
Special rate applies to	Thermal insulation in buildings
	Integral features
	Long-life assets
	Some cars (see 8.19 below)
	Cushion gas
	Solar panels

In addition if for any chargeable period the amount of available qualifying expenditure (minus sale proceeds) on which WDA would otherwise be given in the main pool or the special rate pool would otherwise be less than £1,000, the whole of the pool balance is allowed as WDA for the period. This does not apply to single-asset pools.

Integral features

8.18 The following assets qualify as integral features (*CAA 2001, ss 33A–33B, 104A(1), 104D*):

- electrical systems (including lighting systems);
- cold water systems;
- space or water heating systems, powered systems of ventilation, air cooling or air purification, and any floor or ceiling comprised in such systems;
- lifts, escalators and moving walkways; and
- external solar shading.

Cars

8.19 Special rules apply to cars, as defined at *CAA 2001, s 268A*, which definition excludes:

- motor-cycles (which includes three-wheeled vehicles);
- vehicles of a construction primarily suited for carrying goods (eg vans);
- vehicles of a type not commonly used privately and unsuitable to be so used (such as black cabs, hearses, driving school vehicles fitted with dual controls).

The rate of capital allowances on cars is based on the car's carbon dioxide emissions, as summarised below:

CO_2 emissions: from 2013/14 to 2014/15	*CO_2 emissions: 2015–16 to 2017/18*	*Capital allowances*
Up to 95g/km	Up to 75g/km	FYAs at 100% available
Up to 130g/km	Up to 130g/km	Main rate pool* applies (18%)
Over 130g/km	Over 130g/km	Special rate pool* applies (8%)
		**Unless there is private use, in which case a single-asset pool is required*

The 100% FYA for cars initially applied only for expenditure up to 31 March 2013 (*CAA 2001, s 45D*). It was extended for a further two years to 31 March 2015, but the CO_2 emissions threshold was reduced from 110g/km to 95g/km from 2013/14 and removed FYA from leased cars. The *Finance Act 2015* extended the scheme until 31 March 2018, but further reduced the CO_2 emissions threshold.

For cars with private use the main or special rates apply as above (depending on CO_2 emissions) but the car is retained in a single asset pool. Allowances are restricted for private use.

First-year allowances

8.20 Subject to the general exclusions (see **8.21**), the following types of expenditure may qualify for first-year allowances ('FYAs'), subject to compliance with the detailed requirements of the legislation:

- certain energy-saving plant or machinery (*s 45A–45C*);
- cars with very low CO_2 emissions (*s 45D*);
- zero-emission goods vehicles (*s 45DA*);
- plant or machinery for gas refuelling stations (*s 45E*);
- plant or machinery for use in a ring fence trade (*s 45F*);
- environmentally beneficial plant or machinery (*s 45H–45J*); and
- certain new investment by companies in new plant or machinery in designated assisted areas in Enterprise Zones (*ss 45K–45N*).

8.21 No FYAs are available, for a business of any size (*CAA 2001, s 46(2)*), for:

- expenditure incurred in the final chargeable period;
- cars (other than those with very low CO_2 emissions) (see **8.19**);
- certain ships and railway assets;
- plant or machinery for leasing;

- in certain anti-avoidance cases, where the obtaining of a FYA is linked to a change in the nature or conduct of a trade;
- where an asset was initially acquired for purposes other than those of the qualifying activity;
- where an asset was acquired by way of a gift; and
- where plant or machinery that was provided for long funding leasing starts to be used for other purposes.

Annual investment allowance

8.22 From 1 January 2016 the rate of annual investment allowance (AIA) has been £200,000 per annum.

The rates for earlier years are below:

	Maximum £
1/6 April 2014 – 31 December 2015	500,000
1 January 2013 – 31 March / 5 April 2014	250,000
1 April 2012 – 31 December 2012	25,000
1/6 April 2010 – 31 March / 5 April 2012	100,000

AIA is given for a chargeable period. As a general rule, the annual limit is proportionately increased or decreased for chargeable periods longer or shorter than 12 months (*CAA 2001, s 51A(6)*).

For chargeable periods which straddle a date where there is a change in rate (for example, 5 April 2014 and 31 December 2015), the maximum AIA entitlement is calculated by splitting the chargeable period into two chargeable periods, the first ending with the date before the change in rate, and the second commencing from that date. The maximum AIA available is then calculated according to the transitional rules.

The AIA applies to businesses regardless of size and can be applied to expenditure on long-life assets and integral features as well as on general plant and machinery, but not on cars. Expenditure over the AIA limit will be dealt with within the normal capital allowances regime.

In the context of partnerships, it is important to note that AIA is available only to:

- Individuals;
- Partnerships of which all the members are individuals;
- Companies.

It is not therefore available to any partnership which includes a corporate (or other non-individual) member.

Herd basis for farmers

8.23 Farming businesses (including partnerships) are able to make an irrevocable election to apply a special set of rules to the taxation of a group of living animals or other livestock kept for obtaining products such as milk, wool, etc, or their young (known as a 'herd' regardless of the type of animal). Under these rules the herd is, broadly, treated as a capital asset rather than part of trading stock (*ITTOIA 2005, Pt 2 Ch 8).* Capital allowances are not available, but a 'renewals basis' applies, so that as and when animals are replaced, the cost of replacement is treated as a trading expense and the sale proceeds are brought in as a trading receipt. If all or most of the herd is sold and not replaced, the proceeds represent the sale of a capital asset, which is exempt from capital gains tax since the animals are wasting assets on which capital allowances are not available (*TCGA 1992, s 45*). Herd basis is not available where profits are computed on the cash basis.

The particular significance of herd basis for farming partnerships is that on any change in the membership of a partnership any existing herd basis election ceases to be valid and a new opportunity to make a herd basis election arises. Where a complete sale of the herd is in contemplation this may offer significant tax savings, though the anti-avoidance rule at *ITTOIA 2005, s 127* may need to be considered. Broadly, the rule provides that where there has been a transfer of the herd which is not by way of sale at market value (such as, for example, on a partnership change) between 'bodies of persons' (which includes partnerships) under common control, in circumstances such that a 'herd basis benefit' is the sole or main benefit that might have been expected to accrue, the benefit is effectively to be denied.

Full details of Herd Basis may be found in HMRC guidance at BIM55500.

Chapter 9

Losses

Signposts

- Losses will be calculated in the same way as profits (see **9.1**).
- Losses are divided between the partners according to the loss-sharing ratio of the accounting period. Any subsequent loss relief due is then claimed by each partner individually, usually in his or her personal return (see **9.2 – 9.6**).
- Each partner may choose whether to claim relief for his share of the loss against general income, or to carry it forward against later trading profit shares or, in respect of a loss in any of the first four tax years in which he is a partner, to set the loss against his total income of the three previous tax years (see **9.7**).
- Changes of accounting date and overlap relief can add complications to the computation of a partner's loss (see **9.8 – 9.13**).
- Examples are given of claims for relief under the *Income Tax Act 2007 s 64* (including extension to capital gains) (see **9.14 – 9.19**), *s 72* (see **9.20 – 9.23**), *s 83* (see **9.24 – 9.25**) and *s 89–91* (see **9.28 – 9.30**).
- Where a partnership is transferred to a company solely or mainly in exchange for shares in the company, unrelieved losses of partners taking shares in the company may be carried forward and set against income from the company, provided the business has been carried on and the shares held throughout the tax year for which the claim is made (or, in the tax year in which the transfer takes place, for the whole of the remainder of that year) (see **9.31**).
- Claims to relief are subject to strict time limits (see **9.32 – 9.34**).
- The procedural status of loss claims and the enquiry regime relevant to them has been before the courts on a number of occasions: the position now seems to be established (see **9.35**).
- In making loss claims the effect both on NIC and Tax Credit claims should not be overlooked (see **9.36 – 9.37**).
- There are significant restrictions on the ability to claim relief for partnership losses in certain circumstances (see **9.38 – 9.44**).

9.1 Partnership losses are calculated in the same way as profits.

For partnerships using the cash basis, losses may be carried forward to set against the profits of future years but not carried back or set off 'sideways' against other sources of income.

The remainder of this chapter examines loss reliefs for those partnerships who are *not* using the cash basis.

Division of loss

9.2 The division of the loss will be made between the partners according to the loss-sharing ratio of the accounting period (*Income Tax (Trading and Other Income) Act 2005 ('ITTOIA 2005'), s 850*). Note that partnerships are free to agree that losses and profits are shared in different proportions. Loss relief is claimed by each partner individually, usually in his or her personal return.

9.3 Profits and losses are computed at the partnership level. Where partners divide profits and losses by allocating partnership salaries, priority profit shares or interest on capital before allocating the balance, the result may be that one or more partners shows a notional loss where there is an overall profit, or vice versa. But for tax purposes no partner can claim loss relief if the firm has made a profit, and no partner will have to self-assess a profit where the firm has made a loss. Instead the tax-adjusted profit or loss of the partnership is allocated between those partners who are commercially allocated profit or loss (as the case may be) in proportion to the allocation.

In *PDC Copyprint (South)* [1997] SpC 141, a Special Commissioner upheld this principle. In that case, the partnership agreements provided for two of the equity partners, who were regarded as being the managers of the business, to be entitled to salaries expressed as a first charge on the net trading profits. In the event, the salaries were paid regardless of the profitability. No PAYE was operated on the salaries. The other equity partners, who had little active involvement with the business, sought to increase their loss relief claims for certain years by the salaries paid. Although the report of the judgment is somewhat unclear, the claim was presumed to be on the grounds that the salaries were treated as costs of operating the business. They could not have been appropriations of profit, because no profit actually arose in those years. The Special Commissioner held that the losses must be computed in accordance with the *Taxes Acts*, which prohibit the deduction of partners' salaries in computing taxable profits. It was not open to partners to inflate their loss claims by the payment of salaries to one or more of their number.

Example 9.1 – Partner with negative profit share where partnership has made overall profit, and vice versa

The long-established partnership of Thyme, Sage and Parsley share profits and losses 4:4:2 after payment of salaries as follows: Thyme £21,000, Sage £18,000 and Parsley £16,000.

For the year to 31 December 2015 there is a profit (before salaries) of £8,500 and for the year to 31 December 2016 a loss (before salaries) of £20,000

	Total	*Thyme*	*Sage*	£ *Parsley*
	£	£	£	£
2015/16				
(year to 31.12.15)	8,500			
Salaries	55,000	21,000	18,000	16,000
Balance 4:4:2	(46,500)	(18,600)	(18,600)	(9,300)
	8,500	2,400	(600)	6,700
Eliminate Sage's 'loss' 2,400:6,700		(158)	600	(442)
Taxable profits	8,500	2,242	–	6,258

The elimination of Sage's loss is in the ratio of the other profit shares

	Total	*Thyme*	*Sage*	*Parsley*
	£	£	£	£
Loss of year				
to 31.12.16	20,000			
Salaries	55,000	21,000	18,000	16,000
Balance 4:4:2	(75,000)	(30,000)	(30,000)	(15,000)
	(20,000)	(9,000)	(12,000)	1,000
Eliminate				
Parsley's 'profit'				
9,000:12,000		429	571	(1,000)
Share of loss	(20,000)	(8,571)	(11,429)	–

9.4 These rules may be perceived as creating a degree of unfairness between partners. In **Example 9.1**, Sage gets no relief for his real-world loss of £600 in 2015/16: instead it goes to reduce the taxable profits of Thyme and Parsley. And in 2016/17 Parsley pays no tax on his real-world profit of £1,000: instead the tax losses of Sage and Thyme are reduced. Where there are prior allocations of profit of this kind it may be desirable for the partnership agreement to specify what adjustments if any are to be made between partners to take account of such anomalies.

9.5 It may happen that there is an accounting profit but a tax loss, or vice versa, and the partnership has different profit- and loss-sharing ratios, for example profits are shared 50:50 but losses 75:25.

ITTOIA, s 850 requires that for tax purposes profits or losses are allocated 'in accordance with the rights of the partners to share in the profits of the trade and the liabilities of the partners to share in the losses of the trade'. This can only mean that taxable profits are allocated in accordance with profit-sharing ratios and tax losses are allocated in accordance with loss-sharing ratios, regardless of whether commercially there has been profit or loss.

9.6 A change in the profit/loss-sharing ratio is straightforward; the loss is divided between the partners according to the profit/loss-sharing ratio of the accounting period.

Example 9.2 – Losses and change in profit/loss-sharing ratio

Brad and Leonardo have been in partnership for several years, sharing profits and losses equally. On 1 July 2015, they changed the profit/loss-sharing ratio to 60:40. They make a loss in the year to 30 September 2015 of £80,000.

The loss will be divided as follows:

	Total	*Brad*	*Leonardo*
	£	£	£
1.10.14–30.6.15 (50:50) £80,000 × 9/12	60,000	30,000	30,000
1.7.15–30.9.15 (60:40) £80,000 × 3/12	20,000	12,000	8,000
	80,000	42,000	38,000

9.7 Loss shares are personal to the partners, and each partner may choose whether to claim relief for his share of the loss against general income under the *Income Tax Act 2007 (ITA 2007), s 64* (the *s 64* claim being extended by *ITA 2007, s 71* to include capital gains if the partner so wishes: see **9.17**) or to carry it forward against later trading profit shares under *ITA 2007, s 83*, or, in respect of a loss in any of the first four tax years in which he is a partner, to set the loss against his total income of the three previous tax years, earliest first, under *ITA 2007, s 72* (see **9.20**). See **9.38** regarding the cap on income tax relief for certain losses, which took effect from 6 April 2013. If there is a change of partners, terminal loss relief will be available to a retiring partner, but not to a continuing partner (see **9.28**). Continuing partners will be able to carry unrelieved losses forward.

Interaction of loss relief and overlap relief

9.8 Overlap relief under *ITTOIA 2005, s 220(1)* or *(2)* is available when more than 12 months' profits would otherwise be charged in one tax year, or when a partner leaves the firm, or when the firm ceases trading. The overlap relief is given as a deduction in computing the profits for the relevant period (*ITTOIA 2005, ss 205, 220*). If the overlap relief exceeds the profits against which it is given, the excess represents a loss for which the normal loss reliefs are available.

Example 9.3 – Interaction of loss relief and overlap relief

Barnum and Bailey, who have been equal partners for many years, making up accounts annually to 30 April, are each entitled to overlap relief on profits of £55,000 in respect of the 11 months from 1 May 2007 to 5 April 2008. In 2014/15, they change their accounting date to 31 December, recent profits being as follows:

	£000
Year to 30 April 2013	42
Year to 30 April 2014	30
Eight months to 31 December 2014	10

The position of each partner for 2014/15 is as follows:

	£000
Taxable profits for 20 months to 31.12.2014 (15 + 5)	20
Less overlap relief 8/11 × 55	(40)
Taxable nil, and loss available for relief	(20)

Each partner may claim relief for his loss under *ITA 2007, s 64* in 2014/15 and/or 2013/14, or the loss may be carried forward under *s 83*.

Three months' overlap relief amounting to (£55,000 – £40,000) = £15,000 remains available to each partner.

9.9 Obtaining relief for a loss arising out of overlap relief depends on there being sufficient income to offset it; and, as with other terminal losses, there may be situations where overlap relief available on cessation exceeds the available income.

Choice and change of accounting date

9.10 Problems can also arise if there are losses in the early years of a partnership and the accounts are prepared to a date other than 5 April. This is because the loss is calculated by reference to basis periods rather than tax years.

Example 9.4 – Losses and choice of accounting date

Gail and Hettie set up a partnership as writers and editors on 1 May 2013. Their losses, shared equally, are as follows:

Year ended 30 April 2014	Loss	£2,250
Year ended 30 April 2015	Loss	£10,000

The taxable profits and losses are as follows:

	Gail	*Hettie*
2013/14	£	£
1 May 2013–5 April 2014		
Taxable	0	0
Loss available £2,250 × 340/365 = £2,096	1,048	1,048
2014/15		
1 May 2013–30 April 2014		
Taxable	0	0
Loss available £2,250 less used in 2013/14 £2,096 = £154	77	77
Overlap profits 1 May 2013–5 April 2014	0	0
2015/16		
Year ended 30 April 2015		
Taxable	0	0
Loss available	5,000	5,000

If accounts were drawn up to 5 April 2014 and 5 April 2015 and showed the same losses as above, the assessable profits and losses would be as follows:

	Gail	*Hettie*
2013/14	£	£
1 May 2013–5 April 2014		
Taxable	0	0
Loss available	1,125	1,125
2014/15		
Year ended 5 April 2015		
Taxable	0	0
Loss available	5,000	5,000

This example illustrates that, with a non-5 April year end, loss relief may not be available until one year later than it would have been if a 5 April year end had been used.

9.11 Losses give rise to nil overlap relief. This could result in a large tax bill on cessation if profits are on a rising trend.

Focus

Losses in the early years of trade followed by high profits in the years to cessation could give rise to wasted personal allowances in the initial years and higher rate tax liabilities in later years.

Choosing the most appropriate year end where there are losses is particularly important for claims under *ITA 2007, s 72* (see **9.21**).

Change of accounting date

9.12 A change of accounting date combined with losses and overlap profits gives rise to an interesting result. Any change of accounting date also applies to each individual partner (*ITTOIA 2005, s 853(2)*). Where there is a change of accounting date, the partnership must apply the rules for a change of accounting date as if it were an individual. If the partnership satisfies the relevant conditions in *ITTOIA 2005, s 217* (see **6.2**), the new accounting date will be effective for tax purposes.

If the conditions of *ITTOIA 2005, s 217* are not satisfied, the new accounting date is not effective for tax purposes, and therefore the old accounting date continues to be applied. In the case of new partners, the commencement rules (see **5.2**) are applied in order to determine a basis period, with the modification that the accounting date is taken to be the old, rather than the new, accounting date.

Example 9.5 – Losses and change of accounting date

Sophie and Thelma make losses of £40,000 in the year to 30 June 2015. They change their year end and make further losses in the six months to 31 December 2015 of £25,000. They have overlap profits brought forward of £30,000 (nine months).

The loss arising in 2015/16 is £85,000 (£40,000 + £25,000 + the overlap profits released of £20,000). Overlap profits carried forward are £10,000.

9.13 *ITA 2007, s 62(2)* provides relief for all the loss to be given in the same tax year because losses are to be computed in the same way as profits. If the £40,000 loss had been a profit, *ITA 2007, s 62(2)* provides for that profit to be aggregated with the loss to 31 December 2015. This gives a net loss of £5,000 (£40,000 – £25,000 – £20,000) in 2015/16, with overlap profits to carry forward of £10,000.

Focus

Changing a partnership's year end during a loss-making period can enhance the loss by overlap relief. This may be particularly valuable if the partners can obtain tax relief at higher rates.

ITA 2007, s 64 claim to set off loss against general income

9.14 Relief for trading losses is generally given in the tax year of loss and/or the *previous* tax year (but see **9.38** regarding the cap on relief under *s 64*, which applies from 6 April 2013). It is not necessary for the business to have been carried on in the year of the claim. Relief cannot, however, be given for 'hobby' partnerships.

Example 9.6 – Claim to set off loss against general income (*ITA 2007, s 64*)

ABC, a long-established partnership, makes a profit of £80,000 in the year to 30 September 2014 and a loss of £15,000 in the year to 30 September 2015. The partners will be able to claim relief for their share of the loss against other income in 2015/16 (the year of loss) and/or 2014/15 (the previous year).

9.15 Losses for the purposes of *ss 64* and *83* are calculated in the same way and *for the same periods* as profits (*s 62(2)*). Where basis periods overlap, the loss arising in the overlapping part is treated as belonging to the earlier period and not the later period.

Example 9.7 – Claim to set off loss against general income (*ITA 2007, s 65*)

Fordham joins the Flatwick partnership on 1 July 2014. Accounts are prepared to 30 June 2015, Fordham's share being a loss of £30,000.

Loss relief available to him is:

2014/15	1.7.14 to 5.4.15 – 9/12 × 30,000		£22,500
2015/16	Year ended 30.6.15	30,000	
	Less relating to 2014/15	22,500	£7,500

Fordham can claim relief under *s 64* for the 2014/15 loss in 2014/15 or 2013/14, and for the 2015/16 loss in 2015/16 or 2014/15; the 2014/15 loss takes precedence if relief for losses of both 2014/15 and 2015/16 is claimed in 2014/15.

Under *s 72* (see **9.20**), he could claim relief for the 2014/15 loss in 2011/12, 2012/13 and 2013/14 in that order, and for the 2015/16 loss he could claim relief in 2012/13, 2013/14 and 2014/15 in that order.

9.16 Fordham in **Example 9.7** cannot restrict any particular loss claim to leave in charge to tax sufficient income to utilise personal reliefs or the starting, saving or basic rates of tax.

If the loss for which the claim is made exceeds the statutory total income for the tax year, the excess is available for one of the alternative loss claims. The claim may be made within his self-assessment return or outside it.

Extension of *ITA 2007, s 64* claim to capital gains

9.17 An *ITA 2007, s 64* claim may be extended to include set-off against capital gains, in either or both of the tax year of loss and/or the previous year (*ITA 2007, s 71*). The claim against the partner's income must be made first, so that personal allowances may be wasted. The loss available to set against capital gains is also reduced by any other loss relief claimed, for example, under *s 64* in the previous year or by carry-back under *s 72* in a new business.

9.18 An individual who has income tax losses, but does not have enough other income against which those losses may be set, may be able to treat the unused part as an allowable loss for capital gains tax purposes (*ITA 2007, s 71*; *Taxation of Chargeable Gains Act 1992 (TCGA 1992), ss 261B* and *261C*).

Focus

Income tax losses may be set against capital gains for a given year only if any income for that year has first been covered by the losses arising (see **9.17** above).

9.19 Extending the loss claim to capital gains is not only complex particularly where there are capital losses brought forward but it could waste annual exemptions.

ITA 2007, s 72 claim to carry back new business loss

9.20 *ITA 2007, s 72* enables a loss incurred in any of the first four tax years of a business to be carried back against the claimant's total income of the three previous tax years, earliest first, and tax will be repayable accordingly. Note that from 6 April 2013 a cap applies on the amount of relief available (see **9.38**). Broadly, relief is restricted to £50,000 or 25% of income, whichever is the greater (*ITA 2007, s 24A*).

9.21 Losses for *s 72* claims are calculated by reference to accounting periods. The date to which accounts are made up will affect the extent to which relief is available under *s 72*.

Example 9.8 – Claim to carry back new business loss (*ITA 2007, s 72*) (1)

Partnership starts on 1 May 2012. The periods in respect of which *s 72* claims could be made if losses arise are as follows:

	Accounts to 31 March	*Accounts to 30 April*
2012/13	1.5.12–31.3.13	1.5.12–31.3.13
2013/14	1.4.13–31.3.14	1.4.13–30.4.13
2014/15	1.4.14–31.3.15	1.5.13–30.4.14
2015/16	1.4.15–31.3.16	1.5.14–30.4.15

Thus, there is an extra 11 months in which any losses are eligible for *s 72* relief with a 31 March year end.

9.22 In relation to partnerships, a partner may normally claim under *s 72* in respect of losses made in the first four years in which he or she is involved in the partnership business (ie, whether that is at the commencement of business itself or when he or she joins an existing partnership).

However, a *s 72* claim is not available to someone joining his or her spouse or civil partner in business if the loss is incurred later than the fourth tax year from when the business started (*ITA 2007, s 74(4), (5)*).

Relief is also denied if the business is not being carried out on a commercial basis (*ITA 2007, s 74(1)*). Also, 'sideways reliefs' (that is, relief under *s 64* or *s 72*) is denied to the extent that losses arise in consequence of or otherwise in connection with tax avoidance arrangements (*ITA 2007, s 74ZA*).

Example 9.9 – Claim to carry back new business loss (*ITA 2007, s 72*) (2)

Chris and Dean have been in partnership for several years, sharing profits and losses 60:40. Elmer joined the partnership on 1 September 2014, and the profit- and loss-sharing ratio changed to 60:20:20. The firm's accounts show the following profits and losses:

- Year to 31 December 2014: Loss £100,000;
- Year to 31 December 2015: Profit £50,000.

Losses	*Total*	*Chris*	*Dean*	*Elmer*
	£	£	£	£
1.1.14–31.8.14 – £100,000 × 8/12 (60:40)	66,667	40,000	26,667	
1.9.14–31.12.14 – £100,000 × 4/12 (60:20:20)	33,333	20,000	6,666	6,667
Total losses	100,000	60,000	33,333	6,667
Elmer's losses are computed under the commencement rules so that his result from joining on 1.9.14 to 5.4.15 must be ascertained. Thus: 1.1.15–5.4.15 – £50,000 × 3/12 × 20%				(2,500)
Elmer's net loss				4,167

9.23 Partners are treated as carrying on their own trade. Therefore, when Elmer joins the partnership, he is allocated a share of the loss. The loss may be relieved against Elmer's other income under *ITA 2007, s 64* in 2014/15 and/or 2013/14. Alternatively (or, indeed, after any *s 64* claim if any loss remains unrelieved), it may be relieved under *ITA 2007, s 72* in 2011/12, 2012/13 and 2013/14. Contrast this with the loss relief available to Chris and Dean. Relief will only be available under *ITA 2007, s 64* in 2014/15 and/or 2013/14. If the income is insufficient to utilise the loss fully, the excess can be carried forward (*ITA 2007, s 83*).

Losses carried forward under *ITA 2007, s 83*

9.24 Carrying losses forward is the most straightforward way of obtaining loss relief. The loss must, however, relate to the same trade. In **Example 9.9**, Chris and Dean may carry forward any unused losses and use them against the taxable profits in 2015/16 and subsequent years. The losses will eliminate all the profits for 2015/16, leaving losses to carry forward to 2016/17.

9.25 The disadvantages of carrying forward losses are the delay in obtaining the relief and the risk that the partner might leave the partnership before having utilised the loss.

Interaction with capital allowances

9.26 Capital allowances can be disclaimed or restricted to minimise wasted personal allowances (see **8.15**). This makes it necessary to consider how the losses will be used before the capital allowance claim can be finalised. Since capital allowances are deducted at the partnership level any restriction on capital allowances claimed must also take effect at the partnership level. It is not possible for individual partners to restrict their 'share' of capital allowances in order to achieve the most favourable tax position for themselves. Before allowances are restricted it will therefore be necessary to consider and take account of the position of partners as a whole, and some compromises may be necessary.

Effect on loss claims of changes in partners

9.27 Dealing with losses where there is a change of partner is straightforward because each partner is treated as carrying on his or her own business. Accordingly, a partner, on joining the firm, may claim loss relief under *ITA 2007, s 64, 72* or *83*, depending on his or her circumstances (see also **9.23**) and subject to the cap which came into effect on 6 April 2013 (see **9.38**). A partner leaving the firm can claim terminal loss relief when he or she ceases business, even though the partnership itself continues (*ITA 2007, s 89*).

ITA 2007, ss 89–91 terminal loss claims

9.28 Terminal loss relief is first given against the trading income of the year of cessation, and then the trading income of the previous three tax years, latest first (*ITA 2007, s 89(2)*).

9.29 The terminal loss is the total of:

(a) any loss made in the year in which the trade ceases; and

(b) any loss made in the part of the previous tax year which starts one year before the cessation and ends on 6 April.

Thus on a cessation on 31 December 2015 the relevant 'terminal loss periods' would be:

(a) 6 April 2015 – 31 December 2015; and

(b) 1 January 2015 – 5 April 2015.

Where necessary, the profits of losses of periods of account are apportioned to arrive at the result for each 'terminal loss period'. This will be necessary where the cessation takes place on a date other than the normal accounting date. But no apportionment is made of any overlap relief: that is always deducted in full in arriving at the final year loss (*ITA 2007, s 90(5)*).

If the result of the calculation for either 'terminal loss period' produces a profit, it is treated as nil.

Example 9.10 – Terminal loss relief (*ITA 2007, ss 89–91*)

Partnership which has previously drawn accounts to 30 September annually ceases trading on 30 June 2015, and results for the last two accounting periods are as follows:

Year to 30 September 2014	Profit	£80,000
Nine months to 30 June 2015 (before taking overlap relief of £12,000 into account)	Loss	£24,000

Partners will be taxed on their shares of the profit of £80,000 in 2014/15.

The taxable amount for 2015/16 is nil, since there is a loss in the basis period.

The terminal loss for division between the partners is:

Final year 6.4.2015–30.6.2015			
3/9 × 24,000 loss		£8,000	
100% of overlap relief		£12,000	£20,000
Previous year 1.7.2014–5.4.2015			
1.7.14 – 30.9 14			
3/12 × 80,000 profit	(20,000)		
1.10.14 – 5 4 15			
6/9 × 24,000 loss	16,000	No loss for period	Nil
Total terminal loss available			£20,000

Only £20,000 of the loss can be used in terminal loss claims.

There is, however, a loss of £36,000 for 2015/16 for *s 64* (basis period for final year is from end of previous basis period to date of cessation), for which partners may claim relief for their shares against their total income of 2015/16 and/or 2014/15 instead of or in priority to terminal loss relief (subject to the cap on loss relief under *s 64*, which applies from 6 April 2013, see **9.38**). They cannot, however, claim relief for £20,000 under the terminal loss provisions *and* £36,000 by set-off against any income under *s 64*, as relief for the loss can only be obtained once. Since the *s 64* claim against other income will embrace the trading profits, the best strategy in this case would be to claim the losses under *s 64* against income of 2014/15.

Example 9.11 – Terminal loss relief on partner leaving continuing partnership

Headley leaves the Canterbury partnership on 30 September 2015. He is entitled to overlap relief of £50,000. His share of profits/losses is:

	£000
Profit of year to 30 September 2013	120
Profit of year to 30 September 2014	100
Loss of year to 30 September 2015	(80)

Overlap relief is taken into account in arriving at the result of the final tax year, thus increasing the loss to £130,000. Since the accounting period coincides with Headley's last 12 months of trading, this is the loss available for a terminal loss claim.

Relief for the terminal loss may be given against *trading* income as follows:

		£000
2015/16	Loss, therefore	–
2014/15		100
2013/14	(balance)	30

Alternatively, or in priority to the terminal loss claim, Headley could have claimed relief under *s 64* against his *total* income of 2015/16 and/or 2014/15, but note the cap on reliefs which applies from 6 April 2013 (see **9.38**).

9.30 Although the intention of the current year basis rules is that a business will be taxed over its lifetime on the profits earned, this will not be the case where the loss on cessation is greater than the amounts against which relief may be given, thus resulting in unrelieved losses.

Example 9.12 – Interaction of loss relief and overlap relief (2)

Assume that Headley in **Example 9.11** had had no source of income other than from the business, that income arising in 2015/16 after he left the partnership was covered by his personal allowances, and that, instead of the figures stated in **Example 9.11**, his profit shares in the three years prior to the tax year of cessation had been as follows:

2014/15	£10,000
2013/14	£30,000
2012/13	£60,000

There would be no point in a *s 64* claim for 2015/16, since there is no taxable income. Terminal loss relief would cover only £100,000 of the loss (and personal allowances would be wasted). The remaining £30,000 of the loss would be unrelieved.

Transfer of a business to a company

9.31 Where a partnership business carried on by individuals in partnership is transferred to a company solely or mainly in exchange for shares in the company, unrelieved losses of partners taking shares in the company may be carried forward and set against income from the company provided:

- the business has been carried on by the company throughout the tax year (or, for the year of transfer, the part of the tax year beginning with the transfer and ending on 5 April);
- the shares are held throughout the tax year (or, for the year of transfer, the part of the tax year beginning with the transfer and ending on 5 April).

(*ITA 2007, s 86*).

In practice, HMRC give the relief, provided at least 80% of the shares are retained.

The losses can be used against any income derived from the company including dividends, interest, remuneration, or rent. There is no requirement that the income has any factual connection with the trade transferred – only that the company continues as a matter of fact to carry on the transferred trade, even if that is only a small part of the company's activities.

Relief under *s 86* is not available in respect of a business carried on by a partnership which includes a corporate or other non-individual member.

Time limits for loss claims

9.32 The time limits for the various loss claims are as follows:

ITA 2007, s 64(5)

Set off against income and gains of year of loss and/or previous year. Subject to cap from 6 April 2013 (see **9.38**).	Claim has to be made within 12 months of 31 January following the end of the year of assessment in which the loss arose (22 months after the end of the tax year).

ITA 2007, s 72(3)

Losses incurred during the basis periods for the first four years of assessment can be set off against the income of the three previous tax years, taking earlier years first. Relief is also available to partners joining existing partnerships. Subject to cap from 6 April 2013 (see **9.38**).	Claim has to be made within 12 months of 31 January following the end of the year of assessment in which the loss arose (22 months after the end of the tax year).

ITA 2007, s 83

Carry forward against future profits of same trade.	Four years after the end of the year of assessment in which the loss arose (*FA 2008, s 118* and *Sch 39, para 12*).

ITA 2007, ss 89–91	
Carry back of terminal losses.	
Relief against profits of the year of cessation and the three prior years of assessment (latest years first).	Four years after the end of the year of assessment in which the loss arose (*FA 2008, s 118* and *Sch 39, para 12*).

9.33 Claims under *s 64* may be made either as part of the return or outside it. Claims under *s 72* will usually be made outside the return. The procedure for *s 83* claims is that, once the initial claim establishing the amount of the loss has been made, the loss will be relieved as and when trading profits arise, without the need for any further claims.

Under self-assessment, claims will not be separately agreed but may be subject to consideration in the event of an enquiry.

9.34 Where loss claims are to be made for both of the available years under *ITA 2007, s 64*, the order of priority needs to be established, because it may be beneficial to regard more of the loss as relating to the later year, depending on the other income and gains in the relevant years. Where loss claims are made under both *s 64(1)(a)* and *(b)* in respect of the same loss, the claimant must specify the tax year for which a deduction is to be made first (*ITA 2007, s 64(3)*).

Treatment of carry-back loss claims under self-assessment

9.35 Where a loss is carried back to an earlier year (under *ITA 2007, s 64* or *72* or the terminal loss provisions), then, although the *tax saving* arising from the loss claim is computed as if the loss reduced the income of the earlier year, the *claim* is treated as relating to the tax year of loss (*Taxes Management Act 1970, Sch 1B, para 2*). The legislation states that the claim will be given effect in relation to the loss year, whether by repayment or set-off, or by reducing the balancing payment due on 31 January following the tax year, or otherwise. Interest on overpaid tax is therefore not payable by reference to the payment dates for the carry-back year(s).

It was held in *HMRC v Cotter* [2013] UKSC 69 that the correct route for HMRC to enquire into the carry-back claim in that case was under the *Taxes Management Act 1970, Sch 1A, para 5* as an enquiry into a free-standing claim rather than under *s 9A* as an enquiry into the return for the year to which the relief was carried back. This decision was followed in *R (on the application of Rouse) v HMRC* [2013] UKUT 615 (TCC). However, the Court of Appeal in *R (on the application of De Silva) v HMRC* [2016] EWCA Civ 40 pointed out that the possibility of an enquiry into the later year's return under *s 9A* was not canvassed in *Cotter.* They therefore concluded that, depending on the facts, a carry-back claim may be regarded either as a free-standing claim susceptible of enquiry under *para 5* or as a claim made as part of the return for the later year in which the relevant loss is made for which an enquiry under *s 9A* would be competent.

Effect of loss claims on NICs and tax credit claims

9.36 Losses reduce trading profit for Class 4 National Insurance as well as for income tax purposes.

If trading losses have been set off against non-trading income or capital gains, they will still be carried forward against trading profits in calculating later Class 4 National Insurance liabilities. National Insurance contributions (NICs) are dealt with in **Chapter 24**.

Example 9.13 – Effect of loss claims on NICs

A partner sets off his share of a 2014/15 trading loss against non-trading income under *ITA 2007, s 64*. It amounted to £13,000. His 2015/16 trading profit is £30,000. For the purpose of Class 4 NICs, it will be reduced to £17,000.

9.37 Where there are partnership losses, their effect on tax credit claims should be considered.

Cap on reliefs

9.38 From 6 April 2013, *ITA 2007 s 24A* applies a cap to certain previously unlimited income tax reliefs that may be deducted from income under *ITA 2007, s 24* in any tax year. The cap is set at £50,000 or 25% of income, whichever is greater. In relation to partnership losses, the reliefs affected by the cap are as follows:

(a) *ITA 2007, s 64* (trade loss relief against general income);

(b) *ITA 2007, s 72* (early trade losses relief);

(c) *ITA 2007, s 96* (post-cessation trade relief);

(d) *ITA 2007*, *s 120* (property loss relief against general income); and

(e) *ITA 2007*, *s 125* (post-cessation property relief).

Focus

'Income' for the purposes of the cap is calculated as 'total income liable to income tax' adjusted to add back charitable donations made via payroll giving and to deduct pension contributions relieved at source – this is designed to create a level playing field between those whose deductions are made before they pay income tax, and those whose deductions are made after tax. The result, known as 'adjusted total income', is the measure of income for the purpose of the cap.

If a loss is used partly in one year and partly in another the cap applies separately to each year for which relief is claimed The limit does not apply to relief that is offset against profits from the same trade or property business (such as carry-forward relief or – for trades – terminal loss relief).

Restrictions on relief for partnership losses

Introduction

9.39 Over the past decade or so, successive restrictions have been introduced regarding the extent to which certain partners can claim relief for trading losses. The restrictions apply only to trades and not to professions or investment businesses and they limit the extent to which 'sideways relief' can be claimed against other income or gains for a partner's share of partnership losses. They do not, however, affect the use of losses against profits of the same trade in which the loss arose, whether that relief is by set-off under *s 64*, early years relief under *s 72*, carry-forward under *s 83* or for terminal losses under *s 89*. The restrictions therefore potentially bite on the use of losses against other income and gains under:

- *ITA 2007, s 64* (including its extension to capital gains under *s 71*);
- *ITA 2007, s 72.*

The restrictions are in addition to those generally applying to losses, such as those in *s 66* and *s 72* (no relief unless the trade is commercial) and in *s 74ZA* (no relief for 'tax-generated' losses).

The legislation identifies the following types of partner that are potentially affected by the rules:

- limited partners in Limited Partnerships;
- members of LLPs;
- 'non-active' partners as defined by statute.

The restrictions applying to limited partners and to members of LLPs are dealt with in detail in **Chapters 18** and **19** respectively. Those applying to 'non-active' partners are dealt with below. Note that the restrictions apply cumulatively: a 'non-active' member of an LLP may be affected both by the restrictions applying to him as a member of an LLP and also by those applying to him as a 'non-active' member. There is no such overlap between 'non-active' members and limited partners since the definition of 'non-active' member specifically excludes a limited partner in a Limited Partnership. In addition to the specific restrictions on loss reliefs, the general cap on the deduction of reliefs available against total income which is set out at *ITA 2007, s 24A* may apply.

Non-active partners

9.40 The rules on 'non-active' partners apply to individual partners who do not devote a 'significant amount of time' to the trade in the basis period for the tax year (or, if on commencement or cessation the basis period is less than six months, in the first or last six months of trading as the case may be). A 'significant amount of time' is an average of at least ten hours weekly personally engaged in activities of the trade. Neither a limited partner in a limited partnership (to whom a different set of restrictions apply – see **Chapter 18**) nor a company can be counted as a 'non-active' partner.

The restrictions applying to 'non-active' partners are set out in *ITA 2007, s 103C* and *s 110*.

9.41 Under *ITA 2007, s 103C* the amount of 'sideways relief' given in respect of a trading loss incurred in any tax year by a 'non-active' partner is not to exceed £25,000. This restriction does not, however, apply to so much of the loss as derives from 'qualifying film expenditure' as defined by *s 103D*. Nor does it apply to a trade which consists of the underwriting business of a member of Lloyd's. Although a limited partner is not a 'non-active' partner, *s 103C* is specifically extended to limited partners by *s 103C(1)(b)*.

Under *ITA 2007, s 110* the amount of sideways relief which can (cumulatively) be claimed by a non-active partner for losses made in any of the first four years in which he carries on the trade is restricted to the amount of the partner's contribution to the firm as at the end of the basis period for the relevant tax year. The terms of *s 110* are in fact very similar to those of *s 107* (which applies to members of LLPs and is covered in detail at **Chapter 19**). The main difference is in relation to the definition of the partner's 'contribution to the firm'.

The 'contribution to the firm' is defined for *s 110* purposes as:

- the amount that the member has contributed to the firm as capital, less
- any 'withdrawn capital', less
- any contribution where the financial cost of making the contribution may not be borne by the partner personally; or which (broadly) is financed by limited-recourse or other 'soft' loans; or the main purpose of which is to obtain sideways tax relief, plus
- the amount of the partner's share of undrawn profits

For this purpose, 'withdrawn capital' at any time is defined as the aggregate of any amounts which the individual:

- has previously drawn out or received back;
- draws out or receives back in the following five years;
- is or may be entitled to draw out or receive back at any time when the individual is a partner in the firm;
- is or may be entitled to require another person to reimburse to them.

In each case, amounts count as 'drawn out or received back' whether this is done directly or indirectly; but amounts which are chargeable to income tax as trading profits are excluded.

Where relief is given which proves excessive because of subsequent withdrawals (ie, under the second bullet point above) relief is withdrawn as appropriate. However, since this is possible only by virtue of the usual 'discovery' provisions to which the normal time limits apply it is at least questionable whether (in the absence of carelessness or deliberate understatement) relief could in fact be withdrawn later than four years after the end of the year of assessment concerned.

Where loss relief has been restricted to the member's capital contribution, relief may be obtained for the balance of the loss by making further capital contributions in later tax years. The member is entitled, provided that the conditions for the relief are otherwise met, to relief of up to a maximum of the amount of the additional contribution under the normal sideways loss relief provisions (*ITA 2007, s 113*).

Focus

From 2014/15, *ITA 2007, Pt 4, Ch 3* also provides for no relief to be given for a loss made by an individual in a trade carried on by the individual as a partner in a firm in certain cases where some or all of the loss is allocated to the individual rather than a person who is not an individual (*ITA 2007, s 116A*) (*FA 2014, s 74* and *Sch 17, para 8*) (see **Chapter 17** for further details on the restriction of loss relief for mixed member partnerships).

Trade or profession

9.42 As indicated at **9.39**, the distinction between a trade and profession – previously a historical anachronism – is relevant for determining the loss relief available to a 'non-active' partner. The position is far from clear-cut.

'Trade' is defined in the legislation as including 'any venture in the nature of trade' (*ITA 2007, s 989*). 'Profession or vocation' is not defined and, therefore, whether a particular activity can be treated as a profession is a question of fact to be decided by the courts. The value of the case law is debatable since most of it dates from World War I when the relevance of trade or profession was in point for excess profits duty.

In *IR Commrs v Maxse* (1930) 12 TC 41, Scrutton LJ said that a profession:

> '… involves the idea of an occupation requiring either purely intellectual skill, or if any manual skill, as in painting and sculpture or surgery, skill controlled by the intellectual skill of the operator, as distinguished from an occupation which is substantially the production, or sale, or arrangements for the production or sale of commodities.'

The distinction between the exercise of intellectual skill (profession) and commercial operations (trading) is hard to determine in today's business environment where quasi-professional training and formal qualifications are increasingly features of many businesses which might previously have been thought to be manual trades. **Appendix 6** includes a list of some relevant cases.

Film-related trades

9.43 Specific anti-avoidance provisions apply to prevent abuse by investors forming partnerships to access trading losses (*ITA 2007, ss 115* and *116*).

9.44 Losses arising to partners of certain film partnerships are restricted to being set off against future profits from the partnership's trade only, where the losses are incurred in the first four years that the partner carries on the trade and (*ITA 2007, s 115*). Affected partnerships are those where:

- the loss derives from the partnership which carries on a trade of exploiting films; and
- the partner does not spend a significant amount of time actively working in the trade, ie at least than ten hours per week on average;
- a 'relevant agreement' exists guaranteeing the individual an amount of future income.

Sideways relief for the loss (ie set off against other income) is not available to the individual, except against any of the individual's income which consists of profits of the trade (*ITA 2007, s 115(2)*).

Chapter 10

Joint Ventures and Expense-sharing Arrangements

Signposts

- Care must be taken where a joint business adventure exists but a partnership relationship is not intended (see **10.1 – 10.4**).
- The VAT implications of a joint venture are of particular importance (see **10.5 – 10.7**).
- A checklist of factors which may help minimise the risk of compulsory VAT registration as a partnership is included at **10.8**).

10.1 Reference has already been made to the importance of recording commercial arrangements separately from those relating to the partnership where there are two or more partnerships which inter-trade and have common partners.

10.2 The same care is called for where there is a joint business relationship but a partnership relationship is not intended. As noted at **1.5**, the joint ownership of property or the sharing of gross returns does not of itself create a partnership (*Partnership Act 1890, s 2(1), (2)*).

For example, several traders or professional people might share accommodation and facilities, contributing to the cost in an agreed ratio, but retaining income generated for themselves and paying their own specific direct costs without any right of recovery of those costs from the other traders/professionals. Put like that, the arrangements do not imply a partnership between those concerned. If some variable factors are introduced, however, doubts begin to creep in. For instance, suppose those concerned all carry on the same trade/profession. Sometimes they work together and split fees. Customers/clients move between them. Their marketing is under a common banner. They have joint trade/professional indemnity insurance. They have an agreement that the goodwill of their association passes from one to the other as they leave or others participate in the arrangement, perhaps subject to payment of a predetermined amount or one to be agreed.

Even so, without a common bank account, VAT registration if appropriate, registration with professional bodies and so on, a partnership, as distinct from a business association each member of which is separately taxable, might be difficult to prove. The situation may not, however, be entirely free from doubt and it could cause some anxious thought and cost in rebutting a partnership suggestion by HM Revenue & Customs (HMRC).

10.3 Obviously, every case must be considered on its facts, but the moral is clear: such associations should be adequately documented and, if there is a parallel partnership between all or some of the individuals, that should be dealt with outside the documentation relating to the trading association.

Tax implications

10.4 Thus, if income was banked in a central account because the marketing operation was in the name of, say, 'The Shelby Associates', and then each party to the arrangement took into his or her own separate account that part of the bankings applicable to the income generated by him or her, less an agreed amount to be left in for common expenses, the situation is not free from challenge by HMRC that 'The Shelby Associates' is a partnership and the amounts taken by each associate are drawings on account of the share of profits to be appropriated.

The implications for the joint venture of HMRC claiming that a partnership exists are primarily additional costs and administrative inconvenience. HMRC can only challenge the status of the organisation by means of an enquiry into the affairs of one or all of its members. Given that joint ventures frequently arise in quasi-charitable or non-profit-making associations, this could be a particular burden.

Other implications are penalties for non-submission of partnership returns and incorrectly completed personal returns (see **Appendix 5**). However, the fact that the tax liabilities and the due date for payment are unlikely to differ significantly by trading as a sole trader instead of a partner (if the participators use the same year end) may prevent HMRC enquiries in a majority of cases.

Nevertheless, members of joint ventures should be prudent. The existence of the joint venture should be disclosed on the tax return, together with any commonly used trading names.

VAT implications

10.5 Of greater concern than the direct tax considerations are the VAT implications. When calculating whether each trader has reached the VAT registration threshold, all re-charges between members of the joint venture should be taken into account.

10.6 Care must also be taken not to fall foul of the VAT artificial business splitting rules (see **26.7**). If the combined turnover of the individual members of the joint venture exceeds the registration threshold, HMRC could direct the venture to VAT register.

> **Focus**
>
> There may be penalties for late registration. This may be more likely where some of the members of the joint venture are VAT-registered and others are not. If the venture does not want to register as an entity in its own right, it may be possible for all the individual

members to register for VAT instead. This will depend on the facts of the situation and negotiation with HMRC.

Where a venture is compulsorily registered for VAT, it will be much harder to argue with HMRC that a partnership does not exist and, in this case, the venture should be registered with HMRC as a partnership to avoid the risk of future enquiries and penalties.

10.7 The tribunal case of *Pietro Sorisi v C & E Comrs* [1998] SWTI 1127, 15453, illustrates the VAT implications of two businesses sharing facilities as a joint venture and the need to have accurate agreements reflecting the arrangements between the parties. The appellant ran a hairdressing salon. B, who was the appellant's former employee, operated as a self-employed stylist from the salon. B paid half his takings to the appellant for the use of the facilities and equipment. The two businesses were insured separately, bills were printed on different coloured paper, and the clientele differed. B fixed his own prices but they were included on the salon price list. However, a written agreement drawn up two years after the arrangement started indicated that B provided services to the appellant. Customs & Excise tried to assess B's takings as part of the salon takings.

The tribunal held, in the light of the oral evidence, that the written contract did not reflect the true position: B supplied his services independently and did not receive his takings as agent for the appellant. Although the outcome of this case did not penalise the parties to the joint venture, had they had an agreement which reflected the way that the venture operated, they could have saved the cost and inconvenience of a tribunal hearing. Some businesses sharing facilities will not be so lucky, and it could be upheld that the facts (contrary to the parties' wishes) support the existence of a partnership; see *Tracy Jane Sumner t/a Extravaganza Hair Workshop and Paula Sinead Kiddle* (VAT Tribunal Reference 17784).

The checklist at **10.8** will help sole traders in joint venture/expense-sharing arrangements to prove that they are not in partnership.

Minimising the risk of compulsory VAT registration as a partnership

10.8 In determining whether two (or more) sole traders who work together in a joint venture or expense-sharing arrangement are in fact operating as a partnership, HMRC will have regard to the extent to which the businesses are related and connected by economic, organisational and financial links.

Focus

The following factors will help to prove that a joint venture or expense-sharing arrangement is not a partnership.

Organisation links

- Separate management and control.

- The public can tell that there are two separate businesses, but this may not always be relevant.
- Separate opening hours.
- Separate trading names and logos are advised, but may not always be relevant.
- Separate pricing, charges or tariffs.
- Separate equipment, for example tills or work station.
- Separate insurance.
- Rental agreement in the correct name and paid by the relevant party.
- Responsibility for premises costs is clear.
- Separate staff.
- Separate suppliers.

Financial links

- Separate bank accounts in the correct names.
- Separate cheque-signing arrangements.
- Profits are not shared.
- Drawings can be taken without restriction.
- Separate accounting records are maintained.
- Separate accounts are prepared.
- Each business is viable without support from the other.

Economic links

- Supplying different customers or clients.
- The businesses do not benefit each other, but this would appear to be irrelevant in a husband and wife situation.
- Lack of goodwill attaching to the joint business.

Chapter 11

Spouses, Civil Partners and Family Partnerships

Signposts

- Especial care must be taken when dealing with family partnerships given the possible scope for HMRC challenge (see **11.1 – 11.2**).
- In particular, whilst a well-drawn partnership agreement is important, it is also necessary to show that there is a partnership in substance as well as on paper (see **11.3**).
- Although remuneration paid to a spouse or civil partner as an employee must be commercially justifiable for the work undertaken, there is no similar requirement to justify allocation of profit share (see **11.4 – 11.9**).
- Family partnerships must take care not to fall foul of the settlements provisions in the *Income Tax (Trading and Other Income) Act 2005, Pt 5, Ch 5* (see **11.10 – 11.13**).
- Involvement of minor children in a partnership is particularly fraught (see **11.14 – 11.17**).
- CGT implications of family partnerships should be considered (see **11.18**).

11.1 Family partnerships are usually formed to reflect the genuine contribution of a spouse, civil partner or other family members. However, because they offer scope for substantial tax savings, HMRC may view them with suspicion. HMRC may contend that no partnership exists or that the settlement provisions in *ITTOIA 2005, Pt 5, Ch 5* apply. Some family partnerships may also be adversely affected by the IR35 rules (see **Chapter 28**).

11.2 The general law on the meaning of 'partnership', and the question of whether a partnership exists, is dealt with in **Chapter 1**. Where partners consist of members of the same family, it is particularly important to have evidence that the purported partnership relationship is supported by the facts. There have been numerous cases, many of them involving farming businesses, where the courts have held that, despite the assertions of the parties, no partnership existed.

In *IR Commrs v Williamson* (1928) 14 TC 335, Lord President Clyde summarised the matter as follows (p 340):

> 'The only proof that a partnership exists is proof of the relations of agency and of community in losses and profits and of the sharing in one form or another of the capital of the concern; the only proof of a partnership consists in proof of these things.'

> **Focus**
>
> HMRC are also likely to challenge the existence of the partnership where there are attempts to backdate its commencement. However, they acknowledge in their Business Income Manual at BIM72065 that challenging a spouse's status as a partner, particularly in a trading partnership, can be difficult and may not be cost-effective where there is a signed partnership deed:
>
> > 'It is sometimes overlooked that there is no need for the spouse to contribute capital; or to participate in management; or, in a trading context at least, to be capable of performing the main activity of the business. Indeed to be a partner one need not take an active part in the business at all. Where the spouse has signed a deed declaring an intention to carry on the business and the deed gives a right to share in the profits, and subsequently accounts of the business show that that person has been allocated a share of the profits, there will not usually be much chance of mounting a successful challenge.'

11.3 Clearly, a well-drawn partnership agreement is important. But, in order to show that there is a partnership in substance as well as on paper, the actions of the parties must be consistent with the written agreement, so that VAT registration, bank account signatories, the firm's stationery etc must all reflect what the parties are claiming, and those with whom the partners do business should be made aware that they are dealing with a partnership.

Spouses and civil partners

11.4 One of the aims of the tax planner is to make the best possible use of the personal allowances and basic rate bands available to each spouse or civil partner. This is obviously easier to arrange where there is a family business.

Further advantages of husband and wife, or civil partner, partnerships which should not be overlooked include entitlement of both spouses/partners to entrepreneur's capital gains tax ('CGT') relief, roll-over relief, possible ability to pay higher pension contributions, and the impact on the division of their estates for inheritance tax purposes.

Employment

11.5 If one spouse or partner runs the business and employs the other, the employee spouse's (or partner's) remuneration must satisfy the requirement that it is 'wholly and exclusively for the purposes of the trade, profession or vocation' (*ITTOIA 2005, s 34*). The National Insurance burden is also significantly higher than it would be if both were partners, unless the employed spouse is paid £157 or less per week (for 2017/18). A salary of between £113 and £157 per week attracts no National Insurance liability but entitlement to state benefits is protected (for 2017/18).

> **Focus**
>
> Since 6 April 2015 employers have not been required to pay Class 1 secondary NICs on earnings paid up to the upper earnings limit (£866 per week for 2017/18) to any employee under the age of 21.
>
> In addition, the employment allowance ('EA') enables employers to claim a reduction of up to £3,000 against their secondary NIC liability (see www.gov.uk/claim-employment-allowance for further information).

11.6 Remuneration paid to a spouse or civil partner must not be merely a book entry; the amounts must actually be paid and the spouse or civil partner should be treated in the same way as other employees including being given an employment contract and payslips. The payments (including any benefits provided) must be commercially justifiable for the work undertaken if they are to be tax-deductible for the business.

The provisions of the *National Minimum Wage Act 1998* must always be borne in mind. Helpfully, *reg 58* of the *National Minimum Wage Regulations 2015* provides that national minimum wage does not apply to 'work done by a worker in relation to an employer's family business' if the worker:

(a) is a member of the employer's family;

(b) resides in the family home of the employer; and

(c) participates in the running of the family business.

The problems with this in relation to employment by a partnership are twofold. First, it is doubtful whether a partnership as such can have a 'family' or a 'family home'. Second, 'family business' is not defined and it may be questionable whether a partnership involving a number of unrelated individuals would count as the 'family business' of any of them. It would therefore be unwise to assume that reg 58 has any application to employment by a partnership.

11.7 Taking into account the risks of partnership, it will still be appropriate in some cases for one spouse or civil partner to employ the other, taking advantage, as appropriate, within the constraints of the 'wholly and exclusively' principle, of utilising the employed spouse's personal allowances, lower and basic rate bands, or maximum earnings before NICs apply. Furthermore, as an employee, the spouse or partner could be a member of an executive pension plan, the premiums being paid by the employer and charged as an expense wholly and exclusively for the business in calculating profits, whilst under the tax rules for registered pension funds the employee spouse or partner is not taxable on the benefit provided. As with other benefits, however, any pension benefits should be commensurate with the work done by the employee.

> **Focus**
>
> From April 2015, a spouse or civil partner who is not liable to income tax or not liable above the basic rate for a tax year has been entitled to transfer a small part of their personal allowance to their spouse or civil partner provided that the recipient of the transfer is not liable to income tax above the basic rate. The transferor's personal allowance will be reduced and the transferee's increased by the amount transferred. For 2017/18, the transferrable amount is £1,150. Note that married couples or civil partnerships entitled to claim the married couple's allowance are not entitled to make a transfer.

Partnership

11.8 If, instead of one employing the other, the couple form a partnership, *ITTOIA 2005, s 34* has no relevance and there are no direct provisions in the legislation relating to each spouse's profit share unless it can be argued to be bounteous (see **11.10**). Forming a partnership has other implications. One is that each partner is liable for the partnership debts to the full extent of their personal assets (unless one is a limited partner or a LLP structure is used). Another is that a spouse or civil partner who has been admitted to partnership will have all the rights and powers of a partner in relation to the ownership and conduct of the business; this may cause additional difficulties to the 'active' partner on any future breakdown of the relationship.

11.9 HMRC do now accept that it is often difficult or impossible for them to attack partnership profit shares between family members. The Business Income Manual (BIM 82065) provides the following guidance:

> 'You cannot challenge the apportionment of profits, as you can a wage, by reference to the value of the partners' contribution to the firm's activity. It may be possible in these cases to challenge the spouse's status as a partner, but such a challenge is often very difficult to sustain. It is sometimes overlooked that there is no need for the spouse to contribute capital; or to participate in management; or, in a trading context at least, to be capable of performing the main activity of the business. Indeed to be a partner one need not take an active part in the business at all. Where the spouse has signed a deed declaring an intention to carry on the business and the deed gives a right to share in the profits, and subsequently accounts of the business show that that person has been allocated a share of the profits, there will not usually be much chance of mounting a successful challenge.
>
> 'It is worth emphasising that a partnership is not a sham merely because it is set up to save tax, as indeed the spouse who is deserted by a partner leaving that spouse to meet the firm's liabilities may find to their cost. There will always of course be some cases which will be worth you investigating and challenging, but these are more likely to be found among those where there is no current partnership deed, and particularly where there is a clear attempt to antedate the setting up of a partnership by more than a few months. CTISA Tax (Technical) will be happy to advise on worthwhile cases.'

It might be thought that where a profession or vocation is being carried out that is heavily or even solely dependent on the skill of one of the partners, HMRC would be on stronger ground. They accept that they are not. HMRC guidance reads:

> 'Difficult problems are posed where a taxpayer who is carrying on a profession or vocation (as opposed to a trade), which is dependent on their personal skills or qualifications, purports to take a spouse (who does not possess a like skill or qualification) into partnership. Some professions have internal rules that preclude this; but this is not always the case. You could argue that in such a case a partnership between the husband and wife to carry on the profession or vocation in question would not be possible, but in the light of the judgments in the case of [*Newstead v Frost* (1980) 53 TC 525] (Entertainer entered into an agreement with a company to exploit his artistic talents. Held there was a valid partnership) that still leaves open the possibility that there might be a partnership between them to exploit the spouse's talents for the benefit of both. The Frost case involved a partnership with a company, but the principle is the same.'

11.10 There are, however, a number of circumstances in which the settlements legislation at *ITTOIA 2005, Pt 5, Ch 5* may apply in relation to a partnership between spouse or civil partners.

It is worth first examining the terms of the legislation.

An arrangement whereby A enters into partnership with B on terms which are more favourable to B than A would offer were A dealing on arm's length terms is almost certainly within the statutory definition of a 'settlement' made by A on B–see *ITTOIA 2005, s 620* and *CIR v Plummer [1979] STC 793*. A settlement is 'caught' (ie income arising under it remains taxable on the settlor) if (broadly) the settlor or the settlor's spouse or civil partner is in any way entitled to benefit from the settlement (*ITTOIA 2005, ss 624-5*). Thus on first principles a partnership on uncommercial terms between spouses or civil partners will be caught.

But there is a very important carve-out. By *s 626* the settlement provisions do not apply in respect of an outright gift

(a) of property from which income arises;

(b) made by one spouse to the other or one civil partner to the other; and

(c) meeting conditions A and B.

Condition A is that the gift carries a right to the whole of the income arising from the property transferred. Condition B is that the property itself is not wholly or substantially a right to income.

Thus in the context of partnerships, partnerships under which the spouse or civil partner is a 'full partner' with rights not only to a share of profit but also to a share in the underlying assets will not normally be vulnerable to challenge under the settlements legislation.

Example 11.1 – Settlement legislation does not apply

Mr Alpha and Mr Beta are in partnership as second-hand car dealers. They own the freehold premises through which the partnership trades (valued at £200,000) and routinely carry a stock of 50 used cars. The business is successful and has established goodwill in the locality as a reliable trader. It employs a number of salesmen and office staff. Profits of £100,000 a year are split equally between the partners. They decide to admit their wives to the partnership and amend the partnership agreement in order to split profits and capital equally four ways. Mrs Alpha and Mrs Beta subscribe no new capital and do no work in the partnership. Although this is a bounteous transaction it is an outright gift that is not substantially a right to income and is excluded from the definition of settlement by ITTOIA/S626.

(Based on HMRC guidance at TSEM4215 Example 9)

Example 11.2 – Settlement legislation applies

Mr Y, an architect, commences business as a sole trader. The business is successful and a few years later annual profits are in the region of £80,000. The business is transferred to a new partnership of Mr & Mrs Y. A deed is executed under which income profits are to be shared equally but the rights to share in capital profits belong solely to Mr Y. Mrs Y subscribes no new capital and carries out no work for the partnership. Profits for the year are £80,000 and £40,000 belongs to Mrs Y. This is a bounteous arrangement which consists wholly or mainly in a right in the transfer of a right to income and the exclusion in *s 626* therefore does not apply. The settlements legislation will apply and Mrs Y's share of the profits will continue to be assessed on Mr Y.

(Based on HMRC guidance at TSEM4215 Example 10)

Other adults

Employment

11.11 Exactly the same criteria apply to employment of family members or others on other than commercial terms as apply to employment of spouses or civil partners.

Partnership

11.12 Although entering into a partnership on favourable terms is likely to amount to the making of a settlement within the definition of the legislation, there are normally no tax consequences where the person benefitted is an adult other than the settlor's spouse or civil partner. In particular, it will not normally be possible for HMRC to challenge arrangements whereby the person benefitted is the settlor's adult child, parent or unmarried cohabitee.

Example 11.3 – Settlement legislation does not apply

Mr S is a tax adviser. He lives with Mr T but they are not in a civil partnership. Mr S and Mr T form a partnership to exploit Mr S's talents as tax adviser, sharing assets, profits and losses of the business equally. Mr T has no knowledge of tax, contributes no capital and does no work in the business. Nonetheless the partnership is not within the settlements legislation.

11.13 The exception to the above rule is where the arrangements where the settlor retains an interest, including cases in which the property transferred can in any circumstances revert to the settlor.

Example 11.4 – Settlement legislation does apply

Mr T is in partnership with his wife Mrs T. Their daughter is a university student. The deed is altered to admit the daughter as a partner. All the partners agree that on finishing her course the daughter's interest in the partnership will come to an end. The amendment of the partnership agreement under which the daughter is included without any additional capital or value being added by her is an arrangement with the requisite element of bounty. The gift from the parents is subject to conditions under which the property given will revert to them. The daughter's income is therefore treated as the income of the parents under ITTOIA/S624.

(Based on HMRC guidance at TSEM4215 Example 11)

Minor children

Employment

11.14 Again, as regards deductibility of remuneration in computing taxable profit, similar criteria apply to the employment of children as apply to the employment of adults. School-age children are not entitled to the National Minimum Wage but employment of children at all is subject to strict controls. If in any particular circumstances the employment of children is in breach of the criminal law, *ITTOIA 2005, s 55* (crime-related payments) will deny tax relief for the remuneration though this may be the least of the payer's problems.

Partnership

11.15 There are specific provisions dealing with settlements involving parents and any unmarried child (including step-child) under 18. These treat any income arising under the settlement which would otherwise be treated as the child's as being that of the settlor (*ITTOIA 2005, s 629*). Thus if children under the age of 18 are partners in their parents' business, their profit shares must (if it is to taxed on the children) be capable of being justified by their level of participation in the business, and it must be legal for them to be partners and to be working.

11.16 Partnerships between parents and their minor children are unlikely to be a successful way of diverting income from parent to child. The courts are reluctant to believe that minor children are capable of being genuine business partners, even if they are named as such in the partnership deed. In *Alexander Bulloch & Co v IRC* (1976) 51 TC 563, a mother and her two children traded in partnership as wine and spirit merchants. Two grandchildren aged 15 and 16 were invited to join the firm as partners. Although the grandchildren were at school, they worked in the business at weekends and during school holidays. The family's contention that the grandchildren were partners was rejected by the Court of Session on the grounds of their 'inexperience and immaturity'. The nature of the trade is likely to have been a factor in the decision, as well as the fact that there was no signed partnership deed for the year in question. In the Business Income Manual at BIM82065, HMRC advise that, in some cases (for example, farming or a shop), children aged 15 or 16 might be capable of being partners:

> 'Minors are not, by reason of minority alone, incapable of entering into partnership, although in general while under age they are not personally responsible for the debts of the firm.'

Because of the different law that applies in Scotland, it is unlikely that a person under the age of 16 would be able to enter into a Scottish partnership (*Age of Legal Capacity (Scotland) Act 1991*).

11.17 The legality of the arrangements – whether it is in the particular circumstances of the trade and of the individuals concerned legal for the children to be partners – may sometimes be called into question. But this should not be relevant: tax is levied by reference to what is actually done and not to what legally ought to have been done. Completely illegal businesses can give rise to assessable profits (see for example *Lindsay, Woodward & Hiscox v CIR* [1932] 18 TC 43): a fortiori the unlawful involvement of a person in an otherwise lawful trade is no bar to assessment.

CGT implications of family partnerships

11.18 The introduction of person into a partnership normally results in a change in the asset profit-sharing ratios and therefore a deemed disposal of chargeable assets held by the partnership. Where the parties are not connected the deemed disposal value will be the value at which the assets are recognised in the partnership balance sheet. Where the parties are connected other than by being in partnership (as when family members join the partnership) and a different value would have been used had they not been connected the disposal will be deemed to take effect at the open market value of the interest transferred. For further detail see **Chapter 12**. Thus, if in a family partnership an adult daughter is admitted to partnership without payment for her share of goodwill and business premises, and it is established that, were it not for the family relationship, values of £20,000 and £50,000 would have been attributed to the interests in the assets transferred to her by the other family members, those values will be used and the CGT consequences will follow.

If the partnership is trading partnership and the asset is used wholly for the purpose of the trade it will normally be the case that the transferor(s) and transferee may jointly elect for the otherwise chargeable gain to be deducted from the deemed acquisition cost of the transferee (that is, the said market value) under the business assets gifts relief provisions of *TCGA 1992, s 165*. See **Chapter 15.**

Chapter 12

Capital Gains

Signposts

- The disposal of partnership assets to third parties and transactions between the partners are two areas of capital gains tax that may affect partnerships (see **12.1**).
- Details of disposals of chargeable assets are included in the partnership tax return for the tax year in which the disposal took place. Each partner will then include appropriate details and computations in his or her personal return (see **12.2 – 12.3**).
- Changes in profit-sharing ratios may have CGT implications (see **12.4 – 12.10**).
- Although allowable losses may arise on disposal of partnership assets, merely writing goodwill down in the partnership balance sheet will not of itself found a loss relief claim (see **12.11 – 12.14**).
- Care needs to be taken when ascertaining whether an asset is a 'partnership asset' (see **12.15**).
- In order to compute the gain or loss accruing to a partner on either the disposal of a chargeable asset owned by the partnership or a change in asset surplus-sharing arrangements, it is necessary to calculate each partner's disposal consideration and allowable expenditure by reference to his fractional share in the partnership asset, which may change over time (see **12.16 – 12.22**).
- The *Finance Act 2014* introduced rules to prevent the disposal of assets or income streams by or through a partnership if the main purpose, or one of the main purposes, of the disposal, or any of the steps by which the disposal is effected, is to secure a tax advantage in relation to the charge to income tax or the charge to corporation tax on income (see **12.23**).

12.1 Partnerships are effectively transparent for the purposes of capital gains tax ('CGT'). An interest in a partnership is not itself treated as an asset for CGT purposes. Instead each partner is treated as owning a share in each chargeable asset owned by the partnership (*TCGA 1992, s 59*). This also applies to LLPs which carry on a business with a view to profit (*TCGA 1992, s 59A*). The transparency enjoyed by LLPs ceases to apply on the appointment of a liquidator or in certain other circumstances: for full details see **Chapter 19**.

Where it is necessary to determine the market value of a partner's share in a partnership asset, it is taken to be the relevant fraction of the market value of the entire asset held by the partnership. So, for example, if a partnership owns 100% of the shares in a company and a particular partner has a 10% interest in the partnership, that partner's interest in the shares of the company will be taken to be 10% of the value of the partnership's 100% interest (and not as the value of a 10% interest valued in isolation, which would normally be a substantially lower figure).

There are two aspects of capital gains which affect partnerships: one relates to the disposal of partnership assets to third parties; and the other relates to transactions between the partners in those partnership assets which are chargeable assets for CGT purposes. The detailed guidance for partnership capital gains is to be found in HMRC Statement of Practice SP D12, the current version of which was published on 14 September 2015.

> **Focus**
>
> The *Finance Act 2014* ('*FA 2014*') introduced rules to prevent the disposal of assets or income streams by or through a partnership if the main purpose, or one of the main purposes, of the disposal, or any of the steps by which the disposal is effected, is to secure a tax advantage in relation to the charge to income tax or the charge to corporation tax on income (see **12.23**).

External disposals

12.2 It follows from the transparency of partnerships that any charge to CGT on the disposal of partnership assets arises in the hands of each individual partner and not in the hands of the partnership as such.

Under self-assessment, details of disposals of chargeable assets are to be included in the partnership tax return for the tax year in which the disposal took place. Each partner will then include appropriate details and computations in his or her personal return.

12.3 When the partnership disposes of a partnership asset to an outside party, the entitlement to any surplus on disposal (or the way in which any loss is shared between the partners) depends on the agreement between the partners. A surplus will very often be allocated in the same way as trading profit; but there is nothing to prevent the partners having a different capital profit-sharing ratio from the ratio in which trading, professional, or any other income profits are shared. Indeed the partners may agree different capital profit-sharing ratios for different assets. But the key point is that for CGT purposes proceeds of sale of an asset will be allocated between the partners in accordance with the capital profit-sharing ratio which applies to that particular asset.

Where a surplus on disposal is not allocated between partners, but taken (for example) to an unallocated reserve, the capital profit-sharing ratio will be taken to be the same as the ratio in which other profits are shared.

By the same token, expenditure incurred by a partnership on the acquisition of an asset is allocated between the partners by reference to the capital profit-sharing ratio applying at the time the expenditure in incurred.

Thus each partner will in principle have his own separate identifiable base cost as well as (on eventual disposal) his own separate and identifiable disposal proceeds.

It follows that CGT reliefs also apply to partners separately. The application to partners of entrepreneurs' relief, and roll-over/hold-over relief, are dealt with in **Chapters 13** and **15** respectively.

Transactions between partners

12.4 Although, under the CGT legislation, a person is connected with any person with whom he is in partnership and with the husband, wife, civil partner, or relative of any individual with whom he is in partnership, in relation to partnership assets, a partner is not connected with his fellow partners if the transaction is pursuant to a bona fide commercial arrangement (*TCGA 1992, s 286(4)*; *ITA 2007, s 993*).

Thus, except where the partners are connected other than by partnership (eg father/son) or are otherwise not at arm's length (eg uncle/nephew), HMRC will accept whatever valuation is placed by partners on a transaction between themselves in partnership assets and will not substitute market value.

Where a partner dies in service, any gains arising on the deemed disposal of his or her share of partnership assets occurring by reason of his or her death are exempt from CGT, like any other gains on death.

Focus

The transfer of a share in partnership assets may have to be treated as if made at market value where the partners are connected other than by partnership, but even so, market value will not be substituted if nothing, or no more, as the case may be, would have been paid even if the parties had been at arm's length.

These principles are set out in HMRC Statement of Practice D12, which also applies where two or more existing partnerships come together to form a new one.

12.5 A change in capital profit-sharing ratios between partners is treated as a disposal for CGT purposes. A partner reducing his share is deemed to make a disposal and a partner increasing his share to make an acquisition. The consideration in each case is deemed to be the relevant proportion of the value at which the asset in question appears in the partnership balance sheet. Market value is substituted only where the partners are connected other than by being in partnership: even then, market value will be substituted only if it is considered that the transaction would have been undertaken at market value but for the connection.

It follows that if assets are carried in the balance sheet at a figure which equates to original cost, any change of capital profit-sharing ratios will (although a disposal) not give rise to any gain or loss for CGT purposes.

It also follows that a revaluation of partnership assets does not of itself amount to a disposal for CGT purposes. This is logical: by simply changing the value at which they choose to recognise an asset in the partnership balance sheet, partners have not changed their financial assets. This remains the case even if the revaluation is used to support further borrowings in the partnership which are then drawn down as additional drawings.

12.6 Thus, there will not be a CGT charge by reason *only* of:

(i) cash being withdrawn in excess of the capital introduced and retained profits; or

(ii) assets being revalued and the capital accounts credited with any revaluation surplus in the capital profit-sharing ratio,

or because of a combination of both.

If assets are revalued, however, and a change in capital profit-sharing ratio then takes place, a disposal is deemed to arise in the case of those partners whose shares reduce, whether or not accompanied by a withdrawal of cash. To that extent, the gain on revaluation is regarded as having been realised.

Example 12.1 – Asset revaluation followed by change in capital profit-sharing arrangements

Extract from partnership balance sheet:

Capital accounts	*Total*	*Arthur*	*Bruce*	*Craig*
	£000	*£000*	*£000*	*£000*
Balances	60	20	20	20
Increase in value of premises on revaluation	120	40	40	40
	180	60	60	60
Premises cost	60			
Increase on revaluation	120			
	180			

There is no CGT consequence of the revaluation, since each of Arthur, Bruce and Craig still own exactly what they did before, and the base value for CGT remains at:

Arthur	*Bruce*	*Craig*	*Representing the cost of the asset*
£000	*£000*	*£000*	*£000*
20	20	20	60

Nor is there any CGT consequence on a new partner being introduced unless, on his introduction, there is a change in the capital profit-sharing ratio.

Thus, suppose Denis is introduced as a partner, bringing in capital of £27,000 to the partnership but, notwithstanding an equal income-sharing ratio, the capital profit-sharing ratio remains 1/3, 1/3, 1/3 to Arthur, Bruce and Craig:

	Total	*Arthur*	*Bruce*	*Craig*	*Denis*
Capital accounts:	£	£	£	£	£
Balances	180,000	60,000	60,000	60,000	–
Cash	27,000	–	–	–	27,000
	207,000	60,000	60,000	60,000	27,000
Premises:					
Cost	60,000				
Revaluation	120,000	180,000			
Cash		27,000			
		207,000			

Arthur, Bruce and Craig then withdraw between them the £27,000 which Denis has paid in:

	Total	*Arthur*	*Bruce*	*Craig*	*Denis*
	£	£	£	£	£
Balances	207,000	60,000	60,000	60,000	27,000
Cash withdrawn	(27,000)	(9,000)	(9,000)	(9,000)	–
	180,000	51,000	51,000	51,000	27,000
Premises		180,000			
Cash					
(£27,000 – £27,000)		–			
		180,000			

The introduction of cash by Denis and its withdrawal by Arthur, Bruce and Craig is irrelevant for capital gains purposes. They still each retain a one-third interest in the premises. If the premises were sold for £180,000, the proceeds would be treated for CGT purposes as shared equally between Arthur, Bruce and Craig who each have a CGT base cost of £20,000 and therefore a gain of £40,000.

If, however, the introduction of Denis coincides with a change in the capital profit-sharing ratio, each then having a one-quarter share, then each of Arthur, Bruce and Craig will be treated as having made a part disposal of their interest in the premises at the balance sheet value.

Thus, at a new balance sheet value of £180,000, the position is as follows.

	Arthur	*Bruce*	*Craig*	*Denis*
	£	*£*	*£*	*£*
Was 1/3 each	60,000	60,000	60,000	
Now 1/4 each	45,000	45,000	45,000	45,000
Disposal of 1/12 each	15,000	15,000	15,000	

In reducing their share in the property from one third each to one quarter each, Arthur, Bruce and Craig have each disposed of 25% of their interest in the property.

A CGT disposal arises based on proceeds of £15,000 for each of Arthur, Bruce and Craig whilst Denis has a base cost of £45,000 in respect of his one-quarter share.

This is logical: on a future disposal of the property at £180,000 Arthur, Bruce Craig and Denis will each be treated for CGT purposes as receiving £45,000. No gain will be recognised in the partnership accounts on such a disposal (because the property is being disposed of at the revalued figure at which it appears in the accounts) so Denis will not in fact have benefitted from any part of the gain in economic terms. The gain on the property will in effect be enjoyed by Arthur, Bruce and Craig (to whose capital accounts the revaluation surplus will have been credited), since the revaluation took place before Denis joined the partnership. It is therefore necessary that Denis's base cost must reflect this: treating Denis for CGT purposes as if he had paid for his share of the property at the value at which it appears in the balance sheet achieves this.

In economic terms Arthur, Bruce and Craig will each have enjoyed a gain of £40,000. This is the also the gain on which they are taxed:

	£
Actual proceeds of eventual sale	45,000
Deemed proceeds on change of profit share	15,000
Less original cost	(20,000)
Gain	40,000

A chargeable gain is therefore recognised for each of Arthur, Bruce and Craig at the time of the change of profit-sharing ratios. The gain for each is £10,000, being £15,000 deemed disposal proceeds less £5,000 cost (ie cost of £20,000 each × 25% disposed of).

On a subsequent disposal for £180,000, each would recognise a further gain of £30,000 (ie proceeds of £45,000 less balance of cost £15,000, reconciling with the total gain of £40,000 identified above.

12.7 At first blush it might seem unreasonable that a charge to tax can arise to Arthur, Bruce and Craig when they have not in fact received anything. And, because it seems counter-intuitive, the possibility of a charge to CGT on a change in capital profit-sharing ratios is very often overlooked by partnerships and their advisers. But comparison with achieving the same economic result by way of a payment of cash outside the balance sheet may make it easier to see why a charge is in fact logical.

Example 12.2 – Change in capital profit-sharing arrangements followed by asset revaluation – payment outside accounts by new partner

Suppose in **Example 12.1** that Arthur, Bruce and Craig did not revalue the premises before admitting Denis as a partner but instead required Denis to pay them personally for his share in the increased value of the property at the time of his admission to the partnership. The position would be:

	Arthur	*Bruce*	*Craig*	*Denis*
	£	*£*	*£*	*£*
Property (at original cost) £60,000/3	20,000	20,000	20,000	
Denis gives cash to each (representing 25% of uplift in value to £180,000) of	(10,000)	(10,000)	(10,000)	30,000

It is easy to see why a charge to CGT on Arthur, Bruce and Craig arises here: they have each disposed of a 1/12 interest in the property and have received £10,000 – ie the same outcome as **Example 12.1**. However, consider what happens if the partnership subsequently revalues the property in the partnership balance sheet to £180,000; Arthur, Bruce and Craig each introduce their £10,000 to the partnership, crediting it to their capital accounts; and Dennis draws down his share of the revaluation surplus (funded by the cash that Arthur, Bruce and Craig have introduced). The balance sheet will then look like this:

Capital accounts	*Total*	*Arthur*	*Bruce*	*Craig*	*Denis*
	£000	*£000*	*£000*	*£000*	*£000*
Balances	60	20	20	20	
Increase in value of premises on revaluation	120	30	30	30	30
Capital introduced		10	10	10	(30)
Closing capital	180	60	60	60	-
Premises cost	60				
Increase on revaluation	120				
	180				

The balance sheet position (and the net cash position of the parties) is thus the same as in **Example12.1**. So it is to be expected that the CGT analysis of the two cases is the same – as indeed it is.

12.8 There is, however, no chargeable gain where partners alter the capital profit-sharing ratio between themselves with or without a change in partners where either:

(*a*) the partnership does not own chargeable assets (including goodwill); or

(*b*) the value at which chargeable assets are carried in the balance sheet is not on that occasion (and has not previously been) uplifted and there is no off balance sheet payment by the partners whose capital profit shares are increasing to those whose shares are decreasing.

HMRC will accept the values placed on the transaction by the partners (subject to the caveat at **12.4**), since partners who are not otherwise connected with each other can be expected to act commercially.

12.9 Since an unchanged capital-sharing ratio on the introduction of a new income-sharing partner prevents a CGT charge being triggered, a separate capital-sharing ratio is often useful to enable business premises to be included in partnership accounts as a partnership asset, whilst ensuring that only certain partners have the right to share in future capital surpluses. The *partnership* may then pay interest on borrowing secured on the premises, instead of paying rent to certain partners out of which those partners pay interest on personal borrowing.

12.10 If it is appropriate for those partners entitled to share in capital surpluses to provide the funds for the property, they can borrow personally in order to advance money to the partnership, or to introduce it on capital account for that purpose, then obtaining relief under *ITA 2007, s 398* (loan to invest in partnership) against total personal income as distinct from against rent income only where the premises are owned personally and let to the partnership.

Losses

12.11 GAAP requires assets, including purchased goodwill, to be depreciated or amortised over their useful economic lives, or written down or off as a result of an impairment in their value. Such accounting adjustments do not give rise to capital losses where tangible and intangible assets have been purchased in the past.

Since 1 April 2002, companies, but not individuals, have been able to claim relief for the amortisation of their purchased goodwill and other intangible assets (*CTA 2009, Pt 8*). This relief should be taken into account when considering the pros and cons of incorporation (see **Chapter 16**). For the application of *Pt 8* where a partnership includes one or more companies see **Chapter 17**.

12.12 If nothing is received for goodwill on the retirement of a partner from the partnership, and a loss is thus established compared with cost or March 1982 valuation, the loss may be admissible so long as the lack of payment for the goodwill is not compensated by other consideration.

12.13 HMRC practice, as set out in Statement of Practice D12, of not substituting market value in transactions between partners, unless the partners are otherwise connected persons or not acting at arm's length (and, even in those cases, not to substitute market value if nothing or no more would have been paid if the parties were at arm's length), relies on the principle that partners are commercially minded people. Family and other connections apart, they can be expected to seek meaningful values on transactions between themselves. HMRC's practice as set out in its Statement is thus convenient and sensible, and of much assistance in the movement of partnership shares. That said, there are traps for the unwary, none more than the 'burying' of a surplus on revaluation in a capital account, later overlooked on a change in profit-sharing ratio, and leading to an unintentional non-disclosure of a disposal for CGT purposes.

12.14 Some special care is needed in regard to 'negligible value' claims under *TCGA 1992, s 24* in respect of partnership goodwill. It is not uncommon for partnership agreements to be 'modernised' by providing that all goodwill shall be written out of the balance sheet, and that going forward there shall be no payment demanded of incoming partners in respect of goodwill nor any payment made to outgoing partners. In these circumstances partners owning goodwill who have an acquisition cost (or a 1982 value) might consider that since it will be impossible for them to realise any value for goodwill a 'negligible value' claim should be made so as to crystallise a loss for CGT purposes.

Unfortunately, it is the view of HMRC (see CG28000) that an agreement of this kind does not of itself mean that the goodwill is of negligible value within the meaning of the Act. A claim under *s 24* may be made only if the entire goodwill of the partnership as a whole has become of negligible value. This is a question of fact, and is quite different from an agreement between the partners that they will not, as between themselves, attach any value to goodwill. Of course, it may be that the agreement to treat the goodwill as valueless simply reflects the fact that the goodwill has in the real world actually become valueless: but if a negligible value claim is to be sustained it will be necessary to produce evidence to that effect.

As with any revaluation upwards or downwards, the writing off of the goodwill in the balance sheet will affect the consideration deemed to pass on a future change in capital profit-sharing ratios, including on retirement. Thus a partner who, after goodwill has been written off, disposes of his interest in goodwill on reducing his share of capital profits will realise a loss equal to his acquisition cost.

Partnership assets and 'other' assets

12.15 A 'partnership asset' is an asset owned by all of the partners. An asset that is owned by only some of the partners is not a partnership asset; HMRC guidance (Capital Gains Manual at CG27140) refers to such assets as 'other assets' and says:

> 'There are no hard and fast rules to tell you what are partnership assets and what are other assets. You have to have regard to the facts of the particular case, any documentary evidence and the intentions of the partners. For example, the fact that only one of the partners paid for, and took title to, the assets would suggest these would be other assets. However, if all the partners intended them, or some of them, to be partnership assets then we would regard them as such.'

Focus

Roll-over relief for replacement of business assets (see **Chapter 15**) is available to the owner of assets that are let to a partnership in which he is a partner, if those assets are used for the purposes of the partnership's trade or profession and the other conditions for the relief are met (HMRC Statement of Practice D11). Entrepreneurs' relief is available on the disposal of a share in the partnership assets, either on the introduction of a partner or when a partner reduces their interest (see **Chapter 13**).

Fractional share in a partnership asset

12.16 When a partnership buys an asset, each partner is treated as acquiring a fractional share in it. In order to compute the gain or loss accruing to a partner on either the disposal of a chargeable asset owned by the partnership or a change in asset surplus-sharing arrangements, it is necessary to calculate each partner's disposal consideration and allowable expenditure by reference to his fractional share in the partnership asset.

HMRC guidance sets out a series of tests to determine a partner's fractional share of a partnership asset. Where there is actual consideration for the disposal, HMRC will apply the following tests in the order shown:

- any specific written agreement setting out the allocation of capital assets;
- any written agreement or other evidence setting out how capital profits are to be shared; and
- any written agreement or other evidence setting out how income profits are to be shared.

In the absence of any such agreements or evidence (eg treatment in the accounts), the assets are treated as held equally by all the partners (CG27220).

Focus

Where the market value of a partner's share in a partnership asset is to be ascertained for CGT purposes, it is taken as a fraction of the value of the partnership's entire interest in the asset. There is no discount to take account of the size of the partner's share. For example, if a partner has a one-tenth share in the partnership assets and the partnership owns all of the shares in a company, the value of the partner's interest in the shareholding is one-tenth of the value of the 100% interest held by the partnership (and not the value of a 10% minority interest valued in isolation) (HMRC Statement of Practice D12, para 1).

Allowable expenditure: multiple acquisitions

12.17 Where a partner has built up his fractional share in stages since 6 April 1965, his acquisition cost of the various assets is calculated by pooling the expenditure relating to each asset. Where all or a part of the partner's share was acquired before 6 April 1965, the disposal will normally be identified with shares acquired on a 'first in, first out' basis, but HMRC may accept a different approach where this produces an unreasonable result (eg where there is a temporary change in the shares in a partnership due to a delay between the departure of one partner and the arrival of a new one) (HMRC Statement of Practice D12, para 10; CG27270).

Partnership goodwill

12.18 Where the value of goodwill generated by a partnership is not recognised in the balance sheet and it is customary not to place a value on that goodwill in dealings between the partners, HMRC practice, on a disposal of a partner's interest in that goodwill for actual consideration, is to regard that interest as the same asset as was acquired by the partner when he first became entitled to a share in it (CG27725).

This practice is also applied to purchased goodwill that is not recognised in the balance sheet at a value greater than cost and is not otherwise taken into account in dealings between partners. The interest in purchased goodwill is, treated as acquired on the later of:

- the date of purchase by the partnership; or
- the date when the disposing partner first became entitled to a share in that purchased goodwill (HMRC Statement of Practice D12, para 12).

Disposal of partnership assets

12.19 When a partnership disposes of an asset to an outside party, each partner is treated as making a disposal of his fractional share in that asset. The proceeds of disposal are allocated to the partners in the ratio of their share in asset surpluses at the time of disposal.

If this ratio is not specifically laid down, the allocation follows the destination of the surplus as shown in the partnership accounts, but regard is also had to any agreement outside the accounts. If the surplus is put to a common reserve, the asset surplus-sharing ratio is taken. If no such ratio is specified, regard is had to the ordinary profit-sharing ratio (HMRC Statement of Practice D12, para 2).

Example 12.3 – Disposal of assets

Each of the following partnerships disposes of its chargeable asset to outside parties at arm's length, realising a gain of £90,000. The gain is apportioned among the partners as follows:

Arthur & Co

The partnership agreement states that each of the three partners shall be entitled to share equally in any surplus arising from assets disposed of by the partnership. Each partner is therefore treated as if he had made a gain of £30,000.

Binder & Co

The three partners in Binder & Co have no formal agreement, but interest on capital contributed to the partnership is shown in the accounts at the same sum for each. The inference is that the capital has been equally contributed and can be equally withdrawn, so that the apportioned gain is £30,000 to each partner.

Cooper & Co

The three partners, Abby, Chris and Kate, have no formal agreement and the capital is shown in the accounts as a global sum. The profit-sharing ratio is 3:2:1. Thus the gain is apportioned:

- Abby: £45,000;
- Chris: £30,000; and
- Kate: £15,000.

Part disposals

12.20 If a partnership makes a part disposal, the part disposal rules are applied before the gain is divided among the partners. Where the relief for small part disposals of land is available, the conditions are applied separately in relation to each partner. However, the normal part disposal rules do not apply to changes in fractional partnership shares between the partners.

Partnership assets distributed in kind

12.21 A partnership may distribute one or more assets to one or more of its partners. This is most likely to happen in the dissolution of the partnership when partnership assets, instead of being sold, may be divided up between the partners. But it may also happen when, for whatever reason, the partners decide that an asset will no longer be regarded as a partnership asset but will be transferred to one or more of the partners to be held as a private asset.

A distribution by the partnership is really no more than the extreme case of a change in the capital profit-sharing ratios. However, in the case of a distribution, the interest in the asset changing hands is valued by reference not to the balance sheet value but to the market value (see SP D12 para 3).

Thus a partner to whom the asset is not being distributed will be treated as having disposed of his share for a consideration equal to market value of the asset multiplied by the percentage to which the partner was entitled under the partnership agreement immediately before the distribution. A partner to whom the asset is distributed will not be treated as having made a disposal at the time of the distribution. In fact, his interest in the asset will have increased and his base cost on a future disposal of the asset will be increased by the aggregate amounts treated as consideration received by the partners who do not share in the distribution.

It may be possible to avoid or defer the charge by changing the asset profit-sharing ratios in advance of the distribution of the asset in question.

The same principle applies where a loss arises (HMRC Statement of Practice D12, para 3).

Example 12.4 – CGT on partnership dissolution

A and B carry on a business in partnership and hold equal interests in partnership assets.

The partnership owns a freehold property which stands in the partnership balance sheet at its cost of £400,000.

On the dissolution of the partnership the property is distributed to Partner B.

The market value of the property at the time of the distribution is £640,000.

A will be treated as making a disposal of his 50% interest in the property for a consideration of £320,000. His cost is £200,000 and his gain is therefore £120,000.

B will be treated as making no disposal but as continuing to hold his original 50% interest in the property (cost £200,000) and as acquiring a further 50% for £320,000. His base cost for any future disposal is therefore now £520,000.

12.22 Note that the value which the partners attribute between themselves to the asset on its distribution is not considered. Thus in **Example 12.4**, the wording of SP D12 indicates that A would suffer tax on a gain of £120,000 even if it were agreed between the partners that the property would be transferred to B at its book value of £400,000. This is clearly unfair. There are at least two possible solutions to this. The first is to recognise that A's acquiescing in a transfer at book value is effectively the making of a gift such that a joint hold-over relief claim under the *Taxation of Chargeable Gains Act 1992, s 165* may be in point. The second is that it may be possible to alter the capital profit-sharing ratios under the partnership agreement so as to give B an entitlement to 100% of the profit in advance of transferring the property away from the partnership (without, of course, first revaluing the property). The change would be a deemed disposal by A by under SP D12 the deemed disposal would be at the balance sheet value and no gain would be recognised.

Anti-avoidance: disposal of assets or income streams

12.23 *FA 2014* contains rules designed to prevent the disposal of assets or income streams by or through a partnership if the main purpose, or one of the main purposes, of the disposal, or any of the steps by which the disposal is effected, is to secure a tax advantage in relation to the charge to income tax or the charge to corporation tax on income. Instead, the legislation imposes a charge to income tax on the disposer, similar to the existing rules for disposals of income streams. It applies to arrangements from 1 April 2014 (corporation tax) or 6 April 2014 (income tax) (*FA 2014, s 74* and *Sch 17, Pt 4*).

The arrangements covered by *FA 2014* change are similar to those dealt with by the legislation concerning transfers of income streams (*CTA 2010, Pt 16, Ch1* and *ITA 2007, Pt 13, Ch 5A*). However, the transfer of income stream provisions previously applied to partnerships only in very limited circumstances.

The legislation will apply if directly or indirectly in consequence of or otherwise in connection with an arrangement:

- there is a disposal of an asset (in whole or part) or a right to income by or through a partnership from a member of the partnership or a connected person (the transferor) to another member; and
- the main purpose, or one of the main purposes, of one or more steps taken in effecting the disposal is the obtaining of a tax advantage in relation to the charge to income tax or the charge to corporation tax on income.

'Disposal' takes the same meaning as in *TCGA 1992* and includes both part disposal and in substance disposals such as may be effected by (for example) a change of partnership profit sharing ratios.

The legislation will not apply if the transferor and transferee are relatives.

Where the legislation applies the 'relevant amount' is to be charged to tax as if it were income of the transferor. The relevant amount is the consideration given for the asset or income stream, unless the consideration given is much less than the value of the asset in which case the charge to tax will be based on a deemed market value disposal.

Chapter 13

Entrepreneurs' Relief

Signposts

- Entrepreneurs' relief offers a reduced tax rate of 10% on qualifying gains, with a lifetime limit that is now £10 million (see **13.1 – 13.3**).
- There are seven different categories of disposal which may attract relief including in some circumstances disposals by trustees and disposals of shares in a corporate partner (see **13.4**).
- Examples of the circumstances are set out (see **13.5 – 13.8**).
- Where there is a qualifying disposal, 'associated disposal' relief may apply to a disposal made at broadly the same time as part of the partner's withdrawal from participation in the partnership business. Associated disposal relief rules were significantly changed by the *Finance Act 2015* and again by the *Finance Act 2016* (see **13.9 – 13.11**).
- Relief for disposal of shares in corporate partners was restricted by the *Finance Act 2015* and the *Finance Act 2016*, both having effect from 18 March 2015 (see **13.12**).

Entrepreneurs' relief

13.1 Entrepreneurs' relief operates by applying a reduced rate of capital gains tax ('CGT') to certain 'qualifying business disposals', replacing taper relief with effect from 6 April 2008. Significant changes to entrepreneurs' relief were made by the *Finance Acts* of 2013, 2015 and 2016. It remains the case that entrepreneurs' relief derives some of its basic principles from retirement relief (which existed between 1965 and 1998) and some of the old retirement relief case law can still be in point.

13.2 The relief (which must be claimed on or before the first anniversary of 31 January following the end of the tax year in which the disposal takes place) is limited to the lifetime limit in force at the time of disposal, from which is deducted the amount of any net relevant gains on previous disposals. The limits are as follows (*TCGA 1992, s 169N(4)*):

- £1 million for disposals occurring in the period 6 April 2008 to 5 April 2010;
- £2 million for disposals occurring in the period 6 April 2010 to 22 June 2010;
- £5 million for disposals occurring in the period 23 June 2010 to 5 April 2011; and
- £10 million for disposals occurring on or after 6 April 2011.

13.3 Entrepreneurs' relief is available only to individuals (including individual members of partnerships or LLPs) or, in certain limited circumstances, to trustees. It is not available to companies. It is available on a 'qualifying business disposal', which *TCGA 1992, s 169H* defines as:

(a) a 'material disposal of business assets';

(b) a disposal of 'trust business assets';

(c) a disposal 'associated with a relevant material disposal'.

A 'disposal of business assets' made by an individual is a 'material disposal of business assets' if it is:

(a) a disposal of the whole of part of a trade, profession or vocation conducted on a commercial basis and with a view to the realisation of profits which has been owned by the individual throughout the period of one year ending with the disposal; or

(b) a disposal of (or of interests in) one or more assets in use for the purposes of such a trade etc at the time at which it ceases to be carried on provided the trade etc is owned by the individual for at least one year before cessation and the asset is disposed of within three years after the trade etc ceases; or

(c) a disposal of (or of interests in) share in or securities of a company meeting certain conditions.

Where there is a 'material disposal', certain other disposals made at broadly the same time may qualify for relief for relief as 'associated disposals' – see **13.9** et seq.

There is a disposal of trust business assets where the trustees of a settlement make a disposal of 'settlement business assets', there is a 'qualifying beneficiary' and certain conditions are met (*TCGA 1992, s 169J*).

13.4 For the purposes of applying entrepreneurs' relief to the circumstances of a partnership, *TCGA 1992, s 169I(8)* provides that:

(a) an individual who disposes of (or of interests in) assets used for the purposes of a business carried on by the individual on entering into a partnership which is to carry on the business is to be treated as disposing of a part of the business;

(b) the disposal by an individual of the whole or part of the individual's interest in the assets of a partnership is to be treated as a disposal by the individual of the whole or part of the business carried on by the partnership; and

(c) at any time when a business is carried on by a partnership, the business is to be treated as owned by each individual who is at that time a member of the partnership.

Thus in the context of partnerships, entrepreneurs' relief may potentially be relevant to gains made:

(a) by a partner on the disposal by the partnership of the whole or part of the partnership business;

(b) by a partner on the disposal of the whole or part of an interest in a partnership (including on a change of capital profit-sharing ratios);

(c) by an individual, on actual or deemed disposals when he admits partners into the business for the first time;

(d) by a partner on a disposal, following the cessation of the partnership business, of assets used by the business at the time of cessation;

(e) by certain trustees, in relation to 'trust business assets';

(f) by a partner making an 'associated disposal';

(g) by shareholders of a company which is a member of a partnership in circumstances that the relevant conditions are fulfilled.

> **Focus**
>
> Relief is not confined to sole traders. A partnership business is treated as owned by each individual who is a member of the partnership and the disposal by an individual of his interest in the assets of a partnership is treated as the disposal by the individual of the whole or part of the business carried on by the partnership (*TCGA 1992, s 169I(8)(b), (c)*).
>
> In addition, a sole trader who takes another person into partnership, thus disposing of an interest in the assets of his business, is to be treated as disposing of a part of his business (*TCGA 1992, s 169I(8)(a)*).

How the relief is calculated

13.5 When entrepreneurs' relief was first introduced, it operated by excluding 4/9 of the gain from the charge to tax, leaving 5/9 chargeable. At the then-CGT rate of 18%, this gave an effective tax rate on the gain of 10%. From 23 June 2010, the rules are simplified and the gains qualifying for relief are simply charged at 10%.

When a business is sold, some assets may crystallise gains and other disposals may create losses. Before calculating entrepreneurs' relief, the gains and losses arising on the same business disposal must be aggregated (*TCGA 1992, s 169N(1)*).

Example 13.1 – Disposal of entire business

Lucy has for several years been a partner in a firm of chartered surveyors. The business is sold as a going concern to a public company for cash. Her share of the capital gain on the goodwill is £500,000 and on one property is £250,000 and there is a loss on another property of £50,000. She will be entitled to claim relief on the net gains of £700,000. Note that the size of her interest in the partnership is not relevant.

13.6 Where a sole trader merges his business with an established partnership, the sole trader will be disposing of a fractional share in his 'sole trade' assets to his new partners:

and the partners will be disposing of a fractional share in the partnership assets to the former sole trader. In principle the gains in each case will potentially be covered by entrepreneurs' relief. However, since there will be both a disposal of business assets and an acquisition of business assets, the possibility of a claim to relief under the *Taxation of Chargeable Gains Act 1992, s 152* (replacement of business assets) should also be considered.

Example 13.2 – Disposal to new partner

Brian and Tony have been trading in partnership for some years, sharing profits 60:40 (Brian: Tony). Charles joins the partnership and the profits are to be shared from that point on as 40:30:30 (Brian: Tony: Charles). Under SP D12, Brian has disposed of one-third of his interest in the partnership to Charles, and Tony has disposed of one-quarter of his interest in the partnership to Charles. Entrepreneurs' relief may be claimed in respect of gains arising to Brian and Tony.

The requirement that a business must have been carried on for at least one year if relief is to be available is applied separately to each partner. This means that some partners may qualify and some fail to qualify on the same disposal event.

Example 13.3 – One year of trading required for business to qualify

Rachel and Martyn established a nursery business as a partnership on 1 October 2013. Helen joins the partnership on 1 May 2014, paying £30,000 for her share of the goodwill of the business. Entrepreneurs' relief is not available on the gains realised by Rachel and Martyn, as the business has not been established for at least one year. If Rachel had run the nursery business as a sole trader for some years before Martyn joined as a partner on 1 October 2013, the gains realised by Rachel on 1 May 2014 would qualify for entrepreneurs' relief, but the gain made by Martyn on that date would not qualify.

Cessation of business

13.7 Relief may be claimed by a partner in respect of gains arising on a disposal of assets which were in use for the purposes of the partnership business at the time at which business ceased, provided the partner had been a partner in the business for at least one year before cessation and provided the asset is disposed of within three years of the cessation of the business. The relief applies equally to assets owned by the partnership and to assets owned personally. Although the circumstances in which this relief may be claimed has a superficial similarity to relief under the 'associated disposal' rules which are considered below, the disposal described here remains a 'material disposal' and in particular is not subject to the restrictions on relief which apply to 'associated disposals'.

Example 13.4 – Cessation

Mr and Mrs Last have been trading in partnership as shoe repairers for many years from two shops. One of the shops is a partnership asset shown in the balance sheet. The other is owned personally by Mrs Last. On receiving an offer from a property developer for one of the shops, Mr and Mrs Last decide to close down the business and retire. Assuming both shops are sold within three years of the date the business closes, gains on both the shops will qualify for entrepreneurs' relief.

Trust disposals

13.8 Trustees may in certain circumstances claim entrepreneurs' relief.

It is very important to appreciate that although trustees may be partners in a partnership, the relief is not available in respect of gains made by trustees in that capacity on the disposal of their interest in a partnership in which the trustees are themselves partners. Nor is it available to trustees in their capacity as partners in respect of gains arising when a partnership in which the trustees are partners makes a disposal of a business or part of a business.

Relief is available only in respect of gains on assets owned by the trustees but used by a partnership in which a 'qualifying beneficiary' is a partner. If there is no 'qualifying beneficiary' there can be no relief. Whether the trustees themselves are partners in the partnership is irrelevant.

The relief is given in respect of gains on disposals of 'settlement business assets'. In the context of a partnership, a trust asset is a 'settlement business asset' if:

(a) it is used, throughout a period of at least one year ending not more than three years before the date of disposal, for the purposes of a business carried on by a partnership of which a 'qualifying beneficiary' is or was a member; and

(b) the 'qualifying beneficiary' ceases to carry on the business (either because the partnership ceases to do so or because he ceases to be a partner) on the date of disposal or has done so within three years before that date.

A 'qualifying beneficiary' is one who has an interest in possession (other than for a fixed term) in the 'settlement business asset'. If more than one beneficiary has such an interest, the gain is apportioned and only that part apportioned to the qualifying beneficiary who carries on the business qualifies for relief.

Where the relief is claimed, it counts towards the lifetime limit of the qualifying beneficiary; consequently any claim must be made jointly by the trustees and the qualifying beneficiary.

Example 13.5 – Trust disposal

Adolphus and his sister Cyrene each have a 50% life interest in a family trust which owns farmland. Adolphus (but not Cyrene) is a partner in the partnership which farms the land. Part of the land is re-zoned for residential development and is sold to a developer for £15m. The partnership continues to farm the remainder of the land.

Provided Adolphus has ceased to be a partner before the land is disposed of, entrepreneurs' relief can be claimed in respect of 50% of the gain (the claim to be made jointly by Adolphus and the trustees).

Note that if Adolphus is still a partner at the date of disposal, the conditions for relief are not met.

Associated disposals

13.9 Where a partner disposes of the whole or part of his interest in a partnership in circumstances qualifying for entrepreneurs' relief (a 'material disposal'), a disposal of an asset held personally may qualify for entrepreneurs' relief as an 'associated disposal'. There is no requirement that the 'material disposal' actually gives rise to a gain – merely that the circumstances are such that if there were a gain it would qualify for entrepreneurs' relief. The conditions for 'associated disposal' relief were significantly restricted by the *Finance Act 2015* and again by the *Finance Act 2016,* the effect of which is to make rules which were already complex even more so.

The following sets out the position for disposals after 17 March 2015 – before that date different rules applied for which reference should be made to earlier editions of this book.

13.10 If the material disposal in question is a complete disposal of the partner's interest in the partnership (such as where the partnership business is sold or the partner completely retires) the requirement is that either:

- the interest disposed of is at least a 5% interest in the partnership; or
- the partner's interest in the partnership must have been at least 5% throughout a continuous period of at least three years in the eight years ending with the date of the material disposal.

If the material disposal is a disposal of something less than the partner's complete interest in the business, the material disposal itself must be of at least a 5% interest in the partnership assets.

In each case there must be no 'partnership purchase arrangements' in existence – that is, arrangements whereby the partner making the disposal (or someone connected with him) can re-acquire an interest in (or increase an interest in) the partnership.

Subject to the above restrictions on which material disposals may be taken into account, entrepreneurs' relief is available on the disposal of an asset which:

(a) is disposed of as part of the partner's withdrawal from participation in the business carried on by the partnership (*TCGA 1992, s 169K(3),(5)*);

(b) was used for the purpose of the partnership business for at least one year to the date of disposal of the partnership interest, or the date or cessation of the partnership business if earlier (*TCGA 1992, s 169K(4)*); and

(c) had (if acquired on or after 13 June 2016) been owned by the partner throughout the period of three years ending with the date of disposal (*TCGA 1992 s 169K(4A)*). Where the asset is or has been jointly owned and the extent of the partner's interest in the asset has changed within the three years ending with the date of disposal, an appropriate apportionment of the gain is made and entrepreneurs' relief is available on the proportion of the gain which corresponds to the smallest share owned in the period.

HMRC manuals give some guidance on the interpretation of the phrase 'part of the partner's withdrawal from participation in the business' – see CG63995. It is explicitly stated that it not necessary (in the case of a partial disposal) that the individual should actually reduce the amount of work done in the business, but the associated disposal and the material disposal should be 'part and parcel' of one single withdrawal from participation in the business. This means that there should normally be no significant interval between the two disposals. However, where the partnership ceases to trade HMRC will accept that a disposal is capable of being 'associated' with the material disposal arising on cessation if it takes place within a year after cessation (it may not, by definition, take place before cessation because of the requirement that it is still in use for the purposes of the partnership business on cessation). It will also qualify is if is disposed of:

(a) within three years after cessation provided it has not been leased or used for any other purpose after the cessation of the business; or

(b) in cases where the partnership business has not ceased, within three years of the material disposal provided it has not within that period been used for any purpose other than that of the business.

Example 13.6 – Disposal of partnership interest

Graham is in partnership with his son Tristan, sharing all profits: 7/8ths to Graham, 1/8th to Tristan. Graham owns the office from which the partnership has traded for a number of years. On his 60th birthday, Graham gifts the office to his son, and the profit-sharing ratios are changed to 1/4 to Graham and 3/4 to Tristan, but Graham continues to work full time for the partnership. The disposal of the office to Tristan qualifies as an associated disposal, as Graham has at the same time made a disposal of at least 5% of his interest in the assets of the partnership.

Restrictions

13.11 There are four circumstances in which entrepreneurs' relief on an associated disposal is reduced to such amount as is 'just and reasonable':

(a) The asset has been used by the business for only part of the period of ownership by the individual, in which case the gain taken into account will reflect the period of business use.

(b) Only part of the asset has been used for the purposes of the business, in which case the gain taken into account will reflect the proportion of the asset used for business purposes.

(c) The individual has been concerned in the carrying on of the business (whether as sole trader or as a partner of the partnership) for part only of the time during which the asset was used by the business. This is less likely than situations (a) or (b), but is possible where an individual was a salaried partner before becoming a full partner or perhaps where property is owned by a spouse who is subsequently taken into partnership.

(d) Any payment of rent was made for the use of the asset by the personal company or partnership for a period after 5 April 2008.

The payment of 'rent' in restriction (d) means any form of consideration paid for the use of the asset, including licence fees for the use of intellectual property. Where the rent paid is less than a full market rent for the use of the asset, the gain is restricted proportionately.

Note that these restrictions apply *only* in the context of a claim to 'associated disposal' relief. They are of no relevance where relief is claimed on a 'material disposal' or to a claim by trustees on a disposal of 'settlement business assets'.

Companies in partnership

13.12 Entrepreneurs' relief is available in respect of the disposal of shares in a company where the statutory requirements are fulfilled. Specialist texts should be consulted in regard to the detailed conditions applying to gains on shares: however one of the requirements is that the company in question should be a trading company or the holding company of a trading group throughout a 'relevant period' of one year ending with the date of disposal (or ending on a date falling not earlier than three years before the date of disposal) (*TCGA 1992, s 169I(5)*).

'Trading company' is defined by *s 165A* as 'a company carrying on trading activities whose activities do not include to a substantial extent activities other than trading activities' and 'holding company of a trading group' is defined similarly. Originally, these definitions applied without modification for the purposes of entrepreneurs' relief and hence any company which was a partner in a trading partnership (or a member of a trading LLP) met the definition of trading company.

The legislation was changed by the *Finance Act 2015* to treat activities carried on by a company as a member of a partnership as non-trading activities, thereby excluding corporate partners from entrepreneurs' relief except in the unusual case where the company also carried on its own trade independently of the partnership and the partnership activity was not substantial. The *Finance Act 2016*, backdated to 18 March 2015 (the date of the *Finance Act 2015* changes) reverses the *Finance Act 2015* changes but creates new limitations on the circumstances in which a company trading as a member of a partnership can qualify as a trading company for the purposes of entrepreneurs' relief. It should be noted that these changes apply only for the purposes of entrepreneurs' relief – the definition at *s 165A* remains unaltered in its application to hold-over relief (see **Chapter 15**).

Under the *Finance Act 2016* rules, in relation to an individual's disposal of shares in a company, activities carried on by the company as a member of a partnership do not count as being trading activities of the company if the individual fails either or both of a 'profits and assets' test and 'voting rights' test. Both of these tests are aimed at limiting relief to individuals who have, broadly, indirect ownership of at least 5% of the partnership through their holding in the corporate partner.

More specifically, an individual passes the profits and assets test in relation to a partnership if, throughout the relevant period, the sum of the percentages given by (a), (b) and (c) below is at least 5%, namely:

(a) the percentage which is the individual's direct interest in the assets of the partnership (ie, where the individual is himself a member);

(b) the percentage which the individual holds through companies that are members of the partnership; and

(c) the percentage which the individual holds through companies which in turn hold interests in companies which are members of the partnership.

Where interests are held indirectly the percentage taken is the share of the assets and profits owned by the company multiplied by the share in the company owned by the individual.

A similar test applies in respect of voting rights.

Example 13.7 – Entrepreneurs' relief in respect of corporate member

Graham and Tristan are selling the shares in Isolde Limited. The company has been a member of a trading partnership for many years and has no other activity, and is an equal partner with the other four partners. The shares in Isolde Limited are held by Graham as to 80% and Tristan as to 20%. Both Graham and Tristan fulfil all the other conditions for entrepreneurs' relief.

Graham's indirect interest in the partnership is 16% (that is 80% × 20%) and he passes the 'profits and assets' test and the 'voting rights' test. Tristan's indirect interest is 4% (that is, 20% × 20%) and he fails the test. Isolde is therefore treated as a trading company in relation to Graham's disposal, so that Graham is entitled to claim entrepreneurs' relief, but as a non-trading company in relation to Tristan's disposal, who is therefore denied entrepreneurs' relief.

Chapter 14

Annuities to Retired Partners

Signposts

- Apart from the taxation position, payment of an annuity to a retiring partner may be a cash-efficient way of dealing meaningfully with an outgoing partner (see **14.1**).
- An annuity from the partnership other than a purchased annuity is always taxable as income in the hands of the recipient. The capitalised value of the annuity is also charged to CGT unless certain conditions are fulfilled (see **14.2 – 14.6**).
- The payment of a lump sum in addition to an annuity may bring the capitalised value of the annuity into charge to CGT (see **14.7 – 14.10**).
- The capitalised value of a purchased life annuity is charged to CGT but the annuity itself is only partly chargeable to income tax (see **14.11**).
- The repayment of a partner's capital account will not of itself give rise to a chargeable gain, but if a surplus on a revaluation of chargeable assets has previously been credited there may be CGT implications (see **14.12 – 14.13**).
- A consultancy payment should not be contemplated instead of or as well as an annuity unless the consultancy payment is fully justifiable (see **14.15**).

14.1 The capital gains tax ('CGT') consequences of revaluation of partnership assets, coupled with the change of profit-sharing ratios as partners are introduced, retire, or alter their shares by agreement between themselves, are sometimes avoided by an agreement between the partners that an annuity is paid by the continuing partners to a retiring partner instead of, or in addition to, a payment for his share in the increased value of assets (the cost of the assets being reflected in his capital account).

Apart from the taxation position, this may also be a cash-efficient way of dealing meaningfully with an outgoing partner.

14.2 In the event that an annuity is paid by the partnership, whilst the capitalised value of the annuity is liable to CGT (*TCGA 1992, s 37(3)*), CGT is not charged on that value if it is paid on the retirement of a partner by reason of age or ill health and is in reasonable recognition of past service. The payment must not be a lump sum equivalent or a life annuity which has been purchased by the partnership providing a lump sum (HMRC Statements of Practice D12 (revised 14 September 2015) and 1/89 and 1/79).

14.3 A reasonable amount is regarded as being the appropriate fraction of the average assessable profits of the *best three* of the *last seven years of assessment*, in which the partner was required to devote substantially the whole of his or her time to the partnership.

The relevant profits are the share allocated to the partner in a particular tax year, so that, in cases of varying profit-sharing ratios, he or she might have one of his or her highest years when the firm's profits were lower than normal. The profits for the best years as ascertained are not dynamised by inflation linking.

Profits are those before capital allowances and charges.

14.4 The appropriate fraction depends on the years of service to the firm (or its predecessor) and is as follows (Statement of Practice D12):

Complete years	*Fraction per year*
1–5	1/60
6	8/60
7	16/60
8	24/60
9	32/60
10	2/3

Thus, suppose the average of the best three of the last seven assessments is £82,000. The maximum annuity without CGT implications after ten years of service is £54,667 (2/3rds × £82,000).

Where an annuity is stated not as a fixed sum but as a percentage of future partnership profits, a reasonable estimate of future profits will have to be made in order to determine whether the annuity is likely to fall within the above limits.

14.5 HMRC have previously indicated that, where the amount of an annuity does not contravene this rule at the outset, the rule will not be regarded as having been breached in future years if the annuity (whilst then exceeding the annual permissible limit by reference to the original calculation) has simply kept pace with inflation.

14.6 So long as the annuity is within the prescribed limit, this prevents its capitalised value being regarded as disposal proceeds for CGT. The annuity itself is still charged to income tax. It is received net of basic rate tax. Higher rate (or additional rate) tax may be due, depending on the recipient's other income, or a repayment of tax may be due.

Lump sums

14.7 Originally, the concessional treatment described above applied only where the payment of the annuity was the only consideration paid to the retiring partner. The treatment was however extended in 1979 to certain cases where a lump sum is paid to a partner (or a purchased life annuity is acquired) in addition to the payment of an annuity.

14.8 Where a lump sum is paid in addition to the payment of an annuity (or a purchased life annuity is acquired) the lump sum (or the purchase price of the annuity) will always be taken into account as consideration for CGT purposes. But the capitalised value of the partnership annuity will be left out of account for CGT if the annuity itself plus 1/9th of the lump sum (or purchased life annuity cost) amounts to less than the defined 'reasonable amount'.

14.9 Thus, suppose that, instead of the maximum annuity of £54,667 per annum at **14.4**, a reduced annuity amounting to £50,000 per annum was paid from the partnership, but additionally a lump sum was paid (or a life annuity was purchased for the retiring partner by the partnership at the same cost as the lump sum).

The maximum lump sum which could be paid if the capitalised value of the annuity is to be disregarded is £42,003 (that is, 9 × (£54,667 – £50,000).

If a lump sum of £42,003 was paid (or used to purchase a life annuity), the capitalised value of the £50,000 annuity from the partnership will not become chargeable to CGT because:

	£
The annuity itself	50,000
Plus 1/9th of the lump sum of £42,003	4,667
does not exceed the 'reasonable amount' of	54,667

The reduction of the annuity and part substitution of the lump sum does not therefore affect the CGT position of the annuity.

14.10 The lump sum itself (or purchased life annuity cost) is regarded as proceeds for CGT purposes. The actual CGT payable will depend on the base cost, indexation allowance, taper relief, etc, and also on what other allowances or reliefs are available.

Should, exceptionally, the capitalised value of the partnership annuity have to be regarded as proceeds for CGT purposes, that value can be regarded as acquisition expenditure by those partners responsible for the annuity (Statement of Practice D12).

Purchased annuities

14.11 Whereas the annuity from the partnership is taxable as income in the hands of the recipient (see **14.6**), only part of a purchased annuity is chargeable to income tax, the remainder being regarded as a return of capital. Furthermore, a basic rate taxpayer may formerly have been charged on the income element of a purchased life annuity at the 20% saving rate, whereas he or she would be charged at the basic rate on an annuity from the partnership. In both cases, the appropriate rate of tax would be deducted at source. Higher rate taxpayers are liable to pay the additional 20% (*ITA 2007, ss 12, 16*), and additional rate taxpayers are liable to pay the additional 25%.

Capital accounts

14.12 The repayment of a partner's capital account will not as such give rise to a chargeable gain, but it must be remembered that the capital account balance may include the surplus on a revaluation of chargeable assets, a chargeable gain on which crystallises on a change in capital profit-sharing ratios, whether the amount of the capital account is withdrawn at that time or stays on loan to the partnership (see **Chapter 12**).

Unless, for some reason, a retiring partner retains the same share as before in the partnership chargeable assets (eg he or she may remain as a part-owner of premises), such a change occurs on the retirement of a partner when his or her entitlement to share in a future surplus reduces to 0%, this in itself triggering the chargeable gain.

> **Focus**
>
> The repayment of the capital account may therefore disguise the payment of a lump sum which is represented by the surplus on revaluation which is in the capital account. Care must be taken that it is not overlooked, not only so that any chargeable gains thereon can be calculated, but also to ensure that the capitalised value of the annuity does not have to be reckoned as proceeds for CGT because the formula at **14.9** has been breached.

Example 14.1 – Repayment of capital account affecting capital gains position

Partnership net assets at time of Karen's retirement £50,000

Representing capital accounts:

	Karen	*Bernard*
	£	*£*
Cash introduced and retained profit	10,000	10,000
Introduction of goodwill of £30,000 to balance sheet prior to Karen's retirement, in profit-sharing ratio of 2:1	20,000	10,000
	30,000	20,000

£20,000 is disposal proceeds for CGT on Karen's ceasing to be a partner, not because of the repayment of cash but because of the revaluation followed by a change in profit-sharing ratio, Karen's share reducing from 2/3rds to nil.

The position would be identical if Karen were repaid her capital account of £10,000 plus a separate lump sum of £20,000 on her ceasing to be a partner without the revaluation having first been made.

The accounts would somehow have to reflect the payment to her of the £20,000 and, since there would be no existing credit against which to set it, it would by implication be a payment for goodwill.

14.13 The CGT consequence of a downward movement in capital-sharing ratio is particularly important where the capital account includes a surplus on revaluation of chargeable assets and the amount standing to the account of the partner is to be left on loan to the partnership. The chargeable gain still crystallises and the tax will be payable on the normal due date unless covered by reliefs or able to be paid by instalments (*TCGA 1992, s 280*).

Income tax

14.14 When paying the annuity, the partnership makes the payment net of income tax at the basic rate and retains the tax deducted. Thus, the paying partners get basic rate relief by deduction and retention, and the recipient suffers basic rate tax by deduction at source.

If the paying partners are entitled to relief at higher or additional rates, this is claimed individually in the partners' self-assessment returns. If the recipient is liable at higher or additional rates, he or she will include it in his or her return under self-assessment.

The partnership return must show net partnership charges (including annuities) paid in the tax year (and not the accounting period). Relief is given via the individual and partnership returns. The additional information box on the return should be used to provide an explanation of the payments, particularly in the year in which an annuity starts.

Annuities paid by the partnership to former partners are not deductible in computing taxable profits under the *Income Tax (Taxation of Income) Act 2005 (ITTOIA 2005)*, since relief has already been given as described earlier in this section. The paying partnership will issue form R185 to the recipient, certifying the payment.

Consultancy payments

14.15 A consultancy payment should not be contemplated instead of or as well as an annuity unless the consultancy payment is fully justifiable. It must satisfy the 'wholly and exclusively' rule and, if it does not, it will not only be disallowed in computing profits but will also be regarded as payment for goodwill, with a possible effect on the CGT position of the annuity payments themselves, and/or other CGT consequences. Where a consultancy payment is justifiable, the retired partner will be taxed under *ITTOIA 2005* if he or she is self-employed, or as an employee if not. It is a question of fact whether the consultancy agreement constitutes a contract of service or a contract for services. Increasingly, HMRC find that such agreements are contracts of service taxable as employment income.

Focus

One advantage to the retiring partner of receiving consultancy fees or payments is that it may enable him or her to receive more tax relief on pension payments than would otherwise be the case, as such fees count as qualifying earnings for pension purposes.

Other options

14.16 Problems can arise if a partnership pays an annuity and then later agrees to commute the annuity for a lump sum. The retiring partner will be treated as making a disposal of the right to receive the annuity, and the partners will not obtain either income tax or CGT relief. If a lump sum is to be paid, it should be paid at the outset when the partner retires.

14.17 A retiring partner should not be paid a pension by the continuing partners, since this will not be allowable as a trading expense (being tantamount to payments to acquire the retiring partner's share) whilst still being taxed on the recipient. The annuity route should be followed and partnership dissolution agreements should reflect these arrangements.

Limited liability partnerships

14.18 Where an obligation to pay an annuity is transferred from a partnership to a limited liability partnership (LLP), the members, including incoming members, will be entitled to higher rate relief for their share of the payment, basic rate relief having been obtained by deduction at the time of the payment. The transfer of the annuity obligations are not regarded as chargeable disposals for CGT purposes, provided that the annuitants' rights remain substantially the same (see also **19.38**).

Chapter 15

Capital Gains Tax – Roll-over and Hold-over Relief on Replacement of Business Assets

Signposts

- Any potential for roll-over or hold-over relief under the *Taxation of Chargeable Gains Act 1992, ss 152–158* is assessed at the partner level by reference to the individual circumstances of each partner. This is the case even for partnerships between husband and wife or civil partners (see **15.1 – 15.8**).
- Where the asset is owned by a partner and used by the partnership, the charging of rent is no bar to a claim for relief (see **15.10**).
- Purchase from a retiring partner of his interest in partnership assets may give title to relief (see **15.11 – 15.15**).
- Crystallisation of deferred gains is a particular point to be aware of (see **15.16 – 15.19**).

Availability of relief

15.1 Since, for capital gains tax ('CGT') purposes, those partners entitled to share in capital surpluses each have a share in each chargeable asset, the gains of each partner are independent of the other partners' and each has the possibility of a roll-over or hold-over relief claim under the *Taxation of Capital Gains Act 1992 (TCGA 1992), ss 152–158.*

While the partnership itself reports capital transactions, either with third parties or between the partners themselves, each partner submits an individual capital gains computation reflecting his or her personal circumstances.

Focus

There are three situations where roll-over or hold-over relief might apply:

(a) where a partnership asset is sold to a third party, each of the partners having a chargeable gain by reference to his/her share of the proceeds;

(b) where, because of a change in capital profit-sharing ratios following a revaluation of partnership assets, a chargeable gain arises to a partner whose share reduces; and

(c) where a partner has provided an asset (usually property) for use in the partnership business and he or she disposes of it.

15.2 The available time limit in which to enter into a contract for purchase of the new asset is within 12 months before the contract for the sale of the old asset or within three years after the sale contract (*TCGA 1992, s 152(3)*). HMRC have discretion to extend the time limit, and they have stated that they will usually do so where a taxpayer had a firm intention to acquire the replacement within the time limit, but was prevented from doing so by circumstances outside his control.

Roll-over relief claims must give full details of the assets disposed of and acquired, the dates and the amounts involved. The time limit for making the claim is the later of:

- four years from the end of the tax year in which the disposal of the old assets took place; and
- four years from the end of the tax year in which the replacement assets are acquired.

HMRC Helpsheet 290 provides a form for making the claim though a claim by letter is equally acceptable, provided all the necessary information is included.

There are two kinds of provisional claim to relief.

The first (under *s 152(4)*) is where a contract is entered into before the three-year cut-off date. Relief is then given provisionally, without waiting to ascertain whether the contract is completed and the replacement assets actually acquired. In principle, such a claim can remain provisional for an indefinite period. If the contract is completed the provisional claim becomes final. If it becomes clear that it will never be completed all necessary adjustments (such as withdrawing the relief) are made regardless of any assessment or amendment time limits that would otherwise apply.

The second kind of provisional claim (under *s 153A*) is where a taxpayer declares, in the tax return for the year of the disposal, an intention to enter into a contract before the cut-off date. Relief is then allowed provisionally. If the provisional claim is not superseded by an actual claim (which may be a claim which is itself provisional under *s 154(2)*), it will cease to have effect three years from the due date for the return for the tax year of disposal (eg for a disposal in 2014/15, the return for which is due by 31 January 2016, the provisional relief would no longer apply after 31 January 2019). All necessary adjustments to self-assessments, including interest, will then be made.

15.3 Full relief is available only if the full amount of the proceeds of disposal (net of incidental costs of disposal) is applied in acquiring the new asset (including incidental costs of acquisition). If a part only of the proceeds is re-invested into new assets, the gain is reduced to the amount not reinvested (assuming of course that the amount not reinvested is less than the amount of the gain otherwise arising) and the amount of the reduction in the gain is 'held over' or 'rolled over'.

15.4 The question of whether roll-over or hold-over relief is available depends on the predictable life of the replacement asset. If the replacement has a predictable life of more than 60 years, roll-over relief is available. If the life of the replacement is 60 years or less (called a 'depreciating asset'), hold-over relief is available.

Where roll-over relief applies, the amount of the gain (or, in the case of partial reinvestment, the amount of gain held over) is deducted from the CGT cost of the replacement asset.

Where hold-over relief applies, the amount of the gain (or, in the case of partial reinvestment, the amount of gain rolled over) is deferred until the earliest of the following dates:

(a) the claimant disposes of the 'replacement asset';

(b) the claimant ceases to use the 'replacement asset' for the purposes of a trade carried on by him; and

(c) ten years from the date of acquisition of the 'replacement asset'.

The gain will not, however, crystallise if, at or before that time, a non-depreciating asset has been acquired against which the gain can be rolled over. In this case, the claim to transfer from hold-over to roll-over relief will need to be submitted with the tax return for the year in which the non-depreciating asset is acquired.

Roll-over or hold-over relief applies to the following qualifying assets (*TCGA 1992, s 155*):

- freehold land and buildings or leaseholds, occupied and used for the purposes of the trade or profession (but for this purpose letting property as furnished holiday accommodation is treated as a trade);
- goodwill;
- fixed plant and machinery;
- ships, aircraft and hovercraft;
- spacecraft, space stations and satellites;
- milk and potato quotas;
- ewe and suckler cow premium quotas;
- fish quotas;
- payment entitlements under the single payment scheme for farmers;
- payment entitlements under the basic payment scheme (that is, the scheme of income support for farmers in pursuance of Regulation (EU) No 1307/2013 of the European Parliament and of the Council);
- Lloyd's syndicate rights.

The replacement asset does not have to be in the same category as the asset disposed of, provided they are both qualifying assets. The proceeds of a single disposal could be used to purchase more than one qualifying replacement asset and the proceeds of multiple disposals could be used to purchase a single qualifying replacement asset.

No tracing of actual proceeds through to acquisition is required. Indeed, the relief is in principle available where there are no actual proceeds or no actual acquisition costs (as for example where the market value rule applies to a disposal or to an acquisition or where one qualifying asset is exchanged for another. In the context of partnerships this might apply to a deemed disposal of assets when partnerships merge or a sole trader merges his business into an existing partnership on joining it.

15.5 It should be noted that full relief is potentially due only if the old asset has been used, and used only, for the purposes of the business throughout the period of ownership. But if during that period there has been some degree of non-business use, the legislation provides for the gain to be apportioned such that an appropriate part of the gain may qualify for relief.

15.6 The new asset must on acquisition be taken into use and used only for the purposes of the business. Exceptionally, it may be that circumstances dictate that there is some delay (the new asset may need to be refurbished before being usable, for example, or licensing requirements may delay the bringing into use). However, where the gain is rolled over (as distinct from being held over) there is no provision for the relief to be withdrawn should the asset cease to be used for business purposes, which may on occasion offer some planning opportunities.

Husband/wife and civil partnerships

15.7 The computations are performed at the partner level and not at the partnership level. Thus the comparison between proceeds of the old assets and cost of the new is made by reference to the share that the partner owns in each. This remains the case even for spouses or civil partners. Thus in *Tod v Mudd* (1986) 60 TC 237, the proceeds of business assets owned entirely by the husband were used to buy new business assets owned jointly by husband and wife and roll-over relief was restricted by reference to the share of the new assets owned by the husband. Furthermore, where assets are owned jointly and there is both business and non-business use, it is not possible to 'earmark' one co-owner's share of the asset as being the business element and the other co-owner's as representing the private element. Mr Mudd owned 75% of a property of which business use was 75%: his qualifying expenditure was therefore 75% × 75% of the total cost.

15.8 In a husband/wife or civil partnership situation such as this, the new asset should be acquired by the spouse or civil partner making the earlier gain. Once the roll-over relief and hence the base cost of the new asset is established, a transfer of part of the ownership to the other spouse or civil partner can be considered, using the exemption for inter-spouse or inter-civil partner transfers.

Land and buildings

15.9 Where the replacement assets are land and/or buildings, there is a requirement for the buildings to be occupied as well as used for the purposes of the trade. Thus, in *Anderton v Lamb* (1980) 55 TC 1, farmhouses that were acknowledged to be used for trade purposes were held not to be occupied as such, since the occupation by the farmer's sons was neither essential nor to enable them better to perform their duties. See also HMRC Capital Gains Tax Manual at CG60990.

Assets owned by individual partners

15.10 Since the relief hinges upon use in a business, it is not restricted, in the partnership context, to assets which are owned by the partnership. It is in principle available to partners in respect of assets owned personally but used in the partnership business. Furthermore, unlike 'associated disposal' relief under the entrepreneurs' relief regime, the charging of rent by the partner does not disqualify the asset from relief.

Retiring partners

15.11 There is no automatic claim to roll-over relief when a partnership asset is sold and the proceeds are used to pay out a leaving partner's capital account. The leaving partner has a share of the gain, arising from a sale before he or she goes or a prior revaluation of assets credited to his or her capital account. The question is, do the departing and continuing partners use the proceeds in a qualifying purchase?

15.12 Insofar as the continuing partners are concerned, they may acquire a larger interest in qualifying assets on the departure of the leaving partner, whose share goes down from x% to nil. This may entitle them to roll-over relief, quite apart from any other expenditure which is incurred. Insofar as the departing partner is concerned, it depends on what he or she does with his or her proceeds.

Example 15.1 – Roll-over relief on departure of a partner

(i) Balance sheet of Jim and John

	£		£
Capital:		Properties at cost:	
Jim	80,000	1	50,000
John	80,000	2	90,000
		Net current assets	20,000
	160,000		160,000

(ii) Details of the properties, which are used for trading purposes, are as follows:

		Cost	*Worth*
		£	£
1	Acquired since March 1982	50,000	250,000
2	Acquired before March 1982	90,000	300,000
		140,000	550,000

Jim and John each have identical acquisition dates and base values, capital surpluses being shared equally.

(iii) Jim wishes to leave the partnership, and Property 1 is to be sold to raise cash so that Jim can be paid out.

(iv) The first step is to reflect the revaluation of the properties in the balance sheet, and hence the proper amounts of the partners' capital accounts:

Capital		*Jim*	*John*		
		£	£		£
As 1		80,000	80,000		
Revalued properties					
	£				
	550,000				
	140,000				
	410,000	205,000	205,000		
		285,000	285,000	=	570,000
Being:					
Property 1 at revaluation			250,000		
Property 2 at revaluation			300,000		550,000
Net current assets					20,000
					570,000

Jim will have a chargeable gain if, after this revaluation and without a sale (John raising the money to pay him out by borrowing), Jim's share in the properties reduces by his ceasing to be a partner, and the legal interest in the properties passes entirely to John. In that event, John will not have a chargeable gain, since he has not disposed of anything. Indeed, he has acquired Jim's share in both properties.

(v) If property 1 is sold, then, whilst Jim's position remains the same, a chargeable gain now accrues to John because of his disposal.

The balance sheet becomes:

	£	£
Property 2 at valuation		300,000
Net current liabilities:		
Net current assets before	20,000	
Property 1 sold	250,000	
Jim paid out	(285,000)	(15,000)
Representing John's capital		285,000

(vi) Total chargeable gains by reference to the sale, divisible equally between Jim and John, are:

	£
Proceeds for Property 1	250,000
Cost	50,000
Chargeable gain	200,000

(vii)

- Jim is chargeable on £100,000 (as he would be on Property 1 on a revaluation without a sale).
- John's £100,000 gain is rolled over into his acquisition of Jim's share in Property 2, since his share of the proceeds of Property 1 (£125,000) is less than his deemed acquisition cost of Jim's share of Property 2 (£150,000).

	Jim	*John*
	£	£
Cost of Property 2	45,000	45,000
Revaluation uplift on Jim's departure	105,000	105,000
	150,000	150,000
Disposal from Jim to John	(150,000)	150,000
Per Balance Sheet at 5.		300,000

(viii) Apart from the chargeable gain by reference to the sale, Jim is also chargeable on the disposal of Property 2 resulting from the reduction in his share from one-half to nil:

	£
His share of revalued property	150,000
Value at March 1982, say	(50,000)
Gain	100,000

(ix) John's cost of Property 2 for CGT on a future disposal is:

	£	£
(a) Original cost (rebased to 1982 value)		50,000
(b) Acquisition of Jim's share	150,000	
(c) Roll-over relief on sale of Property 1	(100,000)	
		50,000
		100,000

(x) John's cost of the whole, had there simply been a revaluation and loan money had been raised to pay out Jim, would have been:

Property	*1*	2	*Total*
	£	£	£
Original cost of ½ share to John (rebased to 1982 value for Prop 2)	25,000	50,000	
Jim's share at full valuation on his being paid out	125,000	150,000	
	150,000	200,000	350,000

15.13 If John in **Example 15.1** were later to take Joe into partnership and, on doing so, reduce his capital sharing ratio, a part disposal would thereby arise on which a further gain would arise, (assuming that the properties had not in the interim been revalued downwards in the balance sheet).

15.14 Capital gains will also need to be considered if a partnership splits up, with partners taking various assets in satisfaction of their shares in the partnership. Land and, indeed, other chargeable business assets used for the purposes of a trade may thus be partitioned by the partners, giving rise to both disposals (of assets where the share is reduced) and acquisitions (of assets where the share is increased. In principle, and subject to the rules described above (and in particular the relative values of interests disposed of and acquired) roll-over or hold-over relief may be in point.

15.15 In the event of partnership assets being divided in kind amongst the partners on dissolution, a partner who receives an asset will not be regarded as disposing of his or her previously owned fractional share of it.

The partners' future cost for capital gains tax will therefore be his or her base cost for the share he or she held throughout, plus the appropriate share of the value at which asset was accounted between partners on the dissolution.

Example 15.2 – Division of partnership assets in kind on partnership dissolution

The partnership assets of three equal partners, Penelope, Adelina and Virginia, include three separate properties which are used for the purposes of the trade. The partnership is dissolved, each partner taking one of the properties as part of the amount due to her on dissolution, any difference in entitlement being represented by an adjustment in other assets or cash. The financial particulars of each property are as follows:

	Base value	*Market value*
	£000	*£000*
Property 1 (taken by Penelope)	110	200
Property 2 (taken by Adelina)	127	175
Property 3 (taken by Virginia)	75	225

The position in respect of the properties will be as follows:

Property	*1*	*2*	*3*
	£000	*£000*	*£000*
Market value	200	175	225
Base value	110	127	75
Surplus	90	48	150
Gains on deemed disposals:			
Penelope		16	50
Adelina	30		50
Virginia	30	16	
Deemed proceeds:			
Penelope		58.333	75
Adelina	66.667		75
Virginia	66.667	58.333	
Deemed cost of share acquired:			
Penelope	133.333		
Adelina)		116.667	
Virginia			150

Virginia has deemed proceeds of the old assets of £66,667 (Property 1) and £58,333 (Property 2) and deemed cost of the new asset of £150,000 so she may roll over her gains in full, with the result that the base cost of Property 3 for her will become:

Cost of 1/3 share already owned	25,000
Cost of 2/3 share now acquired	150,000
Gains rolled over	46,000
New base cost carried forward	129,000

Penelope has deemed proceeds of the old assets of £58,333 (Property 2) and £75,000 (Property 3) and deemed cost of the new asset of £133,333 so she too may roll over her gains in full, with the result that the base cost of Property 1 for her will become:

Cost of 1/3 share already owned	36,667
Cost of 2/3 share now acquired	133,333
Gains rolled over	66,000
New base cost carried forward	104,000

Adelina has deemed proceeds of the old assets of £66,667 (Property 1) and £75,000 (Property 3). The deemed cost of the new asset Property 2 is £116,667. Thus she can use £75,000 of the cost of Property 2 to roll-over the whole gain on Property 3. This leaves £41,667 of Property 2 cost remaining. This allows a partial rollover of the gain on

Property 1, leaving £25,000 (the amount of Property 1 proceeds not reinvested) chargeable. Alternatively she could use £66,667 of the cost of Property 2 to roll over the whole gain on Property 1, leaving £50,000 of Property 2 cost remaining. This could be used to make a partial roll-over claim on Property 3, again leaving £25,000 (the amount of Property 3 proceeds not reinvested) chargeable. Her base cost of Property 2 will be:

Cost of 1/3 share already owned	42,333
Cost of 2/3 share now acquired	116,667
Gains rolled over £80,000 – £25,000	55,000
New base cost carried forward	104,000

Crystallisation of deferred gains

15.16 Since each partner has a share in each chargeable asset belonging to the partnership, each will have a separate acquisition cost. This may not be the same for all partners, not only because of different acquisition dates and amounts arising from partnership changes, but also because chargeable gains on the disposal of other assets might have been deducted from the acquisition cost for tax purposes under the roll-over provisions. The accounting records will not usually indicate the lower base cost of the asset, and this must not be forgotten when calculating the chargeable gain on a disposal by one or more of the partners.

15.17 It is even easier to overlook the crystallisation of an earlier chargeable gain which has been held over (on the acquisition of a depreciating asset) for ten years or until the depreciating asset is disposed of or ceases to be used (see **15.3**).

15.18 Rolled-over and held-over gains do not crystallise on a partner's death. Like any other gains on death, they are exempt from CGT.

15.19 When a partner reduces his or her capital profit share, partly or completely, he or she no longer owns a share of the depreciating asset, thus crystallising the held-over gain at that point.

The corollary is that, on such a reduction in capital share or on complete retirement, the other partners have a corresponding acquisition which may itself protect a gain realised by them in the previous three years or the ensuing 12 months.

Example 15.3 – Disposal of share of depreciating asset on retirement – interaction with hold-over relief

Gilder retires from his partnership on 31 December 2014. Several years ago, a gain of £20,000 was held over because of his having acquired a share in short leasehold premises purchased by the partnership.

On his retirement from the partnership, there are two potential CGT events:

(i) the crystallisation of the held-over gain of £20,000; and

(ii) the gain or loss on his disposal to the other partners of his interest in the short leasehold premises (using the special method of computation in *TCGA 1992, s 244* and *Sch 8*, whereby only the depreciated cost can be set off).

The remaining partners will share between themselves, as an acquisition cost, the disposal proceeds at (ii).

Chapter 16

Transfer of a Partnership business to a Company

Signposts

- Given the current relatively low rates of corporation tax in force, incorporating a partnership may be a worthwhile consideration, but there are many more factors which need to be taken into account (see **16.1 – 16.10**).
- A cash-flow advantage may be obtained by incorporating, because tax payments will be delayed (see **16.7**).
- The timing of the cessation will need to be considered carefully to ascertain the profit and loss profile in the closing period of the partnership and the opening year of the company (see **16.11**).
- Treatment of stock, work in progress and capital allowances all need to be considered (see **16.12 – 16.16**)
- CGT may be avoided by retaining chargeable assets (possibly including goodwill, though the matter is not beyond doubt) in the ownership of the former partners and not transferring them to the company (see **16.17 – 16.18**).
- Sale of assets leaving debt outstanding may be attractive. As a result of recent legislative changes Entrepreneurs' Relief will often (but not always) be denied on a disposal of goodwill on incorporation (see **16.19 – 16.21**).
- Relief under the *Taxation of Chargeable Gains Act 1992, s 162* may be available but this depends on the whole of the business being transferred by one or more individuals to a company (see **16.22 – 16.26**)
- Gifts relief under *s 165* should be considered (see **16.27 – 16.30**).
- Other issues to be considered on incorporation include the treatment of existing or prospective partnership annuities (see **16.31 – 16.34**); tax relief on loan interest (see **16.35**); IHT (see **16.36**); and VAT (see **16.37**).
- A list of practical issues to consider on incorporation is given at **16.38**).

Why incorporate?

16.1 There are many reasons why a partnership may wish to 'incorporate' (ie, transfer its business to a limited company): some will be driven by tax incentives; and others, with motives such as image, limited liability and the ability to raise finance, will not. The increase in the audit threshold may have removed one of the administrative burdens faced by some companies, but the incorporation process itself and the additional cost of running a company should not be underestimated, particularly for family businesses. A partnership planning to incorporate in order to achieve limited liability may wish to consider forming a limited liability partnership as an alternative to operating as a company (see **Chapter 19**).

16.2 The differential between personal and corporate tax rates is one obvious incentive to incorporate. For financial years 2017 (commencing 1 April 2017) to 2019, the rate of corporation tax is 19%, with a reduction promised to 17% from FY 2020. This may be compared with personal tax rates ranging up to 45%.

Focus

From April 2016, the dividend tax credit is abolished. There is a dividend tax allowance of £5,000 a year. It remains to be seen whether the proposed reduction in the allowance to £2,000 which was withdrawn because of the 2017 general election will now be reinstated. The rates of tax on dividend income above the allowance are 7.5% for basic rate taxpayers, 32.5% for higher rate taxpayers and 38.1% for additional rate taxpayers.

16.3 A simple comparison of corporation tax and income tax rates is however, only the start of the process. Unlike a partnership, where profits can be withdrawn without further tax charge, profits can only be taken from a company as a salary, dividend, loan repayment or to meet legitimate business expenses. The means by which profits are withdrawn, therefore, potentially affects the tax and NIC position both of the company and of the individual director or shareholders.

16.4 There is no substitute in each case for calculating the likely tax and National Insurance implications of incorporation. The calculation should compare the net income available to partners with their net remuneration from a limited company and the company's tax cost. Each case will depend on the means by which profits are withdrawn, the requirement to retain capital in the business, and the tax position of the proprietors. Generally speaking, in cases where most of the profits of the business are withdrawn for personal expenditure the introduction of the additional 7.5% tax on dividends in excess of the £5,000 exempt amount has severely curtailed the benefits of incorporation. Significant tax savings (or, in most cases, deferral) are now likely to arise only where a significant proportion of the profits are retained within the business for reinvestment as working capital.

16.5 National Insurance has a significant impact on the calculations where profits are withdrawn as salaries. In 2017/18, partners pay Class 2 contributions of £2.85 per week plus Class 4 National Insurance of 9% of profits between £8,164 and £45,000, and 2% thereafter. Directors pay Class 1 contributions of 12% of earnings between £157.01 and £866 per week plus 2% above this limit but, in addition, the company as employer pays secondary Class 1 contributions of 13.8% on earnings above £157 per week.

Employment allowance (by which qualifying employers are able to reduce their Class 1 NIC charge) was increased from £2,000 to £3,000 from April 2016.

> **Focus**
>
> From April 2018, Class 2 NIC is to be abolished. Self-employed people (including partners) will be able to gain access to contributory benefits based on a profits test in Class 4 NICs.

Pros and cons of incorporation

16.6 Depending on the method by which the business is transferred to the company, it is possible that significant loan accounts will be created in favour of the proprietors, representing a combination of undrawn profits of the business and revaluation of business assets. In principle these may subsequently be drawn down with zero or reduced further tax charge. (see **16.20**). The repayment of loan accounts in this way may also increase entitlement to tax credits (see **7.25**). Care is needed here though: the initial creation of the loan accounts may well itself create tax liabilities or affect the availability of other tax reliefs.

16.7 It is sometimes said that a cash-flow advantage may be obtained by incorporating. But the opposite is often the case. It is true that for all but the largest companies tax is payable nine months after the year-end with no in-year payment on account. Contrast this with unincorporated businesses where – although tax is payable ten months after the end of the income tax year, payments on account will very often account for the bulk of the liability.

For a year-end early in the income tax year the period between the period end and payment of tax is much longer than nine months: income tax on the profits of the year ended 30 April 2016 for example will be due for 2016/17 with payments on account due on 31 January 2017, 31 July 2017 and 31 January 2018. Corporation tax for the same period would be due in full on 31 January 2017.

Profits withdrawn from a company by way of dividend will have the same tax payment dates as trading profits of a business with a 5 April year-end.

Profits withdrawn from a company as remuneration will bear PAYE on payment.

Any cash-flow advantage obtained on incorporation must be weighed against the tax liability due on the cessation of the partnership. Although overlap relief will be given, if profits are on a rising trend, the final tax liability could be significant.

16.8 Some reliefs are available only to companies and are denied to partnerships:

- research and development expenditure (*Corporation Tax Act 2009* ('*CTA 2009*'), *s 87*); and
- relief for the amortisation of intangible assets (although not goodwill on incorporation, as it is acquired from a related party) (*CTA 2009, Pt 8*).

16.9 Trading through a company will enable employees, management and possibly directors to be remunerated by share, option and incentive schemes. On the other hand, while admission of an employee to partnership can often be achieved with no immediate or even deferred tax cost, the awarding of shares in a company to an employee will almost always bring with it a charge either under the employment-related securities regime or under the basic employment income rules.

16.10 Partnership cars will be taxed as benefits in kind if provided by the company post-incorporation, which will almost always give a higher tax charge than any disallowance for private use in the partnership. An alternative course of action is for the directors to own the cars personally and claim relief under the authorised mileage scheme: but in many cases this will not cover the full costs of running the car. Further, a failure to transfer partnership cars to the new company may jeopardise relief under *TCGA 1992, s 162*, so the timing of the removal of the cars and their financing will require careful consideration.

Choice of cessation date

16.11 When a partnership is transferred to a limited company, the partnership ceases for tax purposes, and the provisions outlined at **4.14** apply. Overlap relief (if any) will be given against the final taxable profits.

> **Focus**
>
> The timing of the cessation will need to be considered carefully to ascertain the profit and loss profile in the closing period of the partnership and the opening year of the company. It will be necessary to consider whether:
>
> - overlap relief can be used against higher rate tax liabilities;
> - capital allowances can be claimed (see **16.15**);
> - claims for terminal loss relief can be made; incorporation amounts to a cessation for these purposes (see **9.28**); and
> - personal allowances are being wasted.
>
> It may be necessary to perform computations to a variety of dates to determine the best date for incorporation.

Stock and work in progress

16.12 Where work in progress is transferred for money or other valuable consideration to someone who intends to carry on the business and is entitled to deduct the cost as an expense, it is brought in at the amount paid or other valuable consideration given. The fact that the vendor and purchaser may be connected does not affect this. Where a partnership business is transferred to a company for consideration other than for shares, the value attributed to the work in progress in the transaction will be clear and will determine the tax treatment (even if the amount is purely nominal). Where shares form the whole or part of the consideration for the transfer of the business the position is less straightforward.

A value will need to be attached to the shares and part of that value attributed to the transfer of work in progress.

Where stock is transferred, the transfer is deemed to be at market value (since the partnership and the company are 'connected'; but the partnership and the company can jointly elect to substitute the higher of book value and the actual price paid by the company instead (*Income Tax (Trading and Other Income) Act 2005 (ITTOIA 2005), s 178(1)–(4)*; *CTA 2009, s 167(1)–(4)*). The election should be submitted with the tax return for the pre-incorporation period of trading. Where the transfer is wholly or partly in consideration of the issue of shares the position is not clear. Arguably the 'price paid by the company' strictly includes the value of the shares issued. In practice HMRC appear to accept a transfer at book value provided both the partnership and the company use the same value.

Consideration should be given to the effect of the valuation on both the partners' income tax liabilities and the company's corporation tax profits.

Losses

16.13 Unrelieved partnership losses can be carried forward on incorporation under the *Income Tax Act 2007 (ITA 2007, s 86)* provided that certain conditions are met (see **9.31**).

Capital allowances

16.14 Transfer of assets from the partnership to the company at the capital allowances written-down value (WDV) is permitted under the *Capital Allowances Act 2001* ('*CAA 2001*'), *ss 266–267* (plant and machinery) and *ss 567–570* (most other assets) (see **8.13**), so that neither balancing charges nor balancing allowances need arise. An election must be submitted with the final pre-incorporation tax return.

Since the sections are not mandatory, a balancing charge to use up trading losses or a balancing allowance to reduce assessable profits might, however, be preferable.

16.15 For plant and machinery, the capital allowances WDV at the beginning of the basis period before the transfer date is used, so that there is no apportionment of a writing-down allowance (WDA) in the tax year of transfer between the old partnership and the new company. The old partnership does not get any WDA on the assets transferred in the tax year of transfer (*CAA 2001, ss 266–267*: see **Example 8.3**).

16.16 The careful timing of incorporation may be necessary to ensure that the most advantageous result is achieved. This is particularly the case where first-year allowances are involved.

Example 16.1 – Incorporation – capital allowances

Highridge Partnership incurs considerable capital expenditure in September 2014. It prepares its accounts to 30 April 2015. It is advantageous for the partnership to claim the capital allowances.

Incorporation on 1 June 2015 should be considered. The partnership will obtain capital allowances for the year to 30 April 2015 (capital allowances are given for a period of account, not a tax year). No WDAs will be due for the one-month period to cessation, ie 1 May–31 May 2015.

Capital gains tax

16.17 The assets which usually need to be considered for the purposes of capital gains tax (CGT) are:

(a) an interest in the partnership trading premises, whether freehold or leasehold (and, in the case of farming partnerships, any attaching quota); and

(b) goodwill.

The gains on each may be substantial.

16.18 There is no charge to CGT unless the assets are actually transferred, so that premises could be retained by the partners in the shares in which they hold them as partners.

Whether it is possible for partners to retain ownership of goodwill, with the company using it under licence), is a moot point. HMRC's express view (at CG 68030) is that goodwill is not capable of being separated from the business with which it is associated, and that the disposal of a business as a going concern (including, by implication, on incorporation) must involve the transfer of goodwill. However, none of the cases cited by HMRC directly address the case of a business transferred from a partnership to a company in which the former partners continue to be involved. *Castledine v RSM Bentley Jennison* [2011] EWHC 2363 (Ch) contains a useful review of the authorities on the nature and ownership of partnership goodwill; and *Sofra Bakery* [2013] EWHC 1499 (Ch) is an example of a case where the court held that on incorporation goodwill had been retained personally and made available to the company to which the business was transferred.

Sale of assets

16.19 If the individual partnership assets (land, buildings and goodwill) are sold to the company at market value, a capital gain is likely to arise on the excess of market value over base cost. Some assets are not chargeable assets for CGT purposes, such as debtors and vehicles, so no gain arises.

In principle, Entrepreneurs' Relief (see **Chapter 13**) may be available on a disposal of partnerships assets to a company on incorporation of the partnership business. However, for disposals on or after 3 December 2014 *TCGA 1992, s 169LA* must be considered. This was inserted by the *Finance Act 2015* and amended by the *Finance Act 2016* with retrospective effect to its date of introduction. Where the legislation applies, Entrepreneurs' Relief is denied in respect of any gain on goodwill (but only goodwill: unlike the restriction on amortisation relief at the *Corporation Tax 2009, s 849B* the restriction at *s 169LA* does not extend to customer lists, trade marks and other 'relevant assets').

Relief is denied where the transferee is a close company and immediately after the disposal the transferor and any 'relevant connected person' together own 5% or more of the ordinary share capital or voting rights of the transferee or of any company in the same group as the transferee. There is, however, a carve-out to deal with the case where a partnership is transferred to a company as part of the arrangements for sale of the business as a result of which the shares in the transferee company are sold an unconnected purchasing company within 28 days of the transfer of the partnership business to the company.

16.20 The main advantage of selling the assets to the company in this way is the creation of a loan account which can be used to save tax.

Example 16.2 – Sale of goodwill

Paula and Colin are equal partners. They sell the partnership goodwill (which has no allowable cost) to a new company PC Ltd for £80,000. This creates two loan accounts credited with £40,000, which Paula and Colin can draw down. Each former partner will make a capital gain of £40,000. Following changes made by the *Finance Act 2015* entrepreneurs' relief is not due: CGT at the normal rates will be due, so a maximum (assuming no other gains in the year) of £5,780. In the first year of incorporation, the company makes a profit of £150,000, on which corporation tax at 20% amounts to £30,000, leaving a net fund to draw of £120,000. Assuming that each former partner draws all of his or her loan account and £20,000 (as a dividend), and that this is the only income for the year, tax on the dividend will be £300 so the total after-tax amount available will be £53,920.

If Paula and Colin had remained as partners, they would have paid tax and National Insurance on their 50% share of the £150,000 profits amounting to £23,082, leaving them with net cash of £51,918 (for 2016/17).

Paula and Colin are each, therefore, at least £2,002 better off in their first year of incorporation.

16.21 As a transaction between connected persons, the sale of all assets (including goodwill) must be at market value. It may be tempting, in the light of **Example 16.2**, to sell assets at an overvalue to create a larger loan account, though now that entrepreneurs' relief is not always available on goodwill the temptation to overvalue goodwill is considerably reduced. HMRC are likely to refer such cases to the Shares Valuation team, and the valuation of goodwill is a popular enquiry target. Evidence of the valuation should be retained and/or a professional valuation sought. If HMRC successfully argue that there is an overvaluation, it could be treated as a distribution or employment income.

There are various methods of valuation, depending on the type of business concerned, and an expert opinion is likely to be required to justify the valuation of goodwill on incorporation.

Section 162 relief

16.22 If the entire assets of the partnership (with the permitted exception of cash) are exchanged wholly or partly for shares in the company, gains arising on the disposal of those assets which are chargeable can wholly or partly be deferred by being deducted from the base cost of the shares received in exchange (*TCGA 1992, s 162*).

Section 162 relief depends on the whole of the business being transferred by one or more *individuals* to a company. Where the business has one or more corporate partners, the *s 162* relief applies to the individual partners, but not to the corporate partners. Each partner is treated separately.

16.23 Although no claim is required for *s 162* relief, it may be disapplied by election under *s 162A*. Such an election might be desirable where, for example, gains would be covered by the annual exemption.

16.24 Unless the entire assets except cash (non-chargeable assets as well as those which are chargeable assets for CGT) are transferred to the company, relief under *s 162* cannot apply.

Thus, not transferring partnership premises to the company would deny the relief on the transfer of goodwill which is implicit in the transfer of the trade. Cars must also be transferred or removed from the partnership prior to sale. There is, however, no requirement that liabilities must be transferred to the company.

For the relief to apply fully, the consideration must be wholly in the form of shares issued by the company. If consideration other than shares is given (such as cash or loan) partial relief can apply. The partial relief is in the proportion that the value of the shares in the new company bears to the total consideration received for the partnership assets. For this purpose, the assumption of liabilities (although consideration as a matter of law) is, by concession ESC D32, not treated as consideration for the purposes of *s 162*. Thus if all the assets and liabilities of the business are transferred, *s 162* relief is potentially due in full. One point to bear in mind, however, is that if liabilities are very large, such that the market value of shares issued is correspondingly small, it can happen that the market value of the shares is less than the amount of gain which would otherwise be deferred, so that *s 162* has to be restricted accordingly.

Example 16.3 – Incorporation – consideration partly shares, partly cash; effect of not transferring premises

Last balance sheet of partnership:

			Cost	*Now worth*
	£000		*£000*	*£000*
Capital accounts	310	Premises	150	500
		Goodwill	50	1,000
		Net current		

£000		Cost £000	Now worth £000
	Assets	100	100
	Cash balances	10	n/a (cash retained)
310		310	1,600

(i) If shares are received in consideration for the whole undertaking, whether or not the cash is transferred, there need be no CGT on premises or goodwill, since the otherwise chargeable gains can be deducted from the cost of the shares under *s 162.*

Thus, if the cash is not transferred, the value of the shares received in exchange for the entire undertaking will be £1,600,000, from which may be deducted the chargeable gains on the disposal of the goodwill and premises.

(ii) Thus, suppose that the March 1982 value of the premises is £200,000 and of the goodwill £280,000.

	Premises	*Goodwill*	*£000*
Shares received in consideration			1,600
	£000	£000	
Market value on disposal	500	1,000	
March 1982 value	(200)	(280)	
Chargeable gain held over	300	720	1,020
Shares have deemed cost of			580
Which reconciles as:			
March 1982 value			480
Current assets			100
			580

(iii) The partners may, however, be unwilling, or it may be deemed unwise, to lock in to share capital the entire business assets, including the net current assets. To do so denies the facility in future to withdraw monies for, say, taxation payments which have not been provided for in arriving at the net current assets/balances on capital accounts. Shares might therefore be received in part, with cash or loan account for the other part. Thus:

	£000
Cash (or loan account) received for	800
Shares received valued at	800
	1,600

CGT on one half of the calculated gains on the premises and goodwill is not assessed. Those gains are deducted from the base value of the shares.

CGT on the other half of the calculated gains is assessed as follows.

		Shares	*Cash or Loan account*
	£000	*£000*	*£000*
Consideration received	1,600	800	800
Chargeable gains	1,020	510	510
Shares have deemed cost of		290	
Gain			510

If the premises were retained by the vendor partners no relief would be available under *s 162* on the transfer of goodwill, regardless of whether cash, loan or shares were received it. CGT would be charged on the £720,000 gain on the goodwill. (There would obviously be no gain on the premises since there would have been no disposal, of course).

16.25 If full relief is required but net current assets other than cash are not to be locked into share capital, one possible strategy may be to withdraw the maximum possible amount from the business before the time of transfer to corporate status, financed if necessary by external debt. Some or all of the amount withdrawn could after a decent interval be introduced to the company on the directors' loan account, thus achieving the same economic effect as transferring the business partly for loan. Whether over-aggressive use of such 'round-trip' financing could or would be challenged by HMRC remains to be seen.

Example 16.4 – Effect of eliminating net current assets prior to incorporation

Partnership balance sheet figures are as at **Example 16.3** above:

	£000	*£000*	*£000*	*£000*
Capital account	310			
Premises and goodwill		200		
Net current assets			100	
Cash and bank balances				10
Arrange sufficient bank borrowing for withdrawal of	(100)		(90)	(10)
	210	200	10	–

Shares to the reduced value of £1,510,000 will now be issued in consideration of the transfer of the business as a going concern; the company opening balance sheet figures become:

	£000
Premises	500
Goodwill	1,000
Net current assets	100

Less: bank debt taken over	(90)
	1,510
Share capital and premium (in consideration of the entire net assets)	1,510
	1,510

After an interval the £90,000 withdrawn before incorporation could be re-introduced to repay bank borrowings and the balance sheet would be as below.

	£000	*£000*
Premises		500
Goodwill		1,000
Net current assets		100
		1,600
Share capital and premium (in consideration of the entire assets)		1,510
Directors' loan account		90
		1,600

The chargeable gains on the property and goodwill can be rolled over under *s 162*, as in the example above.

Disclaiming s 162 relief

16.26 Incorporation relief applies automatically if the conditions are met.

An election can be made within two years from 31 January following the tax year in which the business was transferred for *s 162* relief not to apply (*TCGA 1992, s 162A*).

Section 165 relief

16.27 Alternatively, if the consideration received for the transfer of assets is less than market value, each partner (individually) may be able to make a claim under *TCGA 1992, s 165* to hold over part of the gain otherwise arising on the transfer. Provided the consideration received does not exceed base cost, the full amount of the gain can be held over. Where the consideration received exceeds the base cost the amount of gain which can be held over is limited to the amount by which the consideration received falls short of the market value. Any election is to be made jointly by the partner concerned and the company.

16.28 One point to be borne in mind with *s 165* relief is that, unlike with *s 162* relief, the company achieves no 'step up' to market value on acquiring the asset. Thus if the asset in question is likely to be sold in the near term, *s 165* may not be the preferred strategy.

16.29 If the business gifts hold-over relief is claimed, then stamp duty or stamp duty land tax could be saved through not transferring the land and buildings to the company.

16.30 When a business is transferred to a limited company as a going concern, wholly or partly for consideration to be satisfied by shares in the company, it will usually not be possible to issue a *number* of shares corresponding exactly with that part of the consideration to be satisfied in shares, since the final value of the business will not be known until after the event. Thus, in **Example 16.3** it would not have been possible before the event to know the amount of the current assets (£100,000) and hence the total consideration (£1,600,000). The value of the assets in excess of the nominal value of the shares issued in consideration is therefore dealt with by the company through a share premium account.

Partnership annuities

16.31 The capitalised value of an annuity paid by continuing partners to a retired partner is not regarded, in the hands of the recipient, as consideration for CGT purposes, so long as its amount is within the limits set out in Statement of Practice D12 (see **Chapter 14**).

When a company acquires the business of a partnership, it would be usual for the company to assume responsibility for the continuing payment of annuities to partners already retired, to whom the present partners have an existing obligation, and also for the payment of annuities in the future to which the present partners would have been entitled under the partnership agreement. The handing on of such existing or future obligations to the company is part of the consideration received by the partners who incorporate.

Following an exchange of correspondence between the Tax Faculty of the ICAEW and the Revenue (see ICAEW Technical Release TAX 7/95), the taxation effect can be summarised as follows.

16.32 Where the business is transferred wholly or partly in exchange for shares, so that *TCGA 1992, s 162* applies to defer the chargeable gains on the disposal of the partnership assets by reducing the acquisition cost of the shares, the taking over by the company of the obligation to pay *existing* annuities falls within ESC D32 (see **16.24**) and is not regarded, for the purposes of *s 162*, as consideration.

16.33 Where the liability taken on by the company is for the payment of *future* annuities to *present* partners, for which there is no existing liability, the future obligation *would* restrict the calculation of *s 162* relief.

16.34 Where *s 165* applies, the assumption of liabilities to pay annuities (whether existing or future obligations) represents actual consideration received and would produce a gain by reference to the value of the liability

The payment of the annuities by the company is deductible as an annual charge in calculating corporation tax liabilities.

Loan interest

16.35 It may happen, on a partnership being transferred to a company, that loans made by partners to the partnership are taken over by the company.

To the extent that the former partners had borrowed in order to loan money to the partnership, they will normally have been entitled to tax relief against total income for any interest paid (*ITA 2007, s 398*). By virtue of *s 410* interest relief continues to be available as long as the loan would have qualified had it been taken out for lending money to the company.

Inheritance tax

16.36 The transfer of a partnership business to a company will not normally be a transfer of value for the purposes of inheritance tax. It will not normally reduce the value of any individual's estate and furthermore there will normally be no gratuitous intent. However, it may nonetheless have IHT consequences insofar as it may affect business property relief under *IHTA 1984, s104*.

Partners can claim business property relief at 100% in respect of transfers of their interests in the partnership (including deemed transfers on death), and at 50% in respect of transfers of assets (such as premises) that are owned personally and used in the partnership business. Where personally owned property is used by a company, the 50% business property relief is available only to a controlling shareholder, and no relief is available at all for assets owned personally by minority shareholders. (Shares of husband and wife, and civil partners, are related property, and the available rate of relief is determined by their joint holdings.)

Value added tax

16.37 The closing down of the old partnership VAT registration, and registration by the company, must not be overlooked.

As to the transfer of assets from the one to the other, there will not generally be any VAT implications so long as both are VAT registered (or register as a result of the transfer) and the business is transferred as a going concern (*Value Added Tax Act 1994 (VATA 1994), s 49*; *Value Added Tax Regulations 1995 (SI 1995/2518), reg 6(1)*; *leaflet 700/9*). In those circumstances, it will usually be possible for the VAT registration number of the partnership to be transferred to the company, if desired.

Practical issues to consider on incorporation

16.38 The following practical issues also need attending to when changing from a partnership to a limited company:

- Form the limited company; check the availability of the intended name; complete all statutory matters.

- Order new stationery.
- Draw up the contract of sale/transfer, shareholder agreements and directors' service agreements (if appropriate).
- Advise banks and set up new accounts.
- Notify hire purchase, leasing companies and financiers and change agreements.
- Notify customers and suppliers.
- Change entries in trade and telephone directories and on the Internet.
- Transfer the title to property or notify landlords.
- Notify rating authorities. Consider the impact on transitional relief for the uniform business rate.
- Transfer insurance cover.
- Check the transferability of farm quotas.
- Advise HMRC for VAT purposes (see **16.37**).
- Notify HMRC of the cessation of the partnership and the incorporation of the company for tax purposes.
- Close down the accounting records of the partnership. Keep all records for five years from 31 January following the end of the tax year in which the cessation occurred.
- Set up new accounting systems for the company.
- The partners should cease to pay Class 2 National Insurance contributions, unless they have other self-employment (irrelevant from April 2018).
- Partnerships operating in the construction industry will require a new gross payments certificate (see **Chapter 29**).
- Ensure that directors' benefits in kind (eg cars) are being taxed correctly.
- Reorganise or set up pension schemes.
- Set up share schemes and management incentives.
- Transfer the PAYE scheme from the partnership to the company.
- Give employees a notice of continuity of employment (*Transfer of Undertakings (Protection of Employment) Regulations 2006, SI 2006/246*).

Chapter 17

Partnerships which include a Corporate Partner and Service Companies

Signposts

- Where a company is a member of the partnership, its taxable profit is based on a computation using corporation tax rules (see **17.1 – 17.3** and **17.7 – 17.10**).
- Where annual interest is paid by a partnership which has a corporate member, tax is by default deductible at source (see **17.4 – 17.6**).
- Special rules apply to 'mixed member' partnerships from 6 April 2014, under which all or part of the profit share of certain corporate partners may be taxed on individual members (see **17.11 – 17.17**).
- There are some restrictions on the use of losses by corporate partners (see **17.18 – 17.20**).
- The *Finance Act 2014* introduced provisions to counter the use of mixed partnerships in creating tax losses for individual members (see **17.21 – 17.23**).
- Where all the members of a partnership are liable to corporation tax, the partnership return should contain details of the partnership's income from all sources for the accounting period covered by the tax return (see **17.24 – 17.29**).
- Partnership service companies are often run alongside a partnership as a means of accumulating profits at a lower rate of tax to fund partnership working capital, but there are some issues to be aware of (see **17.30 – 17.34**).

17.1 A company can be:

- a partner in an ordinary partnership;
- a limited or a general partner in a limited partnership. A limited partnership must have at least one general partner with unlimited liability, though the general partner can itself by a limited liability company (or indeed an LLP);
- a member of a limited liability partnership.

17.2 Where a partnership includes both corporate and individual partners, at least two sets of partnership statements will usually be required: one based on income tax rules, and the other on corporation tax rules. The profit shares for corporate partners will be allocated using the set based on corporation tax principles; the profit shares for individuals will be allocated using the set based on income tax rules. If there would be no difference in the profit computation, only one statement may be required. On the other hand, if non-resident partners are involved, up to four sets of computations may be required.

Note that under current legislation, where a partnership includes a company which is liable to income tax (such as, for example, a non-UK resident company partner in a firm which carries on a UK property business) the profit share of that company is calculated as if the company were an individual. This is clearly anomalous and was identified as such in the Consultation Document 'Partnership taxation: proposals to clarify tax treatment' which was issued in August 2016. Following responses to the Consultation Document, the Government has confirmed an intention to legislate to provide that instead the profit share will be calculated using the rules which would apply if the non-UK resident company was itself carrying on the business. The most obvious effect of this is to remove from such companies the restriction on relief for the costs of a 'dwelling-related loan' imposed by *ITTOIA 2005, s 272A* though there are doubtless also other consequences. The legislative change is itself subject to the outcome of the consultation on 'Non-resident companies chargeable to income tax and non-resident capital gains tax' of March 2017.

Money debts of a partnership

17.3 As stated above, a corporate partner's share of taxable profit is computed by first computing partnership profits using corporation tax rules and then allocating to the corporate partner the appropriate share of the profit so computed.

However, in computing partnership profit no account is taken of any debits or credits which relate to 'money debts' of the partnership (*CTA 2009, s 380*). The normal definition of 'money debt' at *CTA 2009, s 303* applies so this includes among other things any debt which falls to be settled by the payment of money (including therefore any trading debt). Instead, each corporate partner brings into account its share of relevant debits or credits.

For this purpose, the legislation deems that any money debt which is owed by or to the partnership is to be treated as if it were instead owed by or to the corporate partner for the purposes of the trade or business that it carries on, and that everything done by the partnership in relation to the debt has been done by the company (*CTA 2009, s 381*). The corporate partner then computes the debits and credits that arise from applying the loan relationship rules to this deemed situation and brings into account the appropriate proportion of the gross debits and gross credits based on their interest in the partnership.

HMRC's view is that, if the company and the partnership have different accounting dates, or the company and the partnership account in different currencies, the company should imagine itself standing in the shoes of the partnership. There is no reason to pretend that the partnership does not exist. Neither is there any reason to substitute the company's own accounting date or currency for that of the partnership (Corporate Finance Manual at CFM36100).

Where a corporate partner has a loan relationship with the partnership, it will be treated as both creditor and as debtor and will need to bring in both credits (as lender) and its share of the partnerships debits arising from the relationship (or vice versa if it is the borrower under the relationship). Where the corporate partner controls the partnership, either alone or taken together with one or more other company partners connected with it, it may be necessary to adjust the debits and credits under the rules applying to connected party relationships.

Interest paid by a partnership with one or corporate partners

17.4 A partnership of which a company is a member is obliged to deduct basic rate income tax from payments of yearly interest (*Income Tax Act 2007* ('*ITA 2007*'), *s 874*), annual payments and patent royalties (*s 898*), and similar payments. There is however no obligation to deduct tax paid by such a partnership to a company, provided that, at the time that the payment is made, the partnership reasonably believes that the company meets certain conditions (*ITA 2007, Pt 15, Ch 11*).

17.5 The conditions most likely to be encountered are where the payment is made to:

- a UK-resident company;
- a company not resident in the UK which carries on its UK trade through a permanent establishment and the payment is brought into account in computing its UK chargeable profits;
- a local authority;
- a charity;
- a registered pension scheme; or
- a partnership each of whose members qualifies under one of the preceding headings,

17.6 Where the paying partnership is mistaken in its belief that the recipient meets the conditions, it is required to account for the tax which should have been deducted. Further, if the partnership's mistake is considered to have been careless, penalties will be eligible. A partnership should therefore be very cautious in relying on the exemption and should make such enquiries as are necessary and prudent to confirm the position.

Profits

17.7 The company's profit share, share of capital allowances/balancing charges and its charges on income are treated as if the company were carrying on a separate trade of its own. The company includes the relevant amounts in calculating the corporation taxable profits of its own accounting period, apportioning over two periods if its accounting period does not coincide with that of the partnership. For example, if the company has an accounting date of 31 December 2014 and the partnership has a year end of 31 May, it will include in its corporation tax return for 2014 5/12ths of the partnership profit for the year ended 31 May 2014 and 7/12ths of the partnership profit for the year ended 31 May 2015.

17.8 The total shares allocated to individual partners are treated as if they were the profits of a normal partnership of individuals (or, if there is only one individual partner, as if he or she were a sole trader) and self-assessed on the current year basis of assessment. If a loss arises to the individual partners, relief is available in the normal way.

17.9 Having a corporate partner in an accounting year when profits form the basis of assessment for more than one income tax year will not make any difference to the profits potentially taxable on the business, although the share applicable to the corporate partner will reduce those taxable on the individual partners at the outset, with a compensating reduction in overlap relief to be given in the future.

Example 17.1 – Corporate partner – effect on individual partners' self-assessments

First 12 months of partnership of individuals to 30 April 2014, profits £12,000:

		£
2013/14	11/12 × 12,000	11,000
2014/15	Year to 30.4.14	12,000
Potential overlap relief on cessation or change of accounting date		(11,000)
Total potentially taxed profits		12,000

If there is a limited company partner which takes £6,000 of the profit, the assessments become:

	£	£
Profits in accounting year	12,000	
Exclude corporate member's share assessed to corporation tax	6,000	6,000
Leaving for assessment on individual(s)	6,000	
2013/14 11/12 × 6,000	5,500	
2014/15 Year to 30.4.14	6,000	
Potential overlap relief on cessation or change of accounting date	(5,500)	6,000
Total potentially taxed profits		12,000

17.10 **Example 17.2** illustrates some of the issues further.

Example 17.2 – Partnership with corporate member – division of assessable profits

A. The John Brown Partnership carries on a UK trade. Its partners are John Brown Limited, Harpers Stores Limited and Robert Lee. The first £80,000 profit is allocated to Robert Lee and the remaining profits are shared:

- John Brown Limited: 51%
- Harpers Stores Limited: 45%
- Robert Lee: 4%.

The partnership and the two companies were established many years ago and all prepare their accounts to 30 June.

B. For the partnership's accounting period to 30 June 2013, the tax-adjusted profit was £2,080,000. For the year to 30 June 2014, the tax-adjusted profit was £2,350,000.

C. On 1 July 2013 the partnership admitted George Sherman, the partnership agreement providing for a prior charge share of profits for Sherman of £40,000 plus 2% of profits, with Harpers Stores Ltd's share of profits reducing to 43%.

D. The division between the partners of the taxable profit for the year to 30 June 2013 is:

	Total	*John Brown Limited*	*Harpers Stores Limited*	*Robert Lee*
	£	£	£	£
First allocation	80,000			80,000
Share of balance (51:45:4)	2,000,000	1,020,000	900,000	80,000
	2,080,000	1,020,000	900,000	160,000

The profit shares of each company will be incorporated in profits chargeable to corporation tax for the year to 30 June 2013.

E. Robert Lee's profits will be taxed in 2013/14.

F. The division of profits between the partners for the year to 30 June 2014 is:

	Total	*John Brown Limited*	*Harpers Stores Limited*	*Robert Lee*	*George Sherman*
	£	£	£	£	£
First allocation	120,000			80,000	40,000
Share of balance (51:43:4:2)	2,230,000	1,137,300	958,900	89,200	44,600
	2,350,000	1,137,300	958,900	169,200	84,600

The profit shares of the companies will be incorporated in the profits chargeable to corporation tax for the year to 30 June 2014.

Robert Lee's profit share is taxed in 2014/15.

George Sherman's profits for 2013/14 (1 July 2013 to 5 April 2014) are £84,600 × 280/366 = £64,721. The profits for 2014/15 will be £84,600. He will carry forward overlap profits of £64,721.

Mixed member partnerships

17.11 Historically it has been attractive in some cases to combine the tax-efficiency of a company with the flexibility of a partnership by introducing to a partnership of individuals a corporate member in which the individual members have an interest. HMRC's increasing unease at such arrangements culminated in legislation which came into force from 6 April 2014 (subject to certain anti-avoidance rules, which came into force on 5 December 2013) which applies in cases where some members of a partnership are individuals and some are 'non-individuals' – so-called 'mixed member' partnerships. The most common example of a 'non-individual' member is a company and the following paragraphs address this case; but the legislation may also apply, for example, to structures where the 'non-individual' member is a trust. Where it applies, the legislation provides that in certain circumstances the profit share of a 'non-individual' member will be treated as if it were income of an individual member or members (or even in some cases individuals who are not members). It applies to partnerships of all kinds including LLPs. Where income of a corporate member is reallocated to an individual member for tax purposes, *CTA 2009, s1264A* provides that such adjustments as are just and reasonable are made in computing the corporate member's taxable profit.

Note that the legislation falls under the self-assessment regime: it is not for HMRC to identify and apply the situations in which profits are reallocated: partnerships must do this on their own initiative and potentially risk penalties if they fail to apply the legislation because of carelessness or deliberate failure.

The legislation cannot apply where individual members and corporate members are genuinely independent, acting at arm's length and not intending to defer profits or secure a tax advantage.

17.12 In order for the anti-avoidance provisions to apply, one of two alternative conditions (X and Y) must be satisfied (*ITTOIA 2005, s 850C*). Where both conditions are fulfilled, any adjustment is primarily made under the rules for Condition X and any 'Condition X' adjustment is then deducted in making any 'Condition Y' adjustment.

Condition X (*ITTOIA 2005, s 850C(2)*) is that it is 'reasonable to suppose' that amounts representing the 'deferred profit' of an individual member are included in the company's profit share and in consequence the tax is less than it would have been. Where this is the case, so much of the company's profit share as it is reasonable to suppose is attributable to an individual member's 'deferred profit' is treated as income of the individual and not of the company.

An amount is 'deferred profit' of an individual A if it is 'any remuneration or other benefits or returns the provision of which to A has been deferred (whether pending the meeting of any conditions (including conditions which may never be met) or otherwise)' and it includes 'A's share (as determined on a just and reasonable basis) of any remuneration or other benefits or returns the provision of which to A and one or more other persons, taken together, has been deferred (whether pending the meeting of any conditions (including conditions which may never be met) or otherwise).'

Thus A's deferred profit may include a share of profits earmarked for a group of individuals of which he is a member. The fact that A's participation in the earmarked profits is not certain does not prevent their being his 'deferred profit'.

What is 'reasonable to suppose' in particular circumstances is a question of fact. An outcome does not need to be certain; on the other hand one which is improbable should be ignored.

Example 17.3 – Deferred profit

Jones and his team, all members of a professional partnership, are responsible for successful delivery of a potentially very profitable project. Because it is a long-term project, a share of partnership profit is allocated to a corporate member on the understanding that it will be paid out as dividend or bonus to Jones and his team only if they are still with the firm three years later. Jones' share of the profit is expected to be £50,000.

On these facts, it is likely that it will be 'reasonable to suppose' that £50,000 represents Jones' deferred profit. That amount will be taxed on him (and not on the corporate member).

Note that there will be no retrospective adjustment of the charge even in if the event Jones leaves the partnership within three years and actually receives nothing. As to avoiding a double charge on the dividend or bonus if it is in fact paid out, see below.

17.13 *Condition Y* (*ITTOIA 2005, s 850C(3)*) is that the corporate member's profit share exceeds the 'appropriate notional profit'; an individual member or members have 'power to enjoy' those profits; it is reasonable to suppose that the allocation of profits is attributable to that power; and the individual member's profit share and the tax chargeable are both less than they would have been but for the individual's power to enjoy those profits.

The appropriate notional profit is the aggregate of the 'appropriate notional return on capital' and the 'appropriate notional consideration for services' (*ITTOIA 2005, s 850C(10)*).

The appropriate notional return on capital is the return at a commercial rate of interest on the amount which the company has contributed to the partnership as capital (*ITTOIA 2005, s 850C(11)*). For this purpose the definition at *ITA 2007, s 108* is imported. Thus:

- capital is the 'permanent endowment' of the firm;
- capital does not include amounts due on current account;
- undrawn profits are not capital unless they have been added to the 'permanent endowment' by agreement between the members;
- any amount which the member is entitled to withdraw during the lifetime of the partnership is disregarded, as is any amount which the corporate member may require someone else to reimburse. Only 'capital at risk' may be taken into account.

What is a 'commercial rate of interest' depends on all the circumstances and must reflect the level of risk involved. HMRC assert that the rate must be 'reasonable' and assert that 'it is not relevant that an equity return on the same investment might have been much greater'. They suggest that the rate paid by the partnership on money it borrows on the commercial market will determine the 'commercial rate of interest' but this is simplistic, even where such commercial borrowing exists. Commercial borrowing will usually be secured, repayable over an agreed term and will rank ahead of partnership capital. Permanent capital has by definition no fixed repayment date, is unsecured and ranks behind all other creditors; so will reasonably carry a risk premium which, dependent on the nature of the business, may be very considerable. The best estimate of a 'commercial rate of interest' may perhaps be obtained by inviting a bank to quote for finance on the terms that the bank will not get its money back until the business ceases, has no security and ranks behind all other creditors. The rate offered is unlikely to be the 2% suggested in HMRC's guidance!

The 'appropriate notional consideration for services' is the arm's length remuneration for services provided (*ITTOIA 2005, s 850C(15)*), but excluding any services the provision of which involves any partner in the firm (eg services provided via a partner's ownership of the company). In many cases, and in particular where the company is being used either as a 'money box' or as a conduit to route partnership profits tax-efficiently to members of the partnership or their family, there will be little or no appropriate notional profit and the bulk of the corporate member's profit share will be reallocated. An exception would be where the corporate member is making available to the partnership an asset for which it is receiving no other consideration. For example, a corporate member of a farming partnership may own the land on which the trade is conducted and may make this available to the partnership rent-free. An 'appropriate notional consideration for services' would then be an amount of profit share equal to the rental value of the land.

17.14 An individual member is treated as having 'power to enjoy' the profit share of any corporate member with which he or she is connected (other than by being in partnership with the corporate member, of course), but the legislation (*s 850C(18)*) goes much wider than that. The rules are in fact closely based on the 'power to enjoy' test as it is applied for the transfer of assets abroad legislation at *ITA 2007, s 723*. Hence, the 'enjoyment conditions' are satisfied where the profits of the corporate enure to the benefit of the individual, enhance the value of the individual's assets, benefit the individual or where the individual can control the application of the company's profit share. In all cases, the enjoyment conditions are also satisfied if any of these factors apply in relation to persons connected with the individual.

Further, the 'enjoyment conditions' will be satisfied if the individual is a party to arrangements the main purpose, or one of the main purposes, of which is to secure that an amount included in the corporate's profit share is charged to corporation tax rather than income tax (or is otherwise subject to the provisions of the Corporation Tax Acts rather than the provisions of the Income Tax Acts) (*ITTOIA 2005, s 850C(18)(b)*).

17.15 The next question to be asked in *Condition Y* cases is whether it is 'reasonable to suppose' that any part of the company's profit share is attributable to the power of an individual member to enjoy it; if the answer is yes, that part is treated as taxable income of the individual and not of the company. However, the amount reallocated in this way cannot be greater than the excess of the company's profit share over the 'appropriate notional profit' after deducting the amount (if any) already reallocated under Condition X.

In many cases the answer to the question will be obvious. If Mr A and his company A Ltd are in partnership, it will usually be evident that any share of profit allocated to A Ltd will be attributable to Mr A's power to enjoy the income of A Ltd, in the sense that if A Ltd had not been Mr A's company no share of profit would have been allocated to it.

Example 17.4 – Profit share attributable to power to enjoy

Smith is a member of a partnership taking 40% of the profits. By agreement with other members Smith Ltd (a company which is owned by Mrs Smith) is admitted to the partnership. Smith Ltd introduces no capital and provides no services to the partnership. Smith's share of profits reduces to 20% and Smith Ltd takes 20%.

Smith Ltd's appropriate notional profit is nil. Smith has the power to enjoy the profits of Smith Ltd (because he is connected with it). It is reasonable to suppose that the whole of Smith Ltd's profit share is attributable to Smith's power to enjoy it. And but for the mixed member rules the arrangement would reduce the amount of tax payable. Smith Ltd's share of profit is therefore treated as Smith's income.

In other cases, although an individual member has the 'power to enjoy' the profit share of a corporate member, the profit share of the corporate member will not as a matter of fact be attributable to that power and the mixed member rules will not apply.

Example 17.5 – Profit share not attributable to power to enjoy

Dafydd is a member of a partnership. His sister Sîan owns a company Sîan Ltd which is also a member of the partnership. Sîan works full-time for the partnership, proving her services through her company and the share of profit allocated to her company properly reflects the value of that work.

Although Dafydd has 'power to enjoy' the profit share of Sîan Ltd (because he is connected with it) the profits allocated to the company are plainly attributable not to that power but to the genuine work undertaken by Sîan. No part of the company's profit share is therefore taxable on Dafydd.

(Note that on these facts, the profit share of Sîan Ltd does not exceed the 'appropriate notional consideration for services' so there is in any event no excess profit share to be reallocated.)

17.16 *ITTOIA 2005, s 850D* is an anti-avoidance provision which extends the mixed member rules to cover the case where the individual is not in fact a member of the partnership but it is reasonable to suppose that he or she would have been a member but for the existence of the mixed member rules.

The most obvious example is where X, Y and Z together with their respective money-box companies X Ltd, Y Ltd and Z Ltd are in partnership at the time at which the mixed member rules were introduced. Realising that the arrangement is caught by the new rules such that each member is chargeable to tax on the profits of his or her company, X, Y and Z now resign from the partnership, leaving only the companies. In such a case it is clear that the individuals would have been members 'but for' the new rules: the result is that the taxable profits of the companies will continue to be reallocated to the individuals.

Without prejudice to the generality of the phrase, it is in particular 'reasonable to suppose' that an individual A would have been a member of a partnership P1 if A is a member of a partnership P2 which is 'associated' with P1. For this purpose a partnership P2 is 'associated' with a partnership P1 if P2 is a member of P1 or if P2 is a member of a third partnership which is a member of P1 (and so on through as many chains as exist).

It is a question of fact whether in any particular case it is 'reasonable to suppose' that an individual would have been a member of a particular partnership 'but for' the existence of the mixed member rules. Where individuals ceased to be members before the mixed member rules were announced on 5 December 2013, HMRC accept that the cessation cannot as a matter of fact have been attributable to an attempt to circumvent the new rules so the anti-avoidance rule cannot apply. Similarly, where there is clear evidence to show that the decision was made before 5 December but the actual cessation of membership took place on or after 5 December (perhaps because of the need to give notice of resignation from the partnership) the anti-avoidance rules cannot apply.

Equally, where there is no reason to suppose that individuals would personally have been members even if the 'mixed member' rules had never been enacted, it is difficult to see how the anti-avoidance provisions can apply.

Example 17.6 – Anti-avoidance

For many years the members of Accountants LLP have all been companies, each owned by a separate individual who provides his or her services to the LLP via his or her company. This is not a 'mixed member' partnership. Furthermore it is not reasonable to suppose that any of the individuals would have been members but for the existence of the mixed member rules (since they were not members before the mixed member rules existed). The partnership is therefore not within the scope of the anti-avoidance rule.

In April 2017, a new person joins the partnership and to align with the existing structure he, like the existing members, provides his services via a company. Again, it is not reasonable to suppose that the new person would have been a member 'but for' the mixed member rules and he, too, is outwith the scope of the anti-avoidance provision.

17.17 Where the whole or part of the profit share which has in fact been received by a corporate member has been taxed as income of an individual, it would be obviously unreasonable for tax to be charged again when that income is distributed to the individual by the company. There is accordingly a relieving provision at *ITTOIA 2005, s 850E* addressing the case. However, the legislation is far from perfect and is interpreted by HMRC very strictly, leading to pitfalls for the unwary and potentially to double or even triple taxation.

The legislation provides relief where:

- there is an agreement in place in relation to the excess part of the corporate member's profit share;
- as a result of the agreement, the corporate member makes a payment to another person out of the excess part of its profit share; and
- the payment is not made under any arrangements the main purpose, or one of the main purposes, of which is the obtaining of a tax advantage for any person.

The relief is given by providing that payment is not to be:

- income of the recipient;
- taken into account in calculating any profits or losses of the corporate member or otherwise deducted from any income of the corporate member; or
- regarded as a distribution.

The legislation sets out no specific form for the 'agreement' but it is desirable that it should be in writing.

Relief is available only if the payment is made 'as a result of the agreement'. Whether this is the case is a question of fact. Plainly, a payment made before any agreement is entered into cannot as a matter of fact be made 'as a result of the agreement'. This may present a difficulty if a distribution has already been made before the potential application of the mixed member rules has been identified either by the company or by HMRC on enquiry.

Difficulties may also arise if by the time the question of the possible application of the mixed member rules is considered the profits in question are no longer available to be distributed. This may be the case where, for example, the corporate member has used the profit share to fund pension contributions for the individual concerned.

Where there is a single payment which is in excess of the reallocated profit share, no relief will be due. HMRC's view is that such a payment is not itself made 'out of' the profit share, and there is no machinery by which part of the payment can be deemed to be so paid.

Relief is due only in respect of a payment made directly by the corporate member. For example, if the corporate member is a subsidiary and it pays a dividend to its parent, which in turn makes a payment to the individual member, the payment from the parent cannot qualify for relief.

Example 17.7 – Relief for distribution

The members of P LLP are A, B and A Ltd (a company which their spouses own in equal shares). A Ltd provides capital to P LLP and its profit share is considered by A and B to be no more than a commercial rate of return on the capital having regard to the risk attaching to the capital. A Ltd includes its share of profit on its corporation tax returns and pays tax on it. The bulk of the profits of A Ltd are paid out annually as dividend to Mrs A and Mrs B, who pay tax on the dividends.

After a prolonged investigation it is agreed that A Ltd's profit share does in fact exceed a commercial rate of return on its capital. The excess falls to be treated as income of A and B.

There is in these circumstances no scope for giving relief under *ITTOIA 2005, s 850E* to Mrs A and Mrs B. The dividends will remain taxable since they are plainly not paid 'as a result of' an agreement to pay out the reallocated profit share. Furthermore, it is questionable whether the company will meet the requirements to be able to claim overpayment relief under *FA 1998, Sch 18*. It will certainly not do so if the decision is reached later than four years after the end of the company's relevant accounting period.

Losses

17.18 Any tax loss resulting from the partnership's trade is allocated between partners in accordance with the terms of the partnership agreement. Subject to the following special rules, the loss can be utilised by a corporate partner in the same way as any other trading loss, namely by set-off against total profits (*CTA 2010, s 37*) by carry forward against subsequent profits from the same trade (*CTA 2010, s 45*) or (where relevant) by surrender as group relief (*CTA 2010, Pt 5*). Similarly any share of a loss in respect of the partnership's UK property business is set off against total income of the same period or to the extent that this does not utilise the loss carried forward for set-off (*CTA 2010, s 62*); or may be available as group relief.

The extent to which losses may be set-off against total income or surrendered as group relief is restricted in the case of a company which is a limited partner (or in substance a limited partner – see *CTA 2010, s 58*) or a member of an LLP. In each case the aggregate amount of loss for a company's accounting period which may be set off or surrendered is restricted to the amount of the 'company's contribution' to the partnership or LLP as at the end of the period. Where the company and the partnership use the same accounting date, the company's contribution should be apparent from the partnership balance sheet. Where the dates differ, a separate computation will be needed.

Note that these provisions, like the equivalent income tax provisions for individual partners, apply only to trades and have no application to professions or to investment businesses (including property businesses).

Surprisingly, the definition of the 'company's contribution' is slightly different according to whether the limited partnership rules or the LLP rules apply. For details in each case, see **Chapter 18** regarding Limited Partnerships and **Chapter 19** regarding LLPs.

17.19 There are anti-avoidance provisions preventing a corporate partner obtaining relief for trading losses and charges, other than against its share of profits of the trade carried on by the partnership, where there are arrangements in existence whereby such losses or charges are transferred for consideration between the partners or those connected with them (*Corporation Tax Act 2010 (CTA 2010), s 959*). These rules are designed to counter particular avoidance schemes aimed at using partnerships to transfer losses from one company to another in order to circumvent the stringent rules for entitlement to group relief by groups and consortia.

> **Focus**
>
> In *Hamilton & Kinneil (Archerfield Ltd) & Ors* [2014] TC 03485, the appellants argued that support for their interpretation that the legislation was directed in essence at the amount which the company had at risk in the LLP rather than the amount actually contributed was the explanatory notes *to CTA 2010, s 59* and *CTA 2010, s 60*, which make it clear that the purpose of the legislation was to tie loss relief to corporate members to 'the amount the company has at risk'. However, the tribunal found that this did not alter the aspect of the former *Income and Corporation Taxes Act 1988 (ICTA 1988), s 118ZC* under consideration in this appeal and *CTA 2010, ss 59–60* were not intended to effect a change in the legislation in this respect.

17.20 Problems can arise where a company shares in a trading loss of a partnership but then ceases to be a partner without that loss having been relieved against its other corporate profits (using the normal set-off rules of *CTA 2010, s 37* including the extension for terminal losses). Since the remaining loss will be available only against profits of the partnership trade (in which the company no longer has any interest) relief for it will effectively be lost.

Trade loss relief: excess loss allocation to partners who are individuals

17.21 The rules restricting trade loss relief for certain partners are contained in *ITA 2007, Pt 4, Ch 3* (see **Chapter 9**). *FA 2014* introduced a specific restriction aimed at marketed schemes, typically involving a partnership with a corporate member. Specifically, *ITA 2007, s 116A* provides that 'relevant' loss relief is not available where an individual (A) makes a loss in a trade as a partner in a firm, and the loss arises, wholly or partly:

(a) directly or indirectly in consequence of; or

(b) otherwise in connection with

relevant tax avoidance arrangements.

For these purposes, 'relevant tax avoidance arrangements' means arrangements:

(a) to which A is party; and

(b) the main purpose, or one of the main purposes, of which is to secure that losses of a trade are allocated, or otherwise arise, in whole or in part to A, rather than a person who is not an individual, with a view to A obtaining relevant loss relief.

'Relevant loss relief' means:

(a) sideways relief;

(b) carry-forward trade loss relief (*ITA 2007, s 83*);

(c) terminal trade loss relief (*ITA 2007, s 89*); or

(d) capital gains relief.

17.22 A similar provision appears in *ITA 2007, s 127C* restricting loss relief in the same way in respect of UK or overseas property businesses.

17.23 For the treatment of foreign-resident corporate partners, see **Chapter 20**.

Returns

17.24 Where all the members of a partnership are liable to corporation tax (a 'CT Partnership'), the partnership return should contain details of the partnership's income from all sources for the accounting period covered by the tax return. The requirement that 'taxed' income should be returned on a tax year basis does not apply to a CT Partnership. Previously, notes to the partnership return indicated that a CT Partnership should in all cases supply accounts and computations (ie, in the same way as a partnership with turnover in excess of £15,000,000). For 2016/17, the notes have changed: they now specify that 'you should supply the same particulars, accounts and tax computations and fill in the same pages and boxes as for a partnership which has members who are individuals'.

17.25 Where the partnership carries on an investment business and it has a member liable to corporation tax, the partnership will need to calculate the amount of management expenses it has incurred and allocate a share of the expenses to the relevant partners. Where this situation occurs, computations should be provided in the additional information box on the return.

17.26 If the partnership has profits or gains from non-trading loan relationships, exchange fluctuations or financial instruments and one or more members of the partnership are liable to corporation tax, the profits or gains arising from the loan relationship will need to be calculated and allocated to the partners. The computation of profits or gains should be set out in the additional information box on the return.

17.27 If the partnership is a shipping business and any partner is a tonnage tax company, the partnership must complete form CT 600F as if the whole partnership were a tonnage tax company. The form must accompany the partnership tax return. (Instead of being taxed on their shipping profits, tonnage tax companies may choose to be taxed on their tonnage tax profits, calculated by reference to the tonnage of ships operated by the company.)

17.28 Where the partner is a company, the address provided on the return should be its registered office.

17.29 If a partnership contains a company, the filing date for the return cannot be earlier than nine months from the end of the 'relevant period' (for a paper return) or 12 months from the end of the 'relevant period' (for an electronic return) *(TMA 1970, s 12AA(5), (5A),(5B))*.

For a discussion on what this means in practice, see **21.10**.

Service companies

17.30 Partnership service companies that are run alongside a partnership may be an attractive means of accumulating profits at a lower rate of tax to fund partnership working capital. Such a structure gives partners the best of both trading mediums.

> **Focus**
>
> Typically, a service company would employ the partnership's staff, own the premises and generally provide the partnership with administrative services. It is acceptable for a modest mark-up to be applied to the cost of services to recognise, for example, the funding cost and the risk borne. But an excessive mark-up is likely to see the excess disallowed. (see *Stephenson v Payne, Stone, Fraser & Co* (1967) 44 TC 507).

17.31 There are a number of potential tax problems which may arise out of running a service company alongside a partnership.

17.32 Service companies will almost inevitably be close companies, and the consequences of making loans to participators should not be underestimated. Also, attention needs to be paid to the deemed distribution provisions regarding benefits provided to partners.

Both these issues were considered in *Grant v Watton (Inspector of Taxes) and related cases* [1999] STC 330. G was an estate agent. He formed a company of which he was director and controlling shareholder. The company provided services to the estate agency in return for a management fee. There was no written agreement for the services. The Revenue assessed the estate agency (pre-self-assessment) under the former *ICTA 1988, s 160(1)* (now *Income Tax (Earnings and Pensions) Act 2003, Pt 3, Ch 7*) on the basis that G had received a loan in the form of credit from the company. They also assessed the company under former *ICTA 1988, s 419* (now *CTA 2010, s 455*) on the basis that it had made a loan to G as a participator. G and the company lost their appeal against the assessments at the Special Commissioners and appealed to the High Court.

The High Court noted that there was no agreement governing the time when G was to pay for the company's services. The two businesses simply maintained a running account between them. The case therefore hinged on whether these informal arrangements amounted to the provision of credit. It was found that, as a question of fact, the company did provide credit to G and the appeals were dismissed. The lack of a formal agreement stipulating the terms on which services were to be provided and paid for was fatal.

17.33 The problem may not, however, be as serious as it first appears. A charge under *CTA 2010, s 455* only arises nine months after the end of the accounting period. Provided that the credit is paid off by that time, no *s 455* liability arises. And if the credit given is no longer than six months and does not exceed the credit normally given to the company's customers the loan is excluded from *s 455* altogether by *s 456(2)*. Having an agreement providing for monthly payment for the services should reduce the scope for an HMRC challenge in the event of an enquiry. Care must also be taken to ensure that adequate disclosure of the transactions is made on the self-assessment returns to prevent later discovery assessments.

17.34 Where the business is sufficiently substantial to fall within the transfer pricing rules at the *Taxation (International and Other Provisions) Act, s 2010 Pt 4)* (which, despite the title, can apply to purely domestic transactions) care must be taken to avoid *s 174A*. The effect of this provision, introduced to counter and indeed penalise a widely-used avoidance device, is that where a service company under-charges for the services provided to the partnership, the transfer pricing rules will tax the company on the market value of the services, but the partnership will be denied the benefit of a 'compensating adjustment' under *s 174*, thus creating a potential double charge to tax.

Chapter 18

Limited Partnerships

Signposts

- There are various circumstances in which a limited partnership may be the most appropriate trading vehicle (see **18.1**).
- Many limited partnerships will also be 'qualifying partnerships' required to file accounts at Companies House (see **18.2**).
- General partnership law is modified in several respects as regards limited partnerships (see **18.3**).
- Limited partners self-assess their share of partnership profits in the same way as general partners (see **18.4 – 18.6**).
- There are significant restrictions on the way in which limited partners can obtain relief for partnership losses (see **18.7 – 18.9**) or for interest on borrowed money (see **18.10**).
- Restrictions on tax relief for pension contributions need careful consideration (see **18.11**).

18.1 A limited partnership may be attractive where limited liability is sought without the attendant obligation of making the business accounts public, though in many cases such confidentiality is illusory (see **18.2**). Limited partnerships are registered with the Registrar of Companies and governed by the *Limited Partnerships Act 1907* (see **Appendix 2**).

HMRC's Business Income Manual at BIM82101 et seq provides further background information about the legal requirements of a limited partnership.

> **Focus**
>
> A limited partnership is typically attractive to:
>
> - investors contributing capital to a partnership without a desire to be involved with its management;
> - venture capital investment vehicles.
>
> It may also be of interest in specific cases such as:
>
> - a partner who wishes to retire but whose association with the partnership business is important to those continuing.

18.2 A limited partnership is not automatically required to file accounts at Companies House. However, most limited partnerships will in practice be 'qualifying partnerships' and will as such be required to file accounts by reason of *The Partnerships (Accounts) Regulations 2008*. This is because in determining whether a partnership is a 'qualifying partnership' within the meaning of the regulations limited partners are ignored and only general partners are considered. In many cases the only general partners (and therefore the only partners taken into account for the purposes of the regulations) will be companies, with the result that limited partnership will fall to be treated as a qualifying partnership. For further detail on *The Partnership (Accounts) Regulations 2008*, see **1.41**.

18.3 A limited partnership enables an individual's liability to be limited to his or her agreed capital contribution. In return, he or she is not permitted to not take part in the management of the partnership business or bind the firm. If this prohibition is broken for any period of time, the partner becomes liable for all debts and obligations of the firm incurred during that period to the same extent as if a general partner. Furthermore, a limited partner is not able to withdraw capital from the firm for so long as he or she remains a limited partner. If capital is withdrawn, the limited partner becomes liable for the debts and obligations of the firm, up to the amount of capital withdrawn.

There must always be at least one general partner with unlimited liability. But it is perfectly acceptable for the general partner itself to be a limited liability company, giving in effect a limit on the liability for all parties involved in the partnership. See **Chapter 17** for the general tax treatment of partnerships between individuals and companies.

However, although the point has not been tested in the courts, the prohibition on taking part in the management of the partnership business would be likely to extend to involvement via directorship of a general partner. Thus in **Example 18.1**, if Mr or Mrs Jones were to be a director of Kingsclere Limited it is likely that they would lose their limited liability status.

The law as it applies to partnerships is specifically modified in a number of areas in its application to Limited Partnerships so as to recognise the status of the Limited Partner as, in effect, an investor in the business rather than an executive of it. In particular:

(a) A limited partnership is not automatically dissolved by the death or bankruptcy of a limited partner.

(b) On dissolution of a limited partnership its affairs shall be wound up by the general partners unless the court otherwise orders.

(c) Subject to any agreement expressed or implied between the partners:

- any difference arising as to ordinary matters connected with the partnership business may be decided by a majority of the general partners;
- a limited partner may, with the consent of the general partners, assign his share in the partnership, and upon such an assignment the assignee shall become a limited partner with all the rights of the assignor;
- the other partners shall not be entitled to dissolve the partnership by reason of any limited partner suffering his share to be charged for his separate debt;
- a person may be introduced as a partner without the consent of the existing limited partners;
- a limited partner shall not be entitled to dissolve the partnership by notice.

Limited partnerships are not allowed to use the cash basis and simplified expenses regime, which took effect from 2013/14 (see **1.45**).

Example 18.1—Limited partnership of Mr and Mrs Jones and Kingsclere Ltd

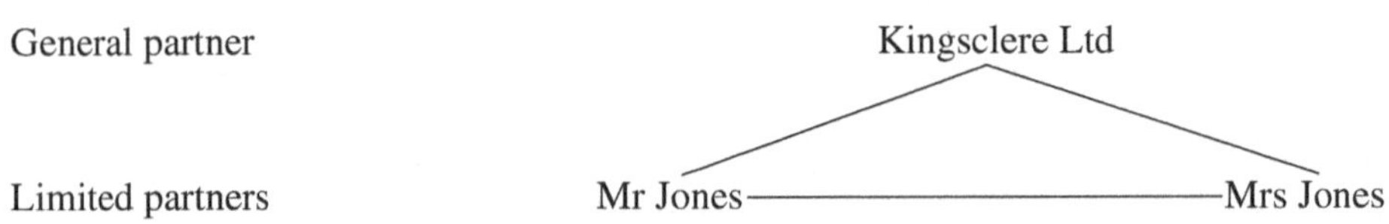

The general partner with unlimited liability for the partnership's liabilities is Kingsclere Ltd. The limited partners are Mr and Mrs Jones, who are also the members and directors of the company.

The general partner manages the firm's business. The limited partners have no rights to take part in the management of the firm.

For the status of a limited partner in relation to National Insurance Contributions ('NICs') before and after 2013/14, see **Chapter 24,** and in relation to pensions see **Chapter 22**.

Taxation of income and gains of limited partnerships

18.4 There are no special rules on the taxation of income or of capital gains of Limited Partnerships.

Limited partners self-assess their share of partnership profits in the same way as general partners. See **Chapters 2, 3,** and **4** regarding the current year basis of assessment and the allocation of profits. The share of profits attributable to a limited company is dealt with under the corporation tax rules as illustrated in **Chapter 17**.

18.5 Similarly, a limited partner who is entitled to share in asset surpluses is taxed on the corresponding share of any chargeable gain of the partnership in the same way as in an ordinary partnership (see **Chapter 12**). Where on the disposal of an asset by a limited partnership a loss arises the normal treatment of partnership losses by reference to the shares in asset surpluses at the time of disposal (see **Chapter 12** and SP D12) would on the face of it apply. However, where the status of limited partners results in their actually suffering a loss which is smaller than the CGT loss (or no loss at all) it seems likely that HMRC may seek to argue, following *Aberdeen Construction Group Ltd v CIR* [1978] STC 127 that CGT is intended to 'tax capital gains and to make allowance for capital losses, each of which ought to be arrived at on normal business principles' and deny relief to the extent that losses allocated to limited partners on that basis are in fact borne by others.

18.6 Other CGT reliefs for partners apply indiscriminately to limited as to ordinary partnerships. In particular a limited partner who meets the statutory conditions may claim roll-over relief on the replacement of business assets, hold-over relief on a gift of business assets or entrepreneurs' relief on a gain on the disposal of qualifying assets, active management of or involvement in the partnership business not being a requirement for any of these reliefs.

Tax relief for trading losses of limited partners

18.7 There are significant restrictions on the amount of trade loss relief available to limited partners to set against their other income and gains ('sideways loss relief'). These restrictions apply not only to limited partners in Limited Partnerships registered under the *Limited Partnership Act 1907* but also to partners in equivalent partnerships formed under the law of an overseas country and to individuals who in substance act as limited partners (that is, who are excluded from management of the firm and are protected or indemnified in respect of exposure to unlimited liability).

The complexity (and indeed the existence) of the restrictions owes much to the ubiquity of Limited Partnership arrangements in artificial tax avoidance arrangements: unfortunately they contain for the most part no motive test and their application is not restricted to tax avoidance arrangements.

The restrictions apply only in regard to 'sideways relief' and do not restrict relief against income derived from the same trade, whether of earlier or later years. Nor do they apply to losses arising from a profession or an investment activity, but only to trading losses. Where relief for a trading loss is given against the general income of another chargeable period which includes both trading income and non-trading income, relief is deemed to be given first against trading income from the same trade.

The reliefs in question are as follows.

For individuals (*Income Tax Act 2007* (*'ITA 2007'*), *s 104*):

(a) deduction of trading losses from general income under *ITA 2007, s 64*;

(b) relief for trading losses against capital gains under the *Taxation of Chargeable Gains Act 1992, s 261B*;

(c) relief for losses in first four years of trade under *ITA 2007, s 72*.

For companies (*Corporation Tax Act 2010* (*'CTA 2010'*), *s 56*):

(a) relief for trading losses against total profits under *CTA 2010, s 37*;

(b) group relief for trading losses under *CTA 2010, s 98*.

18.8 In each case the cumulative amount on which relief may be given must not at any time exceed the partner's 'capital contribution to the firm' as at the end of the basis period.

The 'contribution to the LLP' is defined to be:

- the amount that the member has contributed to the firm as capital;

  less

- any 'withdrawn capital';

  less

- (in the case of an individual but not a company) any contribution where the financial cost of making the contribution may not be borne by the partner personally; or which (broadly) is financed by limited-recourse or other 'soft' loans; or the main purpose of which is to obtain sideways tax relief;

  plus

- the amount of the partner's share of undrawn profits.

For this purpose, 'withdrawn capital' at any time is defined as the aggregate of any amounts which the individual:

- has previously drawn out or received back;
- draws out or receives back in the following five years;
- is or may be entitled to draw out or receive back at any time when the individual is a member of the LLP;
- is or may be entitled to require another person to reimburse to them.

In each case, amounts count as 'drawn out or received back' whether this is done directly or indirectly; but amounts which are chargeable to income tax as trading profits are excluded.

Where relief is given which proves excessive because of subsequent withdrawals (ie, under the second bullet point above) relief is withdrawn as appropriate. However, since this is possible only by virtue of the usual 'discovery' provisions to which the normal time limits apply it is at least questionable whether (in the absence of carelessness or deliberate understatement) relief could in fact be withdrawn later than four years after the end of the year of assessment concerned.

For individuals (but not companies) *ITA 2007, s 103C* applies a further restriction (applied after the restriction under *s 104*) which limits the amount which may be given for a loss arising in any tax year to £25,000: for further details see **Chapter 9**.

Finally, loss relief may further be restricted for individuals by the rule introduced by the *Finance Act 2013*. This rule is not specific to limited partners or to trading losses but generally limits the total of the various deductions at 'Step 2' of the computation of taxable income to the greater of £50,000 and 25% of adjusted total income for the tax year.

Focus

The amount of loss relief claimable by an individual limited partner is limited to the amount of the capital contribution made by the partner concerned to the partnership. A further restriction is then applied limiting the amount to a maximum of £25,000 (*ITA 2007, s 103C*).

Example 18.2 – Restrictions on losses

Joan commences as a partner in a limited partnership in 2012/13. Accounts are drawn to 5 April annually. She invests capital in the partnership as follows:

2012/13: £5,000
2013/14: £10,000

She takes no drawings, and her shares of the adjusted trading results are as follows:

2012/13: £10,000
2013/14: £11,000
2014/15: (£40,000)

Joan has other income of:

2011/12: £6,000
2012/13: £4,000
2013/14: £9,000
2014/15: £25,000

Her loss claim at 5 April 2015 is restricted to her capital contribution £36,000 as follows. And the total amount of the 2014/15 loss which can be relieved using 'sideways reliefs' over all years is further limited to £25,000:

Capital introduced	£15,000 (£5,000 + £10,000)
Profits	£21,000 (£10,000 + £11,000)
	£36,000

Year	*Claim under*	*Available loss*	*Maximum Relief*	*Loss remaining*
		£	*£*	*£*
2011/12	s 72	36,000	6,000	30.000
2012/13	s 72	30,000	4,000	26,000
2013/14	s 72	26,000	9,000	17,000
2014/15	s 64	17,000	17,000	

The cap of £25,000 means that relief could be claimed under *s 72* for the first three years in an aggregate amount of £19,000, leaving £6,000 to be claimed under *s 64* for 2014/15: or the full £25,000 could be claimed under *s 64* for 2014/15, with no *s 72* claim. In either case, £15,000 of loss (£40,000 – £25,000) will be available for carry forward under *ITA 2007, s 83*.

Trade or profession

18.9 The distinction between a trade and profession – previously a historical anachronism – is relevant for determining the loss relief available to a limited partner. The position is far from clear-cut.

'Trade' is defined in the legislation as including 'any venture in the nature of trade' (*ITA 2007, s 989*). 'Profession or vocation' is not defined and, therefore, whether a particular activity can be treated as a profession is a question of fact to be decided by the courts. The value of the case law is debatable since most of it dates from World War I when the relevance of trade or profession was in point for excess profits duty.

In *IR Commrs v Maxse* (1930) 12 TC 41, Scrutton LJ said that a profession:

> '… involves the idea of an occupation requiring either purely intellectual skill, or if any manual skill, as in painting and sculpture or surgery, skill controlled by the intellectual skill of the operator, as distinguished from an occupation which is substantially the production, or sale, or arrangements for the production or sale of commodities.'

The distinction between the exercise of intellectual skill (profession) and commercial operations (trading) is hard to determine in today's business environment where quasi-professional training and formal qualifications are increasingly features of many businesses which might previously have been thought to be manual trades. **Appendix 5** includes a list of some relevant cases.

Borrowing to provide for funds for capital or loan introduction

18.10 Where a limited partner borrows to buy a share in a partnership, contribute money to it as capital or premium or advance money to it (or to repay a loan taken out for any of those purposes) the relief for interest which would otherwise be available under *ITA 2007, s 398* is denied by *ITA 2007, s 399(2)*. However, no similar restriction applies to relief under *s 388* (relief for interest on loans taken to acquire plant or machinery for partnership use).

Pension contributions

18.11 In order for a taxpayer's profit share to qualify as relevant earnings for the purpose of pension contributions, the *Finance Act 2004, s 189(2)* requires the income to be 'immediately derived from the carrying on or exercise of a trade, profession or vocation (whether individually or as a partner *acting personally* in a partnership)'. Thus a limited partner's share of partnership income will not qualify. Given that the income is, as we have seen, now regarded by HMRC as liable to National Insurance Contributions it seems harsh and illogical to deny it the status of relevant earnings: but that appears to be HMRC's current stance. For a limited partner with no other relevant earnings, personal pension contributions qualifying for tax relief will therefore be limited to just £3,600 a year.

Inheritance tax

18.12 Inheritance tax makes no distinction between limited partners and general partners or partners in an ordinary partnership, so that reliefs such as business property relief and agricultural property relief are available in the normal way (see **Chapter 23** and **Appendix 5**).

VAT

18.13 For the special VAT rules governing the registration of limited partnerships for VAT purposes and the exposure of limited partners to VAT liabilities see **Chapter 26**.

Chapter 19

Limited Liability Partnerships

Signposts

- Although introduced to meet the perceived need of the professions for a limited liability vehicle, LLPs are widely used in commerce (see **19.1**).
- In legal form bodies corporate, LLPs are for most tax purposes treated as if they were partnerships (see **19.2 – 19.7**).
- The main benefit of operating through an LLP is that the members obtain limited liability though there are other advantages (see **19.8 – 19.12**) and some disadvantages (see **19.13**).
- A member's share of trading losses is available for tax relief in the usual way but there are significant restrictions on the use of LLP losses (see **19.14 – 19.18**).
- Interest relief (see **19.19**) and relief for double taxation (see **19.20**) are available to members of LLPs in broadly the same way as to partners in a partnership.
- For CGT purposes an LLP has the same transparency as a partnership but care should be taken in regard to the circumstances in which transparency ceases and the consequences of cessation (see **19.22 – 19.24**).
- Unlike a partnership, an LLP can be a member of a VAT group (see **19.25 – 19.26**).
- Special rules may apply to property investment LLPs and investment LLPs (see **19.27**).
- The main difficulties with converting to an LLP are likely to be administrative and organisational, though a number of detailed factors must be addressed (see **19.28 – 19.46**).
- Legislative changes from 6 April 2014 mean that in some cases a salaried member of an LLP will be deemed to be employed by their LLP for tax and NIC (see **19.47 – 19.54**).
- A list of practical issues worth considering when forming an LLP is included at **19.55**.

19.1 Limited liability partnerships ('LLPs') are regulated by the *Limited Liability Partnerships Act 2000* (*LLPA 2000*) and associated regulations, the *Limited Liability Partnerships Regulations 2001* (*SI 2001/1090*) ('*LLPR 2001*') (see **Appendix 3**).

LLPA 2000 applies in England, Wales and Scotland. Although originally introduced under pressure from the professions and expected to be used mainly by professional partnerships, they can be and are used widely for all kinds of business. LLPs were introduced in Northern Ireland in November 2004, with the *Limited Liability Partnerships (Forms) Regulations (Northern Ireland) 2004 (SI 2004/398)* implementing the *Limited Liability Partnerships Act (Northern Ireland) 2002*.

19.2 LLPs are in law bodies corporate and are subject to aspects of company and insolvency law. However, *ITTOIA, s 863* provides that for income tax purposes if an LLP carries on a trade, profession or vocation with a view to profit:

- all the activities of the limited liability partnership are treated as carried on in partnership by its members (and not by the limited liability partnership as such);
- anything done by, to or in relation to the limited liability partnership for the purposes of, or in connection with, any of its activities is treated as done by, to or in relation to the members as partners; and
- the property of the limited liability partnership is treated as held by the members as partnership property.

Similarly, *TCGA 1992, s 59A* provides that where a limited liability partnership carries on a trade or business with a view to profit:

- assets held by the limited liability partnership are treated for the purposes of tax in respect of chargeable gains as held by its members as partners;
- any dealings by the limited liability partnership are treated for those purposes as dealings by its members in partnership (and not by the limited liability partnership as such); and
- tax in respect of chargeable gains accruing to the members of the limited liability partnership on the disposal of any of its assets shall be assessed and charged on them separately.

This treatment continues even after the LLP ceases to carry on any trade, profession or business with a view to profit:

- if the cessation is only temporary; or
- during a period of winding up following a permanent cessation, provided the winding up is not for reasons connected in whole or in part with the avoidance of tax, and the period of winding up is not unreasonably prolonged.

But the commencement of a formal liquidation by the appointment of a liquidator always brings the tax-transparency of an LLP to an end, with the CGT consequences outlined at **19.22** below.

Furthermore, in some circumstances the tax transparency of property investment LLPs is removed (see **19.27** below)

19.3 Thus, unless otherwise provided, the same rules apply to an LLP as to an ordinary partnership. In particular:

- Changes in the composition of an LLP are subject to the usual partnership taxation rules. There will be a cessation only if one would occur in a similar situation in an ordinary partnership (see **Chapter 5**).
- The same cessation and commencement provisions apply to mergers or demergers of LLPs as to ordinary partnerships (see **Chapter 7**).
- Individual members of an LLP are treated in the same way as partners in an ordinary partnership and are liable to Class 2 and Class 4 NICs (*LLPA 2000, s 13*; *Social Security Contributions and Benefits Act 1992, s 15(3A)*).
- Statement of Practice D12 applies to LLPs meeting the requirements of *TCGA 1992, s 59A(1)* in the same way as it applies to other partnerships. For further details, see **Chapters 12** and **13**.
- The administrative rules in the *Taxes Management Act 1970* and elsewhere relating to partnerships and partners apply equally to LLPs and their members.
- Profits and losses of an LLP are allocated between and taxed or relieved on members of an LLP in accordance with the profit-sharing terms of the LLP agreement.
- Taxable profits are computed in accordance with UK GAAP. Cash basis is not available to LLPs.
- For inheritance tax purposes, the members of an LLP are treated as if they were partners in an ordinary partnership (*IHTA 1984, s 267A*, inserted by *LLPA 2000, s 11*). Therefore, the normal inheritance tax provisions apply to lifetime transfers or transfers on death. Reliefs such as business and agricultural property relief apply. Exemptions will also be available, such as *IHTA 1984, s 10*, which provides an exemption for disposals not intended to confer gratuitous benefit.

19.4 The LLP structure is an attractive trading medium for the large firms of accountants, solicitors, architects, consulting engineers and other professionals concerned about the size of claims against them. Forming an LLP should also be seriously considered by new businesses.

19.5 The use of an LLP is not restricted to the professions and it is available to 'two or more persons associated for carrying on a lawful business with a view to profit'. The profit motive means that they are not available to charities or not-for-profit organisations. Furthermore, specific anti-avoidance rules apply to investment LLPs (see **19.27**).

19.6 Unlike a 1907 limited partnership, there is no requirement for an LLP to have one general partner, there is no restriction on the partners' involvement in management, and there is no limit on the maximum number of partners.

19.7 *LLPA 2000* applies only to UK-registered LLPs. A UK branch of an overseas LLP may be taxed either as a company or a partnership but not as an LLP. UK-registered LLPs trading overseas will be taxed according to the tax regime in the relevant country. This may mean that, in some countries, they will be taxed as corporations.

Advantages and disadvantages of the LLP structure

Advantages

19.8 The main benefit of operating through an LLP is that the members obtain limited liability. In a partnership, the partners are personally liable not only for their share of the firm's obligations but for all of its debts to the full extent of their assets. If some partners cannot pay, all the other partners are liable.

19.9 Because an LLP is a separate legal person, a member is not personally or jointly liable for the LLP's debts, and all contracts are between the LLP and its clients or third parties. If the LLP becomes insolvent, a member's personal liability is limited to the amount of their agreed capital contribution plus the value of any personal guarantee. No member is jointly and severally liable for any loss arising from the wrongful acts or omissions of his or her fellow members if they were operating in the ordinary course of the LLP's business, or with the authority of the other members.

19.10 Where negligence is involved, members may still be liable to the full extent of their assets if they have assumed personal responsibility for the advice or work. An LLP could also be liable to the client on the same basis. This risk can be mitigated by correctly worded documents and agreements, and by ensuring that members never take personal responsibility for work or advice. Using the correct terminology is vital. *LLPA 2000* refers to 'members' and not partners, so all LLP documents must use the word 'members' and not 'partners' or 'firm', to prevent limited liability status from being jeopardised. Adequate insurance cover will still be required.

19.11 A member's liability risk in an LLP is a considerable improvement on the situation in a partnership where, in a case of negligence, all the partners are liable to meet the claim on the same basis. For the LLP members, the position is like owning shares in a company. They risk the value of their capital contribution becoming worthless, but their homes and assets are not at risk unless the member is negligent or they have given a personal guarantee. In a disaster scenario, the members will not be worse off than they would have been in an ordinary partnership.

19.12 Some further advantages of operating through an LLP are set out below.

- Unless the 'disguised employment' rules apply from 6 April 2014 (see **19.47**), the members of the LLP are taxed as if they were partners and not employees (or directors) (*LLPA 2000, s 4(4)*). They are therefore not liable to pay PAYE or Class 1 NICs. Distributions (drawings) are not taxed as they would be from a company.
- There is no minimum capital requirement.
- LLPs have unlimited capacity and can enter into contracts and hold property in the same way as an individual (*LLPA 2000, s 1*).
- The LLP has a legal personality separate from that of its members. Its existence continues in spite of changes in its members, meaning that there is no need, for example, to transfer legal title to property on a change of membership.

- It may be easier to recruit new members. Unlimited liability can be a disincentive to many talented people accepting partnership.
- Unlike a 1907 limited partnership, there is no requirement to have one general partner with unlimited liability.

Disadvantages

19.13 The benefits of limited liability combined with a favourable tax treatment should not be underestimated, but they come at a price: increased disclosure. Some disadvantages of operating as an LLP are set out below. The pros and cons should be compared with incorporation (see **Chapter 16**). In most cases, an LLP will be attractive to those who would have formed a partnership rather than a limited company but who ultimately seek the benefit of limited liability.

- There will be costs to set up the LLP (see **19.55**) and ongoing filing fees (see www.companieshouse.gov.uk). The administrative costs in notifying clients and suppliers and transferring bank accounts, leases and agreements should not be underestimated.
- Corporate-type accounts have to be prepared, circulated to each member and filed on a public register within nine months of its year end. A confirmation statement (previously annual return) must be filed annually using form LL CS01.
- The accounts must comply with UK generally accepted accounting principles and with the specific requirements of the relevant LLP regulations (the Limited Liability Partnerships, Partnerships and Groups (Accounts and Audit) (Application of Companies Act 2006) Regulations 2008 (SI 2008/1911); the *Small Limited Liability Partnerships (Accounts) Regulations 2008 (SI 2008/1912)* and the *Large and Medium-sized Limited Liability Partnerships (Accounts) Regulations 2008 (SI 2008/1913)*, as amended from time to time. The regulations were most recently amended by the *Limited Liability Partnerships, Partnerships and Groups (Accounts and Audit) Regulations 2016 (SI 2016/575)*. The regulations are supplemented by the Statement of Recommended Practice ('SORP') issued by the CCAB, the most recent edition of which was issued on 26 January 2017 and is effective for accounting periods beginning on or after 1 January 2016.
- An LLP's accounts are exempt from the requirement to be audited if the LLP is small, ie (for accounting periods beginning on or after 1 January 2016) if it meets at least two of the following conditions: annual turnover is no more than £10.2m the balance sheet total (total assets) no more than £5.1m or 50 or fewer employees on average. An audit will nonetheless be required if the LLP is an authorised insurance company, a banking LLP, an e-money Issuer, a MiFID (Markets in Financial Instruments Directive) investment firm or a UCITS (Undertakings for Collective Instruments in Transferable Securities) management company or is a parent or a subsidiary (unless the LLP is a dormant subsidiary or in a small group). Note that for financial years commencing before 1 January 2016 lower turnover and balance sheet thresholds applied.
- The SORP requires loans and debts due to members (the equivalent of partnership current accounts), to be shown as a liability rather than as part of capital alongside

the partnership capital accounts. This reduces the LLP's net worth and may affect its credit rating and borrowing capacity.

- Where the LLP's profit before members' remuneration exceeds £200,000, there is a duty to report the amount of profit attributable to the highest paid member (but not their name). Other disclosure includes total members' remuneration, total members, average members' remuneration and related party transactions.
- The LLP is regulated in the same way as a limited company and there is more administration than operating through a partnership. For example, membership changes must be notified to the registrar within 14 days (*LLPA 2000, s 9*), and members' home addresses must be notified to Companies House though they do not appear on public file. There is, however, no requirement to hold an AGM.
- The wrongful trading provisions in the *Insolvency Act 1986* apply. Members may be liable to contribute to the LLP's assets if it is wound up and they knew or ought to have known that the firm was insolvent and they failed to take appropriate action. Furthermore, as a result of a provision specifically applied to LLPs, a liquidator may claw back any funds withdrawn by a member (including drawings) in the two-year period leading up to the firm's liquidation, if at the time of the withdrawal, the member knew or ought to have known that the firm could not pay its debts.
- Regular management accounts may be required to rebut any claim of wrongful trading.
- Bankers and creditors may require overdrafts and loans to be renegotiated. They may require fixed and floating charges over debtors and work in progress, or personal guarantees.
- Particularly in the more traditional professions, there may be some remaining reluctance on the part of clients to contract with a limited liability vehicle.
- Some people may lament the loss of the 'partnership spirit' and personal client relationship.
- Tax relief for losses in trading LLPs is restricted (see **19.15**).
- There is no scope for share incentives for staff as there is with a company.
- Anti-avoidance provisions apply to investment property and investment LLPs (see **19.27**).
- Anti-avoidance provisions may apply to 'disguised employment' situations from 6 April 2014 (see **19.48**).

Losses

19.14 The basic rule is that an individual member of an LLP will be entitled to claim loss relief in respect of the share of loss in the usual way. Relief may be claimed by carry-forward against income from the same business in future years (*ITA 2007, s 83*) and (in the case of cessation) terminal loss relief (*s 89*). In addition (or alternatively) a claim may be made for any of the so-called 'sideways reliefs' namely:

- relief against total income for the tax year of the loss or the previous year *(ITA 2007, s 64);*

- 'early years' relief allowing losses made in any of the first four years of business to be carried back against for the income of the preceding three years (*ITA 2007, s 72*);
- relief against capital gains (*TCGA 1992, s 261B*).

Note, however, that from 6 April 2013, *ITA 2007, s 24A* imposes a cap to certain previously unlimited income tax reliefs that may be deducted from income under *s 24*. The cap is set at £50,000 or 25% of income, whichever is greater. Relief under *ss 64* and *72* are affected by this new cap, as indeed is the relief available for interest paid on a loan taken to invest in a partnership or to buy machinery or plant for partnership use.

For losses claimable by corporate members of an LLP, see **Chapter 17**.

Restriction of relief for trading losses of LLP

19.15 Restrictions apply to tax relief for losses arising from trading. It is important to appreciate that these restrictions do not apply to losses which arise from the carrying on of a profession or an investment business. Where the provisions are engaged, the cumulative amount of sideways loss relief for an individual member is restricted (by *ITA 2007, s 107*) to the individual's 'contribution to the LLP' as at the end of the basis period for the relevant tax year. Similar provisions apply to restrict the ability of a company to claim relief under *CTA 2010, s 37* (relief against total profits) or to surrender losses as group relief – see **Chapter 17**.

The 'contribution to the LLP' is defined by *s 108* to be:

- the amount that the member has contributed to the LLP as capital;

  less

- any 'withdrawn capital';

  less

- any contribution where the financial cost of making the contribution may not be borne by the partner personally, or which (broadly) is financed by limited-recourse or other 'soft' loans;

  plus

- the amount of the member's liability on a winding-up, defined as the amount which the member is liable (under the terms of the LLP agreement) to contribute to the assets of the LLP in the event of it being wound up and remains liable to contribute for a period of at least five years beginning with the time at which the amount of the individual's contribution is being calculated (or until it is wound up, if that happens before the end of that period).

For this purpose, 'withdrawn capital' at any time is defined as the aggregate of any amounts which the individual:

- has previously drawn out or received back;

- draws out or receives back in the following five years;
- is or may be entitled to draw out or receive back at any time when the individual is a member of the LLP;
- is or may be entitled to require another person to reimburse to them.

In each case, amounts count as 'drawn out or received back' whether this done directly or indirectly; but amounts which are chargeable to income tax as trading profits are excluded.

Where relief is given which proves excessive because of subsequent withdrawals (ie, under the second bullet point above) relief is withdrawn as appropriate. However, since this is possible only by virtue of the usual 'discovery' provisions to which the normal time limits apply it is at least questionable whether (in the absence of carelessness or deliberate understatement) relief could in fact be withdrawn later than four years after the end of the year of assessment concerned.

In an LLP, the undrawn profits cannot normally be added to the member's subscribed capital because the undrawn profit is generally regarded as a debt of the LLP. However, if the agreement between the members unconditionally and specifically provides that the undrawn profit is part of the member's capital contribution, then the amount can be taken into account.

19.16 Where a member makes a capital contribution to meet a liability for negligence for which he or she is personally responsible, that amount will be taken into account for the purposes of *ITA 2007, s 108*.

Where loss relief has been restricted to the member's capital contribution, relief may be obtained for the balance of the loss by making further capital contributions in later tax years (*ITA 2007, s 109*).

The member is entitled, provided that the conditions for the relief are otherwise met, to relief of up to a maximum of the amount of the additional contribution under the normal sideways loss relief provisions.

Interaction with loss restrictions for non-active members

19.17 For the first four years of trading, losses available to non-active members are restricted by *ITA 2007, s 110*. Where a loss is potentially affected both by *s 107* and by *s 110: s 110* applies and *s 107* does not. Sideways reliefs for non-active members of LLPs may also be restricted under *ITA 2007, s 103C* For detail of both these loss restrictions see **Chapter 9**.

Example 19.1 – Limited liability partnership – losses

Matthew becomes a member of a trading LLP on 6 April 2012 and introduces capital of £100,000. During the year to 5 April 2015, he makes a further capital contribution of £60,000.

His shares of the LLP's losses are as follows:

Year ended 5 April 2013	£60,000
Year ended 5 April 2014	£60,000
Year ended 5 April 2015	£30,000

Matthew is entitled to relief under *ITA 2007, s 64* as follows:

2012/13	£60,000	Unrelieved capital contribution £40,000
2013/14	£40,000	Restricted to capital contribution. £20,000 carried forward
2014/15	£50,000	Loss for year plus loss brought forward

On 6 April 2015, there are unrelieved capital contributions carried forward of £10,000 (capital contributions £160,000 less relief given £150,000).

Trade or profession

19.18 As indicated above, the distinction between a trade and profession – previously a historical anachronism – is relevant for determining the loss relief available to a member of an LLP. The position is far from clear-cut.

'Trade' is defined in the legislation as including 'any venture in the nature of trade' (*ITA 2007, s 989*). 'Profession or vocation' is not defined and, therefore, whether a particular activity can be treated as a profession is a question of fact to be decided by the courts. The value of the case law is debatable since most of it dates from World War I when the relevance of trade or profession was in point for excess profits duty.

In *IR Commrs v Maxse* (1930) 12 TC 41, Scrutton LJ said that a profession:

> '… involves the idea of an occupation requiring either purely intellectual skill, or if any manual skill, as in painting and sculpture or surgery, skill controlled by the intellectual skill of the operator, as distinguished from an occupation which is substantially the production, or sale, or arrangements for the production or sale of commodities.'

The distinction between the exercise of intellectual skill (profession) and commercial operations (trading) is hard to determine in today's business environment where quasi-professional training and formal qualifications are increasingly features of many businesses which might previously have been thought to be manual trades. **Appendix 5** includes a list of some relevant cases.

Interest relief

19.19 Interest relief under *ITA 2007, ss 388* and *s398* will be available provided that the member otherwise meets the conditions for the relief, though this will be subject to the cap imposed by *ITA 2007, s 24A* (see **19.14**). Relief is not, however, available where the LLP is an 'investment LLP' – see **19.27**.

Double tax relief

19.20 Where an overseas tax authority regards a foreign branch of a UK LLP as a body corporate, the UK members will be entitled to claim tax credit relief in respect of their share of the foreign tax paid.

19.21 The members of an LLP, but not the LLP itself, are entitled to relief for any withholding tax on overseas dividends. No relief will be given in respect of taxes paid on the profits out of which the dividend is paid (the underlying taxes), unless the LLP is treated as a body corporate for tax, for example if it is in liquidation.

Capital gains tax

19.22 For CGT purposes an LLP is generally treated in the same way as an ordinary partnership (see Chapter **12**). The exception is where an LLP ceases to be transparent for tax purposes. The most common circumstance in which this will happen is if a liquidator is appointed, but this will also apply if an informal winding-up after permanent cessation of trade is unreasonably prolonged or tainted by tax avoidance – see *TCGA 1992, s 59A*. Thereafter the LLP will be treated for CGT purposes as if it were a company rather than as a partnership. This does not retrospectively affect the treatment of gains made before the liquidation, but any chargeable gains arising on disposals of assets after the commencement of the liquidation etc are computed as if the LLP had never been treated as a partnership. There is however no rebasing on the change of status: the now-opaque LLP is simply treated as having acquired any chargeable assets held at the date of change at the same time and for the same consideration as it actually historically acquired them.

Where business assets roll-over relief has been claimed by rolling over a gain into a share of an asset owned by an LLP, there are special rules to prevent the asset falling out of charge where the LLP cease to be transparent. This would otherwise occur where the replacement assets continue to be owned by the LLP when it goes into liquidation and vest in the liquidator who will compute the gain without reference to any past roll-over relief claims made by the individual members.

In this situation, a tax liability (based on an amount equal to the postponed gain which has not come into charge) will arise on the member when *s 59A* ceases to apply (*TCGA 1992, s 156A*).

19.23 Similar provisions apply to ensure that gains deferred on the gift of business assets under *TCGA 1992, s 165*, or under *TCGA 1992, s 260*, do not fall out of charge when *s 59A* ceases to apply and tax-transparency is lost (*TCGA 1992, s 169A*).

On and from liquidation etc the interest which each of the members has in the LLP as a member (as distinct from as a creditor, eg in respect of undrawn share of profit) is treated in the same way as a shareholding in a company, the acquisition cost of which is the amount of capital subscribed. Hence the realisation of assets by an LLP which is in liquidation can give rise both to gains subject to corporation tax at the LLP level and gains subject to CGT in the hands of members when distributed by the LLP (to the extent that the share of proceeds exceeds the capital contributed by the members).

19.24 The deemed transfers by close companies under the provisions in *IHTA 1984, s 94* cannot apply to an LLP, since any deemed transfer of value is made by the members and not the LLP itself (*Inheritance Tax Act 1984 (IHTA 1984), s 267A*, inserted by *LLPA 2000, s 11*).

VAT

19.25 The LLP is a corporate body and it, rather than its individual members, is liable to register for VAT, subject to the usual rules.

19.26 An LLP can join a VAT group, provided it meets the control conditions in the *Value Added Tax Act 1994, s 43A*.

Investment property and investment LLPs

19.27 To prevent LLPs from being used for purposes for which they were not intended, *FA 2001, s 76* and *Sch 25* included anti-avoidance provisions aimed at property investment LLPs and investment LLPs. The anti-avoidance provisions provide for a two-pronged attack:

- The first of the measures prevents pension funds and other exempt bodies such as insurance companies or friendly societies from obtaining a tax advantage by investing in property through an LLP. If such a company invests in property through an LLP, it will receive a profit share on which tax has not been paid in the LLP and will not be paid in the hands of the exempt body. (Contrast this with a similar investment in a company, where distributions are made out of already taxed income.) Therefore, where a pension fund (or similar body) invests in a *property investment LLP*, it loses its income tax and CGT exemption on receipts from the LLP (*TCGA 1992, s 271(12)*).
- The second measure provides that interest on a loan to buy a share in an *investment LLP* is not eligible for tax relief under *ITA 2007, s 398*.

A *property investment LLP* is defined as one whose business consists wholly or mainly of the making of investments in land and the principal part of whose income is derived therefrom (*ITA 2007, s 1004*).

An *investment LLP* is defined as an LLP whose business consists wholly or mainly of the making of investments and the principal part of whose income is derived therefrom (*ITA 2007, s 399(6)*).

When reviewing whether an LLP is an investment LLP, HMRC will consider a representative period but the view will then apply for the complete period of account (HMRC Business Income Manual BIM72130).

Converting a partnership to an LLP

19.28 For the most part, the tax consequences of transferring a partnership to an LLP are straightforward.

The main difficulties with converting to an LLP are likely to be administrative and organisational, since an agreement between all the partners must be reached. The conversion costs may also be prohibitive for some partnerships.

19.29 In some situations, partial incorporation as an LLP will be appropriate. Where an LLP takes over only part of an ordinary partnership's trade, such an event will constitute a demerger within Statement of Practice SP 9/86 (see **Chapter 7**). The LLP must demonstrate that, as a question of fact, the LLP is recognisably the same business for it to be considered to have succeeded to the trade of the old partnership; otherwise, the cessation and commencement provisions will apply.

19.30 Alternatively, the existing partnership may be used to complete existing contracts, with new contracts being carried out by the LLP. In this case, particular care is required to ensure that the members do not inadvertently assume personal responsibility for their actions by confusing their duties in the two different entities.

Income tax

19.31 The transfer of a partnership to an LLP will be subject to the usual partnership taxation rules. There will only be a cessation if one would occur in a similar situation in an ordinary partnership.

Example 19.2 – Converting a partnership to an LLP – income tax

Able & Co is a long-standing firm of chartered accountants with 20 equal partners. On 1 October 2014, it transfers its business to an LLP.

In transferring its business:

- three partners, A, B and C, retire;
- the other 17 partners become members in Able LLP; and
- two new members, Y and Z, join Able LLP.

The cessation rules apply to A, B and C. They will be entitled to overlap relief (see **5.9**).

The cessation rules do not apply to the 17 continuing partners and they are not entitled to overlap relief.

The commencement rules apply to Y and Z (see **5.1**).

19.32 Where an LLP succeeds to the trade or profession of a partnership, there is no cessation, and no relief for overlap profits will be given. These will be available when the member finally retires from the LLP or on an earlier change of year end, if appropriate.

19.33 The LLP may need to change the accounting policies used by the partnership to comply with the SORP.

Capital allowances

19.34 Where an LLP succeeds to a business previously carried on by a partnership, no balancing charge or allowance will arise.

Interest relief

19.35 Formerly, ESC A43 ensured that partners continued to receive tax relief on interest following certain types of partnership reconstruction. This concession was formalised by *ITA 2007, ss 409(1), (2)* and *410*, and covers a transfer to an LLP.

Partnership annuities

19.36 Each LLP will have to consider the precise terms of its retirement benefit scheme in determining, first, how the payments are to be accounted for and, secondly, their tax treatment (see **Chapter 14**). The payment of a pension, as opposed to an annuity, by the LLP to a former member is to be discouraged, on the basis that it is tantamount to a payment for the acquisition of the retiring members' share (or a payment for goodwill) and therefore not allowable as a trading expense.

19.37 Where an obligation to pay an annuity is transferred from a partnership to an LLP, the members, including incoming members, will be entitled to higher rate relief for their share of the payment, basic rate relief having been obtained by deduction at the time of the payment.

19.38 If the obligation to pay an annuity is not transferred to the LLP and the former partners continue to pay it, they will be entitled to higher rate relief until such time as they cease to be a member of the LLP or the business of the old partnership ceases. Basic rate relief will be obtained by deduction at the time of the payment.

19.39 The transfer of an annuity obligation outlined at **19.37** is not regarded as a chargeable disposal for CGT purposes, provided that the annuitant's rights remain substantially the same.

Example 19.3 – Transfer of annuity

STU partnership with two partners is required to pay a former partner an annuity of £10,000 for the next 15 years. The annuity is paid at the rate of £8,000 net (£10,000 less £2,000 (20%) tax deducted). Each partner declares a gross charge of £5,000 on his or her tax return and receives higher rate tax relief of £1,000 a year. The recipient former partner is taxed on £10,000 with tax deducted of £2,000.

The partnership converts to an LLP on 1 November 2014. The annuity continues to be paid without variation in its terms at the rate of £8,000 net (£10,000 less £2,000 (20%)

tax deducted). Each member declares a gross charge of £5,000 on his or her tax return and receives higher rate tax relief of £1,000 a year. The recipient former partner is taxed on £10,000 with tax deducted of £2,000.

The transfer of the annuity obligation from the partnership to the LLP does not amount to a chargeable disposal.

Capital gains tax

19.40 A transfer of assets between a partnership and an LLP will give rise to a capital gain (or loss) only if, in otherwise identical circumstances, a transfer of assets between one partnership and another would also have CGT consequences.

Inheritance tax

19.41 Incorporation as an LLP does not interrupt entitlement to business property relief or agricultural property relief.

Returns

19.42 Where a partnership incorporates as an LLP during an accounting period (and if the partners so wish), a single partnership return can be submitted, even if the partnership changes its accounting date.

19.43 A PAYE scheme can continue to operate when a partnership incorporates as an LLP.

Stamp duty/stamp duty land tax

19.44 There is no charge to stamp duty or stamp duty land tax ('SDLT') on the incorporation of an LLP provided that:

- the property transferred to the LLP is unchanged before and after the transfer (*LLPA 2000, s 12*);
- the property is transferred to the LLP within one year of incorporation. Those who register LLPs on a protective basis, but are still undecided as to whether or not to use them, could find themselves caught out by this provision; and
- no partners retire or are admitted to the LLP at the time of incorporation. If there are admissions or retirements, *LLPA 2000, s 12(2)* in theory denies relief. Provided that all the other conditions are met, HMRC accept that the duty can be averted by arranging the change of partners the instant before or after incorporation as an LLP. The Stamp Office will need to see the documents to prove that this was the case. They may also call for further information, so particular care is required.

Example 19.4 – Converting a partnership to an LLP – stamp duty/SDLT

Using the facts in **Example 19.2**, Able & Co's balance sheet at 30 September 2013 is as follows:

	£000
Freehold property	5,000
Debtors	1,000
Bank balances	500
Creditors	(2,500)
Net assets	4,000

Provided that all the assets are transferred to the LLP, no SDLT charge will arise.

Provided that A, B and C retire just before the LLP is incorporated, and Y and Z join the LLP shortly after incorporation, the SDLT exemption on incorporation as an LLP is not lost. Care must be taken to ensure that the paperwork supports the facts.

Assuming that the partnership deferred becoming an LLP until 1 December 2013, and on 30 November 2013 its balance sheet was still as above, no charge to SDLT would arise on the freehold property, provided that:

- the freehold property was the same before and after the transfer;
- the transfer takes place before 30 November 2014; and
- there are no partnership changes at the time of incorporation.

(*FA 2003, s 65*)

No charge to SDLT arises on the other balance sheet items, so it makes no difference whether the debtors, creditors and bank balances are retained by the old partnership or transferred to the LLP.

VAT

19.45 Where a partnership changes to an LLP, the transfer of a going concern ('TOGC') rules apply, including those relating to any option to tax.

19.46 Where a general partnership ceases to exist on the creation of an LLP, it may be possible to transfer the VAT number to the LLP.

Anti-avoidance: disguised employment

19.47 The Government announced at the time of the 2013 Budget that is would consult on changes to two aspects of partnership tax rules in order to prevent tax loss, namely:

- disguising employment relationships through limited liability partnerships; and
- certain arrangements involving allocation of profits and losses among partnership members.

The changes, which were subsequently been brought into effect by the *Finance Act 2014 (FA 2014)* took effect from 6 April 2014 (*FA 2014, s 74* and *Sch 17*).

Broadly, the changes affect LLP members who work for LLPs on terms that HMRC view as 'tantamount to employment' (ie disguised employment). They also have an impact on members of LLPs and other partnerships where the members of the partnership consist of members who are chargeable to income tax and others who are not, where it is reasonable to assume that a main purpose of the partnership profit-sharing arrangements is either to secure an income tax advantage for any person or to allocate a partnership loss to a partner with a view to that partner obtaining a reduction in tax liability by way of income tax reliefs or capital gains relief. Profit and loss allocation schemes also cover tax-motivated arrangements whereby one partner transfers profits to another as a result of a revised allocation of profits in return for payment that is not taxed as income (see **Chapter 17** for commentary on the *FA 2014* changes concerning profit and loss allocation).

19.48 Historically, it has been HMRC's view that by law the members of an LLP cannot be employees and are therefore treated as self-employed (but see *Tiffin v Aldridge* below). This, in turn means that lower NIC rates are likely to apply and there will be the ability to defer income tax payments through the standard self-assessment payments regime for the self-employed.

Focus

The employment law case of *Tiffin v Aldridge* [2012] 2 All ER 1113 contains some useful comments. This confirmed that an LLP member could be an 'employee' of the LLP, albeit the claimant in the case was, on the facts, held to be a 'partner (member)'. This was because the membership agreement showed it had been intended to set up a relationship between its signatories that could fairly be regarded – applying traditional partnership law – as a 'partnership' relation between the full equity 'partners' and the fixed share 'partners'. All had to contribute capital; all had a prospect of a share of profit depending on the performance of the LLP, and of a share in surplus on a winding up; all had a voice in the management.

HMRC's view is that there is abuse at both ends of the spectrum, so that 'groups of low paid workers who would normally be regarded as employees are being taken on as LLP members as a condition for their obtaining work' and 'individuals who would normally be regarded as employees in high salary professional areas such as the legal and financial services sectors are benefiting from self-employed status for tax purposes'. The new rules, designed to counter avoidance of tax, only apply to individuals that are members of LLPs, and to fall within the rules they have to satisfy three conditions (A–C) as follows (*ITTOIA 2005, s 863A*):

Condition A

19.49 Condition A is that there are 'relevant arrangements' in place for the individual to perform services as a member of the LLP. 'Relevant arrangements' means arrangements under which amounts are to be, or may be, payable by the LLP in respect of the individual's performance of services for the partnership in his capacity as a member of the partnership. The condition will be met if it is reasonable to expect that at least 80% of the total amount payable by the LLP in respect of the individual's performance, during the relevant period of services for the partnership in the individual's capacity as a member of the partnership, will be disguised salary.

An amount will be treated as 'disguised salary' if it:

(a) is fixed;

(b) is variable, but is varied without reference to the overall amount of the profits or losses of the LLP; or

(c) is not, in practice, affected by the overall amount of those profits or losses.

In many cases, this will not lead to any difficulties as partners in an LLP will be remunerated by reference to the overall profits available.

Focus

There is concern for the treatment of salaried partners or fixed share partners. HMRC's guidance suggests that it is important to ensure that at least 20% of partner remuneration is by reference to the overall partnership profits, but that this can include various points arrangements or pooling arrangements, so long as the overall 'pot' is based on the overall partnership profits.

Condition B

19.50 Condition B is that the person concerned does not have significant influence over the affairs of the partnership (*ITTOIA 2005, s 863C*).

Focus

During the consultation period, this point caused particular concern amongst the larger professional services and law firms, where only a very small proportion of the partners can be said to have any real influence over the affairs of the partnership. HMRC have stated that they do not consider that many of the partners of, for example, the Big 4 accounting firms would have significant influence over the affairs of their firm, so arguably many people will satisfy condition B.

Condition C

19.51 Condition C is that the person's partnership capital is less than 25% of the amount which is reasonably expected to be disguised salary for the tax year (*ITTOIA 2005, s 863D*). In other words, the person concerned has to have at stake capital of at least one quarter of their partnership income to avoid satisfying this test. The partnership capital is determined on 6 April 2014 or at the date of appointment of the partner and then at the beginning of each subsequent tax year or whenever the partnership sharing arrangements change.

Focus

This condition reflects HMRC's views that being in partnership includes having a substantial amount of capital at stake. The test will be accepted as satisfied if there is a firm commitment to contribute capital within three months of 6 April 2014 (ie 5 July 2014), or within two months of becoming a member of an LLP after that date, so long as the capital is actually contributed (*ITTOIA 2005, ss 863E–863F*).

Example 19.5 – Are the disguised employment conditions satisfied?

(Adapted from examples included in HMRC Consultation document: *Partnerships: A review of two aspects of the tax rules*)

(1) Member A receives a salary of £200,000. This is guaranteed so it is payable irrespective of the level of profits or losses. There is no requirement to contribute capital, no right to participate in partnership decisions and no requirement to repay salary in the event that the partnership is not profitable for the period of account.

    On the facts given, Member A is a salaried partner.

(2) Member B receives a salary of £50,000, which may be reduced if the profits are insufficient to pay all the agreed members' salaries. In addition, Member B receives a 10% share of profits remaining after members' salaries have been paid.

    Member B is genuinely exposed to the risk of loss of entitlement to the salary and enjoys the prospect of benefitting from partnership profits. Accordingly, Member B is not a salaried partner.

(3) The facts are as for Example 1, but in addition, Member A will receive 10% share of the profits if the profits exceed a figure that is many times the actual turnover of the business. The intention is that Member A will only ever receive the guaranteed salary, and the profit-sharing entitlement is intended to prevent the legislation from applying. On the facts given, Member A is a salaried member.

19.52 If a person satisfies all three conditions in **19.49 – 19.51** above, then that person is taxed as if they were an employee of the partnership, although their wider legal status as a member of the LLP is not changed. In other words, this is purely a tax measure.

19.53 Under the new legislation, as outlined above, a salaried member will be deemed to be employed by their LLP for tax and NICs purposes. In these circumstances, the LLP will be liable to deduct and pay tax and NICs on any amount paid to the salaried member as if it were employment income for tax and employed earners' earnings for NICs. The LLP will be the secondary contributor for NICs, and will be responsible for paying NICs on earnings and benefits.

19.54 Special anti-avoidance measures ensure that individuals cannot enter into arrangements with the main purpose of avoiding the provisions of the new legislation (new *ITTOIA 2005, s 863G*). This includes situations where a worker provides their services to an LLP through an intermediary which is itself a member of that LLP. In these circumstances, the income of the intermediary from the LLP will be deemed to be the worker's income for tax and NICs purposes. Payment will be regarded as being made to the worker at the point the LLP pays the intermediary for the worker's services.

Consequential changes to the IR35 legislation are designed to prevent double taxation and avoid two separate secondary contributors being liable to pay NICs on the same earnings. Under the new provisions, where an amount is treated as the worker's own remuneration:

- an equivalent amount will not be included in the deemed employment payment calculation;
- there will be no further liability to pay tax and NICs if any of the amount paid by the LLP is subsequently paid as salary to the worker by their intermediary – the amount of these salary payments should not be taken into account in any of the steps of the deemed employment payment calculation;
- the amount disregarded for NICs purposes will not be treated as earnings for any statutory payment entitlement from the personal service company.

The intermediary will be liable to pay tax, NICS and statutory payments in the normal way, applying IR35 legislation when appropriate, on any remuneration received by the intermediary from engagements with clients other than the LLP.

Practical issues to consider when forming an LLP

19.55 The following practical issues are worth considering when changing from a partnership to an LLP:

- Obtain the agreement of the partners to form the LLP.
- Form the LLP (complete form LLP2 and pay the appropriate fee). Take care when buying 'off-the shelf' LLPs, since the 12-month exemption from stamp duty or SDLT may not apply (see **19.44**).
- Complete all statutory matters with the registrar. Appoint at least two 'designated' members and notify Companies House on form LLP 288C within 14 days.
- Choose a name. *LLPA 2000, Sch, Pt I* sets out specific details that must be complied with.

- There is no automatic transfer. A transfer document will be required to transfer assets and goodwill.
- Draw up a members' agreement. There is no obligation to have an agreement (or to publish it) but, in its absence, default regulations apply. These provide for profits and losses to be shared equally (*LLPA 2000, s 5*). Although the original partnership deed could form the basis of the new members' agreement, it should not be used as it stands, and careful alteration will be required.
- Authorisation to operate as an LLP may be required from some professional bodies.
- Advise banks and transfer accounts. Put in place new security arrangements, and complete any necessary Companies House forms to provide details of debentures and charges.
- Notify hire purchase, leasing companies and financiers and change agreements.
- Notify clients, customers and suppliers. Reassure them about the conduct of business in the future.
- Order new stationery.
- Change entries in trade and telephone directories and on the Internet.
- Transfer the title to property or notify landlords. Personal guarantees may be required if their security is lower. Alternatively, if personal guarantees were in place for the partnership, discuss whether they can now be released.
- Notify rating authorities. Consider the impact on transitional relief for the uniform business rate.
- Notify HMRC for both tax and VAT purposes.
- Rename pension schemes.
- Transfer the PAYE scheme from the partnership to the LLP.
- Give employees a notice of continuity of employment (*Transfer of Undertakings (Protection of Employment) Regulations 2006 (SI 2006/246)*).
- Notify other third parties, such as the Data Protection Registrar.
- Wind up the partnership, if appropriate.
- If the partnership is continuing, consider the need for indemnities to any continuing partners.

Chapter 20

Overseas Matters

Signposts

- A partnership as such has no residence status, but the residence status of partners may affect the amount charged to tax and the manner of charging it (see **20.1 – 20.3**).
- The liability to UK tax of non-resident partners (and the ability to claim loss relief) is broadly restricted to UK-source income though there may be room for doubt about exactly what this means in practice (see **20.4 – 20.8**).
- If a non-resident partner or LLP member defaults on paying UK tax due, the partnership or LLP may be liable as the UK agent of the defaulter (see **20.9**).
- Generally, in the case of non-resident partners CGT is computed by reference only to UK assets (whether in computing gains, losses or roll-over relief) (see **20.13 – 20.16**).
- Where a partnership is controlled and managed abroad (for which similar tests apply as for companies) remittance basis may apply to non-domiciled partners and there may be some flexibility in what has to be filed for UK tax purposes (see **20.17 – 20.19**). In addition, special rules apply to double tax relief (see **20.20**) and use of losses (see **20.23**).

Residence and domicile status

20.1 A partnership is not of itself taxable. The concept of residence status is therefore meaningless in the context of partnerships themselves. It follows that a partnership cannot itself claim any benefits as a 'dual resident' under any Double Taxation Convention ('DTC') nor will HMRC normally issue a 'certificate of residence' for the purposes of any DTC. A few DTCs do state that a partnership may be regarded as having a residence status and in those cases a 'certificate of residence' may be issued. In other cases partners may be able to claim treaty benefits and HMRC will assist by providing a 'letter of confirmation' confirming UK-residence status where appropriate – see INTM162110.

Despite the fact that partnerships as such have no residence status under UK law, both the tax liability of members and the mechanics of collecting any liability may be affected by:

- where partners are resident or domiciled;

- where profits arise;
- where the partnership is managed and controlled.

The basis on which partnership trading profit or loss is computed differs as between resident and non-resident partners. The *Income Tax (Trading and Other Income) Act 2005 ('ITTOIA 2005'), s 849* sets out the rules for individuals: *Corporation Taxes Act 2009, s 1259* does the same for companies. In each case the rules can be summarised as follows:

- for any period of account in which the partner is a UK resident, the profits or losses of the trade are calculated as if the firm were a UK resident;
- for any period of account in which the partner is non-UK resident, the profits or losses of the trade are calculated as if the firm were a non-UK resident.

For any tax year that is a split year for residency purposes, as respects a partner, *s 849* will have effect as if the partner were non-UK resident in the overseas part of the year. By definition, 'split-year' treatment cannot apply to a company since by *CTA 2009, s 10* an accounting period ends when a company becomes or ceases to be non-UK-resident.

20.2 Page two of the SA 800 partnership return asks the question whether there are:

- non-resident partners; or
- partners in businesses controlled and managed abroad and who are not UK domiciled, or who are not ordinarily resident in the UK.

The reference to 'ordinary residence' is puzzling in view of the amendments in the *Finance Act 2013* which effectively abolish that status for the purposes of income tax and capital gains tax. The reference to domicile does, however, continue to be of relevance. Note that it is expected that from April 2017, anybody who has been resident in the UK for at least 15 of the previous 20 tax years will be deemed to be domiciled in the UK for income tax and capital gains tax purposes. In addition, from April 2017, individuals born in the UK with UK domicile of origin, will no longer be able to claim non-domicile status for any year for which they are resident in the UK.

Where all the partners are UK resident, the partnership return should show the partnership's worldwide profits. Amounts taxed overseas should be shown separately.

Where all the partners are non-resident, the partnership return should show only profits arising from UK operations.

Where there are both resident and non-resident partners, two partnership statements should be completed: one showing worldwide profits (for the resident partners), and the other showing only the UK profit (for the non-resident partners). For the situation where partnerships are managed and controlled outside the UK, see **20.17**. See also HMRC Helpsheet 380.

Occasionally it may happen that a partnership, although registered in the UK, has no UK resident partners, no income or gains arising in the UK and is managed and controlled outside the UK. In such circumstances, HMRC may agree that a partnership return is not required – see PM41000.

20.3 Following a lengthy period of consultation, the *Finance Act 2013* introduced a new statutory residence test ('SRT') (*FA 2013, s 219* and *Sch 45*). The provisions apply from 6 April 2013. In addition to the SRT, there are provisions to enable tax years to be split into resident and non-resident periods where any one of eight possible 'Cases' applies: previously, this treatment relied on Extra-Statutory Concession. The SRT provisions have three key elements, namely five 'automatic overseas tests', four 'automatic residence tests' and a 'sufficient ties' test. An individual is resident in the UK if (and only if) none of the 'automatic overseas tests' are met and either one of the 'automatic residence tests' is met or the 'sufficient ties test' is met.

A careful and systematic approach to the tests will therefore be required in order to determine an individual's residency status. For further details, see HMRC guidance RDR3: Guidance Note: Statutory Residence Test (SRT).

It is worth noting that the Statutory Residence Test (and with it the abolition of ordinary residence status) is relevant only for tax purposes. It has no application to National Insurance Contributions. Although there is strictly no direct read-across of income tax decisions to Social Security matters, in practice it is likely that in most cases the pre-2013 case law position will be of assistance in determining residence and ordinary residence status for the purposes of National Insurance Contributions.

Non-resident partners

20.4 Non-resident partners will need to complete the non-residence and partnership pages of their personal tax return.

Income tax

20.5 In the case of a non-resident partner, profits or losses of the trade are calculated as if the firm were a non-UK-resident individual (*ITTOIA 2005. s 849(3)*). It follows, from *ITTOIA 2005, s 6*, that a non-resident partner is liable to UK tax on his share of profits:

(a) if the trade is carried on wholly in the UK, on the whole of his profit share; and

(b) if the trade is carried on partly in the UK and partly elsewhere, on his share of profits from the part of the trade carried on in the UK.

Section 849 is applied to other income by *s 851*: so, for example, a non-UK-resident partner is liable to tax in respect of partnership savings and investment income only to the extent that it arises in the UK (*ITTOIA, s368*).

This raises the question what profits arise 'from the part of the trade carried on the UK' where a trade is carried on in the UK and elsewhere. It appears to be HMRC's entrenched view that, regardless of the commercial position, it is necessary for tax purposes that worldwide profits are pooled and that every partner who has a share in the profits of the business is to be regarded, for tax purposes, as having the same proportionate share in profits wherever arising. In HMRC's view, any territorial 'streaming' of profits is to be disregarded for tax purposes.

Example 20.1 – Streaming of profits to non-resident

Henry V LLP carries on business in the UK and in France. Eight members are resident in the UK and two are resident in France. Under the LLP agreement the French-resident members are responsible for managing the French branch and are remunerated exclusively by reference to the profits of the French branch, each taking 30% of the branch profits regardless of the performance of the UK branch. The eight UK-resident members share equally in the whole of the UK branch profits and 40% of the French branch profits.

In 2016 the tax-adjusted profits of the LLP are £1 million attributable to the UK branch and £500,000 attributable to the French branch. Each French member's profit share is therefore £150,000.

HMRC's view is that each French member's entitlement is to £150,000 of the £1.5 million global profit of which one-third arises in France and two-thirds in the UK, and that £100,000 of each French member's profit is liable to UK tax.

20.6 Where the partnership trading partly in the UK and partly abroad includes both resident and non resident partners, two sets of partnership statements will generally be required, one for UK profits and one for overseas profits.

20.7 A non-resident partner, like any other non-resident, may be relieved from liability to UK tax by the terms of any relevant Double Taxation Agreement; and the provisions of the *Income Tax Act, Pt 14, Ch 1 (Limits on Liability to Income Tax of non-UK residents)* may also need to be considered. But these will never remove liability in respect of income arising from a trade (or part of a trade) carried on the UK.

20.8 A non-resident partner cannot claim UK personal allowances, unless he or she is one of the categories qualifying under the *Income Tax Act 2007 (ITA 2007), s 56* (such as a non-resident British citizen or EEA national), or allowances are to be given under the provisions of a double tax treaty.

20.9 Although a partner resident outside the UK is liable to UK tax on trading profits arising in the UK, there may be obvious practical difficulties in the way of HMRC actually collecting tax from him. For this reason, the Taxes Acts make provision (at *ITA 2007, Pt 14, Ch 2C*) for income tax liabilities of a non-resident to be collected from any 'UK representative' of the non-resident. *CTA 2010, Pt 22, Ch 6* makes similar provision in respect of non-resident companies. In relation to partnerships, the partnership itself is treated as the UK representative of the non-resident partners. It may thus be assessed to tax in the name of the non-resident partners. In such circumstances each of the partners is jointly liable for the non-resident partners' tax – this is the only circumstance in which one partner can be liable for another's tax liability. In the case of an LLP, it is the LLP itself which is liable but since in general law members of an LLP are not personally liable for the LLP's liabilities, no personal liability attaches to members.

In either case, a partnership with UK income and non-resident partners may be wise to take a very close interest in the UK tax compliance arrangements of non-resident partners including withholding distributions until evidence that all tax liabilities have been met is available.

This is to be distinguished from the case where a UK-resident member of a partnership or LLP leaves the UK leaving tax debts unpaid. There is in that case no UK representative and no liability on the partnership, partners or LLP.

Basis periods

20.10 Where there is a change of residence (whether because a non-resident partner becomes UK-resident or a UK-resident partner ceases to be UK resident) the partner is treated as ceasing to carry on and immediately re-commence both the notional trade by reference to which his share of trading profits is calculated and the deemed trade by which his share of taxed income is calculated (*ITTOIA, s 852(6)* and *s 854(5)* respectively). Depending on the partnership accounting date, overlap relief will normally be used on the deemed cessation and created on the deemed re-commencement.

Focus

Where there is a change in a partner's residence status, the partnership profit must be apportioned to and from the date of change of residence. For the period of non-residence, the partnership profits must be apportioned between those arising in the UK and those arising overseas. Details of the apportionment should be included with the return or in the additional information box.

Example 20.2 – Change in partner's residence status

Wilhelm is a 10% partner in Windsor LLP, which trades only in the UK, has accounting date 30 June and has the following adjusted profits

30 6 14	£800,000
30.6.15	£1,000,000
30.6.16	£1,200,000
30.6.17	£1,000,000

Wilhelm has been a resident in the UK for many years until leaving the UK for Germany, ceasing to be UK-resident on 30 June 2016. His available overlap relief is £45,000. Wilhelm's assessable profits will be:

Year	Basis period	Amount
2014/15	y/e 30.6.14	£80,000
2015/16	y/e 30.6.15	£100,000
2016/17	y/e 30.6.16 (deemed cessation of old notional trade)	£120,000 less overlap £45,000
2016/17	1.7.16 – 5.4.17 (deemed commencement of new notional trade)	£75,000
2017/18	y/e 30 6 17	£100,000

Wilhelm will now have new overlap relief to carry forward of £75,000.

Losses

20.11 A non-resident partner may claim tax relief for losses in respect of the UK part of the trade in the usual way. This will normally be by carry-forward against subsequent profits of the UK part of the trade but in principle could include offset against other income taxable in the UK if the partner happens to have any such income. A non-resident partner cannot, of course, claim UK tax relief in respect of losses to the extent that they arise from the carrying on of the trade outside the UK.

Where there has been a change of residence (see **20.10** above), trading losses made before the change of residence can be carried forward against trading profits arising after the change of residence in the usual way (*s 852(7)*).

National Insurance

20.12 Non-resident partners are not liable to pay Class 4 NICs (*Social Security (Contributions) Regulations 2001 (SI 2001/1004), reg 91*). A partner is liable to pay Class 2 NICs if he or she is ordinarily resident in the UK, or has been resident in the UK for at least 26 out of the previous 52 weeks (*SI 2001/1004, reg 145(1)(d)*). Class 2 NIC is to be abolished with effect from April 2018.

Capital gains tax

20.13 The general rule is that a person is chargeable to UK CGT in respect of chargeable gains accruing in a year of assessment only if resident in the UK for the year (*TCGA 1992, s 2*). Special rules for temporary non-residents (*s 10A*) and liability of non-residents in respect of ATED-related gains (*s 2B*) or of gains on UK residential property (*s 14B*) are not covered here.

20.14 The exception to the general rule is that if a partnership carries on a trade, profession or vocation in the UK through a branch or agency, a partner who is non-resident is liable to CGT on the disposal of assets used in the UK by the branch or agency (*TCGA 1992, s 10*). If, whilst trading through a UK branch or agency, assets are removed abroad, a CGT charge also arises (*s 25(1)*).

20.15 If a non-resident partner leaves the partnership, he or she will be treated as having disposed of his or her share of UK chargeable assets at their market value for CGT purposes (*TCGA 1992, s 25*). The non-resident partners are also liable to a CGT charge under this section where a UK branch or agency disposes of assets when it ceases business.

20.16 Non-resident partners cannot claim roll-over relief for replacement of business assets under *TCGA 1992, s 152* unless the replacement assets they acquire are within the charge to UK tax at the time they are acquired (*TCGA 1992, s 159*).

Partnerships controlled and managed abroad

20.17 If the partnership is controlled and managed abroad, and is trading wholly or partly outside the UK, then a partner who is a UK-resident individual may make a claim to be taxed on a remittance basis if he is not domiciled in the UK (*ITTOIA 2005, s 857*), subject in appropriate cases to payment of the so-called Remittance Basis User Charge. The partner's share of profits arising in the UK is then taxed in the ordinary way under *ITTOIA 2005, ss 849–856*. Profits of such a partner arising overseas are treated as 'relevant foreign income' taxable on the remittance basis.

20.18 The question whether a partnership is controlled and managed abroad is one of fact. There is little case law directly on the subject but the First Tier Tribunal case of *Mark Higgins Rallying v HMRC* [2011] UKFTT 340 (TC) concluded that the appropriate test is the same as that adopted by the courts in the relation to the residence of companies. This renders relevant the large body of case law on company residence, where 'central management and control' is in point. Thus in determining where a partnership is controlled and managed the first stage is likely to be to identify the forum where control and management is in fact exercised, which may often be plenary meetings of partners or, in a larger partnership, meetings of a management board: and the second may be to identify where meetings take place. The similarities with board meetings of a company are obvious, as too is the importance of differentiating between meetings at which control is genuinely exercised and those which merely rubber-stamp decisions made elsewhere.

In the case of a Limited Partnership, control and management will always reside with the General Partner: so the tax-residence of General Partner will take on a greater degree of significance that that of other members.

20.19 Strictly, a partnership with at least one UK resident partner liable to tax should return its worldwide profits. However HMRC allows (indeed requests) that the Partnership Tax Return of a partnership which is managed and controlled outside the UK to include in its return only UK profits. Non-resident partners will put their share of the UK profit on their own tax returns. The UK resident partners will also put their share of the UK profit on their own tax returns but they will need to supplement this with details of overseas profits as appropriate. This means that where a UK-resident partner is domiciled outside the UK and makes a valid remittance basis claim he will declare overseas profits on a remittance basis; otherwise on an arising basis.

UK-resident partners – overseas profits and gains

20.20 A UK-resident partner is taxable under *ITTOIA 2005* on his share of partnership profits whether earned in the UK or abroad (but subject, in the case of a partner domiciled in the UK, to the possible application of the remittance basis to non-UK profits of a partnership controlled and managed abroad – see **20.17** above). Where any part of the overseas profits have been taxed abroad, they should be separately entered on the partnership tax return. Where appropriate, relief for foreign tax paid on foreign profits may be given under a Double Taxation Treaty. Where no treaty exists, unilateral relief may be available.

It may be that a UK resident may be a member of a partnership controlled and managed outside the UK which has income arising in the UK. In such circumstances, *ITTOIA 2005, s 858(2)* ensures that any provision of a Double Taxation Agreement which might otherwise exempt UK-source income from the charge to tax is dis-applied, so that the UK resident partner's share of the partnership's UK source income remains fully chargeable. See also *Padmore v IRC (No 2)* [2001] STC 280 for further discussion of the point.

This does not preclude a claim to double taxation relief in respect of foreign tax paid on foreign income of the partnership.

20.21 UK-resident partners are liable to CGT on their share of the proceeds of disposal of partnership chargeable assets in both the UK and overseas (*TCGA 1992, s 2*). When the partner leaves the partnership, there will be disposal of his or her share of all partnership assets the tax treatment of which will follow the position described in **Chapter 12**.

20.22 The remittance basis may apply (in the case of partners not domiciled in the UK) to 'foreign chargeable gains' (that is, chargeable gains accruing from the disposal of assets situated outside the UK (*TCGA 1992, s 12*). Chargeable gains are treated as accruing to the partner in any tax year in which any such gains are remitted to the UK.

If the tax year is a split year for residency purposes, the chargeable gains are treated as accruing to the partner in the part of the year (the overseas part or the UK part) in which the foreign chargeable gains are remitted.

Loss relief

20.23 Where a trade is carried on even partly in the UK, relief for losses is available for a UK-resident partner without making any differentiation between losses arising in the UK and losses arising overseas (see **Chapter 9**).

Where a trade is carried on wholly outside the UK, *ITA 2007, s 95* provides that relief (whether by carry-forward or set-off) is available only against foreign income and cannot be 'converted' into a CGT loss under the *Taxation of Chargeable Gains Act 1992, s 261B*. It should be noted that the treatment of profits and losses of a foreign trade is not therefore quite symmetrical. For example, comparing *s 95* (dealing with losses) and *s 857* (dealing with profits – see **20.17** above):

- *s 95* is not limited in its application to partners domiciled outside the UK but applies equally to partners domiciled in the UK or elsewhere;
- *s 95* applies only to trades carried on wholly outside the UK whereas *s 857* can apply to a trade carried on partly within and partly outside the UK.

It might be thought that the additional requirement in *s 857* (absent from *s 95*) that 'control and management' of the trade be outside the UK is a further point of distinction. In practice it probably is not: it is difficult to conceive of the possibility that a trade which is 'controlled and managed' in the UK could at the same time be 'carried on wholly outside the UK'. So in practice *s 95* is probably, like *s 857*, capable of applying only where control and management resides outside the UK.

Partnerships which include a corporate partner

20.24 Where one of the partners is a foreign company, the same rules apply as for non-resident individuals, so that the company is taxed only on its share of the UK profits, usually those arising in the UK through a permanent establishment. A corporate non-resident partner is also taxable on its share of overseas investment income which relates to the UK permanent establishment.

It is arguably anomalous that in the case of a non-resident corporate partner the rules applying should be those relevant to an individual. The Consultation Document 'Partnership Taxation: proposals to clarify tax treatment' issued in August 2016 proposed a change in the law so that the profits, while remaining chargeable to income tax, would be calculated as if a non-resident company were carrying on the relevant business. This change is however deferred pending the outcome of the March 2017 consultation on 'Non-resident companies chargeable to Income Tax and Non-resident Capital Gains Tax'.

20.25 Companies are treated differently from individuals in relation to foreign exchange differences and interest rate and currency contracts. Since 1 October 2002, these have been taxed under the loan relationship regime (*CTA 2009, Pt 5*). For the general treatment of partnerships with a corporate partner, see **Chapter 17**.

Inheritance tax

20.26 UK-domiciled partners are subject to inheritance tax in respect of their assets wherever they are situated, which would include assets of any overseas branch of the partnership business.

Generally, partners who are neither domiciled nor deemed to be domiciled in the UK are subject to inheritance tax only in respect of UK-situs assets. In principle this will include an interest in a UK business, or the UK branch of a business which trades in the UK and elsewhere.

In either case, business property relief may be available, subject to the normal qualifying conditions including the period of ownership, nature of the business and the use of particular assets within the business (see **Chapter 23**). Furthermore, where assets are liable both to UK inheritance tax and to a foreign equivalent, relief for double taxation may be available.

Double taxation relief

20.27 UK-resident partners will normally be entitled to claim either treaty relief or unilateral relief in respect of foreign tax paid on their share of partnership profits arising overseas. Where the foreign tax relates to 'overlap profit' (that is, income for a period which forms part of the basis period for two UK tax years) it is, broadly, available against the UK tax charge for both years (*TIOPA 2010, s 22*). When the overlap profits are deducted on cessation or a later change of accounting date, all or part of the 'double credit' afforded under *s 22* is clawed back under *s 24*.

Similarly, non-UK resident partners may be able to claim relief against any tax charge in their home country for UK tax paid on their share of partnership profits arising in the UK.

Although not quite impossible it would be very unusual for a partnership to carry on business in the UK other than through a permanent establishment. It follows that it will be very rare for a non-resident partner to be able to invoke a double taxation treaty to claim exemption from UK tax on his share of profits arising in the UK.

20.28 Where a non-resident partnership receives dividends or other distributions from a UK company on which it is entitled to a tax credit under a double tax agreement, UK-resident partners are entitled to their shares of the tax credits on the distributions (*ITTOIA 2005, s 858(3)*). The reform of the taxation of UK dividends and the abolition of tax credits make this provision redundant from April 2016.

European economic interest grouping

20.29 An European economic interest grouping ('EEIG') is a form of business entity (*European Council Regulation 2137/85*) which may be used by businesses in the European Community (since 1 July 1989) for certain commercial activities, usually processing and packing. Although it is not generally constituted as a partnership, the tax treatment is similar. Like a partnership, the profits are taxable in the hands of its members. A trade carried on by the members is treated as if it is carried on in partnership, subject to the normal rules of income tax and CGT.

An EEIG registered in Great Britain and Northern Ireland is required to collect and account for tax. Its manager must complete a partnership return. References to partnerships are deemed to include groupings.

The future of European Economic Interest Groupings after the UK's proposed withdrawal from the European Union remains to be seen.

Chapter 21

Partnership Tax Returns, Enquiries and Administration

Signposts

- Partnerships are required to submit a partnership return form SA800 each year which include a statement of 'partnership share' allocating income between partners (see **21.1 – 21.15**).
- The filing dates for partnership returns are normally the same as for individuals (see **21.8**) but may be extended where there is a corporate partner (see **21.10**).
- Individual partners are responsible for paying the tax due on their share of partnership profits. Where a partner disagrees with the amount of 'partnership share' allocated the disagreement should be disclosed on his personal return (see **21.16**).
- Partnership returns are subject to the same enquiry procedures as personal returns including the possibility of 'discovery' once the enquiry window has closed though there are a number of procedural differences and ambiguities (see **21.21 – 21.42**).

Partnership tax returns

21.1 Since a partnership is not itself chargeable to tax, the provisions at the *Taxes Management Act 1970* (*'TMA 1970'*), *s 7* (notification of liability) do not apply to partnerships. It is, however, good practice to notify HMRC of the existence of a partnership so that it may be brought into HMRC's systems in good time for a reference number to be allocated and a return to be issued at the normal time. Form SA400 may be used for this purpose. SA401 is used for notifying details of individual partners and SA402 for corporate partners. SA400 is not needed for an LLP, the existence of which will be automatically notified to HMRC by Companies House when the LLP is formed; but SA401 and SA402 remain relevant for LLPs.

21.2 By virtue of the *TMA 1970, s 12AA(1)* HMRC may require the making of a partnership return to facilitate the establishment of the amounts in which each partner is chargeable to income tax (or, for corporate partners, corporation tax). This may be done either under *s 12AA(2)* or *s 12AA(3)*.

A notice under *s 12AA(2)* is given to 'the partners' (normally in practice issued in the name of the partnership) and requires 'such person as is identified in accordance with rules given with the notice or a successor of his' to make and deliver a return. In fact, the standard form of notice served by HMRC (form SA316) does not actually set out or enclose any rules. Although this might call into question the validity of the notice in penalty proceedings for failure to comply with the notice, in practice most partnerships very wisely comply with the notice regardless of any deficiency in form.

Alternatively a notice may be given under *s 12AA(3)* 'to any partner' requiring the partner or a successor of his to make and deliver a return. Where a notice is given under *s 12AA(3)* it may be given to any partner, or separate notices may be given to each partner or to such partners as HMRC think fit.

One interesting point of distinction between notices under *s 12AA(2)* and *s 12AA(3)* is that while both may require 'such information as may reasonably be required' together with the delivery of 'such accounts and statements as may reasonably be required', it is only a notice under *s 12AA(2)* that may further require 'such documents relating to information contained in the return' as may reasonably be required.

HMRC procedures assume the existence of a 'nominated' or 'representative' partner with whom HMRC will deal. Indeed HMRC guidance goes so far as to say (incorrectly) that 'the members of a partnership are required by *s 12AA(2)* to nominate a partner who will act for the partnership in relation to a return, claim or other matter' (PM20200) and form SA 400 both identifies and is signed by the 'nominated partner'. Regardless of whether it is strictly necessary for a partnership to 'nominate' a partner in this way it is clearly sensible for a partnership to do so, and for any partnership agreement to set out how this is to be done.

Where a partner has been 'nominated' it will normally be that partner who files the return, whether it is addressed to him by name or to the partnership.

21.3 The partnership return (SA800) comprises an eight-page core tax return showing trading profits and untaxed interest and alternative finance receipts from UK banks or building societies. If the partnership has received other income or has disposed of chargeable assets, details will need to be shown on the relevant supplementary pages for UK property income, foreign income, chargeable disposals or other income as appropriate.

Where a partnership (or more likely an LLP) registered in the UK has no UK resident partners, no income or gains arising in the UK and is managed and controlled outside the UK, HMRC may agree that no partnership return is required (see PM41000 and also **Chapter 20**).

Where a partnership has more than one trade, HMRC require the completion of separate trading and professional income pages (PT1–4) for each trade. Where there are two or more trades, the individual partners must complete multiple partnership pages with their personal self-assessment returns.

21.4 As well as giving details of trading income and untaxed interest (together with details of other income and disposals, if appropriate) the partnership return includes a short partnership statement which shows, for each partner, his or her name, address, National Insurance number, unique tax reference number ('UTR') and date of admission to or retirement from the partnership if it occurred during the year or the preceding year. It also states the individual partner's share of profits, losses, adjustments on change of basis ('catch-up charges'), construction industry tax deductions, tax deducted and partnership charges. Where a partnership carries on two or more separate trades, a separate partnership statement will be prepared for each trade.

A partnership return will be treated as incomplete and rejected by HMRC if it does not contain all details (including UTR) of each partner. Failure by a partner to obtain a UTR or to pass it on to the 'nominated partner' making the return will not be regarded as a 'reasonable excuse' for failure to complete a partnership tax return. Since such a failure will result in penalties being levied on all partners (and not just the partner whose UTR is missing) this may be regarded as containing an element of unfairness; but HMRC's position is clearly set out at PM20410.

21.5 Where a partnership carries on a trade or profession, the return normally requires completion of 'Standard Accounts Information' which, as the name suggests, presents the information which would normally be found in a set of accounts in a standardised format. However, if the turnover of the business exceeds £15 million HMRC require submission of full accounts and tax computations, with only limited information required to be entered on the face of the tax return itself.

21.6 The return will normally cover the trading and professional income for the accounting period(s) ending within the relevant tax year unless the partnership ceased in the period (in which case the basis period runs from the end of the previous year's basis period until the date of cessation).

If the partnership carries on a trade, other untaxed non-trading income (ie, income from which UK tax has not been deducted at source) is reported by reference to the same basis period as for the trade. If it does not carry on a trade, all income is reported on a strict 'tax year' basis. Whether or not the partnership carries on a trade 'taxed' non-trading income is always reported on a strict 'tax year' basis.

21.7 Computations of partnership capital gains are not required since, amongst other things, different partners may have, in relation to the same partnership asset, different acquisition costs or dates of acquisition. However, although computations are not required, details of disposals must be provided. Since capital gains are always assessed (as regards individuals) on a tax year basis, care must be taken to ensure that disposals are always reported on that basis. Thus, if a disposal occurs in January 2017, it must be notified on the 2016/17 partnership return, even if the partnership's year end is 30 April and the partnership thus reports on the 2016/17 return its trading profits for the year to 30 April 2016. This remains the case even though at the time by which the return is required to be filed in January 2018 the accounting period in which the disposal occurred may not have ended and accounts may not be available. It appears that the requirement to return disposals on a tax year basis applies even in the case of 'CT Partnerships' (ie, partnerships all the members of which are companies).

21.8 A notice requiring a partnership to file a tax return is normally issued on or shortly after 6 April following the end of the tax year. Where this is the case the return must normally be submitted by 31 October next following the end of the tax year if submitted on paper and by 31 January if submitted electronically (*TMA 1970, s 12AA(4A) and (4B)*). But if for any reason the notice requiring a return is issued late, the deadlines are in each case extended so that they will always fall at least three months after the date the notice is issued. Thus if a notice is given on, say, 31 August, a paper return will be in time if filed by 30 November and if a notice is given on, say, 31 December a paper or an electronic return will be in time if filed by 31 March (*TMA 1970, s 12AA(4D) and (4E))*.

21.9 One point to note is that HMRC's free on-line software does not allow for filing of a partnership return. A partnership must therefore either file a paper return or purchase proprietary software to file electronically (or of course appoint an agent with access to such software. In *Creative Eye Photography LLP & Helipix LLP v HMRC* [2017] UKFTT 399 (TC) one of the members of the LLP had attached a pdf copy of the partnership return to the personal tax return that had been filed electronically. When this was done for 2010/11; HMRC had levied a penalty for failure to file a partnership return but had cancelled the penalty on appeal. When the same thing happened for 2011/12, HMRC declined to cancel the penalty. Before the Tribunal the taxpayer argued that the cancellation of the penalty for 2010/11 meant that it was reasonable for them to have supposed that this was an acceptable way to file a partnership tax return. The Tribunal made it clear that it agreed with HMRC that 'filing' in this way was not in fact acceptable. However, the Tribunal agreed that the taxpayers had a reasonable excuse and allowed the appeal – HMRC should have made that clear in writing to the taxpayers when cancelling the 2010/11 penalty that a partnership return must either be filed on paper or using commercially available software: attaching a pdf to a personal return would not do.

21.10 If a partnership contains a company, the filing date for the return cannot be earlier than nine months from the end of the 'relevant period' (for a paper return) or 12 months from the end of the 'relevant period' (for an electronic return) *(TMA 1970, s 12AA(5), (5A), (5B))*.

The 'relevant period' is defined as 'the period in respect of which the return is required' (*TMA 1970, s 12AA(5D)*). The difficulty with that definition is that by *s 12AA(8)* a return may (and normally does) 'require different information, accounts and statements for different periods'. For example, a return normally requires details of the trading profit for the accounting period ending in the tax year but the details of taxed income required are those for the tax year itself (see **21.6** above). And disposals of assets are always returned on a tax year basis. There is, therefore, strictly no single 'period in respect of which the return is required'. Nonetheless HMRC express the view at PTRG31 that the relevant period will normally be taken to be the partnership's accounting period, but will be the tax year itself where:

- the partnership makes up its accounts to 5 April; or
- there are no partnership accounts ending in the year; or
- the partnership is an investment partnership which does not carry on a trade or profession.

Thus in HMRC's view, except in the three special cases above, *s 12AA(5)* in practice extends the filing date only if the accounting date falls after 31 January. However, in the writer's view this is not necessarily correct. It is at least arguable that the definition of 'relevant period' in *s 12AA(5D)* will always result in the 'relevant period' being the tax year itself (since that is always one of the periods for which the return is required, even if in any particular case there is no income and there are no disposals to be returned for that period). That would have the result that the earliest filing date for a return filed by a partnership containing a company can never be before 5 January following the tax year (for a paper return) or 5 April (for an electronic return).

While it is not recommended that this interpretation should be relied upon as a planning point (it will always be safer to file before the date which HMRC considers, rightly or wrongly, to be the filing date) it may offer a means of challenging any penalty levied in respect of a return filed 'late' (in HMRC's view) but before 5 January or 5 April as appropriate.

Whichever interpretation is correct, it will be the case that if the partnership filing date is extended under *s 12AA(5)* the partnership filing date will fall later than the date on which individual members of the partnership must file their personal tax returns.

In such cases it may be that the partnership tax return can be completed and submitted before the formal filing date, but where this is not possible, each individual partner will have to include in his or her personal return an estimate of the share of partnership profits, and correct the estimate if necessary when the final figure becomes available on filing of the partnership return.

Penalties will apply if the partnership return is not submitted on time (*Finance Act 2009* ('*FA 2009*'), *s 106, Sch 55*).

21.11 If the partnership return contains provisional figures and cannot be completed with final figures in time for it to be submitted by the due date, the relevant box on the return must be ticked and the following information provided in the additional information space:

- which figures are provisional (give box numbers);
- why the final figures could not be provided; and
- the date when final figures will be available.

In the Tax Return Guide, HMRC advise that, in this case, the return will not be rejected as incomplete. It does not, however, regard pressure of work (in relation to the partnership or its advisers) or the complexity of its affairs as a valid reason for entering provisional figures.

The provisional numbers entered on the return must be as accurate as possible. Detailed workings should be retained to refute a later allegation of negligence, in the event that the final figure turns out to be significantly different. The partnership must also make every effort to supply the final figures as soon as possible.

21.12 Provisional numbers are not the same as estimates and valuations. Where figures are entered on the return and there is a degree of uncertainty about them, but no further amendment will be made, the numbers affected and their basis of calculation should be drawn to HMRC's attention in the additional information box.

21.13 If, after a return has been made, it is found to be incorrect, it may be amended by the partner who made the return or by his successor under *TMA 1970, s 12ABA*. But this may be done only within an 'amendment window' which expires 12 months after the 'filing date' (which means the latest date by which the return was required to be filed, not the date on which the return was actually filed).

Following an amendment of the return, HMRC will issue an 'amendment notice' to each partner affected by the amendment, the effect of which is to amend the partner's personal return by increasing or decreasing the amount of tax payable as appropriate. There is no right of appeal on the part of the partner against such a consequential 'amendment notice'. It appears that if the partner receiving such an 'amendment notice' disagrees with it, his only remedy is to invoke *s 9ZA* (within the time limit for doing so, which is 12 months from the filing date) and amend his return back to the original figures. HMRC would then have the right to give notice of enquiry into the personal return as amended. If the 'amendment notice' is issued after the time limit for amending the return (which is possible if the time limit has expired between the time at which the partnership gives the notice to HMRC under *s 12ABA* and the time at which HMRC issue the 'amendment notice' to the partner) it would seem that any challenge could be made only using the process of judicial review.

If an amendment is made under *s 12ABA* after HMRC have issued a notice enquiring into the return the amendment is, in effect, held in suspense and is not given effect until the enquiry is concluded when it is normally taken into account in the conclusions stated in the enquiry notice (*TMA 1970, s 12AD*).

If an error is discovered outside of the 'amendment window' which has resulted in an *understatement* of partnership income the partner filing the return is unable to amend the return but is nonetheless obliged to notify HMRC that the return is incorrect. Normally HMRC would then make a 'discovery' amendment to the partnership tax return under *s 30B*. For the processes involved in *s 30B*, including rights of appeal and the effect on partners' personal returns, see **21.39** below.

In either case, HMRC may be expected to consider whether the inaccuracy in the original return was attributable to carelessness or deliberate failure on the part of the partner filing it and to consider what penalties if any may be exigible in respect of the inaccuracy.

21.14 If an error is discovered outside of the 'amendment window' which has resulted in an *overstatement* of partnership income resulting in one of more of the partners overpaying tax, it may be possible to make a claim under *TMA 1970, Sch 1AB* for relief for overpaid tax, subject to the limitations and exclusions contained in *para 2*. The time limit for the claim is four years from the end of the year of assessment. A single claim is made (under *para 5*) on behalf of all the partners by a 'relevant partner' who must be nominated for the purpose by all the partners who were partners in the partnership during the affected period (or by their personal representatives).

21.15 Until the *Finance Act 2013*, there was no machinery for HMRC to withdraw a notice requiring a return to be filed. *TMA 1970, s 12AAA* remedies that omission by providing that if a partner who has been served with a notice to file a partnership return considers that the issue of the notice is inappropriate he may request HMRC to withdraw the notice. Such a request may not be made after the return in question has been filed, but subject to that may be made:

- in respect of partnerships involving a company, within the period of two years after the end of 'the period in respect of which the return under s 12AA was required'. As to the meaning and ambiguity of that phrase, see **21.10** above;
- in respect of other partnerships, within the period of two years from the end of the year of assessment to which the notice relates.

In either case HMRC are empowered in exceptional circumstances to agree a longer period.

On receipt of such a request, HMRC may or may not decide to withdraw the notice and to cancel any penalty incurred for failure to comply with it. The decision is entirely within HMRC's discretion – if HMRC decide not to comply with a request that a notice should be withdrawn the legislation does not lay down any appeal procedure. And if HMRC do agree to withdraw a notice this does not preclude the issue of further notice requiring a return for the relevant year if HMRC subsequently conclude that a return is, after all, required.

Personal tax returns

21.16 Each partner is responsible for transferring the information on the partnership return to his or her self-assessment return. An individual partner should not normally make any alteration or amendment to the figures and details supplied on the partnership return but should ensure that the personal tax return matches the partnership statement. It will, therefore, be necessary for the partnership return to include any adjustments to partnership profit required by reason of any matters dealt with by a partner personally, such as partnership-related expenses incurred and borne personally or capital allowances on assets owned personally and used within the partnership.

It may happen that a partner believes that the figure of profit that is allocated to him or her on the partnership return is incorrect. This may be either because there is disagreement as to the quantum of the partnership profit for tax purposes or because there is disagreement as to how the partnership profit is allocated for tax purposes. On the face of it this puts the partner in an impossible position: *TMA 1970, s 8(1B)* requires him to include on his return 'each amount which, in any relevant [partnership] statement is stated to be equal to his share of any income [etc]' but *s 8(2)* requires him to include on his return a declaration that it is to the best of his knowledge correct and complete.

This was the quandary before the Tribunal in *Morgan v CIR*; *Self v CIR* [2009] UKFTT 78 (TC). In the event the Tribunal held that the figures allocated to the relevant partners on the partnership return were correct. But the Chairman expressed (albeit as *obiter dicta*) the view that where a partner disagreed with the accuracy of the figure of taxable profit allocated to him or her on the partnership statement the correct procedure was for the partner to self-assess on the basis of the amount believed to be the correct figure but also to disclose in the return the amount shown in the partnership statement.

The comments made by the First-tier Tribunal in *Morgan* and *Self* are now reflected in HMRC guidance at EM7025. But despite this, HMRC took the case of *King v HMRC*

[2016] UKFTT 0409 in which they effectively argued that their own guidance in EM7025 was incorrect. Although, as a First-tier Tribunal decision, *Morgan* and *Self* was not binding on the Tribunal in *King*, the decision was followed:

> 'Therefore, despite clearly being obiter, the observations of Dr Brice on s 8 TMA in Morgan and Self were made after hearing argument on the issue from experienced leading counsel on both sides and, as such, should not be dismissed lightly. Rather, having carefully considered what she said, particularly at [74], I would adopt her reasoning and agree that the purpose of s 8 TMA is to establish the right amount of tax.'

Thus where an individual partner disagrees with the amount allocated to him in the partnership return, best practice would be that the partner should:

- enter on the return as the share of partnership profits the amount that he considers to be correct;
- make a note in the white space identifying:
  - the amount shown as profit allocated to him in the partnership return;
  - a statement of the difference between that figure and the figure included in the personal return;
  - an explanation as to why the partnership return is considered incorrect and the personal return correct.

The second Finance Bill of 2017 proposes to reverse the position established by Morgan and Self by introducing a mechanism to allow any dispute between partners as to the allocation of profit between them to be referred for adjudication to the First-Tier Tax Tribunal. This change will apply to returns relating to the tax year 2018/19 or any subsequent tax year. This will apply only to disputes as to how the taxable profit is allocated: if the dispute is about the quantum of the partnership taxable profit the usual appeal processes described in this chapter will apply.

A claim for relief for interest on borrowing by a partner personally for introduction of capital to the partnership or purchase of a share in a partnership is, however, a personal claim by the partner against his or her statutory total income, not an adjustment to his or her partnership share and is entered on the individual partner's tax return (see **Chapter 3**). For the effect that this may have on the procedure under which HMRC may enquire into such claims, see **21.27** below.

Tax payments

21.17 Partnerships do not receive taxpayer statements of account, because they do not pay tax. Each individual partner is responsible for paying the tax due on his or her share of partnership profits (and other income) along with any tax due on other income and gains. The partner will pay the tax in the usual way, namely two payments on account of the tax liabilities if appropriate on 31 January in the tax year and 31 July after the end of the tax year, with a balancing payment due on 31 January after the end of the tax year.

21.18 Although tax on partnership profits is a liability of each partner and not of the partnership, a partnership may as a matter of convenience wish to pay tax on behalf of the partners. Where this is done it is important that details are given to HMRC of how any payment is to be apportioned between the various partners. Such an arrangement (which is entirely a matter of private agreement between the partners) is often encountered in conjunction with the partnership's retaining tax due on the partnership income by way of a tax reserve (see **Chapter 27**).

21.19 Where an amount of tax becomes payable by or repayable to a partner as a result of a taxpayer amendment to a partnership return made under *s 12ABA* (see **21.13** above) or an HMRC correction under *s 12ABB* (see **21.21** below) the due date for paying (or repaying) the tax is the later of:

(a) the normal due date;

(b) 30 days after the 'amendment notice' is issued to the partner by HMRC.

Records

21.20 Partnerships (along with other taxpayers) are required to keep the records that are needed to make their returns until five years and ten months from the end of the relevant tax year or, if later, the date of completion of enquiries into the return or the date of expiry of the time limit for making enquiries (*TMA 1970, s 12B*). There are similar record-keeping requirements in relation to claims that are not made in the return (*TMA 1970, Sch 1A*). There is a penalty of up to £3,000 for failing to comply with the record-keeping requirements (*TMA 1970, s 12B(5), Sch 1A, para 2A(4)*).

Enquiries

21.21 An officer of HMRC may correct any obvious errors or omissions, whether of principle or arithmetic, in a partnership return, or anything else in the return that the officer has reason to believe is incorrect in the light of the information available to him. This can be done only within nine months after the date on which the return is delivered or (if the correction is required in consequence of an amendment made to the return by the taxpayer) within nine months after the date of the amendment. Any 'correction' is made by giving notice to the partner who made the return or to his successor (*TMA 1970, s 12ABB(3)*). The partner to whom the correction notice is given (or his successor) has the unfettered right to reject the correction notice within 30 days of its issue: if this right is exercised the correction notice and any consequent amendments are of no effect.

Where the partnership return is 'corrected' in this way, HMRC will also amend each partner's personal return by issuing an 'amendment notice'. This will not normally be done until the 30 day period for rejection of the 'correction' by the partnership has expired. There is no right of appeal by a partner against an amendment notice issued following a correction under *s 12ABB*. It is suggested that the position is similar to an amendment notice issued following a taxpayer amendment under *s 12ABA* (see **21.13** above) such that if the partner receiving such an amendment notice disagrees with it, his only remedy is to invoke *s 9ZA* and amend his return back to the original figures (if within time to do so) or to seek judicial review (if the time limit for a 'taxpayer amendment' under *s 9ZA* has passed).

21.22 Quite separately from the 'correction' procedure described at **21.21**, HMRC may enquire into any partnership return by sending a notice of enquiry to the partner who made and delivered the return or to any successor. Any enquiry must be made within strict time limits, namely:

- If the return was delivered to HMRC on or before the filing date, HMRC have up to the end of the period of 12 months after the day on which the return was delivered to commence enquiry proceedings.
- If the return was delivered after the filing date, HMRC have up to and including the quarter day next following the first anniversary of the day on which the return was delivered to commence proceedings.
- If the return is amended under *TMA 1970, s 12ABA*, the time limit is up to and including the quarter day next following the first anniversary of the day on which the amendment was made.

For this purpose, the quarter days are 31 January, 30 April, 31 July and 31 October (*TMA 1970, s 12AC(2)*).

21.23 There is no particular formality about the giving of the notice. According to the Special Commissioner in *Flaxmode Ltd v HMRC* [2008] STC (SCD) 666, 'all that is needed is something in writing which informs the taxpayer than an enquiry is underway'. *Section 12ABB(2)* does, however, specify that the notice must be given to the person 'who made or delivered the return, or to his successor'. In the case of *Sword Service and others v HMRC* [2016] EWHC 1473 (Admin) the validity of enquiry notices was challenged on the grounds that they had not been served on the partners making the returns. This was an avoidance case involving a large number of general partnerships and LLPs where there had been some confusion as to which of the companies formed by the promoters ('the FCP group') were members of (or had filed returns for) which of the partnerships. The court took a broad view of the matter, citing *Flaxmode* and observing that 'the reality from early on with this tax avoidance scheme was that the FCP group knew that HMRC would be enquiring into the tax returns of the partnerships associated with it'. On the facts of the case, the partners making and delivering the tax returns 'did not receive formal notices of the enquiry, but since they knew of the enquiry that is sufficient for the purposes of the legislation'.

21.24 Where an enquiry is made into a partnership return it is HMRC's normal practice to notify each partner of that fact by letter. This is not a legal requirement but is regarded by HMRC as good 'customer service'.

21.25 A notice of enquiry into the partnership return is considered to be the only basis on which any matter relating to the partnership may be enquired into. Thus if HMRC issue an enquiry notice under *TMA 1970, s 9A* in respect of the personal tax return of a partner, that enquiry is limited to non-partnership aspects of the person's affairs.

21.26 The giving of notice of enquiry into a partnership return is deemed to constitute the giving of notice of enquiry into the return of each of the partners, under *s 12AC(6)*. This deemed enquiry notice is valid even if the time limit for issuing an actual notice has passed. This might be the case if the partner's tax return has been filed on time but the partnership return is filed late.

It is HMRC's view (as expressed at EM 7050) that the deemed enquiry notice 'exists simply to ensure that HMRC is able to make any adjustments to the self assessments of the partners arising from any amendments to the partnership statement as a result of the enquiry into the partnership return' and that if HMRC wish in addition to make enquiries into the non-partnership aspects of a partner's tax return a separate 'actual' enquiry notice must be issued to the partner under *s 9A* in addition to the deemed enquiry notice under s 12AC(6). In the light of *s 9A(3)* which provides that a return which has been the subject of one notice of enquiry may not be the subject of another, HMRC's view is at best questionable. In particular, *s 9A(3)* would seem to give grounds to question the validity of a purported enquiry into 'non-partnership' aspects of a partner's tax return which is commenced after an enquiry into the partnership return for the same year has been concluded.

Focus

All partners' returns will remain open until the partnership enquiry is complete. It should be noted that an enquiry into the personal returns of one of the partners will not automatically open up the partnership statement for enquiry, but unexplained funds or irregularities involving partnership transactions could trigger further enquiries or be persuasive in respect of other partners.

21.27 The uncertain scope of a deemed enquiry notice under *s 12AC* can also cause some difficulty for HMRC, as may be evidenced in film partnership cases such as *Eclipse Film Partners No 35 LLP v HMRC* [2015] EWCA Civ 95. The tax planning in this case depended upon tax relief being available to members of an LLP in respect of interest paid on very substantial loans which they had, as individuals, taken out in order to invest in the LLP. That tax relief in turn depended upon whether the LLP was carrying on a trade. HMRC raised an enquiry into the LLP's return and had closed the enquiry with a closure notice concluding that the LLP was not carrying on a trade, a conclusion that was upheld, ultimately by the Court of Appeal. The difficulty, from HMRC's point of view, is that the question whether the LLP was or was not carrying on a trade had, on the facts of the case, very little effect on the LLP itself. It is at least arguable that the claims for relief for loan interest are purely personal tax matters with no direct connection to the partnership so that any challenge to the availability of tax relief for the interest needs to be challenged not by an enquiry into the LLP return (and the consequent deemed enquiry notices on the partners) but by actual enquiry notices served on each of the partners personally. This aspect of the case is understood to be continuing at the time of writing.

21.28 HMRC differentiate between an 'aspect' enquiry into a partnership return and a 'full' enquiry. An 'aspect' enquiry' is an enquiry into one or more discrete aspects of the return (typically an enquiry into some technical aspect of the return). A 'full' enquiry is likely to involve a review of the books and records of the business with a view to testing the underlying accuracy of the return.

The terms 'aspect' and 'full' enquiry are used for departmental convenience and do not appear in the statute. As a matter of law there is no differentiation between the two types of enquiry: HMRC either issue a notice of enquiry or they do not. However, it is HMRC's normal practice in the case of a 'full' enquiry to issue actual enquiry notices to each of the partners under *s 9A* with a view to looking closely at all aspects of each partner's tax affairs as well as those of the partnership: in effect enquiries into the partners will run concurrently with enquiries into the partnership. In the case of an 'aspect' enquiry, it is likely that separate *s 9A* notices will not be issued and the examination of the tax affairs of the partners will be limited to partnership aspects.

21.29 A partnership enquiry is completed when HMRC issue a closure notice under *TMA 1970, s 28B(1)* informing the partnership (or, more specifically, the person to whom the enquiry notice was given or his successor) that the enquiry is complete and stating either:

- that no amendment to the return is required; or
- the amendments required to give effect to HMRC's conclusions.

During the course of the enquiry the partner to whom the notice of enquiry was given (which will of course be the partner who made the return, or his successor) has the right to apply to the tribunal for a direction requiring HMRC to issue a closure notice within a specified period. Any such application is heard in the same way as an appeal.

A right of appeal against the partnership closure notice is given by *TMA 1970, s 31*. Although the appeal right would normally be exercised by the person to whom the closure notice is issued, *Gibbs v HMRC* [2013] UKFTT 236 (TC) indicates that any partner has the right to appeal.

21.30 When a closure notice is given amending a partnership return, HMRC must give a notice amending the individual partners' returns (both personal and corporate) (*TMA 1970, s 28B(4)*) so as to give effect to the conclusions stated in the closure notice. Although the legislation is not explicit, it seems to be a necessary implication that the issue of the amendment notice also has the effect of terminating the separate 'deemed enquiry' into the partner's return which is deemed to have been opened by the issue of the partnership enquiry notice. Any additional tax becomes payable (and any overpayment becomes repayable) 30 days after the amendment notice is given.

A partner has no separate right of appeal against an amendment notice (see *King and others v HMRC* [2016] UKFTT 409 (TC)). Where the amendment notice increases the amount of tax payable by the partner the absence of any right to appeal against the issue of the notice inevitably means that there is no right to seek postponement of the tax resulting from its issue, even where the partnership closure notice itself is appealed. Contrast this with position where an enquiry into a personal return is concluded with a closure notice under *s 28A* against which an appeal is made, where *TMA 1970, s 55* gives a right to apply for postponement of tax pending resolution of the appeal. For this reason HMRC will normally defer issuing amendment notices under *s 28B(4)* until the partnership position becomes final either on expiry of the appeal period with no appeal having been made or on the final resolution of the appeal by the Tribunal (see EM7205).

It is HMRC's view that an amendment notice is capable of amending only 'partnership aspects' of the partner's return. Thus if, for example, the partnership enquiry is into the proceeds of disposal of a partnership asset, any amendment notice is capable of amending the share of proceeds brought into a partner's personal tax return, but is not capable of making other amendments to the partner's capital gains tax computation (such as the allowable cost). See EM7015.

21.31 Any appeal against a partnership closure notice may be settled by agreement (*TMA 1970, s 54*) between the person making the appeal and HMRC. Where this happens, the same consequences ensue as if the Tribunal had heard the appeal and had given a decision corresponding with the terms of the agreement.

In *De Silva* [2016] EWCA Civ 40 an appeal in a limited partnership case involving tax avoidance had been settled by agreement between the general partner and HMRC to the effect that the amount of the tax losses stated in the partnership tax return would be substantially reduced. It was held in the High Court that 'the Claimants' (who were limited partners in the partnership) 'were not parties to the partnership settlement agreement and so were not directly bound by its terms'. But this was reversed by the Court of Appeal, which held that there was no dispute as to the fact that the general partner had power to bind the partners such that 'the partnership settlement agreement was contractually binding upon the Appellants as limited partners and they were bound by its provisions, including the agreement only to claim limited sums by way of relief in respect of partnership losses.'

21.32 The *De Silva* case referred to above also gives helpful guidance and analysis on the substantive and procedural issues which can arise in partnership loss cases.

Mr De Silva had made claims in his tax returns for 1998/99 and 1999/2000 to set off against his income for the year his share of the partnership tax losses shown in the partnership tax returns for later years and repayments had been made. No enquiry had been made by HMRC into the loss claims under the provisions of *TMA 1970, Sch 1A* and by the time the case came to court the time limit for making any enquiry under that provision had long since expired.

Subsequently, however, an enquiry was made into the tax returns of the partnerships for the years in which the losses arose, with consequential deemed enquiries into the tax returns of the partners for the relevant years. That enquiry had been concluded by agreement between HMRC and the general partner on behalf of the partnership under *TMA 1970, s 54* to the effect that partnership losses should be reduced. Mr De Silva sought to argue that despite the agreement to restrict the partnership losses, no amendment could now be made to claims to loss relief he had made. Any enquiry, it was argued, should have been made into the claim as a 'free-standing' claim under *Sch 1A*.

It was held by the Court of Appeal that any loss claim necessarily involves the inclusion of the loss in the tax return for the year in which the loss is said to have been made. It therefore followed that it would always be open to HMRC to frame its enquiry into the amount of the loss as an enquiry into the tax return for the year of loss. The Court of Appeal approved the

High Court's description of Mr De Silva's claim in the earlier years as an 'inchoate' claim which could 'only ultimately be made good if the Appellants also eventually included their shares of the partnership trading losses in their own individual returns for the periods in which those losses actually arose'. Thus the effect of the reduction in the losses as a result of the conclusion of the enquiry into the later years was that only the reduced amount of loss relief was available and the self-assessments were to be amended accordingly.

21.33 Normally, where in the course of an enquiry HMRC conclude that the taxpayer's self-assessment is understated, and that unless the assessment is immediately amended there is likely to be a loss of tax to the Crown, HMRC have the power to make a 'jeopardy amendment' under *TMA 1970, s 9C*. This would normally be contemplated only where HMRC suspect that a taxpayer is considering taking steps to avoid payment such as leaving the country, disposing of assets, applying for bankruptcy etc such that immediate amendment is necessary to protect the revenue.

Because a partnership is not itself liable to tax, the rules on 'jeopardy amendments' do not apply to partnerships. However, if there is, alongside the partnership enquiry, an enquiry into a partner's personal return (as will normally be the case for a 'full' partnership enquiry) HMRC may be able to make a 'jeopardy amendment' to the partner's self-assessment. Any decision to proceed under *s 9C* must be made in respect of each partner separately by reference to the risk of a loss of tax from that specific partner.

21.34 It is important for partnerships to take all steps to minimise the risk of an enquiry by:

- keeping good accounting records;
- undertaking a careful review of the accounts and returns prior to submission, particularly with regard to compliance with generally accepted accounting practices (GAAP), where appropriate (see **Chapter 1**);
- submitting returns on time; and
- making adequate disclosure in the return to prevent a later discovery assessment (see **21.39**).

21.35 HMRC use information from a variety of sources in deciding whether to commence an enquiry, including third-party sources (registers and applications) and informal sources such as tip-offs. More likely, however, the enquiry will arise from a review of the accounts, the business sector in which the partnership operates, or random selection.

21.36 HMRC have the same rights to call for partnership documents and records as for individuals. Penalties can be imposed for failure to produce documents subject to a right of appeal. Often the main focus of the enquiry is an attempt to prove that the accounting records do not support the entries on the return or are in some way deficient.

21.37 If the partnership and HMRC cannot agree on a matter raised in an enquiry, it is possible to refer the case to the tribunal at any time during the enquiry process if they jointly decide to do so (*TMA 1970, s 28ZA*).

HMRC's power to review earlier years

21.38 No valid enquiry notice may be issued once the 'enquiry window' has closed.

21.39 However, under *TMA 1970, s 30B* HMRC may amend a partnership return where they 'discover' outside the 'enquiry window' that partnership profits have been understated However, they may do so in only two circumstances.

The first is where the understatement has been brought about carelessly or deliberately by any person who was a partner in the relevant period or by someone acting on behalf of such a person.

The second is where, at the time when the 'enquiry window' closed (or any enquiry into the return was completed) HMRC could not have been reasonably expected, on the basis of the information then available, to have been aware of the understatement. *Section 30B* specifies certain documents which are deemed to be available. As to the matters of which HMRC could be 'reasonably expected' to be aware at any particular time, there has been much case law. An exhaustive discussion of 'discovery' lies outside the scope of this book: reference should be made, as a starting-point, to HMRC guidance at EM3250.

The normal rights of appeal apply to a 'discovery amendment' under *s 30B.* Although the appeal right would normally be exercised by the partner who filed the partnership return, *Gibbs v HMRC [2013] UKFTT 236 (TC)* indicates that any partner has the right to appeal.

21.40 Following a 'discovery amendment' HMRC will make whatever amendments to the personal returns of the separate partners are required in order to give effect to the 'discovery amendment' under *s 30B(2).* As with 'consequential amendments' under *s 28B(4),* partners have no separate right of appeal against personal 'discovery amendments'. Because there is (as with 'consequential amendments' under *s 28B(4)*) no machinery to allow postponement of tax charged by such an amendment it is HMRC's practice not to make these amendments until after any appeal against the partnership 'discovery amendment' has been finally determined or the appeal period has expired without any appeal having been made. .

There is no statutory time limit for making a 'discovery amendment' to a partnership return under *s 30B(1).* Nor, as a matter of strict law, is there any time limit for making a 'consequential discovery amendment' to a partner's return under *s 30B(2)* since the amendment is not strictly speaking an 'assessment' to which the time limits in *s 34–s 36* apply. But in practice HMRC regard their ability to make adjustments to partners' self assessments as restricted by the normal time limit of four years after the end of the relevant tax year for making assessments – see EM7101. Where the understatement is attributable to the person's carelessness the time limit is extended to six years: and where it is brought about deliberately, to 20 years. The carelessness or deliberate failure must normally be that of the person assessed. However, the effect of *TMA 1970, s 36(1B)* and *s 36(2)* is that carelessness or deliberate failure in respect of the partnership position by any partner (such as the partner filing the tax return) is deemed to be that of all the partners, opening the door to these extended time limits.

Although HMRC's position is not completely clear, it appears that HMRC regard the time limits as applying by reference to the date on which the discovery amendment notice is served on the partnership under *s 30B(1)* rather than that on which consequential discovery amendment notices are served on partners under *s 30B(2)*. For example, for a discovery relating to tax year 2014/15 and not involving carelessness or deliberate failure, it appears that HMRC would regard themselves as able to serve partner notices under *s 30B(2)* at any time, provided a partnership notice under *s 30B(1)* had been issued before 6 April 2019.

21.41 As to penalties, there are fixed and tax-based penalties for failure or delay in filing returns, and for careless or deliberate misconduct in submitting accounts and computations.

Penalties are not charged on the partnership. Each individual partner will be liable to the various fixed penalties and to tax-geared penalties, calculated by reference to the partner's circumstances and tax rates, a separate offer in settlement being required from each partner. Details of the penalties are given in **Appendix 6**.

21.42 To prevent a later allegation by HMRC that they had been given inadequate information, it is important to disclose all the relevant details on the return. The additional information box should be used if appropriate.

Additional disclosure may include:

- estimates;
- balancing numbers;
- private use proportions;
- the composition of numbers on the return, particularly if specifically required by HMRC;
- accounting policies;
- capital and current account movements, partner by partner;
- an explanation for low profits, losses or inconsistent results with the previous period;
- key transactions occurring in the period; and
- capital allowances computations.

It is a moot point whether accounts need to be submitted with the partnership return. HMRC indicate that these are only required where the turnover exceeds £15m. However, many of the above points could be disclosed simply by submitting the accounts along with the return. Where the accounts add nothing to the information on the return, their submission is debatable.

Focus

Where accounts (or any additional information) are submitted with the return, it is important to draw this to HMRC's attention in the additional information box on the return, and to indicate what additional information they contain that might be useful for the HMRC officer.

Penalties

21.43 The partners (not the partnership) can be penalised for:

- failing to file the partnership return by the due date;
- carelessly or deliberately filing an incorrect return.

Details of the penalties are set out in **Appendix 6**.

Chapter 22

Providing for Pensions and Life Assurance

Signposts

- Taxable share of partnership business income normally creates an entitlement to make pension contributions (see **22.1 – 22.2**).
- The annual allowance for pension contributions is £40,000 but is further restricted for those with incomes, including pensions contributions, above £150,000 (see **22.3**).
- Subject to certain conditions, any unused annual allowance may be carried forward for up to three tax years (see **22.3**).
- Tax relief on contributions above £3,600 is dependent upon the existence of 'relevant UK earnings' (see **22.4**).
- From 6 April 2016 the lifetime allowance is reduced to £1 million (see **22.5**).
- Self-invested schemes are one of several methods of allowing a group of partners to pool their resources and direct where some or all of the funds are held (see **22.7 – 22.12**).
- Term assurance policies, written on a discretionary trust basis, may be worth considering but the tax treatment of contributions and treatment of any recoveries should be carefully considered (see **22.13 – 22.15**).
- The changes to pensions introduced by the *Finance Act 2014* may offer increased flexibility (see **22.16 – 22.18**).

22.1 From 6 April 2006, a single set of simplified rules came into effect around how pensions are taxed, designed to offer simpler and more flexible retirement arrangements. The tax treatment for all types of approved schemes, including occupational schemes, small self-administered schemes ('SSASs'), personal pensions, self-invested personal pensions ('SIPPs') and retirement annuity contracts have been amalgamated into the rules for registered pension schemes. In addition, the tax treatment of unapproved schemes was changed (*Finance Act 2004* (*'FA 2004'*), *ss 149–284* and *Schs 28–36*).

22.2 The collapse of pension providers and continuing poor annuity rates caused deep mistrust of the pensions industry; but, despite these problems, pensions remain the main vehicle for long-term saving, and tax relief seems set to continue.

Broadly, partners paying personal pension premiums receive basic rate tax relief by paying contributions net of basic rate tax (which is reclaimed from HMRC by the pension scheme). Any higher rate relief is given in the computation of tax under self-assessment by extending the basic rate band appropriately.

Annual allowance

22.3 Contributions may be paid by (*FA 2004, ss 188, 196*):

- the scheme member;
- the member's current or former employer; or
- a third party on behalf of the member,

up to an annual maximum amount of £40,000. An 'annual allowance charge' is charged on contributions in excess of the annual allowance. This is levied at the 'appropriate rate' (ie broadly the individual's marginal tax rate) (*FA 2004, s 227*). An individual with an annual allowance charge of over £2,000 will in most cases be able to elect for his pension scheme to pay the liability instead, with scheme benefits being actuarially reduced accordingly (*FA 2004, s 237B*).

Any unused annual allowance for up to three tax years preceding the current tax year may be added to the annual allowance available for the current tax year, if it arises for a tax year in which the individual was a member of a registered pension scheme (even if the pension input amount for that year was nil).

From April 2016, the benefits of pensions tax relief are restricted for those with incomes, including pension contributions, over £150,000 by tapering away their annual allowance. For every £2 of adjusted income over £150,000, an individual's annual allowance will be reduced by £1 to a minimum of £10,000. To ensure the measure is significantly targeted, individuals with income, excluding pension contributions, below £110,000 will not have their annual allowance tapered.

Those individuals who access flexible income from their pension funds via drawdown or taking an uncrystallised funds pension lump sum ('UFPLS') will still be allowed to contribute to their pension plans but will now be subject to the Money Purchase Annual Allowance of £10,000 rather than the normal £40,000. Individuals who remain in Capped Drawdown can still contribute up to £40,000 per annum.

Tax relief

22.4 The basic rule is that tax relief is available for contributions up to the full amount of 'relevant UK earnings' for the year – broadly, income from employment, self-employment or furnished holiday lettings but only (in the case of a partnership) where the partner is 'acting personally' in the partnership. Profit share of a limited partner (who is by definition not 'acting personally') does not therefore count as 'relevant UK earnings'.

However, the amount on which tax relief is available is underpinned by a 'basic amount' of £3,600, which applies regardless of whether the individual has any 'relevant UK earnings' at all. This means that partners with low profits, or who are on a career break, can pay personal pension contributions and secure tax relief by deduction of source at the basic rate.

It may happen that contributions on which basic rate tax relief has been obtained on payment turn out to be excess of 'relevant UK earnings' (but within the annual allowance). This may occur, for example, where contributions are made early in the year in anticipation of receiving 'relevant UK earnings' for the year which do not in the event materialise. Where this happens the onus is on the individual to contact the administrator of the pension scheme to ensure that the scheme's claim to recover basic rate tax is restricted as necessary.

Lifetime allowance

22.5 There is a single lifetime allowance on the amount of pension savings that can benefit from tax relief. The value of the lifetime allowance for 2016/17 is £1 million, though in some cases there may be transitional protections in place to ensure that the successive reductions from the lifetime allowances which have previously applied are not effectively retrospective. The new lifetime allowance will be indexed annually in line with CPI from 6 April 2018.

The lifetime allowance applies to everyone, irrespective of the type of scheme to which they belong. Different forms of calculation are needed to establish an individual's entitlement.

There is a lifetime allowance charge of 25% on funds in excess of the lifetime allowance which are used to provide a pension. If funds in excess of the lifetime allowance are taken as a lump sum, there is a lifetime allowance charge (*FA 2004, s 215*) of 55%.

Focus

It was announced in the summer 2015 Budget that the Government will consult on whether and how to undertake a wider reform of pensions tax relief to encourage saving into pensions in the longer term. One suggestion is whether pensions should be put on a footing similar to individual savings accounts, ie 'taxed-exempt-exempt' ('TEE'). The consultation document suggests that the government is not trying to remove its financial encouragement for pensions provisions, and recognises the need for both members and employers to be encouraged to make proper pensions provision. The financial prize to the exchequer of moving to a 'TEE' basis would be significant, even if only from a cashflow point of view.

22.6 In a partnership situation, the partnership could allocate a prior slice of profit to each partner and require him or her to use it to provide for retirement by paying appropriate qualifying premiums, other partners then being absolved legally and morally from providing for that partner on his ceasing to be a partner.

There is a view that provision in this way should be a requirement of the partnership agreement, but it may be difficult to enforce because of the differing views amongst partners on how their retirement should be provided for.

A possible compromise is for partners' capital to be repaid by instalments in the several years before their retirement, enabling them, if they wish, to use those funds to pay qualifying premiums. The tax relief will reduce their tax liabilities, which in itself gives them more cash availability. Pension payments can then continue at up to £3,600 (gross) if the partner so desires.

Self-invested schemes

22.7 Self-invested schemes allow a group of partners to pool their resources and direct where some or all of the funds are held. Contribution limits, tax relief and benefits are governed by the rules for self-employed pensions.

There are three types of scheme: SIPPs, private funds and friendly societies. All schemes are subject to tight rules and regulations. Partnerships will require specialist advice before a scheme is set up.

Self-invested personal pensions

22.8 SIPPs are similar to small self-administered schemes and are offered by insurance and pension companies and actuaries. Investment advice may be provided by an investment adviser or the partners (if they have the necessary expertise). Hybrid schemes, where the fund is partly insured, are also possible.

> **Focus**
>
> Two or more partnerships could combine to form one self-invested personal pension scheme, allowing larger funds to be accumulated.

Private funds

22.9 These are insured schemes with an insurance company. The funds can be managed by the partners or an adviser.

Friendly societies

22.10 Seven or more partners can set up a friendly society governed by the *Friendly Societies Act 1992* and the *Trustee Investments Act 1961*. This avoids the need to involve an insurance company. Members can include salaried partners but not employees. The partners usually act as trustees. Running a friendly society may involve the partners in considerable amounts of administrative time.

Premiums and costs

22.11 One of the main problems with self-invested schemes is that a minimum level of initial and ongoing premiums is usually required. Administrative charges and fees for investment advice can also be high.

Owning property

22.12 Members must not be able to benefit from the investment prior to retirement and transactions with members and connected persons are prohibited. This precludes the purchase of property already owned by the partnership. However, the pension scheme may purchase commercial property and subsequently let it to the partnership on commercial terms. Further problems can also arise when partners retire or leave the scheme, as the existing partners have to find funds to pay pensions or transfers. If the membership of the scheme falls, there may also be funding difficulties.

Term assurance in favour of other partners

22.13 A term assurance policy held on the life of one partner by or in trust for other partners produces an asset in the hands of the partners owning the policy, not the partner whose life is insured, thus providing a capital sum for them to introduce to their own credit and using the cash generated to pay out the capital account, etc of the deceased partner.

Example 22.1 – Term assurance on other partners' lives – capital

Each of the lives of the partners in the Pilcher partnership is covered for £300,000, the proceeds payable to the surviving partners in the event of the death of any partner.

The capital of each partner is £300,000 and the expressed purpose of the policy is to provide funds for repayment of capital on the death of a partner. No claim to tax relief has been made in respect of the premiums paid.

Eric dies, being at that time one of 11 partners. The ten remaining partners receive the £300,000 sum assured between them and pay it into the firm to the credit of their capital accounts. The cash is then paid out to clear Eric's capital account.

The bank balance remains constant, and so does the partnership capital, but it is now held by ten partners excluding Eric, each of whom has a part of the policy proceeds to his credit, which has enabled each of the partners to introduce funds without the difficulty of having to raise them.

It is unlikely in these circumstances that the £300,000 received on Eric's death would be treated as taxable income of the business.

22.14 It is possible for such policies to be written on a discretionary trust basis, to avoid the complications which partnership changes would otherwise create.

22.15 The deductibility in computing profits of premiums on policies on the lives of partners and the taxability of any recoveries should be considered carefully.

Premiums will be deductible in computing profits of a trade or profession carried on by a partnership only if the expenditure is incurred 'wholly and exclusively' for the purposes of the trade or profession. This is likely to be the case only where the insurance is term cover (ie, with no surrender or investment value) taken out solely to provide funds to compensate for a loss of partnership income that it is foreseen may result from the death of a key partner.

Where tax relief has been claimed for the premiums any recovery will be taxable as business income of the partnership on the 'filling a hole' principle enunciated in *London & Thames Oil Wharves Ltd v Attwooll* [1966] 43 TC 491.

Generally speaking, where premiums do not pass the test for deductibility set out above, any recoveries will not be taken into account as business receipts. But this is subject to the caveat (see BIM 45525) that even where relief has not been claimed for the premiums 'whether particular receipts are part of trading income is a separate matter of law to the deductibility of expenditure. No assurance can be given that any future receipt will be excluded from trading income even though the premiums are not allowable.'

Where a policy is taken out in order to provide the necessary money to fund a return of capital or the repayment of a loan which will fall due on a partner's death, the premium will not be deductible and the recovery will not normally rank as a business receipt.

To minimise the risk of difficulty should the insured event occur, it is desirable that the reason for taking out cover and the purpose to which it was intended that any receipt should be applied should be documented (and of course that any receipt should demonstrably be applied to the stated purpose). Where it is likely that any receipt will be taxable, this will need to be taken into account in deciding the amount of cover required.

Where the proceeds of life insurance policies are not trading receipts, liability may arise under the chargeable events legislation in the *Income Tax (Trading and Other Income) Act 2005, Pt 4, Ch 9* – see also Statement of Practice SP6/92.

Example 22.2 – Term assurance on other partners' lives – income

The lives of the partners in the Polcher partnership are insured by the partnership for varying amounts, the amounts reflecting the income-generating skills of each partner, the expenses to which the partnership would be put in securing a replacement and the expected short-term loss of income that the partnership would suffer from the loss of the partner pending recruitment of a replacement. The amounts vary from £500,000 for a senior tax partner down to £100,000 for a junior audit partner.

It is likely that in these circumstances tax relief would be available for the premiums. Whether or not relief is actually claimed for them, it is likely that any receipt under the policy would be taken into account as income of the partnership business.

Weighing up the options

22.16 An objection to funding for retirement through tax-relievable premiums to a personal pension had previously been that the available lump sum at retirement is limited. It is now possible to take the entire pension fund as a lump sum with up to 25% of a pension pot, subject to the Lifetime Allowance, as tax-free. Withdrawals in excess of the 25% limit are charged to marginal rate tax. For individuals now looking to take pension benefits there are the following main options:

- With 'flexible drawdown' there is no limit on the amount that can be drawn from the pot each year, but the investor must be mindful that taking large sums out might mean paying tax at the additional rate. There is also the danger of depleting the pension fund too quickly. Taking an uncrystallised funds pension lump sum ('UFPLS') usually from a plan which does not offer 'flexible drawdown' allows the whole fund to be taken as a lump sum with 25% free of tax and the balance subject to marginal rate tax.
- Purchasing an annuity where a fixed sum of money is paid each year, although it will now be possible to set up a flexible annuity if desired so that the income can be varied.

Regardless of total pension wealth, those aged 55 or over can take any pot worth less than £10,000 as a lump sum as this is classified as a 'small pot' subject to a maximum number of three.

There will be substantially more flexibility. People who continue to want the security of an annuity will be able to purchase one and people who want greater control over their finances can drawdown their pension as they see fit. Those who want to keep their pension invested and drawdown from it over time will be able to do so. It will also be possible to leave the entire remaining pension fund on death to dependants or beneficiaries and this will not be subject to IHT. The beneficiaries will also be able to draw the fund flexibly to minimise their personal tax position. This makes the pension fund an important part of inter-generational planning.

22.17 Where partners are restricted by the annual and lifetime allowances (see **22.3** and **22.5**), they should consider additional tax-efficient means of retirement funding, such as Individual Savings Accounts (ISAs).

22.18 Many partnerships of doctors and dentists have special rules for pension contributions because of the requirement to pay NHS pension contributions. The rules are complicated and expert advice will be necessary.

Chapter 23

Inheritance Tax

Signposts

- A partnership interest forms part of an individual's estate for IHT (see **23.1**).
- A lifetime transfer of a partnership interest will often (if a transfer of value at all) be a Potentially Exempt Transfer (see **23.2 – 23.6**).
- Business property relief ('BPR') or agricultural property relief ('APR') will be due in appropriate circumstances (see **23.7 – 23.17**).
- Care should be taken with 'excepted assets' (see **23.9**); assets held outside the partnership (see **23.10**) and investments (see **23.12**).
- Loss of relief may be an issue after retirement or (where there is a binding contract for sale) on death (see **23.13 – 23.15**).
- Although agricultural property relief is limited to agricultural value, BPR may be available to cover any excess over agricultural value (see **23.16 – 23.18**).

Partnership transfers generally

23.1 An interest in a partnership forms part of an individual's estate for inheritance tax ('IHT') purposes so in principle a disposal (including a deemed disposal on death) of such an interest may be relevant for IHT purposes. The principal complications which arise are to do with what reliefs if any are available in respect of interests in partnerships or assets used for the purposes of a partnership business.

23.2 A lifetime transfer of an interest in a partnership between individuals is usually (like other transfers between individuals) a potentially exempt transfer (*Inheritance Tax Act 1984* (*'IHTA 1984'*)*, s 3A*). Transfers to a trust will not (with the exception of certain special types of trust) qualify as PETs but will be immediately chargeable.

23.3 A transfer is not, however, a transfer of value at all if it is shown that it was not intended, and was not made in a transaction intended, to confer any gratuitous benefit on any person and either:

(a) that it was made in a transaction at arm's length between persons not connected with each other; or

(b) that it was such as might be expected to be made in a transaction at arm's length between persons not connected with each other (*IHTA 1984, s 10*).

23.4 Whilst a person is connected with his or her partner, he or she will not be so connected in relation to transfers of partnership assets pursuant to bona fide commercial arrangements (*Taxation of Chargeable Gains Act 1992, s 286,* applied by *IHTA 1984, s 270*).

23.5 Thus, if partnership shares pass partly or in their entirety under bona fide commercial arrangements, there should not be any exposure to inheritance tax.

23.6 Where there is a family connection, HMRC may look more closely at whether transfers between partners are such as might be expected to be made in a transaction at arm's length between unconnected persons. But transactions between family members may nonetheless be commercial as for example where:

(a) shares increase or decrease according to workload and partners' contributions to the running of the partnership;

(b) shares increase or decrease in consideration for partners' obligations under the partnership deed; or

(c) shares pass to younger members in consideration of the obligations which they have undertaken and the more onerous conditions under which they have worked in earlier years.

Business and agricultural property relief

23.7 If a transfer is (or becomes) chargeable the availability of business or agricultural property relief will need to be considered.

Business Property Relief ('BPR')

23.8 In the context of partnerships, the most pertinent definitions of 'relevant business property' qualifying for BPR are those at *IHTA 1984, s 105(1)(a) (d)* and *(e)*:

- property consisting of a business or an interest in a business;
- any land, building, machinery or plant which immediately before the transfer was used wholly or mainly for the purposes of a business carried on by a company of which the transferor then had control or by a partnership of which he was then a partner;
- any land or building, machinery or plant which immediately before the transfer was used wholly or mainly for the purposes of a business carried on by the transferor and was settled property in which he was then beneficially entitled to an interest in possession.

The rate of relief available for the first category is 100% and for the others 50%.

> **Focus**
>
> Partnerships whose business is wholly or mainly dealing in securities, stocks or shares, land or buildings or making or holding investments do not qualify for business property relief. Nor do assets held outside the partnership and used for such a business.

23.9 Should the partnership property include 'excepted assets' relief will not be available to the extent that the value of the partner's interest in the partnership is attributable to such assets (*IHTA 1984, s112*).

'Excepted assets' are assets which are neither:

(a) used wholly or mainly for the purposes of the business concerned throughout the whole of the last two years of the period during which the asset has been owned by the partnership; nor

(b) required at the time of the transfer for future use for those purposes.

It should be noted how this rule applies in the case of a 'hybrid' business – that is to say, a business which is mainly qualifying in nature but which includes some elements which would (if they were the main part of business) disqualify the business from relief. An example would be a partnership which, in addition to its trade, carries on investment activities. In such a case the 'business' for the purposes of the excepted asset test is considered to be the business as a whole (ie, including both the 'qualifying' and 'non-qualifying' parts) so that an asset used in the non-qualifying part is nonetheless not an 'excepted asset'.

Thus in the context of a partnership, the assets most at risk are normally excessive cash balances which cannot be demonstrated to be needed for future business use, or (exceptionally) assets which are not used at all in any part of the global business activities of the partnership.

23.10 Having regard to the fact that assets held outside a partnership qualify for only 50% relief whereas the partnership interest (and therefore the assets forming part of the partnership assets) qualifies for 100% relief, there is potentially a considerable advantage in putting assets into the partnership. However, the commercial risks must justify it. A well-drafted partnership agreement should ensure that a partner transferring assets to a partnership in these circumstances remains entitled to any capital growth and is compensated (perhaps through enhanced profit share) for any lost income. Further, the cost of stamp duty land tax arising on a transfer of land and buildings should not be overlooked.

23.11 *IHTA 1984, s 106* provides that property is not 'relevant business property' qualifying for business property relief in relation to a transfer of value unless it was owned by the transferor throughout the two years immediately preceding the transfer. The rule is relaxed in special situations including:

(a) where the property replaced other business property (*IHTA 1984, s 107*);

(b) where the property was acquired on the death of a previous owner (*IHTA 1984, s 108*);

(c) where the property was acquired on an earlier transfer qualifying for BPR (*IHTA 1984, s 109*).

In the context of a share in a partnership, the two-year rule means that the partnership share must have been owned for two years (or that the business in question was conducted as a sole trade for part of the period and as a partnership for the remainder of the period). It is not necessary that any particular asset held by the partnership must have been owned for the two-year period.

In the context of an asset owned outside the partnership, the two-year rule means that the asset in question must have been owned for two years. It is not necessary that the partnership in which it is used has been carried on for two years.

23.12 Business property relief will be denied where the business consists wholly or mainly of the holding of investments (*IHTA 1984, s 105*). Sometimes it is difficult to say where the line is to be drawn, as a whole string of caravan park cases have demonstrated, with *Hall (Executors of Hall deceased) v CIR* [1997] STC (SCD) 126 an example of a case going one way and *Furness v CIR* [1999] STC (SCD) 232 the other.

23.13 When a partner retires from a partnership he obviously ceases to own an interest in the business. Instead he becomes a creditor of the partnership for any capital or current account balances remaining unpaid (*Beckman v IRC* [2000] STC (SCD) 59). The timing of retirement is therefore critical.

Furthermore, business property relief is not available where at the time of death a binding contract for sale has been entered into. This may occasionally cause difficulties where a partnership agreement provides that on the death of a partner the interest of the deceased partner is required to be sold by his executors and acquired by the surviving partners. Usually, careful drafting (perhaps using put and call options) can get round the problem: but the issue should be addressed whenever a partnership agreement is being drafted. Relief should, for example, remain potentially available on a partner's death where:

(a) A double option agreement is entered into under which the surviving partners have an option to buy and the deceased's personal representatives an option to sell, such options to be exercised within a stated period after the partner's death.

(b) The partnership determines on the death. Partnership assets are realised and the deceased's estate is entitled to a share of the proceeds.

(c) The partnership continues, with the personal representatives being entitled to represent the deceased.

(d) The partnership continues, with the deceased's partnership share falling into his estate but with an option for the other partners to acquire it, either on valuation or by a formula.

(e) The partnership continues, with the share of the deceased partner accruing to the surviving partners and the estate entitled to payment, either on valuation or by a formula (accruer arrangement).

The careful wording of partnership agreements is, therefore, important.

23.14 Where there has been a potentially exempt lifetime gift of a partnership share (or any other business property) which subsequently becomes chargeable because the donor dies within seven years of the gift, business property relief will need to be considered. The relief will be available only if:

(a) the original or qualifying replacement property is still owned by the donee at the donor's death (or, if the donee has in the meantime died, at his own death); and

(b) the property is still relevant business property (ignoring the two-year rule) at the time of the donor's or donee's earlier death.

This prevents the relief applying where property was relevant business property when given away, but subsequently ceases to be so.

Insofar as replacement property is concerned, there is a three-year period after the disposal, or such longer period as HMRC allow, during which the consideration for the sale can be reapplied in acquiring replacement property. The relief is still available if the transferor dies within the permitted period after the sale and before the replacement has taken place (*IHTA 1984, s 113B*).

Family partnerships

23.15 As indicated in **23.13**, in order for the gift of a partnership capital account to qualify for business property relief, the donor must still be a partner, rather than a mere creditor. Such gifts are most likely to occur in family partnerships, and therefore retirement should not take place until after the capital account has been transferred. It is important that there is no binding agreement or arrangement in force to this effect lest the relief be jeopardised.

Agricultural property relief

23.16 Agricultural property relief may apply in one of three ways:

(a) The partnership may own and occupy agricultural property, the partnership share of the donor/deceased partner reflecting his or her interest in that property.

(b) The partnership may own agricultural property occupied by someone else for the purpose of agriculture.

(c) A partner may personally own agricultural property which is occupied by the partnership of which he or she is a member.

23.17 As with business property relief, agricultural property relief requires a minimum ownership period. Relief does not apply to property unless either:

(a) it was occupied by the transferor for the purposes of agriculture throughout the period of two years ending with the date of the transfer or

(b) it was owned by the transferor throughout the period of seven years ending with the date of the transfer and was throughout that period occupied (whether by the transferor or by someone else) for the purposes of agriculture.

Land may in principle meet the qualifying conditions for both agricultural property relief and business property relief. Agricultural property relief is given only in respect of the agricultural value of the property. Where the property has value in excess of its agricultural value (typically development value) business property relief is available if appropriate.

Similarly, agricultural property may not meet the ownership conditions for agricultural property relief but may meet the slightly different ownership conditions applying to business property relief. For example, the land may have been acquired by a long-established partnership less than two years before the date of death. In such circumstances business property relief would be due.

Capital Gains Tax hold-over relief

23.18 In some circumstances agricultural property will meet the conditions of the *Taxation of Chargeable Gains Act 1992, s 165(2)* and hold-over relief will be available under *s 165*. Where it does not (as will be the case where the property is let) title to hold-over relief will be via the *Taxation of Chargeable Gains Act 1992, Sch 7, Pt I*. In such a case hold-over relief is available in full and is not be restricted to the gain attributable to agricultural value.

Transfer to company

23.19 A disadvantage of trading through a partnership is the difficulty of transferring parts of the business to the next generation. For this reason, when inheritance tax planning becomes an issue, incorporation of the partnership should be considered.

In that event, the comparative rates of business property relief on assets held within/outside the partnership/company should not be overlooked (see **23.10**). For the position on transfer of a partnership trade to a company, see **Chapter 16**.

Wills

23.20 A partnership share is, in theory, a bundle of rights which can be disposed of as the partner wishes. However, many partnership agreements include specific conditions about what will happen to the partnership share in the event of a partner's death. For example, the deed may state that the share of the deceased partner will accrue to the surviving partners, subject to payment calculated by an agreed formula.

> **Focus**
>
> Care should be taken to ensure that the wording of the deed does not deny business property relief, and partners should ensure that their wills are consistent with the partnership agreement.

Chapter 24

National Insurance

> **Signposts**
>
> - Partners, including the members of a limited liability partnership, will normally be liable to pay Class 2 and Class 4 NICs if they are over 16 and under state pension age (see **24.1**).
> - Extra care must be taken when considering NICs for sleeping and/or inactive partners (see **24.4**).
> - Class 2 NICs will be collected through self-assessment from April 2016, for the 2015/16 tax year onwards (see **24.8**).
> - Like other employers, partnerships may be liable to pay Class 1 and Class 1A contributions in respect of employees (see **24.5 – 24.7**).
> - From April 2018, Class 2 NICs are to be abolished and Class 4 reformed (see **24.13**).

National Insurance

General position

24.1 As self-employed individuals, partners, including the members of a limited liability partnership, will normally be liable to pay Class 2 and Class 4 NICs if they are over 16 and under state pension age. If they employ staff, they will also be liable as employers for the collection and payment of Class 1 NICs.

Consultation ran from December 2015 until February 2016 on the abolition of Class 2 National Insurance and the reform of Class 4 National Insurance, and the March 2016 Budget announced the abolition of Class 2 NIC from April 2018. Despite the proposed abolition there has nonetheless meanwhile been a major change to the collection procedure for Class 2 NICs which, for tax years 2015/16 onwards, has been collected as part of the tax self-assessment regime.

The results of the consultation were published in December 2016 confirming the abolition of Class 2 NIC and making changes to Class 4 NIC which are detailed at **24.13** below.

24.2 The general rules as to whether a partnership exists, and whether a particular individual is a partner, apply for National Insurance as for income tax. The term 'sleeping partner' is not a term of art but is often used to denote someone who as a matter of fact takes no active part in a partnership business (see **24.4**). A 'limited partner' is one who is defined as such in a Limited Partnership and is precluded from taking any part in the management of the business.

24.3 To be liable to Class 2 NICs as self-employed earners, partners must be 'gainfully employed in Great Britain otherwise than in employed earner's employment' (ie otherwise than as an employee) (*Social Security Contributions and Benefits Act 1992 (SSCBA 1992), s 2(1)(b)*). Liability to Class 4 NICs arises on profits or gains 'immediately derived' by the individual from carrying on one or more trades, professions or vocations and chargeable under the *Income Tax (Taxation of Other Income) Act 2005* ('*ITTOIA 2005*'), *s 15(1)*). The Class 2 net is thus wider than that for Class 4, and activities that constitute a 'business', such as the commercial letting of property, would give a Class 2 liability even though there was no Class 4 liability.

24.4 HMRC now consider that sleeping and inactive limited partners (see **24.2**) are (and have always been) liable to pay Class 2 NICs as self-employed earners and Class 4 NICs in respect of their taxable profits. This view represents a change from that previously held by HMRC and the Department for Work and Pensions ('DWP'). The revised view is enforced with effect from 6 April 2013. In relation to earlier years sleeping or limited partners who have not paid Class 2 or Class 4 NICs will not be pursued to pay contributions, but contributions already paid will not be refunded. Where contributions have not been paid on the basis of HMRC's previous view of the law, it may now be possible for partners to make voluntary payments in order to secure contributory benefit entitlements.

In relation to the payment of Class 2 NICs from 6 April 2013, sleeping and limited partners must check their Class 2 NICs position, and those who are not already paying Class 2 NICs should take appropriate steps to remedy the position.

> **Focus**
>
> For the purposes of Class 2 NICs, a change to the regulations (*Social Security Contributions (Limited Liability Partnership) Regulations 2014 (SI 2014/3159)*) took effect from April 2015 to ensure that for the avoidance of doubt the position of inactive members of LLPs follows that of sleeping partners and limited partners in Limited Partnerships.

Class 1 and Class 1A NICs

24.5 If the partners employ staff, they will be liable for collecting and accounting for employees' Class 1 primary NICs and for paying Class 1 employer's secondary NICs. They will also be liable to pay Class 1A NICs on most employee benefits in kind and are responsible for any Class 1B NICs in respect of amounts within a PAYE Settlement Agreement.

> **Focus**
>
> From April 2016, eligible employers have been able to reduce their employer Class 1 NICs liability by up to £3,000 per tax year, (previously £2,000). This measure is partly to counteract the additional costs to small businesses from the introduction of a National Living Wage (NLW).

The responsibility for payment of the contributions is a joint liability of the partners.

24.6 Partners with income from relevant engagements under the IR35 rules are liable to Class 1 NICs in respect of the deemed employment payment (see **Chapter 28**) as are salaried members of LLPs who are within the scope of the *Finance Act 2014* provisions.

24.7 If a partner is a director of a company in the circumstances that Extra Statutory Concession A37 applies (see **2.8**) the same treatment applies for NIC purposes with the result that Class 1 NICs are payable neither by the director nor by the company (*Social Security (Contributions) Regulations 2001 (SI 2001/1004), reg 27*).

Class 2 NICs

24.8 Class 2 NICs are due from each partner if his or her share of profits exceeds the 'small profits threshold' (£6,025 for 2017/18). Class 2 NICs for tax years 2015/16 onwards are collected under self-assessment in broadly the same way as Class 4 contributions and are calculated at the rate of £2.85 (2017/18) for each week during which the partner was a member of the partnership. Married women may be exempt from paying Class 2 NICs if they so elected before 11 May 1977 and have not subsequently revoked the election or lost the right to exemption.

Class 2 NICs are to be abolished from April 2018.

Class 4 NICs

24.9 In order to arrive at a partner's liability for Class 4 NICs, their profit share is determined according to income tax rules (*SSCBA 1992, Sch 2, para 2*), and is aggregated with their profit share, if any, from any other trade or profession carried on (*SSCBA 1992, Sch 2, para 4*). The profit limits for Class 4 contributions then apply separately to the aggregate profits of each partner (including husband/wife and civil partners) and contributions are collected as part of each individual partner's self-assessment. They are collected as part of his or her tax payments on account and balancing payment.

24.10 For 2017/18, Class 4 NIC is payable at the rate of 9% on profits between £8,164 and £45,000 and at 2% on profits above £45,000.

24.11 The same provisions for charging interest on unpaid Class 4 contributions apply as for income tax, and the same provisions for penalties for cases of careless or deliberate inaccuracy in a return.

24.12 If a partner suffers trading losses, they will be taken into account in arriving at his or her profit shares as for income tax. Where income tax relief is claimed against non-trading sources of income, or capital gains, under the *Income Tax Act 2007* (*'ITA 2007'*), *s 64* or *s 72*, the loss so relieved remains available to reduce the partner's later profits to calculate Class 4 NICs (*SSCBA 1992, Sch 2, para 3*).

24.13 The results of the consultation on abolition of Class 2 contributions and reforming Class 4 contributions have the following implications for partnerships:

- From 2018–19, self-employed individuals (including partners) will be able to gain access to contributory benefits based on a profits test in Class 4 NICs. This will enable self-employed individuals to continue to gain access to the new State Pension, contributory Employment and Support Allowance ('ESA') and Bereavement Support Payment ('BSP').
- A new zero-rate band will be introduced into Class 4 NICs on profits between the Small Profits Limit ('SPL') (which replaces the Class 2 Small Profits Threshold) and the Lower Profits Limit ('LPL') (£8,060 in 2016–17). Class 4 NICs will be treated as having been paid on these profits. This means that everyone who was previously liable to pay Class 2 NICs based on their profits will be able to gain access to benefits through Class 4 NICs, whether paid or treated as paid. They will be able to gain a qualifying year for benefit entitlement purposes for each tax year in which their profits are above the SPL.
- The Standard Rate of Maternity Allowance ('MA') for the self-employed (including partners) will be accessed using Class 3 voluntary NICs.
- People with profits below the SPL will continue to be able to gain access to the new State Pension, through earnings subject to payment of Class 1 Primary (employee) NICs; through NICs credits; or through payment of Class 3 voluntary NICs.
- The government will also enable self-employed individuals who (because of their profit levels) would not gain access to contributory ESA through Class 4 NICs to do so using Class 3 voluntary NICs.
- Transitional arrangements will be introduced to enable individuals with low profits, share fishermen and volunteer development workers to rely on their contribution record in the years prior to Class 2 abolition for longer than usual when claiming contribution-based Jobseeker's Allowance and contributory ESA. The transitional arrangements will remain in place until 1 January 2022.

Chapter 25

Stamp Duty Land Tax

Signposts

- Partnership assets are treated for stamp duty land tax purposes as held by all the partners, and land transactions entered into for the purposes of a partnership are treated as entered into by or on behalf of the partners (see **25.1 – 25.6**).
- Special and complex rules apply to transfers of property to a partnership by a partner (see **25.7 – 25.11**); transfers of an interest in a partnership (see **25.12 – 25.16**) and to transfers of property from a partnership to a partner (see **25.17**).

Introduction

25.1 Stamp duty land tax ('SDLT') applies to any 'land transaction'. This is defined (*Finance Act 2003, s 43*) as 'any acquisition of a chargeable interest', (including the grant, creation, surrender or variation of one). 'Chargeable interest' is further defined by *s 48* as:

(a) an estate, interest, right or power in or over land in England and Wales or Northern Ireland; or

(b) the benefit of an obligation, restriction or condition affecting the value of any such estate, interest, right or power, other than an 'exempt interest' (meaning principally a security interest such as that held by a mortgagee or charge-holder, a licence or tenancy).

SDLT does not apply to transactions involving land in Scotland; instead land and buildings transaction tax applies, the principles of which are broadly similar to SDLT.

Special rules apply to 'alternative finance arrangements' – broadly arrangements compliant with the requirements of Sharia law.

As a broad generality, SDLT is charged on a land transaction by applying the appropriate percentage to the relevant consideration. In the case of leases, relevant consideration is derived from the net present value of rental payments payable over the term of the lease. And, where property is subject to a mortgage, assumption of liability for the mortgage debt will as a matter of law constitute the giving of consideration.

25.2 For SDLT purposes a 'partnership' includes not only a partnership within the *Partnership Act 1890*, a limited partnership registered under the *Limited Partnerships Act 1907* and a limited liability partnership formed under the *Limited Liability Partnerships Act 2000*: it also extends to any firm or entity of a similar character formed under the law of a country or territory outside the UK.

A partnership relationship will exist only if a 'business' is being carried on. HMRC do not necessarily accept that the mere joint holding of property constitutes a partnership. Where they do not, the special rules on partnership SDLT do not apply and SDLT is instead computed in the normal way. The question whether property ownership is a 'business' arises in a number of areas including the applicability of CGT incorporation relief under *TCGA 1992, s 162*. An indication of the factors to be considered is given in, for example, *E M Ramsay v HMRC* [2013] UKUT 0226 (TCC).

25.3 The treatment of partnership transactions is among the most complex areas of SDLT and the rules have undergone frequent change over the years since SDLT was introduced in 2003. Notwithstanding the frequent tinkering with the rules the legislation continues to contain areas of uncertainty. The following gives an outline of the principal provisions regarding partnerships, which are to be found in the *Finance Act 2003, Sch 15*. For a full explanation and discussion of all the complexities of the law in this area it is recommended that a specialist SDLT text be consulted.

25.4 Chargeable interests held by or on behalf of a partnership are treated for SDLT purposes as held by or on behalf of the partners, and land transactions entered into for the purposes of a partnership are treated as entered into by or on behalf of the partners (and not by the partnership as such). This is the case irrespective of whether the partnership has a legal personality or is a body corporate under the law of the country in which it is formed (*FA 2003, s 104* and *Sch 15, Pt 1*).

The partnership is treated as continuing, regardless of changes in composition, as long as one partner continues.

25.5 By the *Finance Act 2003, Sch 15, para 7* the liability to pay SDLT together with any associated interest and penalties is a joint and several liability of all those partners (or members of an LLP) who were partners (or members) as at the effective date of the land transaction to which the tax relates (as regards liability for tax and interest) or the date when the penalty arose or the act giving rise to the penalty occurred (as regards liability for penalties). In other words, a partner joining a partnership is not fixed with liability for unpaid SDLT in respect of a land purchase which occurred before he joined, though he may be liable (for example) for an ongoing daily penalty for a failure to render an SDLT return in respect of such a land purchase which continues after he has joined the partnership.

The legislation envisages that partners may nominate and notify to HMRC a 'representative partner' to act on behalf of the partnership, (and in particular to make and sign partnership SDLT returns).

25.6 Purchases of land by the partnership are therefore reasonably straightforward in SDLT terms, though it should be noted that where the purchase is of residential property, liability to the additional 3% surcharge for 'additional dwellings' by a partnership or by a member of a partnership is an area which may require especial care. However, the main complexities in regard to partnerships arise with *Pt 3* of *Sch 15* – 'Transactions to which special provisions apply'.

Transactions to which special provisions apply: Schedule 15 Part 3

25.7 Special provisions apply to:

(a) the transfer of a chargeable interest to a partnership by a partner or a person connected with a partner;

(b) the transfer of an interest in a partnership;

(c) the transfer of a chargeable interest from a partnership to a partner or a person connected with a partner.

Transfer of a chargeable interest to a partnership by a partner or a person connected with a partner

25.8 Although it is not within S*ch 15* it is appropriate to mention first the special rule in *FA 2003, s 65* which applies where a chargeable interest is transferred from a general partnership to an LLP in connection with its incorporation. Such a transfer is exempt from SDLT provided that:

- the property is transferred to the LLP within one year of its incorporation. Those who register an LLP on a protective basis, but are still undecided as to whether or not to use it, could find themselves caught out by this provision;
- at the 'relevant time' (usually immediately before the incorporation of the LLP) the partners in the partnership comprise all of the people who are (or who are to be) members of the LLP (and no-one else); and
- the proportions in which the partners/members own the chargeable interest immediately after the transfer are the same as those in which they own it immediately before the transfer (or, if this is not the case, that the change in the proportions has not arisen as part of any scheme or arrangement of which the main purpose, or one of the main purposes, is avoidance of liability to any duty or tax).

So in the simplest case, where (for example) three partners owning partnership property in equal shares transfer the partnership business including the property to a new LLP which they also own in equal shares, no SDLT will be due.

25.9 Subject to the special rule described above, the transfer of a chargeable interest to a partnership by a partner or a person connected with a partner (or a person who become a partner as a result of the transfer) will in principle give rise to a charge to SDLT (*FA 2003, Sch 15, para 10*). However, the broad aim of the legislation here is to 'look through' the partnership to the partners so as to identify the value that is actually changing hands and to charge SDLT only on that amount.

The simplest example is where an individual transfers a chargeable interest to a partnership with whose members he or she is otherwise unconnected. The amount on which SDLT is charged is in that case the percentage of the market value of the asset which is equal to the percentage which he gives up. That is, the difference between the 100% of the asset which he owns at the outset and the share of the asset which he owns (via his membership of the partnership) after the transfer.

Example 25.1 – Transfer from an individual to a partnership on joining

Smith owns a property. He joins a partnership in which he takes a 25% share and on joining it transfers to the partnership as partner's capital a property worth £400,000.

Smith has effectively given up 75% of the value in the property. SDLT is due on 75% × £400,000 = £300,000. Note that the value which the partners attribute to the property is irrelevant: SDLT will be due by reference to a percentage of the market value.

The same SDLT would be payable if Smith were already a 25% member of the partnership and was selling the property to the LLP for value. Again, he would be giving up a 75% interest and SDLT would be due on 75% of the value (regardless of the selling price).

For this purpose (as for *Sch 15* generally) the shares in which partners are treated as owning partnership assets are determined by reference to the shares in which income profits of the partnership are allocated (*Sch 15, para 34*). This may of course be different from the shares in which capital profits are allocated (which is what is relevant for CGT purposes) and may be a trap for the unwary.

Taking a slightly more complex case, where the individual who is making the transfer is connected with other members of the partnership, regard is had not only to share of the asset which he himself owns (via his membership of the partnership) after the transfer but also to that owned by partners connected with him.

Example 25.2 – Transfer to a partnership involving a connected person

If in **Example 25.1** Smith's civil partner Jones was also a member of the partnership, with a 15% share of profits, Smith would be regarded as having effectively given up 60% (that is, 100% – 25% – 15%) of the property so that SDLT would be due on 60% × £400,000 = £240,000.

25.10 A charge to SDLT can arise where land has been transferred into a partnership by a partner and within three years of the date of transfer a 'qualifying event' occurs. This is defined as the transferor:

(a) withdrawing from the partnership any money or money's worth other than income profit; or

(b) obtaining repayment of any loan he has made to the partnership.

In such circumstances the 'qualifying event' is treated as a chargeable transaction and the chargeable consideration is taken to be the amount of the withdrawal or repayment up to the market value of the chargeable interest transferred (less any amount previously chargeable).

25.11 If the partnership to which the chargeable interest is a property-investment partnership (PIP) an election can be made to disapply the treatment described in **25.13** below and instead to pay SDLT by reference to the full market value of the chargeable interest transferred (*Sch 15, para 12A*). Although such an election would initially seem counter-intuitive, the advantage of making the election is that it will avoid any subsequent charge as described under **25.10** and will also reduce the amount of SDLT payable on a subsequent transfer of an interest in the PIP (see **25.13** below).

For this purpose a PIP is not, as might reasonably be supposed, simply a partnership which invests in property. Instead, it is defined (by *Sch 15, para 14(8)*) as a partnership whose sole or main activity is investing or dealing in chargeable interests (whether or not that activity also involves the carrying out of construction operations on the land in question). A property developing partnership and a land dealing partnership will therefore both be PIPs.

Transfer of an interest in a partnership

25.12 SDLT is in principle payable on the transfer of an interest in a PIP where the partnership property includes a chargeable interest. This includes not only the case where a person becomes a partner but also the case where one partner's share reduces (including a reduction to zero on leaving the partnership) and the share of another partner or partners increases. Any person whose partnership share increases (including any new partner) is treated as the 'purchaser' for SDLT purposes and is answerable for the relevant SDLT.

A transfer of an interest in a partnership other than a PIP is not subject to SDLT (regardless of the amount of chargeable property held within the partnership).

25.13 On a transfer of an interest in a PIP, SDLT is chargeable on the proportion changing hands of the market value of 'relevant partnership property'. Thus if a partner in a PIP having a 10% share in the partnership retires from the partnership, the remaining partners will suffer a charge to SDLT on 10% of the 'relevant partnership property'.

25.14 What is included in (or excluded from) 'relevant partnership property' depends on the type of transfer, styled either a 'Type A' transfer or a 'Type B' transfer.

25.15 A Type A transfer is one where:

- a partner's share is acquired (in whole or part) by another person (either an existing or a new partner) for consideration in money or money's worth; or
- a person becomes a partner; the interest of an existing partner reduces (or ceases) and money or money's worth is withdrawn from the partnership by the existing partner (other than out of resources available to the partnership prior to the transfer).

For a Type A transfer the 'relevant partnership property' taken into account is every chargeable interest held by the partnership immediately after the transfer of the partnership interest except for:

- any chargeable interest transferred to the partnership in connection with the transfer;
- leases at a market rent; and

- any chargeable interest that is not attributable economically to the partnership interest transferred.

25.16 Any other transfer is styled a Type B transfer. In the case of a Type B transfer the 'relevant partnership property' excludes (in addition to the exclusions for a Type A transfer):

- any chargeable interest transferred to the partnership on or before 22 July 2004;
- any chargeable interest for which the *para 12A* election has been made (see **25.10** above); and
- any other chargeable interest which was transferred to the partnership other than by a partner or a person connected with a partner (ie, those dealt with under **25.8** et seq above).

Transfer of a chargeable interest from a partnership to a partner or a person connected with a partner

25.17 As with a transfer to a partnership, the transfer of a chargeable interest from a partnership to a partner or a person connected with a partner (or to a person who ceases to be a partner as a result of the transfer) will in principle give rise to a charge to SDLT (*FA 2003, Sch 15, para 18*). As with transfers the other way, the broad aim of the legislation is to 'look through' the partnership to the partners so as to identify the value that is actually changing hands and to charge SDLT on that amount.

Thus on a transfer of land from a partnership consisting of husband and wife (or other connected parties) to a company controlled by those persons (or by any one of them) no SDLT is payable (including in the particular case where a business is incorporated). This may be thought anomalous given that there is no corresponding SDLT relief on the incorporation of a sole trade. Those contemplating taking advantage of the anomaly by converting a sole trade to a partnership shortly before incorporation would however be well advised to contemplate the anti-avoidance rules at the *Finance Act 2003, s 75A et seq*.

Chapter 26

Value Added Tax

Signposts

- Registration is normally in the name of the partnership and is independent of the VAT status or history of any of the partners themselves (see **26.1 – 26.6**). The rule is modified in some circumstances for limited partnerships (see **26.9**).
- Care needs to be taken not to fall foul of the 'business splitting' rules (see **26.7**).
- Joint ownership of land may need to be registered as a partnership for VAT purposes even where no partnership is recognised for direct tax purposes (see **26.8**).
- In making cost-sharing arrangements, care is needed to avoid a VAT charge (see **26.10**).
- Partners are jointly liable for VAT owed by the firm (see **26.11**).
- Do not overlook the need to charge VAT as appropriate on service charges or other recharges between businesses (see **26.12**).
- Where a partner accepts any office in the course of the partnership activities it may be necessary to charge VAT on remuneration, even where the income tax concession at ESC A37 does not apply (see **26.14**).

Legislative framework

26.1 The legislative framework for the value added tax ('VAT') treatment of partnerships (including limited liability partnerships ('LLPs') which are treated as bodies corporate) is to be found in the *Value Added Tax Act 1994* ('*VATA 1994*'), *s 45*, which refers to 'persons carrying on a business in partnership'. The general law outlined in **Chapter 1** applies to determine whether a partnership exists.

Registration

26.2 As we have seen from **Chapter 1**, an English partnership is not a 'person'. Since the edifice of VAT is constructed on the foundation of 'taxable persons' (*VATA 1994, s 3*) it is strictly speaking the partners in a partnership who are registrable. However *VATA 1994,* *s 45* provides that VAT registration may be (and in practice usually is) in the name of the firm rather than of all the partners, and that changes in the partners are ignored in deciding whether goods or services are supplied to or by them. In determining whether the VAT registration threshold is reached, therefore, the cumulative turnover would be considered despite changes in partners. If, however, there is a change from sole trader to partnership, or vice versa, this involves two separate 'entities' for VAT purposes (see **26.5**), so that the transferor's turnover would not be taken into account.

Any joint registration of partners (whether in the name of the partners or of the partnership) is separate from any registration of any of the partners individually in their own name in respect of any 'sole trade' business which they may conduct.

26.3 Under the *Value Added Tax Regulations 1995 (SI 1995/2518), reg 7*, partners are jointly and severally liable for giving any notice required by the legislation. When a partnership registers for VAT, details of the partners are given on form VAT 2 and signed by each partner.

26.4 Where a partner joins or leaves a partnership, this does not affect the VAT registration. There is strictly speaking no absolute legal obligation to notify a change of partners. However it is nonetheless very important that partnership changes should be notified to HMRC promptly since failure to do so will result in a continuing liability to VAT (see **26.11**).

The treatment of partnership mergers is dealt with in **Chapter 7**.

26.5 Where a sole trader takes in one or more partners, or one or more partners retires leaving a sole trader, this denotes a change in business entity for VAT purposes. If the transferor is VAT registered, the change must be notified to HMRC within 30 days and the transferor's VAT registration will be cancelled. An application may, however, be made (on form VAT 68: www.gov.uk/government/publications/vat-request-for-transfer-of-a-registration-number-vat68) for the VAT registration to be transferred.

26.6 Since it is persons who are registered for VAT rather than businesses, partnerships carrying on different businesses but with identical members will normally have only one VAT registration. (*HMC&E v Glassborow* [1974] STC 142). However, *Saunders v Customs and Excise Comrs* [1980] VATTR 53 shows the exception to that rule: in that case the same two individuals were the only members of two limited partnerships. One was the general partner of one partnership and the other was the general partner of the other partnership. It was held that separate registrations were necessary.

Furthermore, the position is different in Scotland. A Scottish partnership, unlike an English one, is a legal person. In principle therefore it would be possible for two individuals to enter into a number of Scottish partnerships each of them governed by a separate partnership agreement: each partnership would be a separate person for VAT purposes.

Partnerships with some but not all members in common will have separate VAT registrations, unless action is taken by HMRC under the 'business splitting' rules (see **26.7**).

Care needs to be taken, however, when the members in the businesses change. If, for example, someone carried on a non-registered business as a sole trader, and a registered business in partnership with someone else, and his or her business partner retired or died, the VAT registration would then cover both businesses because they would be operated by the same person.

26.7 In order to prevent people from avoiding the need to register for VAT by splitting what is essentially a single business that would have a turnover in excess of the VAT threshold into one or more separate businesses controlled by different persons (eg husband running one and wife the other), *VATA 1994, Sch 2, para 1* enables HMRC to make a direction that those named in the direction shall be treated as a single taxable person. The named person is then liable to be registered with effect from the date of the direction, or such later date as is specified. A direction will not be made unless HMRC are satisfied that avoiding VAT registration was a main reason for splitting the business. In making a direction, they will also take into account the extent to which the businesses have organisational, financial or economic links.

Focus

Business splitting can therefore be an effective way of avoiding the need to register for VAT unless and until an HMRC direction is made. HMRC have, however, successfully assessed businesses retrospectively by arguing that there has in fact only been one business throughout (see *Burrell (t/a The Firm) v Customs and Excise Comrs* [1997] STC 1413, which has been much cited in subsequent cases). It should also be borne in mind that, if a direction is made, the viability of the enterprise could be in question if the impact of VAT registration has not been appraised.

For a consideration of when there is and is not a partnership for VAT purposes, see **10.8**.

Jointly-owned land

26.8 A partnership may be treated as existing for VAT purposes where no partnership is recognised for direct tax purposes. In particular the treatment may diverge where land is held jointly. For direct tax purposes, joint ownership and letting of land will not normally be treated as a partnership (see **Chapter 1**). But for VAT purposes, HMRC considers that where joint owners of land exploit the land (eg for letting) any VAT registration must be in joint names and therefore as a partnership. As with other partnerships, where the joint owners are already registered as the partners in another firm (as where a business partnership sublets land as a subsidiary activity), no separate registration is required and any VAT will be accounted for under the existing VAT registration.

The *Law of Property Act 1925* restricts the names appearing on legal title to land to a maximum of four. Where the legal owners hold on behalf of a larger number of beneficial owners the VAT registration will be in the name of the beneficial owners (or a partnership name if there is one).

Limited partnerships

26.9 Because a limited partner is debarred from any involvement in the management and running of the partnership business, it was held in *Saunders v HMC&E* [1980] VATTR 53 that limited partners do not 'count' for VAT purposes. They have no liability for VAT debts of the partnership and they are ignored in registering the partnership. Any registration of a limited partnership is therefore in the name of the general partners only. It follows that where a company is the general partner of a number of limited partnerships (and is in each case the only general partner) there will be a single VAT registration which will encompass each of the limited partnerships concerned as well as any 'sole trade' business conducted by the general partner in its own right.

As with an ordinary partnership, a Scottish limited partnership is a legal person and is registrable in its own name.

Cost-sharing arrangements

26.10 As to the VAT consequences of cost-sharing arrangements falling short of partnership, see *Durham Aged Mineworkers' Homes Association v HMC&E* [1994] STC 553. In this case a charity and a company shared headquarters, office accommodation and staff. The charity held the freehold of the accommodation and paid all the bills for the office accommodation, other administrative overheads and staff training and travel and charged 50% of these costs to the company. The company employed and paid all staff and charged 50% of the costs of the headquarters staff and 100% of certain other staff to the charity. There was no express contract between the two entities covering this sharing of costs and they did not invoice each other in respect of them.

HM Customs and Excise had contended that the charity was making taxable supplies to the company and that VAT was due. Reversing the decision of the VAT Tribunal, the High Court held that, on the uncontested evidence of the parties, there was an implied agreement that expenses would be shared and that the charity would, in paying for supplies, act as principal as regards its own agreed share and as agent for the company in respect of the company's share.

In similar cases, to avoid conflict and difficulty, it is advisable for the terms of the agreement (and in particular the fact that payment is being made as agent) to be fully documented.

VAT liability

26.11 Partners are jointly liable for VAT owed by the firm. Where a partner leaves the firm, their liability ceases not on the date of their leaving but on the date the change is notified to HMRC (*VATA 1994, s 45(2)*). (See **26.4** as to notification of partnership changes.) It is therefore important for a retiring partner to ensure prompt notification; otherwise, he or she may find that they are liable for VAT bills that relate to periods after they have left the firm (and this could be particularly painful if, say, the remaining partners are unable to pay).

This is exactly what happened in *Customs and Excise Comrs v Jamieson* [2002] STC 1418. The respondent and her husband had run a pub in partnership. In August 1999, she left the marriage. Customs served a statutory demand on her for unpaid VAT for the period ending 31 August 1999 and subsequent periods. The respondent claimed that the partnership was dissolved when she left. The High Court held that, under *VATA 1994, s 45(2)*, the partnership continued until February 2000 when Customs were informed of the dissolution.

The liability of someone who is a partner for only part of a VAT return period is 'such proportion of the firm's liability as may be just' (*VATA 1994, s 45(5)*).

26.12 For a variety of reasons, a partnership might run alongside a limited company, the directors/shareholders and the partners being the same or substantially the same people. Thus, a particularly risky part of a business might more appropriately be conducted through a limited company, whereas a partnership is the better medium for the main operation. Again, a management or service company may be appropriate to run the administration of a professional practice or other partnership situation.

In these cases, as with any other where the same people are concerned with the businesses, it is easy to overlook that VAT has to be charged on any supplies or services from one to the other. In many cases both businesses may be in a full VAT recovery position: but even where that is so, technical offences arise, even though there may not be any loss of tax to HMRC, if proper invoices are not raised and VAT accountability properly controlled. In other cases the VAT recovery position of the businesses may be different and there may be a substantive VAT effect. In such situations a group VAT registration may be considered provided the control conditions in *VATA 1994, s 43A* are met. In this regard it should be noted that an LLP (as a 'body corporate') is capable of being a member of a group, but a general partnership or limited partnership is not.

Default surcharge

26.13 Partnership problems have been successfully cited as a reasonable excuse for paying VAT late; see *Stanley Long and Partners* LON/02/354 (17812). A dispute arose between the partners in a firm of chartered surveyors which resulted in the matter going to arbitration. Mr Long was responsible for the payment of VAT, but all cheques had to be countersigned by Mr Chapman whom he was trying to dismiss. Checks by Mr Chapman's advisers resulted in the payment of VAT being delayed. The tribunal held that Mr Long had a reasonable excuse for late payment and the default surcharge was cancelled.

Professional partnerships

26.14 Reference has been made (in **Chapter 2**) to fees from personal appointments being brought into the partnership accounts for income tax purposes. Generally, if the appointment is ancillary to the trade, profession or vocation, the services will be regarded as supplied by the partnership, and VAT will have to be added to the supply. The relevant provision is *VATA 1994, s 94(4)*. This provides that 'where a person, in the course or furtherance of a trade profession or vocation, accepts any office, services supplied by him as the holder of that office are treated as supplied in the course or furtherance of the trade, profession or vocation.' Note that *s 94(4)* applies only to offices, not employments; but it applies even if the conditions for ESC A37 are not fulfilled (or the benefit of ESC A37 is not taken) such that the income from the office in question is charged to tax as employment income of the individual concerned. On other words in cases where *s 94(4)* applies it is not possible to avoid the imposition of VAT by accepting or procuring that the income is treated as employment income rather than as business income of the partnership.

The mere fact that the income in question has been received by the partnership and included in its accounts is not conclusive as to liability under *s 94*. It must be established both that the income arises from the holding of an 'office' and also that the holding of the office is undertaken 'in the course or furtherance of a profession'.

The term 'office' is not defined for VAT purposes but it is generally understood to mean a position which exists independently of the persons holding it from time to time – for example a company director, secretary of an organisation, etc. Assistance on an ad hoc basis may, depending on its terms, amount to 'employment' but it will seldom if ever amount to the holding of an 'office'. Specifically, salaried judicial appointments whether full- or part-time are regarded as 'employments' and not as 'offices' (see VBN40000 et seq). In a few cases such as Notaries Public and Commissioners for Oaths there is a legal or regulatory prohibition on sharing fees with others. By definition such income cannot arise in the course of a profession carried on in partnership and *s 94(4)* will apply to such income only in the case of a sole trade.

Subject to the above, where an equity partner in a firm (but not a salaried partner who is an employee of the firm) is appointed to an office which involves the provision by him or her of the same kind of professional services as those provided by the firm, *s 94(4)* will apply, requiring VAT to be accounted for, unless the appointment can be shown to have been made in a private capacity. This is likely to be the case where the partner is appointed on grounds of his or her personal merit, occupational expertise or experience, or standing in the community as distinct from professional expertise.

One of the most useful cases to have come before the VAT Tribunal has been *Birketts (a firm) v C & E Comrs* [2002] SWTI 12, 35 (17515) which dealt with a number of kinds of fee received by a firm of solicitors in respect of offices held by various equity and salaried partners and included in the firm's accounts.

In respect of the specific appointments, the tribunal found as follows:

Member of board of local building society	Expected to give legal advice. Therefore, the appointment was accepted in furtherance of the partner's profession.	VATable
Non-executive director of local NHS Trust	Appointed due to personal merit and standing, not professional expertise.	Not VATable
Vice chairman of the Family Health Services Authority	Appointed due to personal merit and standing, not professional expertise.	Not VATable
Non-executive director of a regional hospital NHS Trust	Appointed due to personal merit and standing, not professional expertise.	Not VATable

Legal adviser to a charity (salaried partner)	Accepted personally, as she was not an equity partner. If she had been, the fees would be VATable.	Not VATable
Chairman of the Insolvency Practitioners Tribunal		Outside the scope of VAT
Former clerk to the General Commissioners		Outside the scope of VAT

VAT and the self-assessment tax return

26.15 Where the partnership is VAT registered, the tax return requires the partnership to indicate whether its accounts figures include or exclude VAT. Where the inclusive approach is used, the net payment to HMRC must be entered on the return form.

Where the partnership registered (or deregistered) for VAT during the year, the following details should be disclosed in the additional information box:

- a note that the partnership registered/deregistered during the year;
- the date of registration/deregistration; and
- whether the sales and expenses from the date of registration (or prior to deregistration) are shown on the return inclusive or exclusive of VAT.

Where VAT distorts any of the figures on the Standard Accounts Information because the partnership makes zero-rated supplies, is partially exempt or uses a special scheme, details should also be disclosed on the return.

26.16 If the partnership uses the flat rate scheme (*VATA 1994, s 26B*; *FA 2002, s 23*; *SI 1995/2518*), income and expenses must be entered on the return, either all net of VAT (method 1) or all inclusive of VAT (method 2).

Where method 1 is adopted, the balance on the VAT account should be entered in Box 3.50 where it exceeds the VAT paid under the scheme. An entry should be made in Box 3.63 where the balance cannot be recovered. Where method 2 is used, the net payment to HMRC is entered as an expense in Box 3.63.

Chapter 27

Provision for Taxation in Partnership Accounts

Signposts

- Although not a legal requirement, there are many situations when it is prudent to include a tax reserve in the partnership accounts (see **27.1 – 27.5**).
- There may be a greater logic in having a tax reserve in partnerships that do not have a 5 April year end (see **27.6**).

27.1 Under the current year basis of assessment and self-assessment, each partner is individually responsible for the tax on his or her share of the partnership profits. Since there is no partnership liability as such there is no requirement to reserve or provide for it in partnership accounts and many partnerships manage very well without doing so.

27.2 There are, however, situations when it may be considered prudent to include a tax reserve in the partnership accounts and have the partnership pay the partners' tax liabilities with a partnership cheque. Tax reserves prevent partners overdrawing their current accounts and avoid the potentially embarrassing situation arising whereby an imprudent partner is unable to settle his tax liability when it arises. Many partners find tax provisions administratively convenient. However, since partnership tax reserves are not a legal requirement and because tax liabilities are personal to the partners, where tax is held on reserve, it should be with the agreement of all partners. Full details of the tax reserve and its calculation should be documented in the partnership agreement.

If tax reserves are to be used three very important points must always be borne in mind. The first is the obvious one that creating a tax reserve does nothing to ensure that funds are available to pay the tax when it is due. To do that requires the earmarking of cash, either notionally in the partnership general bank account, or by paying funds into a partnership tax reserve account maintained in parallel with the reserve. Alternatively there may be an unused overdraft facility which can be used. The main thing is to recognise that the question of funding the liabilities for which the reserve has been created is properly considered.

The second point is that if the aim of the reserve and reserve account is to remove from partners the worry and responsibility of dealing with tax on their share of partnership profits, it is important that the liabilities are accurately identified. Explaining to a partner at the last minute that the reserve is not in fact adequate to meet tax bills that he thought were taken care of is a recipe for partnership conflict. A badly-handled tax reserve policy is likely to be worse than no tax reserve policy at all.

The third point is that the creation of a tax reserve (with or without earmarking funds in a tax account) is a private arrangement between the partners in which HMRC has no part. It does not transfer the legal liability to pay tax from the partner to the partnership and if the unthinkable happens and the partnership is unable to meet the tax obligations of a partner when they fall due, the partner will nonetheless be obligated to do so. The partner, in relation to the partnership's promise to meet his tax bill out of profits held back for that purpose, is in effect only a creditor of the partnership and is at much at risk as any other creditor.

27.3 Although we speak of a partnership tax reserve it is really nothing of the kind. Tax liabilities are personal to partners and the 'partnership tax reserve' is effectively an earmarking of part of each partner's capital or current account, to be held back and made available only to meet that partner's tax liabilities. Logically, therefore, it is only tax on the partnership income which needs to be taken into account. If a partner has a significant source of untaxed income or large capital gains outside the partnership, it will not normally be appropriate for that to be reflected in any partnership tax reserve. It follows that such a partner will need to ensure that he has made arrangements independently of the partnership to fund such other tax liabilities, and it is important that this is understood by the partner.

27.4 To achieve the objective – which is to give partners the assurance that there will be both sufficient capital or current account and sufficient cash to pay the tax bill when it comes – it will be desirable to quantify each partner's liability as accurately as possible. While it may be simpler to use estimated allowances and tax rates or simply calculate the provision as a flat percentage of profits this will inevitably provide only a rough approximation of the liability and may require a partner to provide some funds personally when tax falls due for payment, which may undermine some of the benefits of creating a reserve.

March or 5 April year end

Example 27.1 – Provision for tax in partnership accounts – 31 March or 5 April year end

Robin and Mel have a year end of 31 March. The partnership profits are £60,000 for the year ended 31 March 2015, shared equally. The partners' tax liabilities are as follows:

	Robin	*Mel*
	£	*£*
Profits	30,000	30,000
Allowances and reliefs (say)	(5,600)	(6,500)
Tax (say)	5,100	4,900
National Insurance (say)	1,980	1,980
Reserve required total £13,960	£7,080	£6,880

The partnership accounts to 31 March 2015 would include a tax reserve of £13,960, created by debiting to the partners' current accounts as shown above. When tax is paid by the partnership, it will be debited to the relevant partner's share of the tax reserve.

On 31 January 2015, the partnership paid £2,000 on account for Robin and £3,000 for Mel for the tax year 2014/15. Similar payments will be due on 31 July 2015, with the balance due on 31 January 2016. The tax reserve required in the balance sheet at 31 March 2015 would thus be:

	Robin	*Mel*
	£	£
Tax due 2014/2015	7,080	6,880
Less: payment on account 31.1.15	(2,000)	(3,000)
Reserve required total £8,960	5,080	3,880

The partners' tax reserve accounts will reflect the following entries:

	Robin	*Mel*
	£	£
Accounts to 31.3.15		
Tax reserve 2014/15	7,080	6,880
Tax paid 31.1.15 (1st payment on account 2014/15)	2,000	3,000
Reserve carried forward at 31 March 2015	5,080	3,880
Accounts to 31.3.16		
Tax reserve brought forward	5,080	3,880
Tax paid 31.7.15 (2nd payment on account 2014/15)	(2,000)	(3,000)
Tax paid 31.1.16 (balancing payment 2014/15)	(3,080)	(880)
Tax paid 31.1.16 (1st payment on account 2015/16, ie 50% of the 2014/2015 tax liability)	(3,540)	(3,440)

The reserve for the year ended 31 March 2016 will then be created and the process will continue.

27.5 Tax reserves for partnerships with a 31 March or 5 April year end will therefore consist of the payment on account due on 31 July and the balancing payment due on 31 January following the tax year.

Other year ends

27.6 Where partnerships have a year end that does not coincide with the tax year, the first period of account will form the basis period for more than one tax year: and in cash-flow terms the tax which will need to be recognised in the first year's account will need to be increased accordingly. .

Example 27.2 – Provision for tax in partnership accounts – other year ends

Clark and Anita start a solicitors' practice on 1 June 2014, sharing profits equally. The accounts to 31 May 2015 show a profit of £20,000. They expect to make profits in the year to 31 May 2016 of £80,000.

Tax year basis

Tax year	*Accounts year*	*Period taxed*	*Months taxed*	*Profit (£)*
2014/15	1.6.14–31.5.15	1.6.14–5.4.15	10 months 5 days	16,930
2015/16	1.6.14–31.5.15	1.6.14–31.5.15	12	20,000
2016/17	1.6.15–31.5.16	1.6.15–31.5.16	12	80,000

Overlap profits are £16,930, shared equally.

The partners' tax liabilities are as follows:

	Clark	*Anita*
2014/15 (tax due 31.1.16)	£	£
Profits	8,465	8,465
Allowances and reliefs (say)	(5,600)	(5,600)
Tax (say)	550	550
National Insurance (say)	270	270
Reserve required total £1,640	820	820
2015/16 (tax due 31.1.16, 31.7.16 and 31.1.17)		
Profits	10,000	10,000
Allowances and reliefs (say)	(5,800)	(5,800)
Tax (say)	900	900
National Insurance (say)	430	430
Reserve required total £2,660	1,330	1,330
2016/17 (tax due 31.1.17, 31.7.17 and 31.1.18)		
Profits	40,000	40,000
Allowances and reliefs (say)	(5,800)	(5,800)
Tax (say)	8,550	8,550
National Insurance (say)	2,160	2,160
Reserve required total £21,420	10,710	10,710

On this basis, the tax reserve will be:

- in the accounts to 31 May 2015 (covering two tax years): £4,300 (£1,640 + £2,660); and
- in the accounts to 31 May 2016 (covering one tax year): £21,420.

Paying the tax

27.7 Where the partnership settles its partners' tax liabilities, care must be taken with the means of payment. The individual partners' liabilities should preferably be settled by separate cheques, each bearing the correct taxpayer reference number. Where one cheque or transfer is issued on behalf of the whole partnership, it must be clearly split down into the individual partners' tax payments, showing each taxpayer's reference number.

Other provisions

Deferred tax

27.8 In some situations, a provision for deferred tax might be appropriate.

The circumstances in which a provision for deferred tax might arise are limited, but they might include those where:

(a) claims for capital allowances have reduced the written-down values below the realisable value of the partnership assets. There is, therefore, potentially a balancing charge which will fall on the continuing partners, for example because an election for written-down values to be carried forward through changes of ownership has been made; or

(b) work in progress has been included in accounts at a basis of valuation higher than cost (in order to preserve equity between incoming, continuing and outgoing partners), and is therefore reflected in capital/current account balances, but there has been a computational adjustment to reduce the taxable profits to accord with GAAP.

General provisions

27.9 The accounts might include a general provision, eg for bad debts or for costs permitted under UK GAAP. Partners will have borne their share of any such provision by a reduction in their profit entitlement and hence in their capital/current account balances, but in some cases no equivalent reduction will have been made in taxable profits.

When the provision is subsequently released or used, the then partners will have the advantage arising.

A reverse provision within the deferred tax principle will maintain equity between the partners.

No provision

27.10 Tax provisions are by no means universal. Many partnerships make no tax provision. The tax payments are simply charged against the partners' current accounts when the payments are made to HMRC by the partnership. And in some cases, the partnership as such takes no part at all in payment of partners tax: instead partners are left to make their own arrangements to meet their tax liabilities out of drawings. Sometimes there is a middle way, with partners left to settle their tax liabilities personally, but with a supplementary cash distribution in January and July to assist in funding.

27.11 **Example 27.2** illustrates the effect of not providing for partners' tax. If the partnership simply paid the partners' tax liabilities but did not provide for the liability to do so, the partnership accounts to 31 May 2015 would show no tax paid or provided, because none of the tax will be due until 31 January 2016. The accounts to 31 May 2016 would show the payment made on 31 January 2016 of £820 for each partner plus payments on account for 2015/16 of £410 per partner. Partners could easily be deceived as to the true extent of their financial resources by there being no tax provision.

In summary, if partners can be relied upon both to understand the implications of partnership taxation (if necessary by taking advice) and to make their own arrangements to provide the necessary funds, the partnership can confidently withdraw from the field and leave it to partners. But in cases where partners either do not understand the quantum and timing of tax liabilities arising or wilfully fail to make provision to meet them, it may be wise to take the matter 'in house' with a partnership tax reserve and reserve account.

Chapter 28

IR35 and Managed Service Companies

Signposts

- Although large partnerships are unlikely to be affected by the IR35 rules, smaller partnerships and in particular family partnerships may be caught (see **28.1 – 28.2**).
- The partnership is responsible for complying with IR35 and must use the tests determining the boundary between employment and self-employment to identify any relevant engagements (see **28.3**).
- Where IR35 applies detailed computational rules must be followed. Special care is needed where the accounting year end is other than 5 April (see **28.4 – 28.6**).
- In consequence of the *Finance Act 2014* changes to salaried partners in LLPs, the IR35 legislation has also been amended from April 2014 to prevent double taxation and excessive NICs payable (see **28.7**).
- Deemed salaries must be reported to HMRC. For most partnerships this will now be done under the real-time information regime (see **28.8 – 28.10**).
- A partnership may in some circumstances fall within the definition either of a 'Managed Service Company' or of an 'MSC Provider'. In either case, liability in respect of deemed remuneration may arise (see **28.11 – 28.14**).

IR35

28.1 The IR35 regime, named after the press release announcing reform of the provision of personal services (which followed the 1999 Budget speech), does not apply only to companies. Partnerships may be caught by the rules where a partner personally performs services for another person and the circumstances are such that if the contract were between the client and the individual partner the relationship would be one of employment (*Income Tax (Earnings and Pensions Act 2003* ('*ITEPA 2003*'), *s 49*). The rules may also apply to a partnership if the person performing the services ('the worker') is an employee of the partnership and a member of the partnership is an associate of the worker.

Example 28.1 – IR35 – services provided other than by a partner

James is an employee of a partnership the members of which are his wife and his father. James is paid a nominal salary. The only business of the partnership is to provide the services of James to a single client for an annual fee of £350,000. The terms of the agreement between the partnership and the client are such that if James had contracted directly with the client he would have been an employee.

Despite the fact that James is not a partner, the contract is within the scope of IR35.

The Government has long considered that the IR35 rules in their present form do not fully achieve their objective partly because they are difficult and expensive for HMRC to enforce. HMRC have estimated the rate of non-compliance as up to 90% and the annual loss to the Exchequer as something in excess of £400m. Consultation on options for improvement the effectiveness of the rules ran from July to September 2015. The intractability of the problem may be judged by the fact that as at summer 2017 HMRC's considered response to the consultation is still awaited.

Focus

Large partnerships are unlikely to be affected by the rules, but family, husband and wife, or civil partner partnerships may be. Such partnerships may face considerable difficulties in determining whether a particular contract falls within the definition of a relevant engagement, and in applying the complex calculations if it does.

28.2 A partnership is potentially vulnerable in relation to such a contract as is described in **28.1** where:

- the partner concerned, alone or with one or more relatives (including for this purpose the cohabitee of an unmarried partner (*ITEPA 2003, s 61(4)*), is entitled to 60% or more of the partnership profits (*ITEPA 2003, s 52(2)*); or
- all or most of the partnership profits derive from the provision of services under such a contract to a single client (or associates of that client); or
- the profit-sharing arrangements of the partnership provide for the income of any of the partners to be based on the amount of income that they generate from such a contract (*ITEPA 2003, s 52*).

The rules also apply to payments or benefits received (or receivable) by the worker in a capacity other than as a member of the partnership if the payment or benefit is received directly from the partnership and it can reasonably be taken to represent the worker's earnings from a relevant engagement (*ITEPA 2003, s 52(3)*).

See **28.7** regarding limited liability partnerships.

Example 28.2 – IR35 – contract not caught by the provisions

James, a partner in a firm of tax consultants, is seconded by the partnership to the Treasury for two years. The terms of the engagement are such that if James had entered into it personally he would have been an employee. The income from the engagement (£100,000 a year) is paid into the partnership. The partnership profits are £500,000. James is entitled to a 12% profit share, which amounts to £60,000 but he receives no further payment of benefit from the partnership in respect of his work at the Treasury.

None of the three conditions in **28.2** apply, and the engagement is therefore not a relevant engagement.

Contrast this with **Example 28.3**.

Example 28.3 – IR35 – contract caught by the provisions (relevant engagement)

Frank and Joanne are husband and wife and operate in partnership as consulting engineers. Joanne spent the majority of the tax year on maternity leave and only brought in £5,000 of fees. Frank worked mainly on one large contract for Bee Ltd. The terms of the contract with Bee Ltd are such that if Frank had been engaged directly he would have been regarded as an employee. Frank generates £80,000 from the contract and £5,000 from other clients. Frank and Joanne share profits equally.

The engagement with Bee Ltd would appear to be a relevant engagement caught by the rules and conditions in **28.2**. If it is a relevant engagement, it will affect both Frank personally and the partnership.

Frank will be deemed to have employment earnings in addition to trading profits. This may complicate his National Insurance and pension position.

Employment status

28.3 Usually the key issue in determining whether IR35 applies in any particular cases is deciding whether the relationship would have been one of employment had it been entered into directly by the worker involved. For these purposes the same tests (and the same case law) are relevant as in any 'employment status' matter, with the additional difficulty that in an IR35 situation one is reviewing not the legal effect of the arrangements actually entered but the legal effect of the arrangements which would hypothetically have been entered had there been a contract between the worker and the client. Entire books could be written on employment status. HMRC's guidance in its Employment Status Manual may profitably be studied.

Previously HMRC have published a range of guidance specific to IR35, including Tax Bulletin 45 issued at the time the IR35 rules were introduced in 2000, and latterly a number of 'example scenarios' developed in conjunction with the IR35 Forum. Some of these are now to be found, along with general guidance on IR35, at ESM3001 et seq. See also HMRC guidance at https://www.gov.uk/guidance/ir35-find-out-if-it-applies and the associated helpline including details on how to access HMRC's 'Contract Review Service'.

Calculations

28.4 Where a partnership receives income under one or more relevant engagements in any income tax year, it is deemed to make an 'employment payment' to the worker concerned and PAYE and NIC is due accordingly. In a case where the worker is an employee, the deemed employment payment is in addition to any emoluments actually paid to the worker by the partnership: in a case where the worker is a partner the deemed employment payment has no regard to what actual payments or drawings were made by the partnership to the partner.

The payment is normally deemed to be made on 5 April in the year but where the partnership ceases to trade or the worker (if a partner) resigns from the partnership or (if an employee) ceases to be employed by the partnership the deemed employment payment is treated as made immediately before the cessation or resignation (*ITEPA 2003, s 57*).

Where the partnership operates in the construction industry and payments are made under deduction of tax at source, the partnership is treated as receiving the payments gross for the purposes of the deemed calculation (*ITEPA 2003, s 54(2)*).

28.5 In calculating the deemed salary on which the partnership is required to pay PAYE and National Insurance, the following expenses can be deducted:

- a flat-rate deduction of 5% of the gross value of relevant engagements;
- expenses paid by the partnership which would have been deductible in computing employment income if the partner had been employed and had paid the expenses out of the earnings;
- capital allowances that could have been claimed by the worker under the *Capital Allowances Act 2001* ('*CAA 2001*'), *s 262* if the worker had been an employee;
- contributions to registered pension schemes;
- employers' National Insurance on the deemed payment; and
- payments already subject to PAYE (in the case where the worker is an employee).

(*ITEPA 2003, s 54*)

Example 28.4 – IR35 – deemed salary and effect on partnership profits

The facts are those in **Example 28.3**. The partnership incurs £2,000 of travel costs which would be deductible under the provisions relating to employees. The other partnership expenses are £1,500 relating to the contract with Bee Ltd which would not be deductible under the provisions relating to employees and £1,000 relating to the other income of £10,000. For the purposes of this computation we make the important assumption that the partnership draws accounts to 5 April.

Deemed salary – Frank	£
Income from relevant engagement	80,000
Less: 5% of the gross contract payment	(4,000)
Less: expenses	(2,000)
Deemed salary including employers' NIC	74,000
Less: employers' NIC on the deemed payment (13.8%)	(8,974)
Deemed salary	65,026
Partnership profits	
Turnover	90,000
Less: expenses	(4,500)
Less: deemed salary	(65,026)
Less: employers' NIC on deemed payment	(8,974)
Taxable partnership profits (split 50:50)	11,500

Frank will be taxed on a deemed salary of £65,026 plus partnership profits of £5,750. Joanne will be taxed on partnership profits of £5,750 and will not fully utilise her personal allowance or the starting and basic rate bands of tax. Changing the partnership agreement to give Joanne a partnership salary or a higher profit share could mitigate the effect of this.

Focus

Care must be taken not to fall foul of special rules for calculating the partnership taxable profits. Where a partnership makes a deemed employment payment, the payment itself and the employers' National Insurance on the payment are deducted in computing the partnership profits; however, the deduction can only reduce the profits to nil, it cannot create a loss. Furthermore, no deduction will be allowed for expenses incurred by the partnership in connection with relevant engagements which exceed the amounts which would have been deductible from employment earnings under *ITEPA 2003, s 336* plus the 5% allowance (*ITTOIA 2005, s 164*).

In **Example 28.4**, this means that the partnership could have obtained a deduction for up to £6,000 of expenses incurred in connection with the relevant engagement (£2,000 plus £4,000) if it had incurred those expenses and they were otherwise deductible as being incurred wholly and exclusively for the purposes of the business. This is in addition to any expenses that are related not to the relevant engagement but to its other work, which remain deductible in full.

Accounting date pitfall

28.6 Great care is needed with the accounting date. In computing profits of the partnership, tax relief is given for the deemed employment payment in the partnership accounting year in which it is deemed to be made. In **Example 28.4** we have assumed a 5 April accounting date. If the accounting date had been 31 March, the deemed employment payment would still have been deemed to have been paid on 5 April, giving Frank taxable employment income of £65,026. However, no relief would have been given in the accounts to 31 March for the payment, so the partnership profit would be £85,500. Of course, relief would have been given in the following accounting period for the deemed employment payment deemed to have been paid on 5 April; but the bunching of income in the first year may be extremely disadvantageous. This may particularly need to be borne in mind where the 'relevant engagement' is a one-off contract made in the course of a business that normally operates outside IR35.

Limited liability partnerships

28.7 The *Finance Act 2014* ('*FA 2014*') introduced new rules (*ITTOIA 2005, s 863A*) affecting limited liability partnership ('LLP') members who work for LLPs on terms that HMRC view as 'tantamount to employment' (ie disguised employment). These rules treat members who are within the rules as being employees of the LLP. These are reinforced by *ITTOIA 2005, s 863G* which ensures that individuals cannot avoid the new rules by (for example) providing their services to an LLP through an intermediary which is itself a member of that LLP. In these circumstances, the income of the intermediary from the LLP will be deemed to be employment income of the individual arising from an employment with the LLP. In other words, the interposed company is 'looked through'.

IR35 compliance

28.8 Deemed salaries must be reported to HMRC. The vast majority of employers are now legally required to report payroll information in real time. Under real time information ('RTI'), payments of deemed salary made should be reported on a full payment submission ('FPS') on or before the time of payment. In most cases the deemed payment date will be 5 April though there are circumstances in which the date will fall earlier in the tax year (see **28.4** above). The final FPS will include a specific question to indicate that the intermediaries' legislation has been operated. Where IR35 has been operated, the question on the FPS should be answered positively and this in turn, will alert HMRC that the scheme falls into the special arrangements for IR35.

28.9 In order to avoid an interest charge, the PAYE and National Insurance on the deemed salary should be paid over to HMRC by 19 April following the end of the tax year. However, the final figures for income and the allowable deductions may not be known until after 5 April. A further complication also arises over tax codes: partners do not usually have tax codes, so, unless one has been obtained, it is likely that tax at the basic rate will be deducted under PAYE, leaving the partner to pay the higher rate tax.

28.10 Failure to comply with the IR35 rules is dealt with under the normal PAYE and National Insurance rules for employers.

Managed Service Companies

28.11 The Managed Service Company ('MSC') legislation has much in common with the IR35 legislation. Indeed, the main reason for introduction of the MSC code was to deal with businesses which were in fact within the IR35 rules but which were ignoring them with apparent impunity.

Although one would reasonably expect that the first requirement of a 'managed service company' would be that it should be a company, the definition in fact extends to any body corporate or partnership. In principle therefore a partnership (or more likely an LLP) may be an MSC.

28.12 Very broadly, under a typical MSC structure a number of individuals become partners in a partnership (or, more commonly, shareholders in a company) but take no active involvement in the administration of the business, which is instead under the effective control of an 'MSC provider'. Each worker simply provides his or her services to clients of the MSC and is remunerated by profit share (if the MSC is a partnership) or dividend together with a small element of salary (if the MSC is a company). It is this involvement of an 'MSC provider' which is fundamental to the MSC rules and which differentiates an MSC from an IR35 business. The full statutory definition of the required involvement is that the MSC provider:

(a) benefits financially on an ongoing basis from the provision of the services of the individual;

(b) influences or controls the provision of those services;

(c) influences or controls the way in which payments to the individual (or associates of the individual) are made;

(d) influences or controls the company's finances or any of its activities; or

(e) gives or promotes an undertaking to make good any tax loss.

(ITEPA 2003, s 61B(2))

A person does not become an MSC provider merely by virtue of providing legal or accountancy services in a professional capacity (*ITEPA 2003, s 61B(3)*) but this does not mean that mere possession of a professional qualification is an amulet that protects against becoming an MSC provider. Some comfort can be gained from the list (at ESM3515) of businesses which HMRC confirm 'are not a MSC Provider by virtue of the activity described':

- a firm of accountants carrying on a business of being accountants (irrespective of the percentage of the client base which is individuals operating through service companies);
- a tax advisor carrying on the business of being a tax advisor generally;
- a company formation agent;
- a chartered secretary;
- an employment business/agency undertaking its core business of placing work seekers (including those operating through companies) with end clients;
- service providers providing services to companies generally, for example, insurance companies, payroll bureaux etc;
- a trade association operating in the service sector.

On the other hand, the following would be regarded as MSCs:

- a service provider carrying on a business specifically of marketing and/or providing corporate solutions and services to individuals providing their services to end clients;
- a firm of accountants carrying on a discernable part of their business specifically to market and/or provide corporate solutions and services to individuals providing their services to end clients (in this case the firm would only be an MSC provider in respect of that discernable part of the business);
- a business which terms itself a tax advisor, service provider, or whatever but which specifically markets and/or markets corporate solutions and services to individuals providing their services to individuals.

28.13 In many cases MSC arrangements would already be within the scope of IR35. But MSCs are taken outside the scope of IR35 and instead subjected to a more onerous regime. The main differences between MSCs and IR35 businesses are:

- The MSC rules do not require any investigation as to whether a direct engagement with the worker would have been a contract of employment. They apply if the services of an individual are provided (directly or indirectly) by an MSC, the individual (or an associate of the individual) receives (from any person) a payment or benefit which can reasonably be taken to be in respect of the services and the payment or benefit is not otherwise treated as earnings.
- The full amount of any payment made by an MSC to a worker is treated as employment income, subject only to deduction of allowable expenses incurred by the worker. The 5% deduction for notional expenses applicable under IR35 is not available to an MSC.
- PAYE is required to be operated on a real-time basis as and when payments are made rather than on a deemed payment made on the last day of the tax year.
- If the MSC itself does not account for the tax and NIC due under PAYE in respect of payments made to workers, 'Debt Transfer' provisions (*ITEPA 2003, s 688A*) allow HMRC to instead collect the amounts from certain other persons.

28.14 It is the 'Debt Transfer' rules that are probably in practice the main weapon in HMRC's armoury in countering perceived abuse using MSCs. It is alleged that historically, even if a business was considered to be within IR35, it was often a lengthy and time-consuming process for HMRC to establish the fact of liability and all too often by the time the liability was established the workers had moved on to another company in the promoter's stable and there were no assets left in the IR35 business to meet the PAYE obligations. By fixing liability on those who promote the arrangements HMRC aim to discourage their use or at worst to collect the tax legally due.

Thus, in respect of a payment made by an MSC to any individual, the 'Debt Transfer' rules allow HMRC to collect tax from:

(a) a director or other office-holder, or an associate, of the MSC;

(b) an MSC provider;

(c) a person who (directly or indirectly) has encouraged or been actively involved in the provision by the MSC of the services of the individual; and

(d) a director or other office holder, or an associate, of a person (other than an individual) who is within paragraph (b) or (c) above.

However, HMRC can recover from a person in category (c) (or a director, office holder or associate of such a person) only if there is no person in the first two categories from whom recovery is practicable.

For this purpose 'associate' is defined, in relation to a company, as a person connected with the company. In relation to a partnership, 'associate' means any associate of a member of the partnership but if an MSC is a partnership and a person is an associate of another person by virtue only of being a member of the partnership, he is to be treated in relation to the MSC as if he were not an associate of that other person (*ITEPA 2003, s 61I*).

Services to the public sector through intermediaries

28.15 Neither IR35 nor the MSC rules apply in a case where the rules at *ITEPA 2003, Ch 10* (workers' services provided to public sector through intermediaries) that were introduced by the *Finance Act 2017* apply. Further guidance on the new rules is at https://www.gov.uk/guidance/public-authorities-using-a-personal-service-company.

Chapter 29

Construction Industry Partnerships

Signposts

- All businesses in the construction industry (individuals, partnerships and companies) are subject to the Construction Industry Scheme (see **29.1 – 29.3**).
- The business, turnover and compliance tests apply to partnerships as to other businesses with appropriate modifications which in some cases disadvantage partnerships compared with other business structures (see **29.4 – 29.8**).
- There are specific provisions in the legislation to ensure that the Construction Industry Scheme interacts with the IR35 rules (see **29.9**).

29.1 All businesses in the construction industry (individuals, partnerships and companies) are subject to the Construction Industry Scheme ('CIS'). This applies not only to construction work but also to work including installation (of most items from heating systems to shop fittings), repairs, decorating and demolition. The legislation governing the CIS is contained in the *Finance Act 2004* ('*FA 2004*') and the *Income Tax (Construction Industry Scheme) Regulations 2005 (SI 2005/2045*). Broadly, the rules provide for a verification service run by HMRC, periodic returns and an employment status declaration.

29.2 'Contractors' for these purposes include construction firms and any other business involved in construction work, although private householders and businesses spending less than £1m per annum on construction work are excluded (*FA 2004, s 59*).

A subcontractor is any business which has agreed to carry out construction operations for a contractor – whether by doing the operations itself, or by having them done by its own employees, or in any other way.

29.3 HMRC will only authorise a contractor to make gross payments to a partnership where the following conditions are satisfied.

The business test

29.4 To satisfy this condition, the partnership must provide evidence that it is carrying on a business in the UK which:

(a) consists of or includes the carrying out of construction operations or the furnishing or arranging for the furnishing of labour in carrying out construction operations, and

(b) is, to a substantial extent, carried on by means of an account with a bank.

Evidence prescribed to satisfy the business test is as follows (*SI 2005/2045, reg 27*):

- the business address;
- invoices, contracts or purchase orders for construction work carried out by the applicant;
- details of payments for construction work;
- the books and accounts of the business; and
- details of the business bank account, including bank statements.

The turnover test

29.5 The partnership must satisfy HMRC that, in the year following the making of the application as a partnership, the net business turnover from construction work (ie after deducting the cost of any materials) is £30,000 a year or more multiplied by the number of partners. For a husband and wife team, for instance, it would be £60,000.

29.6 An alternative test for partnerships and companies is that the business has an annual net turnover from construction work (after deducting the cost of materials) of £100,000 or more.

The compliance test

29.7 Not only the partnership but also each of the partners individually must have kept their tax affairs up to date during the 'qualifying period' (the period of 12 months ending with the date of the application in question). This means they must have paid all tax liabilities, including any PAYE and subcontractor deductions, and submitted all tax returns on time. HMRC will not accept an application where tax affairs are brought to date just prior to submitting an application.

This means that in cases where some partners meet the compliance test but others do not, the only way in which gross payment status can be achieved by the partnership may be to eject the non-compliant partners from the partnership, perhaps with a view to re-admitting them when their compliance record passes muster.

Applicants seeking registration for gross payment will be able to pass the compliance test even though they have failed to pay, or have paid late, an amount of tax due under the *Taxes Acts* or the *Taxes Management Act 1970*, where that amount is small. In this situation, 'small' is taken to mean less than £100.

Special problems for partnerships

29.8 Where a company is not authorised to receive gross payments, tax deducted under the Construction Industry Scheme can be set off against tax due from the company under PAYE or in respect of Construction Industry payments which the company itself makes. But this does not apply to partnerships: for a partnership any CIS tax deducted must be treated as income tax paid in respect of trading profits of the partnership. This may give a partnership a significant cash-flow disadvantage compared to a company.

Interaction with IR35

29.9 In some circumstances a deduction may be made under the CIS rules from an amount received by a partnership in respect of something which is also a 'relevant engagement' under the IR35 rules (see **Chapter 28**). Where this happens, *ITEPA 2003, s 54(2)* provides that IR35 applies in the first instance as if the CIS deduction had not been made and the payment had been received gross.

Tax returns

29.10 Tax deducted via the CIS must be shown in Box 3.97 on the return and Box 24 on the partnership statement.

If the partnership does not qualify for gross payment from contractors, it should provide HMRC with:

- the name and address of the contractor;
- the month that the payment was made;
- the gross payment; and
- the tax deducted.

Under the CIS, contractors must provide a written statement to every subcontractor from whom a deduction has been made within 14 days of the end of each tax month. A tax month runs from the 6th of one month to the 5th of the next month, so the statement must be provided by the 19th of the month. If any statements have been lost, the partnership should ask the contractor to supply them with photocopies. If the contractor does not, it is recommended that an explanation be provided on the partnership return.

Appendix 1

Partnership Act 1890

1890 Chapter 39 – Royal Assent 14 August 1890

ARRANGEMENT OF SECTIONS

Section

Nature of Partnership

1 Definition of partnership

(1) Partnership is the relation which subsists between persons carrying on a business in common with a view of profit.

(2) But the relation between members of any company or association which is–

(a) Registered as a company under the Companies Act, 1862, or any other Act of Parliament for the time being in force and relating to the registration of joint stock companies; or

(b) Formed or incorporated by or in pursuance of any other Act of Parliament or letters patent, or Royal Charter:

is not a partnership within the meaning of this Act.

2 Rules for determining existence of a partnership

In determining whether a partnership does or does not exist, regard shall be had to the following rules:

(1) Joint tenancy, tenancy in common, joint property, common property, or part ownership does not of itself create a partnership as to anything so held or owned, whether the tenants or owners do or do not share any profits made by the use thereof.

(2) The sharing of gross returns does not of itself create a partnership, whether the persons sharing such returns have or have not a joint or common right or interest in any property from which or from the use of which the returns are derived.

(3) The receipt by a person of a share of the profits of a business is *prima facie* evidence that he is a partner in the business, but the receipt of such a share, or of a payment contingent on or varying with the profits of a business, does not of itself make him a partner in the business; and in particular–

(a) The receipt by a person of a debt or other liquidated amount by instalments, or otherwise out of the accruing profits of a business does not of itself make him a partner in the business or liable as such;

(b) A contract for the remuneration of a servant or agent of a person engaged in a business by a share of the profits of the business does not of itself make the servant or agent a partner in the business or liable as such;

(c) A person being the widow or child of a deceased partner, and receiving by way of annuity a portion of the profits made in the business in which the deceased person was a partner, is not by reason only of such receipt a partner in the business or liable as such;

(d) The advance of money by way of loan to a person engaged or about to engage in any business on a contract with that person that the lender shall receive a rate of interest varying with the profits, or shall receive a share of the profits arising from carrying on the business, does not of itself make the lender a partner with the person or persons carrying on the business or liable as such. Provided that the contract is in writing, and signed by or on behalf of all the parties thereto;

(e) A person receiving by way of annuity or otherwise a portion of the profits of a business in consideration of the sale by him of the goodwill of the business is not by reason only of such receipt a partner in the business or liable as such.

3 Postponement of rights of person lending or selling in consideration of share of profits in case of insolvency

In the event of any person to whom money has been advanced by way of loan upon such a contract as is mentioned in the last foregoing section, or of any buyer of a goodwill in consideration of a share of the profits of the business, being adjudged a bankrupt, entering into an arrangement to pay his creditors less than [100p] in the pound, or dying in insolvent circumstances, the lender of the loan shall not be entitled to recover anything in respect of his loan, and the seller of the goodwill shall not be entitled to recover anything in respect of the share of profits contracted for, until the claims of the other creditors of the borrower or buyer for valuable consideration in money or money's worth have been satisfied.

4 Meaning of firm

(1) Persons who have entered into partnership with one another are for the purposes of this Act called collectively a firm, and the name under which their business is carried on is called the firm-name.

(2) In Scotland a firm is a legal person distinct from the partners of whom it is composed, but an individual partner may be charged on a decree or diligence directed against the firm, and on payment of the debts is entitled to relief *pro rata* from the firm and its other members.

Relations of Partners to persons dealing with them

5 Power of partner to bind the firm

Every partner is an agent of the firm and his other partners for the purpose of the business of the partnership; and the acts of every partner who does any act for carrying on in the usual way business of the kind carried on by the firm of which he is a member bind the firm and his partners, unless the partner so acting has in fact no authority to act for the firm in the particular matter, and the person with whom he is dealing either knows that he has no authority, or does not know or believe him to be a partner.

6 Partners bound by acts on behalf of firm

An act or instrument relating to the business of the firm and done or executed in the firm-name, or in any other manner showing an intention to bind the firm, by any person thereto authorised, whether a partner or not, is binding on the firm and all the partners.

Provided that this section shall not affect any general rule of law relating to the execution of deeds or negotiable instruments.

7 Partner using credit of firm for private purposes

Where one partner pledges the credit of the firm for a purpose apparently not connected with the firm's ordinary course of business, the firm is not bound, unless he is in fact specially authorised by the other partners; but this section does not affect any personal liability incurred by an individual partner.

8 Effect of notice that firm will not be bound by acts of partner

If it has been agreed between the partners that any restriction shall be placed on the power of any one or more of them to bind the firm, no act done in contravention of the agreement is binding on the firm with respect to persons having notice of the agreement.

9 Liability of partners

Every partner in a firm is liable jointly with the other partners, and in Scotland severally also, for all debts and obligations of the firm incurred while he is a partner; and after his death his estate is also severally liable in a due course of administration for such debts and obligations, so far as they remain unsatisfied, but subject in England or [Northern Ireland] to the prior payment of his separate debts.

10 Liability of the firm for wrongs

Where, by any wrongful act or omission of any partner acting in the ordinary course of the business of the firm, or with the authority of his co-partners, loss or injury is caused to any person not being a partner in the firm, or any penalty is incurred, the firm is liable therefor to the same extent as the partner so acting or omitting to act.

11 Misapplication of money or property received for or in custody of the firm

In the following cases; namely–

(a) Where one partner acting within the scope of his apparent authority receives the money or property of a third person and misapplies it; and

(b) Where a firm in the course of its business receives money or property of a third person, and the money or property so received is misapplied by one or more of the partners while it is in the custody of the firm;

the firm is liable to make good the loss.

12 Liability for wrongs joint and several

Every partner is liable jointly with his co-partners and also severally for everything for which the firm while he is a partner therein becomes liable under either of the two last preceding sections.

13 Improper employment of trust-property for partnership purposes

If a partner, being a trustee, improperly employs trust-property in the business or on the account of the partnership, no other partner is liable for the trust-property to the persons beneficially interested therein.

Provided as follows:–

(1) This section shall not affect any liability incurred by any partner by reason of his having notice of a breach of trust; and

(2) Nothing in this section shall prevent trust money from being followed and recovered from the firm if still in its possession or under its control.

14 Persons liable by 'holding out'

(1) Every one who by words spoken or written or by conduct represents himself, or who knowingly suffers himself to be represented, as a partner in a particular firm, is liable as a partner to any one who has on the faith of any such representation given credit to the firm, whether the representation has or has not been made or communicated to the person so giving credit by or with the knowledge of the apparent partner making the representation or suffering it to be made.

(2) Provided that where after a partner's death the partnership business is continued in the old firm-name, the continued use of that name or of the deceased partner's name as part thereof shall not of itself make his executors or administrators estate or effects liable for any partnership debts contracted after his death.

15 Admissions and representations of partners

An admission or representation made by any partner concerning the partnership affairs, and in the ordinary course of its business, is evidence against the firm.

16 Notice to acting partner to be notice to the firm

Notice to any partner who habitually acts in the partnership business of any matter relating to partnership affairs operates as notice to the firm, except in the case of a fraud on the firm committed by or with the consent of that partner.

17 Liabilities of incoming and outgoing partners

(1) A person who is admitted as a partner into an existing firm does not thereby become liable to the creditors of the firm for anything done before he became a partner.

(2) A partner who retires from a firm does not thereby cease to be liable for partnership debts or obligations incurred before his retirement.

(3) A retiring partner may be discharged from any existing liabilities, by an agreement to that effect between himself and the members of the firm as newly constituted and the creditors, and this agreement may be either express or inferred as a fact from the course of dealing between the creditors and the firm as newly constituted.

18 Revocation of continuing guaranty by change in firm

A continuing guaranty or cautionary obligation given either to a firm or to a third person in respect of the transactions of a firm is, in the absence of agreement to the contrary, revoked as to future transactions by any change in the constitution of the firm to which, or of the firm in respect of the transactions of which, the guaranty or obligation was given.

Relations of Partners to one another

19 Variation by consent of terms of partnership

The mutual rights and duties of partners, whether ascertained by agreement or defined by this Act, may be varied by the consent of all the partners, and such consent may be either express or inferred from a course of dealing.

20 Partnership property

(1) All property and rights and interests in property originally brought into the partnership stock or acquired, whether by purchase or otherwise, on account of the firm or for the purposes and in the course of the partnership business, are called in this Act partnership property, and must be held and applied by the partners exclusively for the purposes of the partnership and in accordance with the partnership agreement.

(2) Provided that the legal estate or interest in any land, or in Scotland the title to and interest in any heritable estate, which belongs to the partnership shall devolve according to the nature and tenure thereof, and the general rules of law thereto applicable, but in trust, so far as necessary, for the persons beneficially interested in the land under this section.

(3) Where co-owners of an estate or interest in any land, or in Scotland of any heritable estate, not being itself partnership property, are partners as to profits made by the use of that land or estate, and purchase other land or estate out of the profits to be used in like manner, the land or estate so purchased belongs to them, in the absence of an agreement to the contrary, not as partners but as co-owners for the same respective estates and interests as are held by them in the land or estate first mentioned at the date of the purchase.

21 Property bought with partnership money

Unless the contrary intention appears, property bought with money belonging to the firm is deemed to have been bought on account of the firm.

22 Conversion into personal estate of land held as partnership property

Where land or any heritable interest therein has become partnership property, it shall, unless the contrary intention appears, be treated as between the partners (including the representatives of a deceased partner), and also as between the heirs of a deceased partner and his executors or administrators, as personal or moveable and not real or heritable estate.

[Section 22 has been repealed in England and Wales.]

23 Procedure against partnership property for a partner's separate judgment debt

(1) A writ of execution shall not issue against any partnership property except on a judgment against the firm.

(2) The High Court, or a judge thereof, or a county court, may, on the application by summons of any judgment creditor of a partner, make an order charging that partners' interest in the partnership property and profits with payment of the amount of the judgment debt and interest thereon, and may by the same or a subsequent order appoint a receiver of that partner's share of profits (whether already declared or accruing), and of any other money which may be coming to him in respect of the partnership, and direct all accounts and inquiries, and give all other orders and directions which might have been directed or given if the charge had been made in favour of the judgment creditor by the partner, or which the circumstances of the case may require.

(3) The other partner or partners shall be at liberty at any time to redeem the interest charged, or in case of a sale being directed, to purchase the same.

(4) [Repealed.]

(5) This section shall not apply to Scotland.

24 Rules as to interests and duties of partners subject to special agreement

The interests of partners in the partnership property and their rights and duties in relation to the partnership shall be determined, subject to any agreement express or implied between the partners, by the following rules:

(1) All the partners are entitled to share equally in the capital and profits of the business, and must contribute equally towards the losses whether of capital or otherwise sustained by the firm.

(2) The firm must indemnify every partner in respect of payments made and personal liabilities incurred by him–

(a) In the ordinary and proper conduct of the business of the firm; or,

(b) In or about anything necessarily done for the preservation of the business or property of the firm.

(3) A partner making, for the purpose of the partnership, any actual payment or advance beyond the amount of capital which he has agreed to subscribe, is

entitled to interest at the rate of five per cent. per annum from the date of the payment or advance.

(4) A partner is not entitled, before the ascertainment of profits, to interest on the capital subscribed by him.

(5) Every partner may take part in the management of the partnership business.

(6) No partner shall be entitled to remuneration for acting in the partnership business.

(7) No person may be introduced as a partner without the consent of all existing partners.

(8) Any difference arising as to ordinary matters connected with the partnership business may be decided by a majority of the partners, but no change may be made in the nature of the partnership business without the consent of all existing partners.

(9) The partnership books are to be kept at the place of business of the partnership (or the principal place, if there is more than one), and every partner may, when he thinks fit, have access to and inspect and copy any of them.

25 Expulsion of partner

No majority of the partners can expel any partner unless a power to do so has been conferred by express agreement between the partners.

26 Retirement from partnership at will

(1) Where no fixed term has been agreed upon for the duration of the partnership, any partner may determine the partnership at any time on giving notice of his intention so to do to all the other partners.

(2) Where the partnership has originally been constituted by deed, a notice in writing, signed by the partner giving it, shall be sufficient for this purpose.

27 Where partnership for term is continued over, continuance on old terms presumed

(1) Where a partnership entered into for a fixed term is continued after the term has expired, and without any express new agreement, the rights and duties of the partners remain the same as they were at the expiration of the term, so far as is consistent with the incidents of a partnership at will.

(2) A continuance of the business by the partners or such of them as habitually acted therein during the term, without any settlement or liquidation of the partnership affairs, is presumed to be a continuance of the partnership.

28 Duty of partners to render accounts, etc.

Partners are bound to render true accounts and full information of all things affecting the partnership to any partner or his legal representatives.

29 Accountability of partners for private profits

(1) Every partner must account to the firm for any benefit derived by him without the consent of the other partners from any transaction concerning the partnership, or from any use by him of the partnership property name or business connexion.

(2) This section applies also to transactions undertaken after a partnership has been dissolved by the death of a partner, and before the affairs thereof have been completely wound up, either by any surviving partner or by the representatives of the deceased partner.

30 Duty of partner not to compete with firm

If a partner, without the consent of the other partners, carries on any business of the same nature as and competing with that of the firm, he must account for and pay over to the firm all profits made by him in that business.

31 Rights of assignee of share in partnership

(1) An assignment by any partner of his share in the partnership, either absolute or by way of mortgage or redeemable charge, does not, as against the other partners, entitle the assignee, during the continuance of the partnership, to interfere in the management or administration of the partnership business or affairs, or to require any accounts of the partnership transactions, or to inspect the partnership books, but entitles the assignee only to receive the share of profits to which the assigning partner would otherwise be entitled, and the assignee must accept the account of profits agreed to by the partners.

(2) In case of a dissolution of the partnership, whether as respects all the partners or as respects the assigning partner, the assignee is entitled to receive the share of the partnership assets to which the assigning partner is entitled as between himself and the other partners, and, for the purpose of ascertaining that share, to an account as from the date of the dissolution.

Dissolution of partnership, and its consequences

32 Dissolution by expiration or notice

Subject to an agreement between the partners a partnership is dissolved–

(a) If entered into for a fixed term, by the expiration of that term;

(b) If entered into for a single adventure or undertaking, by the termination of that adventure or undertaking;

(c) If entered into for an undefined time, by any partner giving notice to the other or others of his intention to dissolve the partnership.

In the last-mentioned case the partnership is dissolved as from the date mentioned in the notice as the date of dissolution, or, if no date is so mentioned, as from the date of the communication of the notice.

33 Dissolution by bankruptcy, death or charge

(1) Subject to any agreement between the partners, every partnership is dissolved as regards all the partners by the death or bankruptcy of any partner.

(2) A partnership may, at the option of the other partners, be dissolved if any partner suffers his share of the partnership property to be charged under this Act for his separate debt.

34 Dissolution by illegality of partnership

A partnership is in every case dissolved by the happening of any event which makes it unlawful for the business of the firm to be carried on or for the members of the firm to carry it on in partnership.

35 Dissolution by the Court

On application by a partner the Court may decree a dissolution of the partnership in any of the following cases:

(a) [Repealed in England and Wales.]

(b) When a partner, other than the partner suing, becomes in any other way permanently incapable of performing his part of the partnership contract;

(c) When a partner, other than the partner suing, has been guilty of such conduct as, in the opinion of the Court, regard being had to the nature of the business, is calculated to prejudicially affect the carrying on of the business;

(d) When a partner, other than the partner suing, wilfully or persistently commits a breach of the partnership agreement, or otherwise so conducts himself in matters relating to the partnership business that it is not reasonably practicable for the other partner or partners to carry on the business in partnership with him;

(e) When the business of the partnership can only be carried on at a loss;

(f) Whenever in any case circumstances have arisen which, in the opinion of the Court, render it just and equitable that the partnership be dissolved.

36 Rights of persons dealing with firm against apparent members of firm

(1) Where a person deals with a firm after a change in its constitution he is entitled to treat all apparent members of the old firm as still being members of the firm until he has notice of the change.

(2) An advertisement in the London Gazette as to a firm whose principal place of business is in England or Wales, in the Edinburgh Gazette as to a firm whose principal place of business is in Scotland, and in the [Belfast Gazette] as to a firm whose principal place of business is in [Northern Ireland], shall be notice as to persons who had not dealings with the firm before the date of the dissolution or change so advertised.

(3) The estate of a partner who dies, or who becomes bankrupt, or of a partner who, not having been known to the person dealing with the firm to be a partner, retires from the firm, is not liable for partnership debts contracted after the date of the death, bankruptcy, or retirement respectively.

37 Right of partners to notify dissolution

On the dissolution of a partnership or retirement of a partner any partner may publicly notify the same, and may require the other partner or partners to concur for that purpose in all necessary or proper acts, if any, which cannot be done without his or their concurrence.

38 Continuing authority of partners for purposes of winding up

After the dissolution of a partnership the authority of each partner to bind the firm, and the other rights and obligations of the partners, continue notwithstanding the dissolution so far as may be necessary to wind up the affairs of the partnership, and to complete transactions begun but unfinished at the time of the dissolution, but not otherwise.

Provided that the firm is in no case bound by the acts of a partner who has become bankrupt; but this proviso does not affect the liability of any person who has after the bankruptcy represented himself or knowingly suffered himself to be represented as a partner of the bankrupt.

39 Rights of partners as to application of partnership property

On the dissolution of a partnership every partner is entitled, as against the other partners in the firm, and all persons claiming through them in respect of their interests as partners, to have the property of the partnership applied in payment of the debts and liabilities of the firm, and to have the surplus assets after such payment applied in payment of what may be due to the partners respectively after deducting what may be due from them as partners to the firm; and for that purpose any partner or his representatives may on the termination of the partnership apply to the Court to wind up the business and affairs of the firm.

40 Apportionment of premium where partnership prematurely dissolved

Where one partner has paid a premium to another on entering into a partnership for a fixed term, and the partnership is dissolved before the expiration of that term otherwise than by the death of a partner, the Court may order the repayment of the premium, or of such part thereof as it thinks just, having regard to the terms of the partnership contract and to the length of time during which the partnership has continued; unless

(a) the dissolution is, in the judgment of the Court, wholly or chiefly due to the misconduct of the partner who paid the premium, or

(b) the partnership has been dissolved by an agreement containing no provision for a return of any part of the premium.

41 Rights where partnership dissolved for fraud or misrepresentation

Where a partnership contract is rescinded on the ground of the fraud or misrepresentation of one of the parties thereto, the party entitled to rescind is, without prejudice to any other right, entitled–

(a) to a lien on, or right of retention of, the surplus of the partnership assets, after satisfying the partnership liabilities, for any sum of money paid by him for the purchase of a share in the partnership and for any capital contributed by him, and is

(b) to stand in the place of the creditors of the firm for any payments made by him in respect of the partnership liabilities, and

(c) to be indemnified by the person guilty of the fraud or making the representation against all the debts and liabilities of the firm.

42 Right of outgoing partner in certain cases to share profits made after dissolution

(1) Where any member of a firm has died or otherwise ceased to be a partner, and the surviving or continuing partners carry on the business of the firm with its capital or assets without any final settlement of accounts as between the firm and the outgoing partner or his estate, then, in the absence of any agreement to the contrary, the outgoing partner or his estate is entitled at the option of himself or his representatives to such share of the profits made since the dissolution as the Court may find to be attributable to the use of his share of the partnership assets, or to interest at the rate of five per cent. per annum on the amount of his share of the partnership assets.

(2) Provided that where by the partnership contract an option is given to surviving or continuing partners to purchase the interest of a deceased or outgoing partner, and that option is duly exercised, the estate of the deceased partner, or the outgoing partner or his estate, as the case may be, is not entitled to any further or other share of profits; but if any partner assuming to act in exercise of the option does not in all material respects comply with the terms thereof, he is liable to account under the foregoing provisions of this section.

43 Retiring or deceased partner's share to be a debt

Subject to any agreement between the partners, the amount due from surviving or continuing partners to an outgoing partner or the representatives of a deceased partner in respect of the outgoing or deceased partner's share is a debt accruing at the date of the dissolution or death.

44 Rule for distribution of assets on final settlement of accounts

In setting accounts between the partners after a dissolution of partnership, the following rules shall, subject to any agreement, be observed:

(a) Losses, including losses and deficiencies of capital, shall be paid first out of profits, next out of capital, and lastly, if necessary, by the partners individually in the proportion in which they were entitled to share profits:

(b) The assets of the firm including the sums, if any, contributed by the partners to make up losses or deficiencies of capital, shall be applied in the following manner and order:

1. In paying the debts and liabilities of the firm to persons who are not partners therein.
2. In paying to each partner rateably what is due from the firm to him for advances as distinguished from capital.
3. In paying to each partner rateably what is due from the firm to him in respect of capital.
4. The ultimate residue, if any, shall be divided among the partners in the proportion in which the profits are divisible.

Supplemental

45 Definitions of 'court' and 'business'

In this Act, unless the contrary intention appears–

The expression 'court' includes every court and judge having jurisdiction in the case:

The expression 'business' includes every trade, occupation, or profession.

46 Saving for rules of equity and common law

The rules of equity and of common law applicable to partnership shall continue in force except so far as they are inconsistent with the express provisions of this Act.

47 Provision as to bankruptcy in Scotland

(1) In the application of this Act to Scotland the bankruptcy of a firm or of an individual shall mean sequestration under the Bankruptcy (Scotland) Acts, and also in the case of an individual the issue against him of a decree of cessio bonorum.

(2) Nothing in this Act shall alter the rules of the law of Scotland relating to the bankruptcy of a firm or of the individual partners thereof.

48 Repeal

[. . .]

49 Commencement of Act

[. . .]

50 Short title

This Act may be cited as the Partnership Act, 1890.

Appendix 2

Limited Partnerships Act 1907

1907 Chapter 24 – Royal Assent 28 August 1907

ARRANGEMENT OF SECTIONS

1 Short title

This Act may be cited for all purposes as the Limited Partnerships Act, 1907.

2 Commencement of Act

[Repealed.]

3 Interpretation of terms

In the construction of this Act the following words and expressions shall have the meanings respectively assigned to them in this section, unless there be something in the subject or context repugnant to such construction:

'Firm,' 'firm name,' and 'business' have the same meanings as in the Partnership Act, 1890:

'General partner' shall mean any partner who is not a limited partner as defined by this Act.

4 Definition and constitution of limited partnership

(1) [. . . Words repealed] Limited partnerships may be formed in the manner and subject to the conditions by this Act provided.

(2) A limited partnership [. . . Words repealed] must consist of one or more persons called general partners, who shall be liable for all debts and obligations of the firm, and one or more persons to be called limited partners, who shall at the time of entering into such partnership contribute thereto a sum or sums as capital or property valued at a stated amount, and who shall not be liable for the debts or obligations of the firm beyond the amount so contributed.

(3) A limited partner shall not during the continuance of the partnership, either directly or indirectly, draw out or receive back any part of his contribution, and if he does so draw out or receive back any such part shall be liable for the debts and obligations of the firm up to the amount so drawn out or received back.

(4) A body corporate may be a limited partner.

5 Registration of limited partnership required

Every limited partnership must be registered as such in accordance with the provisions of this Act, or in default thereof it shall be deemed to be a general partnership, and every limited partner shall be deemed to be a general partner.

6 Modifications of general law in case of limited partnerships

(1) A limited partner shall not take part in the management of the partnership business, and shall not have power to bind the firm.

Provided that a limited partner may by himself or his agent at any time inspect the books of the firm and examine into the state and prospects of the partnership business, and may advise with the partners thereon.

If a limited partner takes part in the management of the partnership business he shall be liable for all debts and obligations of the firm incurred while he so takes part in the management as though he were a general partner.

(2) A limited partnership shall not be dissolved by the death or bankruptcy of a limited partner, and the lunacy of a limited partner shall not be a ground for dissolution of the partnership by the court unless the lunatic's share cannot be otherwise ascertained and realised.

(3) In the event of the dissolution of a limited partnership its affairs shall be wound up by the general partners unless the court otherwise orders.

(4) [Repealed.]

(5) Subject to any agreement expressed or implied between the partners–

(a) Any difference arising as to ordinary matters connected with the partnership business may be decided by a majority of the general partners;

(b) A limited partner may, with the consent of the general partners, assign his share in the partnership, and upon such an assignment the assignee shall become a limited partner with all the rights of the assignor;

(c) The other partners shall not be entitled to dissolve the partnership by reason of any limited partner suffering his share to be charged for his separate debt;

(d) A person may be introduced as a partner without the consent of the existing limited partners;

(e) A limited partner shall not be entitled to dissolve the partnership by notice.

7 Law as to private partnerships to apply where not excluded by this Act

Subject to the provisions of this Act, the Partnership Act, 1890, and the rules of equity and of common law applicable to partnerships, except so far as they are inconsistent with the express provisions of the last-mentioned Act, shall apply to limited partnerships.

8 Manner and particulars of registration

The registration of a limited partnership shall be effected by sending by post or delivering to the registrar at the register office in that part of the United Kingdom in which the principal place of business of the limited partnership is situated or proposed to be situated a statement signed by the partners containing the following particulars–

(a) The firm name;

(b) The general nature of the business;

(c) The principal place of business;

(d) The full name of each of the partners;

(e) The term, if any, for which the partnership is entered into, and the date of its commencement;

(f) A statement that the partnership is limited, and the description of every limited partner as such;

(g) The sum contributed by each limited partner, and whether paid in cash or how otherwise.

9 Registration of changes in partnerships

(1) If during the continuance of a limited partnership any change is made or occurs in–

(a) the firm name,

(b) the general, nature of the business,

(c) the principal place of business,

(d) the partners or the name of any partner,

(e) the term or character of the partnership,

(f) the sum contributed by any limited partner,

(g) the liability of any partner by reason of his becoming a limited instead of a general partner or a general instead of a limited partner, a statement, signed by the firm, specifying the nature of the change shall within seven days be sent by post or delivered to the registrar at the register office in that part of the United Kingdom in which the partnership is registered.

(2) If default is made in compliance with the requirements of this section each of the general partners shall on conviction under the [Magistrates' Courts Act 1952] be liable to a fine not exceeding one pound for each day during which the default continues.

10 Advertisement in Gazette of statement of general partner becoming a limited partner and of assignment of share of limited partner

(1) Notice of any arrangement or transaction under which any person will cease to be a general partner in any firm, and will become a limited partner in that firm, or under which the share of a limited partner in a firm will be assigned to any person, shall be forthwith advertised in the Gazette, and until notice of the arrangement or transaction is so advertised, the arrangement or transaction shall, for the purposes of this Act, be deemed to be of no effect.

(2) For the purposes of this section, the expression 'the Gazette' means–

In the case of a limited partnership registered in England, the London Gazette;

In the case of a limited partnership registered in Scotland, the Edinburgh Gazette;

In the case of a limited partnership registered in Ireland, the [Belfast Gazette].

11 [Repealed.]

12 [Repealed.]

13 Registrar to file statement and issue certificate of registration

On receiving any statement made in pursuance of this Act the registrar shall cause the same to be filed, and he shall send by post to the firm from whom such statement shall have been received a certificate of the registration thereof.

14 Register and index to be kept

At each of the register offices herein-after referred to the registrar shall keep, in proper books to be provided for the purpose, a register and an index of all the limited partnerships registered as aforesaid, and of all the statements registered in relation to such partnerships.

15 Registrar of joint stock companies to be registrar under Act

The registrar of joint stock companies shall be the registrar of limited partnerships, and the several offices for the registration of joint stock companies in London, Edinburgh, and [Belfast] shall be the offices for the registration of limited partnerships carrying on business within those parts of the United Kingdom in which they are respectively situated.

16 Inspection of statements registered

(1) Any person may inspect the statements filed by the registrar in the register offices aforesaid, [. . . Words repealed] and any person may require a certificate of the registration of any limited partnership, or a copy of or extract from any registered statement, to be certified by the registrar [. . . Words repealed].

(2) A certificate of registration, or a copy of or extract from any statement registered under this Act, if duly certified to be a true copy under the hand of the registrar or one of the assistant registrars (whom it shall not be necessary to prove to be the registrar or assistant registrar) shall, in all legal proceedings, civil or criminal, and in all cases whatsoever be received in evidence.

17 Power of Board of Trade to make rules

The Board of Trade may make rules [. . . Words repealed] concerning any of the following matters–

(a) [Repealed.]

(b) The duties or additional duties to be performed by the registrar for the purposes of this Act;

(c) The performance by assistant registrars and other officers of acts by this Act required to be done by the registrar;

(d) The forms to be used for the purposes of this Act;

(e) Generally the conduct and regulation of registration under this Act and any matters incidental thereto.

Appendix 3

Limited Liability Partnerships Act 2000

Chapter 12 – Royal Assent 20 July 2000

ARRANGEMENT OF SECTIONS

Schedule: Names and registered offices.
Part II – Names.
Part II – Registered offices.

An Act to make provision for limited liability partnerships.

[20th July 2000]

BE IT ENACTED by the Queen's most Excellent Majesty, by and with the advice and consent of the Lords Spiritual and Temporal, and Commons, in this present Parliament assembled, and by the authority of the same, as follows:–

Introductory

1 Limited liability partnerships

(1) There shall be a new form of legal entity to be known as a limited liability partnership.

(2) A limited liability partnership is a body corporate (with legal personality separate from that of its members) which is formed by being incorporated under this Act; and–

(a) in the following provisions of this Act (except in the phrase 'overseas limited liability partnership'), and

(b) in any other enactment (except where provision is made to the contrary or the context otherwise requires),

references to a limited liability partnership are to such a body corporate.

(3) A limited liability partnership has unlimited capacity.

(4) The members of a limited liability partnership have such liability to contribute to its assets in the event of its being wound up as is provided for by virtue of this Act.

(5) Accordingly, except as far as otherwise provided by this Act or any other enactment, the law relating to partnerships does not apply to a limited liability partnership.

(6) The Schedule (which makes provision about the names and registered offices of limited liability partnerships) has effect.

Incorporation

2 Incorporation document etc

(1) For a limited liability partnership to be incorporated–

(a) two or more persons associated for carrying on a lawful business with a view to profit must have subscribed their names to an incorporation document,

(b) there must have been delivered to the registrar either the incorporation document or a copy authenticated in a manner approved by him, and

(c) there must have been so delivered a statement in a form approved by the registrar, made by either a solicitor engaged in the formation of the limited liability partnership or anyone who subscribed his name to the incorporation document, that the requirement imposed by paragraph (*a*) has been complied with.

(2) The incorporation document must–

(a) be in a form approved by the registrar (or as near to such a form as circumstances allow),

(b) state the name of the limited liability partnership,

(c) state whether the registered office of the limited liability partnership is to be situated in England and Wales, in Wales or in Scotland,

(d) state the address of that registered office,

(e) state the name and address of each of the persons who are to be members of the limited liability partnership on incorporation, and

(f) either specify which of those persons are to be designated members or state that every person who from time to time is a member of the limited liability partnership is a designated member.

(2A) Where a confidentiality order, made under section 723B of the Companies Act 1985 as applied to … limited liability partnerships, is in force in respect of any individual named as a member of a limited liability partnership under subsection (2) that subsection shall have effect as if the reference to the address of the individual were a reference to the address for the time being notified by him under the Limited Liability Partnerships (Particulars of Usual Residential Address) (Confidentiality Orders) Regulations 2002 to any limited partnership of which he is a member or if he is not such a member either the address specified in his application for a confidentiality order or the address last notified by him under such a confidentiality order as the case may be.

(2B) Where the incorporation document or a copy of such delivered under this section includes an address specified in reliance on subsection (2A) there shall be delivered with it or the copy of it a statement in a form approved by the registrar containing particulars of the usual residential address of the member whose address is so specified.

[Note: the '…' indicate editorial removal of the superfluous word 'a'.]

(3) If a person makes a false statement under subsection (1)(*c*) which he–

(a) knows to be false, or

(b) does not believe to be true,

he commits an offence.

(4) A person guilty of an offence under subsection (3) is liable–

(a) on summary conviction, to imprisonment for a period not exceeding six months or a fine not exceeding the statutory maximum, or to both, or

(b) on conviction on indictment, to imprisonment for a period not exceeding two years or a fine, or to both.

3 Incorporation by registration

(1) When the requirements imposed by paragraphs (*b*) and (*c*) of subsection (1) of section 2 have been complied with, the registrar shall retain the incorporation document or copy delivered to him and, unless the requirement imposed by paragraph (*a*) of that subsection has not been complied with, he shall–

(a) register the incorporation document or copy, and

(b) give a certificate that the limited liability partnership is incorporated by the name specified in the incorporation document.

(2) The registrar may accept the statement delivered under paragraph (*c*) of subsection (1) of section 2 as sufficient evidence that the requirement imposed by paragraph (*a*) of that subsection has been complied with.

(3) The certificate shall either be signed by the registrar or be authenticated by his official seal.

(4) The certificate is conclusive evidence that the requirements of section 2 are complied with and that the limited liability partnership is incorporated by the name specified in the incorporation document.

Membership

4 Members

(1) On the incorporation of a limited liability partnership its members are the persons who subscribed their names to the incorporation document (other than any who have died or been dissolved).

(2) Any other person may become a member of a limited liability partnership by and in accordance with an agreement with the existing members.

(3) A person may cease to be a member of a limited liability partnership (as well as by death or dissolution) in accordance with an agreement with the other members or, in the absence of agreement with the other members as to cessation of membership, by giving reasonable notice to the other members.

(4) A member of a limited liability partnership shall not be regarded for any purpose as employed by the limited liability partnership unless, if he and the other members were partners in a partnership, he would be regarded for that purpose as employed by the partnership.

5 Relationship of members etc

(1) Except as far as otherwise provided by this Act or any other enactment, the mutual rights and duties of the members of a limited liability partnership, and the mutual rights and duties of a limited liability partnership and its members, shall be governed–

(a) by agreement between the members, or between the limited liability partnership and its members, or

(b) in the absence of agreement as to any matter, by any provision made in relation to that matter by regulations under section 15(*c*).

(2) An agreement made before the incorporation of a limited liability partnership between the persons who subscribe their names to the incorporation document may impose obligations on the limited liability partnership (to take effect at any time after its incorporation).

6 Members as agents

(1) Every member of a limited liability partnership is the agent of the limited liability partnership.

(2) But a limited liability partnership is not bound by anything done by a member in dealing with a person if–

(a) the member in fact has no authority to act for the limited liability partnership by doing that thing, and

(b) the person knows that he has no authority or does not know or believe him to be a member of the limited liability partnership.

(3) Where a person has ceased to be a member of a limited liability partnership, the former member is to be regarded (in relation to any person dealing with the limited liability partnership) as still being a member of the limited liability partnership unless–

(a) the person has notice that the former member has ceased to be a member of the limited liability partnership, or

(b) notice that the former member has ceased to be a member of the limited liability partnership has been delivered to the registrar.

(4) Where a member of a limited liability partnership is liable to any person (other than another member of the limited liability partnership) as a result of a wrongful act or omission of his in the course of the business of the limited liability partnership or with its authority, the limited liability partnership is liable to the same extent as the member.

7 Ex-members

(1) This section applies where a member of a limited liability partnership has either ceased to be a member or–

(a) has died,

(b) has become bankrupt or had his estate sequestrated or has been wound up,

(c) has granted a trust deed for the benefit of his creditors, or

(d) has assigned the whole or any part of his share in the limited liability partnership (absolutely or by way of charge or security).

(2) In such an event the former member or–

(a) his personal representative,

(b) his trustee in bankruptcy or permanent or interim trustee (within the meaning of the Bankruptcy (Scotland) Act 1985) or liquidator,

(c) his trustee under the trust deed for the benefit of his creditors, or

(d) his assignee,

may not interfere in the management or administration of any business or affairs of the limited liability partnership.

(3) But subsection (2) does not affect any right to receive an amount from the limited liability partnership in that event.

8 Designated members

(1) If the incorporation document specifies who are to be designated members–

(a) they are designated members on incorporation, and

(b) any member may become a designated member by and in accordance with an agreement with the other members,

and a member may cease to be a designated member in accordance with an agreement with the other members.

(2) But if there would otherwise be no designated members, or only one, every member is a designated member.

(3) f the incorporation document states that every person who from time to time is a member of the limited liability partnership is a designated member, every member is a designated member.

(4) A limited liability partnership may at any time deliver to the registrar–

(a) notice that specified members are to be designated members, or

(b) notice that every person who from time to time is a member of the limited liability partnership is a designated member,

and, once it is delivered, subsection (1) (apart from paragraph (*a*)) and subsection (2), or subsection (3), shall have effect as if that were stated in the incorporation document.

(5) A notice delivered under subsection (4)–

(a) shall be in a form approved by the registrar, and

(b) shall be signed by a designated member of the limited liability partnership or authenticated in a manner approved by the registrar.

(6) A person ceases to be a designated member if he ceases to be a member.

9 Registration of membership changes

(1) A limited liability partnership must ensure that–

(a) where a person becomes or ceases to be a member or designated member, notice is delivered to the registrar within fourteen days, and

(b) where there is any change in the name or address of a member, notice is delivered to the registrar within 28 days.

(2) Where all the members from time to time of a limited liability partnership are designated members, subsection (1)(*a*) does not require notice that a person has become or ceased to be a designated member as well as a member.

(3) A notice delivered under subsection (1)–

(a) shall be in a form approved by the registrar, and

(b) shall be signed by a designated member of the limited liability partnership or authenticated in a manner approved by the registrar,

and, if it relates to a person becoming a member or designated member, shall contain a statement that he consents to becoming a member or designated member signed by him or authenticated in a manner approved by the registrar.

(3A) Where a confidentiality order under section 723B of the Companies Act 1985 as applied to limited liability partnerships is made in respect of an existing member, the limited liability partnership must ensure that there is delivered within 28 days to the registrar notice in a form approved by the registrar containing the address for the time being notified to it by the member under the Limited Liability Partnerships (Particulars of Usual Residential Address) (Confidentiality Orders) Regulations 2002.

(3B) Where such a confidentiality order is in force in respect of a member the requirement in subsection (1)(b) to notify a change in the address of a member shall be read in relation to that member as a requirement to deliver to the registrar within 28 days, notice of–

(a) any change in the usual residential address of that member; and

(b) any change in the usual address for the time being notified to the limited liability partnership by the member under the Limited Liability Partnerships (Particulars of Usual Residential Address) (Confidentiality Orders) Regulations 2002,

and the registrar may approve different forms for the notification of each kind of address.

(4) If a limited liability partnership fails to comply with subsection (1), the partnership and every designated member commits an offence.

(5) But it is a defence for a designated member charged with an offence under subsection (4) to prove that he took all reasonable steps for securing that subsection (1) was complied with.

(6) A person guilty of an offence under subsection (4) is liable on summary conviction to a fine not exceeding level 5 on the standard scale

Taxation

10 Income tax and chargeable gains

(1) In the Income and Corporation Taxes Act 1988, after section 118 insert–

'Limited liability partnerships

118ZA Treatment of limited liability partnerships.

For the purposes of the Tax Acts, a trade, profession or business carried on by a limited liability partnership with a view to profit shall be treated as carried on in partnership by its members (and not by the limited liability partnership as such); and, accordingly, the property of the limited liability partnership shall be treated for those purposes as partnership property.

118ZB Restriction on relief.

Sections 117 and 118 have effect in relation to a member of a limited liability partnership as in relation to a limited partner, but subject to sections 118ZC and 118ZD.

118ZC Member's contribution to trade.

(1) Subsection (3) of section 117 does not have effect in relation to a member of a limited liability partnership.

(2) But, for the purposes of that section and section 118, such a member's contribution to a trade at any time ('the relevant time') is the greater of–

(a) the amount subscribed by him, and

(b) the amount of his liability on a winding up.

(3) The amount subscribed by a member of a limited liability partnership is the amount which he has contributed to the limited liability partnership as capital, less so much of that amount (if any) as–

(a) he has previously, directly or indirectly, drawn out or received back,

(b) he so draws out or receives back during the period of five years beginning with the relevant time,

(c) he is or may be entitled so to draw out or receive back at any time when he is a member of the limited liability partnership, or

(d) he is or may be entitled to require another person to reimburse to him.

(4) The amount of the liability of a member of a limited liability partnership on a winding up is the amount which–

(a) he is liable to contribute to the assets of the limited liability partnership in the event of its being wound up, and

(b) he remains liable so to contribute for the period of at least five years beginning with the relevant time (or until it is wound up, if that happens before the end of that period).

118ZD Carry forward of unrelieved losses.

(1) Where amounts relating to a trade carried on by a member of a limited liability partnership are, in any one or more chargeable periods, prevented from being given or allowed by section 117 or 118 as it applies otherwise than by virtue of this section (his 'total unrelieved loss'), subsection (2) applies in each subsequent chargeable period in which–

(a) he carries on the trade as a member of the limited liability partnership, and

(b) any of his total unrelieved loss remains outstanding.

(2) Sections 380, 381, 393A(1) and 403 (and sections 117 and 118 as they apply in relation to those sections) shall have effect in the subsequent chargeable period as if–

(a) any loss sustained or incurred by the member in the trade in that chargeable period were increased by an amount equal to so much of his total unrelieved loss as remains outstanding in that period, or

(b) (if no loss is so sustained or incurred) a loss of that amount were so sustained or incurred.

(3) To ascertain whether any (and, if so, how much) of a member's total unrelieved loss remains outstanding in the subsequent chargeable period, deduct from the amount of his total unrelieved loss the aggregate of–

(a) any relief given under any provision of the Tax Acts (otherwise than as a result of subsection (2)) in respect of his total unrelieved loss in that or any previous chargeable period, and

(b) any amount given or allowed in respect of his total unrelieved loss as a result of subsection (2) in any previous chargeable period (or which would have been so given or allowed had a claim been made).'

(4) In section 362(2)(a) of that Act (loan to buy into partnership), after 'partner' insert 'in a limited partnership registered under the Limited Partnerships Act 1907'.

(3) In the Taxation of Chargeable Gains Act 1992, after section 59 insert–

'59A Limited liability partnerships.

(1) Where a limited liability partnership carries on a trade or business with a view to profit–

(a) assets held by the limited liability partnership shall be treated for the purposes of tax in respect of chargeable gains as held by its members as partners, and

(b) any dealings by the limited liability partnership shall be treated for those purposes as dealings by its members in partnership (and not by the limited liability partnership as such),

and tax in respect of chargeable gains accruing to the members of the limited liability partnership on the disposal of any of its assets shall be assessed and charged on them separately.

(2) Where subsection (1) ceases to apply in relation to a limited liability partnership with the effect that tax is assessed and charged–

(a) on the limited liability partnership (as a company) in respect of chargeable gains accruing on the disposal of any of its assets, and

(b) on the members in respect of chargeable gains accruing on the disposal of any of their capital interests in the limited liability partnership,

it shall be assessed and charged on the limited liability partnership as if subsection (1) had never applied in relation to it.

(3) Neither the commencement of the application of subsection (1) nor the cessation of its application in relation to a limited liability partnership is to be taken as giving rise to the disposal of any assets by it or any of its members.'

(4) After section 156 of that Act insert–

'156A Cessation of trade by limited liability partnership.

(1) Where, immediately before the time of cessation of trade, a member of a limited liability partnership holds an asset, or an interest in an asset, acquired by him for a consideration treated as reduced under section 152 or 153, he shall be treated as if a chargeable gain equal to the amount of the reduction accrued to him immediately before that time.

(2) Where, as a result of section 154(2), a chargeable gain on the disposal of an asset, or an interest in an asset, by a member of a limited liability partnership has not accrued before the time of cessation of trade, the member shall be treated as if the chargeable gain accrued immediately before that time.

(3) In this section 'the time of cessation of trade', in relation to a limited liability partnership, means the time when section 59A(1) ceases to apply in relation to the limited liability partnership.'

11 Inheritance tax

In the Inheritance Tax Act 1984, after section 267 insert–

'267A Limited liability partnerships.

For the purposes of this Act and any other enactments relating to inheritance tax–

(a) property to which a limited liability partnership is entitled, or which it occupies or uses, shall be treated as property to which its members are entitled, or which they occupy or use, as partners,

(b) any business carried on by a limited liability partnership shall be treated as carried on in partnership by its members,

(c) incorporation, change in membership or dissolution of a limited liability partnership shall be treated as formation, alteration or dissolution of a partnership, and

(d) any transfer of value made by or to a limited liability partnership shall be treated as made by or to its members in partnership (and not by or to the limited liability partnership as such).'

12 Stamp duty

(1) Stamp duty shall not be chargeable on an instrument by which property is conveyed or transferred by a person to a limited liability partnership in connection with its incorporation within the period of one year beginning with the date of incorporation if the following two conditions are satisfied.

(2) The first condition is that at the relevant time the person–

(a) is a partner in a partnership comprised of all the persons who are or are to be members of the limited liability partnership (and no-one else), or

(b) holds the property conveyed or transferred as nominee or bare trustee for one or more of the partners in such a partnership.

(3) The second condition is that–

(a) the proportions of the property conveyed or transferred to which the persons mentioned in subsection (2)(*a*) are entitled immediately after the conveyance or transfer are the same as those to which they were entitled at the relevant time, or

(b) none of the differences in those proportions has arisen as part of a scheme or arrangement of which the main purpose, or one of the main purposes, is avoidance of liability to any duty or tax.

(4) For the purposes of subsection (2) a person holds property as bare trustee for a partner if the partner has the exclusive right (subject only to satisfying any outstanding charge, lien or other right of the trustee to resort to the property

for payment of duty, taxes, costs or other outgoings) to direct how the property shall be dealt with.

(5) In this section 'the relevant time' means–

(a) if the person who conveyed or transferred the property to the limited liability partnership acquired the property after its incorporation, immediately after he acquired the property, and

(b) in any other case, immediately before its incorporation.

(6) An instrument in respect of which stamp duty is not chargeable by virtue of subsection (1) shall not be taken to be duly stamped unless–

(a) it has, in accordance with section 12 of the Stamp Act 1891, been stamped with a particular stamp denoting that it is not chargeable with any duty or that it is duly stamped, or

(b) it is stamped with the duty to which it would be liable apart from that subsection.

13 Class 4 national insurance contributions

In section 15 of the Social Security Contributions and Benefits Act 1992 and section 15 of the Social Security Contributions and Benefits (Northern Ireland) Act 1992 (Class 4 contributions), after subsection (3) insert–

'(3A) Where income tax is (or would be) charged on a member of a limited liability partnership in respect of profits or gains arising from the carrying on of a trade or profession by the limited liability partnership, Class 4 contributions shall be payable by him if they would be payable were the trade or profession carried on in partnership by the members.'

Regulations

14 Insolvency and winding up

(1) Regulations shall make provision about the insolvency and winding up of limited liability partnerships by applying or incorporating, with such modifications as appear appropriate, Parts I to IV, VI and VII of the Insolvency Act 1986.

(2) Regulations may make other provision about the insolvency and winding up of limited liability partnerships, and provision about the insolvency and winding up of oversea limited liability partnerships, by–

(a) applying or incorporating, with such modifications as appear appropriate, any law relating to the insolvency or winding up of companies or other corporations which would not otherwise have effect in relation to them, or

(b) providing for any law relating to the insolvency or winding up of companies or other corporations which would otherwise have effect in relation to them not to apply to them or to apply to them with such modifications as appear appropriate.

(3) In this Act 'oversea limited liability partnership' means a body incorporated or otherwise established outside Great Britain and having such connection with Great Britain, and such other features, as regulations may prescribe.

15 Application of company law etc

Regulations may make provision about limited liability partnerships and oversea limited liability partnerships (not being provision about insolvency or winding up) by–

(a) applying or incorporating, with such modifications as appear appropriate, any law relating to companies or other corporations which would not otherwise have effect in relation to them,

(b) providing for any law relating to companies or other corporations which would otherwise have effect in relation to them not to apply to them or to apply to them with such modifications as appear appropriate, or

(c) applying or incorporating, with such modifications as appear appropriate, any law relating to partnerships.

16 Consequential amendments

(1) Regulations may make in any enactment such amendments or repeals as appear appropriate in consequence of this Act or regulations made under it.

(2) The regulations may, in particular, make amendments and repeals affecting companies or other corporations or partnerships.

17 General

(1) In this Act 'regulations' means regulations made by the Secretary of State by statutory instrument.

(2) Regulations under this Act may in particular–

(a) make provision for dealing with non-compliance with any of the regulations (including the creation of criminal offences),

(b) impose fees (which shall be paid into the Consolidated Fund), and

(c) provide for the exercise of functions by persons prescribed by the regulations.

(3) Regulations under this Act may–

(a) contain any appropriate consequential, incidental, supplementary or transitional provisions or savings, and

(b) make different provision for different purposes.

(4) No regulations to which this subsection applies shall be made unless a draft of the statutory instrument containing the regulations (whether or not together with other provisions) has been laid before, and approved by a resolution of, each House of Parliament.

(5) Subsection (4) applies to–

(a) regulations under section 14(2) not consisting entirely of the application or incorporation (with or without modifications) of provisions contained in or made under the Insolvency Act 1986,

(b) regulations under section 15 not consisting entirely of the application or incorporation (with or without modifications) of provisions contained in or made under Part I, Chapter VIII of Part V, Part VII, Parts XI to XIII, Parts XVI to XVIII, Part XX or Parts XXIV to XXVI of the Companies Act 1985,

(c) regulations under section 14 or 15 making provision about oversea limited liability partnerships, and

(d) regulations under section 16.

(6) A statutory instrument containing regulations under this Act shall (unless a draft of it has been approved by a resolution of each House of Parliament) be subject to annulment in pursuance of a resolution of either House of Parliament.

Supplementary

18 Interpretation

In this Act–

'address', in relation to a member of a limited liability partnership, means–

(a) if an individual, his usual residential address, and

(b) if a corporation or Scottish firm, its registered or principal office,

'business' includes every trade, profession and occupation,

'designated member' shall be construed in accordance with section 8,

'enactment' includes subordinate legislation (within the meaning of the Interpretation Act 1978),

'incorporation document' shall be construed in accordance with section 2,

'limited liability partnership' has the meaning given by section 1(2),

'member' shall be construed in accordance with section 4,

'modifications' includes additions and omissions,

'name', in relation to a member of a limited liability partnership, means–

(a) if an individual, his forename and surname (or, in the case of a peer or other person usually known by a title, his title instead of or in addition to either or both his forename and surname), and

(b) if a corporation or Scottish firm, its corporate or firm name,

'oversea limited liability partnership' has the meaning given by section 14(3),

'the registrar' means–

(a) if the registered office of the limited liability partnership is, or is to be, situated in England and Wales or in Wales, the registrar or other officer performing under the Companies Act 1985 the duty of registration of companies in England and Wales, and

(b) if its registered office is, or is to be, situated in Scotland, the registrar or other officer performing under that Act the duty of registration of companies in Scotland, and

'regulations' has the meaning given by section 17(1).

19 Commencement, extent and short title

(1) The preceding provisions of this Act shall come into force on such day as the Secretary of State may by order made by statutory instrument appoint; and different days may be appointed for different purposes.

(2) The Secretary of State may by order made by statutory instrument make any transitional provisions and savings which appear appropriate in connection with the coming into force of any provision of this Act.

(3) For the purposes of the Scotland Act 1998 this Act shall be taken to be a pre-commencement enactment within the meaning of that Act.

(4) Apart from sections 10 to 13 (and this section), this Act does not extend to Northern Ireland.

(5) This Act may be cited as the Limited Liability Partnerships Act 2000.

Schedule – Names and registered offices

Part I NAMES

Index of names

1 In section 714(1) of the Companies Act 1985 (index of names), after paragraph (*d*) insert–

'(*da*) limited liability partnerships incorporated under the Limited Liability Partnerships Act 2000,'.

Name to indicate status

2 (1) The name of a limited liability partnership must end with–

(a) the expression 'limited liability partnership', or

(b) the abbreviation 'llp' or 'LLP'.

(2) But if the incorporation document for a limited liability partnership states that the registered office is to be situated in Wales, its name must end with–

(a) one of the expressions 'limited liability partnership' and 'partneriaeth atebolrwydd cyfyngedig', or

(b) one of the abbreviations 'llp', 'LLP', 'pac' and 'PAC'.

Registration of names

3 (1) A limited liability partnership shall not be registered by a name–

(a) which includes, otherwise than at the end of the name, either of the expressions 'limited liability partnership' and 'partneriaeth atebolrwydd cyfyngedig' or any of the abbreviations 'llp', 'LLP', 'pac' and 'PAC',

(b) which is the same as a name appearing in the index kept under section 714(1) of the Companies Act 1985,

(c) the use of which by the limited liability partnership would in the opinion of the Secretary of State constitute a criminal offence, or

(d) which in the opinion of the Secretary of State is offensive.

(2) Except with the approval of the Secretary of State, a limited liability partnership shall not be registered by a name which–

(a) in the opinion of the Secretary of State would be likely to give the impression that it is connected in any way with Her Majesty's Government or with any local authority, or

(b) includes any word or expression for the time being specified in regulations under section 29 of the Companies Act 1985 (names needing approval),

and in paragraph (a) 'local authority' means any local authority within the meaning of the Local Government Act 1972 or the Local Government etc. (Scotland) Act 1994, the Common Council of the City of London or the Council of the Isles of Scilly.

Change of name

4 (1) A limited liability partnership may change its name at any time.

(2) Where a limited liability partnership has been registered by a name which–

(a) is the same as or, in the opinion of the Secretary of State, too like a name appearing at the time of registration in the index kept under section 714(1) of the Companies Act 1985, or

(b) is the same as or, in the opinion of the Secretary of State, too like a name which should have appeared in the index at that time,

the Secretary of State may within twelve months of that time in writing direct the limited liability partnership to change its name within such period as he may specify.

(3) If it appears to the Secretary of State–

(a) that misleading information has been given for the purpose of the registration of a limited liability partnership by a particular name, or

(b) that undertakings or assurances have been given for that purpose and have not been fulfilled,

he may, within five years of the date of its registration by that name, in writing direct the limited liability partnership to change its name within such period as he may specify.

(4) If in the Secretary of State's opinion the name by which a limited liability partnership is registered gives so misleading an indication of the nature of its activities as to be likely to cause harm to the public, he may in writing direct the limited liability partnership to change its name within such period as he may specify.

(5) But the limited liability partnership may, within three weeks from the date of the direction apply to the court to set it aside and the court may set the direction aside or confirm it and, if it confirms it, shall specify the period within which it must be complied with.

(6) In sub-paragraph (5) 'the court' means–

(a) if the registered office of the limited liability partnership is situated in England and Wales or in Wales, the High Court, and

(b) if it is situated in Scotland, the Court of Session.

(7) Where a direction has been given under sub-paragraph (2), (3) or (4) specifying a period within which a limited liability partnership is to change its name, the Secretary of State may at any time before that period ends extend it by a further direction in writing.

(8) If a limited liability partnership fails to comply with a direction under this paragraph–

(a) the limited liability partnership, and

(b) any designated member in default,

commits an offence.

(9) A person guilty of an offence under sub-paragraph (8) is liable on summary conviction to a fine not exceeding level 3 on the standard scale.

Notification of change of name

5 (1) Where a limited liability partnership changes its name it shall deliver notice of the change to the registrar.

(2) A notice delivered under sub-paragraph (1)–

(a) shall be in a form approved by the registrar, and

(b) shall be signed by a designated member of the limited liability partnership or authenticated in a manner approved by the registrar.

(3) Where the registrar receives a notice under sub-paragraph (2) he shall (unless the new name is one by which a limited liability partnership may not be registered)–

(a) enter the new name in the index kept under section 714(1) of the Companies Act 1985, and

(b) issue a certificate of the change of name.

(4) The change of name has effect from the date on which the certificate is issued.

Effect of change of name

6 A change of name by a limited liability partnership does not–

(a) affect any of its rights or duties,

(b) render defective any legal proceedings by or against it,

and any legal proceedings that might have been commenced or continued against it by its former name may be commenced or continued against it by its new name.

Improper use of 'limited liability partnership' etc.

7 (1) If any person carries on a business under a name or title which includes as the last words–

(a) the expression 'limited liability partnership' or 'partneriaeth atebolrwydd cyfyngedig', or

(b) any contraction or imitation of either of those expressions,

that person, unless a limited liability partnership or oversea limited liability partnership, commits an offence.

(2) A person guilty of an offence under sub-paragraph (1) is liable on summary conviction to a fine not exceeding level 3 on the standard scale.

Similarity of names

8 In determining for the purposes of this Part whether one name is the same as another there are to be disregarded–

(1) the definite article as the first word of the name,

(2) any of the following (or their Welsh equivalents or abbreviations of them or their Welsh equivalents) at the end of the name–

'limited liability partnership',

'company',

'and company',

'company limited',

'and company limited',

'limited',

'unlimited',

'public limited company',

'community interest company',

'community interest public limited company',

'investment company with variable capital', and

'open-ended investment company', and

(3) type and case of letters, accents, spaces between letters and punctuation marks,

and 'and' and '&' are to be taken as the same.

Part II REGISTERED OFFICES

Situation of registered office

9 (1) A limited liability partnership shall–

(a) at all times have a registered office situated in England and Wales or in Wales, or

(b) at all times have a registered office situated in Scotland,

to which communications and notices may be addressed.

(2) On the incorporation of a limited liability partnership the situation of its registered office shall be that stated in the incorporation document.

(3) Where the registered office of a limited liability partnership is situated in Wales, but the incorporation document does not state that it is to be situated in Wales (as opposed to England and Wales), the limited liability partnership may deliver notice to the registrar stating that its registered office is to be situated in Wales.

(4) A notice delivered under sub-paragraph (3)–

(a) shall be in a form approved by the registrar, and

(b) shall be signed by a designated member of the limited liability partnership or authenticated in a manner approved by the registrar.

Change of registered office

10 (1) A limited liability partnership may change its registered office by delivering notice of the change to the registrar.

(2) A notice delivered under sub-paragraph (1)–

(a) shall be in a form approved by the registrar, and

(b) shall be signed by a designated member of the limited liability partnership or authenticated in a manner approved by the registrar.

Appendix 4

Partnership Agreement – Main Clauses Having a Taxation Effect

The importance of having a written partnership agreement was emphasised in **Chapter 1**. The following headings indicate the main clauses affecting taxation to be included in such an agreement. Limited liability partnerships should have a members' agreement (see **Chapter 23**).

Profit-sharing

- Profit-sharing ratios (see **Chapter 7**).
- Contributions to the cost of partners' cars, telephones and other expenses (see **Chapter 2**).
- Changes to profit-sharing ratios as a result of paying a deemed salary under IR35 (see **Chapter 28**).
- Guaranteed profit shares (see **Chapter 7**).
- Salaried partners (see **Chapter 1**).
- Profit entitlement during periods of absence and sickness; treatment of payments due under any sickness policies.

Admissions and retirements

- Confirmation that, even if accounts are prepared to a date which does not coincide with a normal accounting date for the purposes of equity between incoming and outgoing partners, that this will not be adopted as a new accounting date for tax purposes (see **Chapter 5**).
- Entitlement on leaving the partnership to undrawn profits, capital account repayments and goodwill (including its valuation) (see **Chapter 5**).
- Pensions and annuities for retiring partners (see **Chapters 16** and **22**).
- Asset revaluations on admission or retirement (see **Chapter 12**).
- Right or option of the continuing partners to acquire an outgoing partner's share and on what basis (see **Chapter 12**).
- Buy and sell agreements on the death of a partner (see **Chapters 12** and **23**).

Accounting

- Basis of accounting and accounting policies, particularly the means of valuing work in progress (see **Chapter 7**).

- Maintaining separate capital and current accounts (see **Chapter 1**).
- The accounting date (see **Chapter 4**).
- Changes to the accounting date (see **Chapter 6**).

Tax reserves

- Whether a tax reserve will be maintained, how it will be calculated and the circumstances in which it will be used (see **Chapter 27**).
- Tax reserves on admission or retirement (see **Chapters 5** and **27**).

Capital accounts

- Capital contributions and the date when required (see **Chapter 2**).
- Capital surplus-sharing ratio and ownership of partnership assets such as property (see **Chapter 12**).
- Assets owned personally by the partners (see **Chapter 2**).

Duty to the partnership

- Other business interests (see **Chapter 1**).
- Employments, salaries and fees (see **Chapter 3**).
- Retaining income outside the partnership (see **Chapter 3**).

Pensions and insurance

- The requirement for partners to contribute to pensions and the amount (see **Chapter 22**).
- Partnership annuities (see **Chapter 14**).
- Life insurance, dependants and permanent health arrangements (see **Chapter 22**).

Indemnities

- Indemnities to incoming partners for liabilities incurred before joining the partnership including the catching-up charge, and with regard to fraudulent or negligent conduct and the implications for enquiries and discovery assessments (see **Chapters 5** and **21**).
- Indemnities to retiring partners regarding the partnership debts (see **Chapter 5**).
- Indemnity by retiring partner with regard to liabilities prior to retirement and with regard to fraudulent or negligent conduct and the implications for enquiries and discovery assessments (see **Chapters 5** and **22**).

Administration

- How the tax will be paid, by the partners individually or by the partnership (see **Chapter 27**).
- Providing timely information to partners to enable them to complete their tax returns (see **Chapter 21**).
- Partners are required to provide timely information to the partnership for claims such as assets used personally (see **Chapter 2**).
- The partner responsible for signing the partnership return (see **Chapter 21**).
- Dealing with HMRC enquiries, including notification and updates to the individual partners (see **Chapter 21**).

Cases Illustrating the Distinction between Trade and Profession

Occupation	Trade/ Profession	Case	Comments
Tax adviser	Trade	*Currie v CIR* 12 TC 245	Not an accountant
Stockbrokers	Trade	*Kowloon Stock Exchange Ltd v Commr of Inland Revenue* [1984] STC 602, PC	Hong Kong case
Insurance broker	Trade	*Durant v CIR* 12 TC 245	
Auctioneers	Trade	*CIR v Peter McIntyre Ltd* 1926 12 TC 1006, CS	
Land and estate agents, auctioneers and valuers	Profession	*Escritt and Barrell v CIR* [1947] 26 ATC 33	Reversing the decision of the Commissioners
Dance band leader	Trade	*Loss v CIR* [1945] 2 All ER 683	
Optician	Trade	*Webster v CIR* [1942] 2 All ER 517	Selling spectacles – eye testing was ancillary
Optician	Trade	*Neild v CIR* 1948 27 ATC 328, CA	
Optician	Profession	*Carr v CIR* [1944] 2 All ER 163	Useful guidance on the definition of profession
Freelance journalist	Profession	*CIR v Maxse* 12 TC 41	
Freelance photographer	Profession	*Cecil v CIR* 36 TLR 164	Quoted in *Currie v CIR*
Dramatist	Profession	*Billan v Griffith* 1941 23 TC 757	
Actress	Profession	*Davies v Braithwaite* (1931) 18 TC 198	

Penalties in Connection with Partnership Matters

Failure to file partnership return by filing date (2010/11 and later years)

(*FA 2009, s 106, Sch 55*)

A penalty in respect of the failure is payable by every relevant partner. 'Relevant partner' means a person who was a partner in the partnership to which the return relates at any time during the period in respect of which the return was required.

Period	Penalty	Notes
Up to three months late	£100 per partner	Fixed penalty. A £100 penalty is payable by each partner.
More than three months late	£10 per partner per day	Daily penalties apply for up to 90 days (maximum £900). The penalty is payable by each partner.
More than six months late	£300 per partner	The tax-geared penalties which normally apply to returns more than six months late (and again if they are more than 12 months late) do not apply to partnership returns (because there is no 'amount of tax' shown on a partnership return).
More than 12 months late:	£300 per partner	

Notes

(1) The penalties shown above relate to the failure to file the partnership return. In addition, the non-availability of information regarding share of partnership profits may mean that individual partners may not be able to file their own self-assessment returns at the correct time. If this is the case personal penalties will be incurred in addition to those shown above. Partners in this position will be able to avoid penalties for failure to file their personal return by including an estimate of their partnership on their personal return and amending the return when the final figure is available.

(2) Penalty reductions – HMRC may reduce a penalty in 'special circumstances' (*FA 2009, Sch 55, para 16*). In addition, a defence of 'reasonable excuse' may be available (*Sch 55, para 23*).

Failure to keep or retain tax records

(*FA 2008, s 115, Sch 37*)

(1) The maximum penalty for failing to keep and preserve records (in accordance with *TMA 1970, s 12B*) is £3,000 per tax year (or accounting period) (*s 12B(5)*). The penalty may be charged separately on each partner.

(2) The record-keeping requirements introduced in *FA 2008* apply for direct tax (and VAT) purposes from 1 April 2009 (*SI 2009/402*), and for other taxes and duties generally from 1 April 2010 (*SI 2010/815*).

Inaccurate partnership return

Where a partnership is inaccurate because of carelessness or deliberate failure, leading to a loss of tax, a penalty is potentially chargeable in the usual way. The penalty is chargeable not on the partnership or on the partner actually making the return but on each of the partners whose tax liability is affected (despite the fact that those partners may not as a matter of fact have been personally careless or been a party to any deliberate understatement).

Penalties are charged by reference to the normal penalty loadings and the usual reductions for disclosure:

For 'category 1' inaccuracies, the penalty ranges are as below:

	Minimum		**Maximum**
	Unprompted	**Prompted**	
Carelessness	0%	15%	30%
Deliberate but not concealed	20%	35%	70%
Deliberate and concealed	30%	50%	100%

In each case the percentages are increased by one-half for 'category 2' disclosures and are doubled for 'category 3' disclosures.

Information and inspection powers

(*FA 2008, s 113, Sch 36*)

Failure to comply with an information notice or obstruction (*FA 2008, Sch 36, paras 39, 40, 50*)	
Initial penalty	£300
Continued failure	Up to £60 per day on which failure or obstruction continues
	Higher penalties may in certain circumstances be award by the First-tier Tribunal or the Upper Tribunal
Inaccurate information and documents (*FA 2008, Sch 36, para 40A*)	Up to £3,000 for each inaccuracy

Notes

(1) The basic rule is that an information notice (a) may be given only to a 'person' and (b) must be in relation to the tax affairs of a 'person'. A notice served on a partnership as such will therefore be invalid. Instead it will normally be served on the designated partner and any penalty for non-compliance will be due only from the designated partner.

(2) There is a special rule (*para 37(3)*) which permits a third party notice which is given in order to check the tax position of more than one of the partners in a partnership (in their capacity as such) to be given in the partnership name. *Paragraph 37* also contains other modifications to the rules where a notice is served on one partner in relation to the affairs of one or more of the other partners.

(3) Penalties for the above offences do not arise if there is a 'reasonable excuse' for the failure or obstruction (*FA 2008, Sch 36, para 45*).

Appendix 7

Inheritance Tax – Business and Agricultural Property Relief

Business property relief (IHTA 1984, Part V Chapter I)

1. The relief applies to 'relevant business property', which is defined as follows, the rate of relief being as stated:

	Rate of relief
A sole trader's business, or a partnership share, including professions and vocations	100%
Unquoted securities of a company which (either by themselves or with other unquoted securities or unquoted shares of the company) give control	100%
Any unquoted shares in a company	100%
Quoted shares or securities which, together with any related property, give the transferor control immediately before the transfer	50%
Land, buildings, plant or machinery which immediately before the transfer were used wholly or mainly for the purposes of a business carried on by a company controlled by the transferor, or by a partnership of which he was a partner	50%
Land, buildings, plant or machinery which immediately before the transfer were used wholly or mainly for the purposes of a business carried on by the transferor and were settled property in which he then had an interest in possession	50%

By *s 105(1ZA)* shares and securities are 'quoted' if and only if they are listed on a recognised stock exchange (which does not include the UK's Alternative Investment Market (AIM)).

2. Interests in the following types of business do not qualify as relevant business property:

   - dealing in securities, stocks or shares (except for UK market makers and discount houses);
   - dealing in land or buildings; and
   - making or holding investments (except where the business is acting as holding company of one or more trading companies).

3. Business property relief is not available on otherwise qualifying property to the extent that the value of the property is attributable to *excepted assets*, ie assets which

were neither used wholly or mainly for the purposes of the business throughout the two years preceding the transfer, nor required at the time of the transfer for future use for those purposes.

4. The relevant business property must have been owned by the transferor throughout the two years preceding the transfer or be qualifying replacement property which, together with the original property, was owned by the transferor for periods adding up to at least two years within the five years immediately preceding the transfer. The two-year rule does not apply if the property was eligible for business property relief on an earlier transfer and either the earlier or later transfer was made on the death of the transferor.

5. To qualify for the 50% relief on controlling holdings in quoted companies, it is only necessary for the *shares transferred* to have been owned for the two-year period, the control requirement being satisfied if control is held immediately before the transfer. The 100% rate of relief on unquoted holdings is available on the transfer of *any* unquoted shares that have been owned for two years.

Agricultural property relief (IHTA 1984, Part V Chapter II)

1. The relief applies to the transfer of agricultural property, that is: agricultural land or pasture; woodland and any building used in the intensive rearing of livestock or fish if the occupation of the woodland or building is ancillary to that of the agricultural land or pasture; such cottages, farm buildings and farmhouses occupied with the agricultural land as are of a character appropriate to the property; land or buildings used for the cultivation of short rotation coppice.

   The rate of relief deductible from the *agricultural* value of the property (net of any loan secured on the property) is as follows:

	Rate of relief
Where the transferor had the right to vacant possession immediately before the transfer (or the right to obtain such possession within the next twelve months, extended to 24 months by Extra-statutory concession F17, or (also by concession F17) where the property is valued broadly at vacant possession value despite the tenancy)*	100%
Where the land is let on a tenancy which commences on or after 1 September 1995 (including successions to tenancies following the death of the previous tenant on or after that date)	100%
Where the transferor has been beneficially entitled to his interest in the property since before 10 March 1981 and satisfies certain conditions (see 2 below)	100%
Where farmland and related buildings have been dedicated to wildlife habitats under the Government's Habitat Schemes (*IHTA 1984, s 124C*).	100%
Otherwise	50%

   * Where there is a partnership in which the landowner is a partner and which occupies agricultural land held outside the partnership under licence, with no partnership agreement or document prescribing the terms of occupation of the land, a potential

problem may arise. The Capital Taxes Office considers that, in the absence of a deed, there is a partnership governed by the *Partnership Act 1890*. In such cases, the partnership can only be terminated on the next accounting date by giving notice which may take it beyond the 12-month period. Until the partnership can be terminated, the vacant possession in 12-months test is not satisfied and 100% agricultural property relief could be denied. A partnership agreement stipulating that the landowner is entitled to vacant possession within 12 months will solve the problem.

2. Relief at the 100% rate is given on the agricultural value of certain tenanted property where the transferor was beneficially entitled to his interest before 10 March 1981, and:

   (i) if he had disposed of it before then, he would have been entitled to the 50% relief available at that time (now 100%), and

   (ii) the relief would not have been restricted by the then limits of £250,000/1,000 acres, and

   (iii) the interest from 10 March 1981 neither gave vacant possession rights nor failed to give them because of an act or omission of the transferor since that date.

   (IHTA 1984, s 116(3))

3. As with business property relief, provision is made for the relief to be given on qualifying replacement property.

4. Subject to the rules for replacement property, the agricultural property must at the time of the transfer have been either occupied by the transferor for the purposes of agriculture throughout the two years before the transfer or owned by the transferor throughout the seven years before the transfer and occupied for the purposes of agriculture by him or another throughout that period. Occasional non-agricultural use, such as using the land for a country fair, would not jeopardise the 'purposes of agriculture' rule, but permanently using the land for equestrian activities could deny a partner agricultural property relief, although he or she may be entitled to business property relief (see 5).

   The two-year/seven-year rules do not apply where the property was eligible for relief on an earlier transfer and either the earlier or later transfer was made on the death of the transferor.

5. Where agricultural property also satisfies the conditions for business property relief, business property relief is available in respect of the non-agricultural value (*IHTA 1984, s 114*).

Interaction with capital gains tax

Farm land and buildings which qualify for inheritance tax agricultural property relief are qualifying assets for the purpose of a claim for gift hold-over relief for capital gains tax under *TCGA 1992, s 165*. Two points should be noted:

(*a*) this enables relief to be claimed on agricultural land held as an investment; and

(*b*) the hold-over relief is not restricted by reference to the agricultural value.

Provisions applicable to both reliefs

1. If the transferor dies within seven years after making the transfer, business or agricultural property relief is only available when calculating the tax or additional tax payable as a result of the death if (*IHTA 1984, ss 113A, 124A*):

   (i) the original property or qualifying replacement property has been retained by the transferee up to the date of death, and

   (ii) the property is still relevant business or agricultural property at that time. Except that, for shares transferred out of a controlling holding, it is only necessary for the transferee to retain the shares he was given (which may not give control). In order for unquoted shares to qualify, they must still be unquoted when the donor dies.

2. To the extent that the original transfer was covered by annual exemptions, whether the balance was chargeable at the time or potentially exempt, it is considered that the business or agricultural property relief relating to that part of the transfer is not affected by the death of the donor within seven years, since the seven-year rule only affects chargeable transfers or potentially exempt transfers, and not transfers that were completely exempt.

3. The reliefs are applied automatically without the need for a claim, and are given before applying any other relief, for example annual exemptions.

4. If the transferee dies before the donor then the property must qualify at the date of the transferee's death instead of the transferor's.

5. Proportionate relief is available where only part of the property is owned at the date of death (*IHTA 1984, ss 113A, 124A*).

6. Where the property had been acquired on a spouse's death, the respective periods of ownership and/or occupation are aggregated to determine whether the ownership/occupation requirements are satisfied (*IHTA 1984, ss 108, 120*).

7. Property that is subject to a *binding contract for sale* at the time of the transfer is not relevant business or agricultural property unless (*IHTA 1984, ss 113, 124*):

   (*a*) the sale is to a company that is to carry on the business, the consideration being wholly or mainly shares or securities in the company (which, in the case of agricultural property relief, will give the transferor control of the company), or

   (*b*) the property is shares or securities of a company and the sale is made for the purpose of reconstruction or amalgamation.

8. Where business or agricultural property forms part of an estate at death, the benefit of the relief will be lost if the property is left to an exempt beneficiary. Even if it is not left to an exempt beneficiary, part of the relief will be wasted where there are exempt legacies and the business or agricultural property forms part of the residue of the estate, rather than being left as a specific gift, because the relief is then regarded as applying to the whole estate, including the exempt part of it, so that again relief is wasted to the extent that it is allocated to the exempt legacies.

Index

[All references are to paragraph number and appendices]